Child Sexual Abuse Reported by Adult Survivors

Child Sexual Abuse Reported by Adult Survivors is a wide-ranging and timely critical history and analysis of legal responses to 'historical' or 'non-recent' child sexual abuse (NRCSA) in England and Wales, Ireland and Australia, each of which represents an evolving and progressive approach to this important and complex issue.

The book examines the emergence of NRCSA as a distinctive social, political and legal phenomenon in each country and explores the legal responses developed to address its unprecedented challenges. Courts and parliaments in each country have reformed existing doctrine and practice and have created new ways of holding state and private actors accountable and new ways of addressing survivors' injuries. Criminal law, tort law, public inquiries and state reparations have all been to the forefront of these new legal responses, which have transformed law's engagement with NRCSA survivors and understandings of justice itself. However, despite this undeniable progress, the book identifies ways in which the legal responses developed in each country fail to deliver accountability and recognition to NRCSA survivors and argues that such failures betray the law's inherent ambivalence to delivering justice for these survivors.

Creating new insights into legal responses to this complex contemporary legal, social and political problem, this book will be of great interest to academic lawyers, political scientists and historians, as well as those working on related topics in criminology, sociology, social policy, cultural studies and gender studies.

Sinéad Ring is an Assistant Professor at the School of Law and Criminology, Maynooth University where she teaches courses on crime, evidence, gender and sexuality and law, and state responses to historical gendered violence. She has published widely on sexual violence and the law, with a particular focus on the legal issues relating to non-recent child sexual abuse.

Kate Gleeson is an Associate Professor of Law at Macquarie University and Chair of Full Stop Australia, which aims to put a full stop to sexual, domestic and family violence.

Kim Stevenson is an Emeritus Professor of Law, Crime and History in the School of Society and Culture at the University of Plymouth. She has published widely on aspects of the criminal law with specialist expertise in the contemporary and historical contexts of the legal regulation and criminalization of sexual behaviour and offending. She is Lead General Editor Routledge SOLON Explorations in Crime and Criminal Justice Histories and Co Founder SOLON Promoting Interdisciplinary Studies in Law, Crime and History.

Routledge SOLON Explorations in Crime and Criminal Justice Histories

This series is a collaboration between Routledge and the SOLON consortium (promoting studies in law, crime and history), to present cutting edge interdisciplinary research in crime and criminal justice history, through monographs and thematic collected editions which reflect on key issues and dilemmas in criminology and socio-legal studies by locating them within a historical dimension. The emphasis here is on inspiring use of historical and historiographical methodological approaches to the contextualising and understanding of current priorities and problems. This series aims to highlight the best, most innovative interdisciplinary work from both new and established scholars in the field, through focusing on the enduring historical resonances to current core criminological and socio-legal issues.

Edited by Kim Stevenson, University of Plymouth; Judith Rowbotham, University of Plymouth; David Nash, Oxford Brookes University, David J. Cox, University of Wolverhampton and Zoe Alker, University of Liverpool.

Policing Suspicion
Proactive Policing in London, 1780–1850
Eleanor Bland

Infanticide
Expert Evidence and Testimony in Child Murder Cases, 1688–1955
Rachel Dixon-Goodall

The Limits of Criminological Positivism
The Movement for Criminal Law Reform in the West, 1870–1940
Michele Pifferi

Child Sexual Abuse Reported by Adult Survivors
Legal Responses in England and Wales, Ireland and Australia
Sinéad Ring, Kate Gleeson and Kim Stevenson

For more information about this series, please visit: www.routledge.com/Routledge-SOLON-Explorations-in-Crime-and-Criminal-Justice-Histories/book-series/HCCJ

Child Sexual Abuse Reported by Adult Survivors

Legal Responses in England and Wales, Ireland and Australia

Sinéad Ring, Kate Gleeson and Kim Stevenson

Routledge
Taylor & Francis Group
LONDON AND NEW YORK

First published 2022
by Routledge
4 Park Square, Milton Park, Abingdon, Oxon OX14 4RN

and by Routledge
605 Third Avenue, New York, NY 10158

Routledge is an imprint of the Taylor & Francis Group, an informa business

British Library Cataloguing-in-Publication Data
A catalogue record for this book is available from the British Library

Library of Congress Cataloging-in-Publication Data
A catalog record has been requested for this book

ISBN: 978-1-138-60535-0 (hbk)
ISBN: 978-1-032-25364-0 (pbk)
ISBN: 978-0-429-46816-2 (ebk)

DOI: 10.4324/9780429468162

Typeset in Times New Roman
by Newgen Publishing UK

This book is dedicated to all those victims and survivors of non-recent child sexual abuse who have come forward to recount their experiences and the professionals who supported them.

Contents

Acknowledgements

This book has its origins in a workshop organized by Sinéad and held at the Centre for Sexuality, Race and Gender Justice at the University of Kent in 2017. We further developed our ideas at the conference "From Trauma to Protection: The Twentieth Century as the Children's Century" at the University of Warwick in 2018. Thanks to colleagues at Kent and Warwick for providing us with these spaces to collaborate.

Thanks to: Adair Donaldson, Aidan O'Callaghan, Andrew Burke, Angela Sdrinis, Ann Barker, Antonia Porter, Aravinda Kosaraju, Clíona Saidléar, David Doyle, Diarmuid Griffin, Dick Baston, Erika Rackley, Gordon Lynch, Graham Turnbull, Joan and Des Bruton, Judy Courtin, Karen Fitzsimons, knowmore legal, Máiréad Enright, Maria Drakopoulou, Michael Doherty, Miriam and Oliver Ring, Olivia Ronan, Peter McGrath, Peter O'Brien, Philippa White, Rape and Domestic Violence Services Australia, Rosemary Hunter, The Francis Forbes Society for Australian Legal History, Thomas Macreadi, The final-year LLB law students at the University of Plymouth who opted for my Sex Power and Legal Control module (KS), Toni Williams, Tuart Place, Vicky Conway, Vinita Joseph and Viv Waller.

Sinéad would like to particularly thank her wife Claire for her support throughout the writing process and baby Evelyn for being herself.

Finally, thanks to the Routledge SOLON General Editors and to Routledge for the opportunity to publish this book. We are grateful to the reviewers for their helpful feedback and to Lydia de Cruz for her professionalism and kindness.

Abbreviations

CC	Confidential Committee
CICA	Commission to Inquire into Child Sexual Abuse (Ireland)
CICS	Criminal Injuries Compensation Scheme (England and Wales)
CJ	Chief Justice
CLAA 1885	Criminal Law Amendment Act 1885 (England and Wales, Ireland)
CLAN	Care Leavers Australasia Network
CPTSD	Complex Post-Traumatic Stress Disorder
CSA	child sexual abuse
CSE	child sexual exploitation
ECHR	European Convention on Human Rights
DPP	Director of Public Prosecutions
EU	European Union
IC	Investigation Committee
IICSA	Independent Inquiry into Child Sexual Abuse (England and Wales)
ISPCC	Irish Society for the Prevention of Cruelty to Children
J	Justice
NSPCC	National Society for the Prevention of Cruelty to Children
NRS	National Redress Scheme (Australia)
NRCSA	non-recent child sexual abuse
NSW	New South Wales
OAPA 1861	Offences Against the Person Act 1861 (England and Wales, Ireland)
POIA 1908	Punishment of Incest Act 1908 (England and Wales, Ireland)
PTSD	Post-traumatic Stress Disorder
RTÉ	Raidió Teilifís Éireann
QC	Queen's Counsel
s	section

SC	Senior Counsel
SOA 2003	Sexual Offences Act 2003 (England and Wales)
ss	sections
TOR	Terms of Reference
UNCRC	United Nations Convention on the Rights of the Child
UK	United Kingdom
WA	Western Australia

All materials including reports relating to each public inquiry's work are on their websites:

CICA:	www.childabusecommission.ie
IICSA:	www.iicsa.org.uk
Royal Commission:	www.childabuseroyalcommission.gov.au

1 Introduction

Introduction

Adults seeking justice for the sexual abuse they suffered as children is one of the most important social, political and legal phenomena of the twenty-first century. Since the closing decades of the last century, Western countries have been faced with waves of revelations about sexual abuse perpetrated in past decades on large numbers of children by adults. Societies across Europe, North America and in Australia and New Zealand have been rocked by the gravity of the abuse revealed and by the sheer scale of the problem. Most shocking have been the actions of former pillars of society, including teachers, politicians, entertainers, clerics and politicians. Before the emergence of non-recent child sexual abuse (NRCSA)[1] as a social, legal and political issue, no country ever had to grapple with the challenges it poses, but today almost every Western country has been forced to face up to these challenges. Survivors of NRCSA have sought justice for the crimes they have suffered. Together with their advocates, survivors have come to law, demanding recognition of their abuse and for those responsible to be held accountable. This simple and legitimate demand in fact provokes unprecedented challenges to what were long-established norms of practice and doctrine in common law countries, such as historical hostility on the part of legal institutions, and legal doctrine, to recognizing sexual violence against children as a major social problem, or to seeing its impacts on victims as meriting a serious legal response. Significant challenges flow from the interval of time between the abuse and the survivor's decision to seek a legal response. Traditionally, any 'delay' of the magnitude involved in NRCSA cases (usually over two decades, and sometimes as much as five decades) has been seen by lawyers as exceeding the institutional capabilities of the law; no court or jury or inquiry could ever judge events that were deemed too remote in time. However, parliaments and courts have been forced by survivors and advocates to reckon with these and other challenges inherent in NRCSA cases and to reform existing legal responses to address these challenges. Survivors have sought justice through each of the main legal domains. They have made complaints to the police, prompting a criminal investigation and possible criminal prosecution and trial. They have pursued

DOI: 10.4324/9780429468162-1

individual abusers, abusive organizations and even state agencies through civil litigation. Survivors of sexual abuse in institutions have highlighted the roles of private organizations and the state itself in widespread child sexual abuse (CSA). Governments have responded using statutory public inquiries to write national official accounts and have established financial redress schemes and associated reparative measures underpinned by law. In each of these domains (criminal law/civil law/public inquiries/state reparations), courts and/or parliaments have introduced important reforms to how the law deals with the issues at the heart of NRCSA cases. The emergence of NRCSA as a distinct and significant legal, social and political phenomenon has come against the backdrop of important broader cultural shifts including: greater openness about domestic and sexual violence; heightened awareness of individual rights to be vindicated by the state (most pertinently rights to bodily integrity, dignity and privacy, as well as the right to a legal remedy for infringement of one's rights); the rise of 'the victim' as a significant actor in legal and political discourse;[2] the increasing importance of testimony and memory as justifications for legal and political action;[3] the neoliberal transformation of modern Western governance from the 1970s onwards;[4] increased attention to individual and state responsibility for historical injustices; the changing role of organized religion and other institutions in society and changing social attitudes towards sex, sexuality and gender roles.

This book examines law's engagement with NRCSA in three common law countries, England and Wales, Ireland and Australia. It argues that the reformed and new legal responses developed to address the legal and political challenges of NRCSA are truly revolutionary responses. Courts and parliaments in each country have reformed existing doctrine and practice and have created new ways of holding state and private actors accountable and new ways of addressing survivors' injuries. Although the changes have not been straightforward or uncontroversial, we argue that they are unprecedented exercises in delivering justice to NRCSA survivors. At the same time, legal responses to NRCSA have transformed understandings of justice itself. However, despite this undeniable progress, the book identifies ways in which the legal responses developed in each country fail to deliver accountability and recognition to NRCSA survivors and argues that these failures betray the law's inherent ambivalence to delivering justice for these survivors.

To appreciate why the reformed legal responses to NRCSA are so significant, and to understand the law's continued ambivalence to delivering justice for NRCSA survivors, we need to understand where the problem of NRCSA originated, which is of course in the past. Hence, in this book, although we are concerned with NRCSA, we establish the conditions and parameters of the past that allowed CSA to occur and for welfare and justice responses to fail to address it at the time. Part I of this book explores how each country came to acknowledge the prevalence and significance of NRCSA, and how law and policy on child welfare and CSA have changed since the mid-nineteenth century in each. We highlight the pivotal role of survivors' activism in prompting new forms of established legal responses, which we also situate within broader developments, such as the intense media and public focus on NRSCA and child protection 'scandals', the rise of victims' rights discourse and seismic shifts in how governments perceived their role in child welfare and in how they perceived children. Child welfare in the past in each country has been shaped by a focus on class and race, a strictly policed gender order and nationalist ideas about the role of children in society. State intervention in children's lives centred on institutionalization of children from colonized and marginalized families or forced migration (from England to Australia).[5] Historically, the problem of sexual offending against children was known about and taken seriously in all three countries, but it was subordinated to other policy priorities. Children were not seen as rights-holders until late in the twentieth century with the adoption of the United Nations Convention on the Rights of the Child (UNCRC) in 1989, establishing that children have the right to protection from sexual and other forms of exploitation.[6] Along with the United Nations Declaration of Basic Principles of Justice for Victims of Crime and Abuse of Power 1985, the UNCRC was instrumental in shaping modern responses to child abuse. Rights discourse helped to re-frame children's suffering as a criminal wrong requiring state action, and ultimately the foundation of political claims for recognition.

Part II of this book begins by focussing on what justice may mean in the context of NRCSA. Chapter 6 identifies the core components of justice for NRCSA survivors as involving accountability (of the abuser, the abusive organization or the state) and recognition of the survivor's legal subjectivity and belonging to a broader community that take their experiences seriously. These insights underpin the analysis in the remaining chapters which explore key controversies at the heart of each form of legal response: criminal trials; civil litigation; statutory public inquiries and associated reparative responses of the state including financial redress. In each of these domains, survivors in each country[7] have had to struggle constantly over years, sometimes decades, for justice. We do not provide a comprehensive coverage of all the relevant legal issues, which are complex, but instead, we focus on legal dilemmas that have faced the courts, legislatures and governments. We focus on the challenges posed by the passage of time inherent to NRCSA and how these have been met by legal responses.[8] The defining legal concern in NRCSA cases is a significant interval of time between the abuse and the survivor's decision to disclose their abuse and seek a legal response. Recent research conducted for the Independent Inquiry into Institutional Responses to Child Sexual Abuse in England and Wales (IICSA) indicates that two thirds of CSA survivors do not disclose contemporaneously.[9] The Australian Royal Commission into Institutional Responses to Child Sexual Abuse found that on average, a survivor may take 23.9 years to disclose.[10] NRCSA has presented important new challenges to both the criminal and civil justice systems where the interval of time is generally not a consideration in proceedings that do not involve NRCSA. Courts and parliaments in each country have come to understand this delay and its implications for evidence and procedure (and for the award of damages in civil litigation) through the 'politics of trauma'.[11] Psychological trauma caused by abuse can cause enduring feelings of distress, shame and self-blame, and in some people, it may mean that they are not able to think about the sexual abuse until decades later. For others, the harms of the abuse, such as inability to work or form stable relationships, may not become apparent until well into adulthood. In examining public inquiries and state reparations for institutional abuse (Chapters 10 and 11), we draw on theories of transitional justice to consider broader political goals of truth telling, accountability, redress and non-repetition in this context. We are interested in how law may have been implicated in political efforts to construe NRCSA as a problem contained to the past rather than part of an ongoing present for survivors, their families and society. We also examine how a focus on institutional abuse in public inquiries has sidelined questions about other forms of NRCSA, most importantly, abuse within families.

Scope and structure of this book

The point of examining NRCSA and legal responses to it in England and Wales, Ireland and Australia is not to determine which country has provided the best or most preferable responses, but to explore, through comparative and historically contextualized discussion of legal doctrine, how they have developed in different ways and ask what insights and lessons might be gleaned from this comparison. Drawing on our respective disciplinary backgrounds,[12] we understand these countries as having connected histories,[13] with circulations, exchanges and interactions of legal concepts and ideas about race, gender and sexuality linking them. Each is a common law jurisdiction and each professes a commitment to human rights.[14] Each country has initiated important politico-legal responses in the form of landmark public inquiries. Ireland was the first country in the world to address 'historical abuse' on a national scale when it established the Commission to Inquire into Child Abuse (2000–2009) ('the CICA'), which examined NRCSA alongside other forms of non-recent child abuse. Australia was the first federal state to deliver a national response and it established the first Royal Commission into Institutional Responses to Child Sexual Abuse (2013–2017) ('the Royal Commission'). Informed by both these examples, the IICSA was established in 2015 in response to institutional NRCSA at local, regional, national and international levels and is about to publish its final report in 2022. Each country has also been confronted with the challenges of delivering state redress schemes to survivors of sexual abuse in state institutions.[15] The three countries also share a connected history involving religious institutions, especially through the many Catholic organizations that operated between them.[16] Institutional structures are a further commonality such as the forced migration of children from England and Wales to Australia,[17] or the establishment of industrial schools by the British administration in Ireland and Australia in the nineteenth century.

In a departure from much research in this field, we consider all forms of NRCSA, including incest and other abuses committed in familial and kinship settings, as well as abuse in institutional settings such as care homes, industrial schools and day schools and in religious settings. To our knowledge, this is the first book to take such an expansive approach to NRCSA and legal responses to it.

NRCSA is a complex contemporary social issue that presents unprecedented challenges to the law. This book shows that the legal responses developed to respond to these challenges have been innovative and radical, but there remain important gaps of accountability and recognition that must be addressed if survivors are to achieve the justice to which they are entitled.

Notes

1 Throughout this book, we use the term 'non-recent child sexual abuse' ('NRCSA') to refer to the sexual abuse of a child that is reported by the victim-survivor at some point after they have reached adulthood. We use this term instead of the more commonplace 'historical child sexual abuse', because the latter wrongly implies the abuse occurred at some distant point in the past, and is of historical, not contemporary relevance. On the contrary, as this book argues, the adult who seeks a legal response for their childhood sexual abuse is not historical, but a contemporary legal subject with rights and entitlements to access justice. Key terms used in the book are defined in the Appendix.

2 J. Doak, *Victims' Rights, Human Rights and Criminal Justice: Reconceiving the Role of Third Parties* (Oxford: Hart Publishing, 2008).

3 N. Whittier, *The Politics of Child Sexual Abuse. Emotion, Social Movements, and the State* (Oxford: Oxford University Press, 2009).

4 Ibid.

5 G. Lynch, *UK Child Migration to Australia, 1945-1970. A Study in Policy Failure* (Palgrave MacMillan, 2021).

6 Articles 34 and 36.

7 For the sake of simplicity, throughout this book we refer to three countries. We understand that this is inaccurate and that Wales is a country in its own right with its own political and social identity. We note that England and Wales share a legal system and social context in addressing NRCSA. We considered that the alternatives of 'case studies' and 'jurisdictions' were also inaccurate and more confusing. We apologize to Wales for this linguistic compromise.

8 The book is not about survivors' experiences of engaging legal responses but about the contexts in which the responses have emerged and the legal issues in themselves. On survivors' experiences, see J.M. Balboni, *Clergy Sexual Abuse Litigation: Survivors Seeking Justice* (London: First Forum Press, 2011); P. Lundy, "'I Just Want Justice': A Critical Analysis of the Historical Institutional Abuse Inquiry in Northern Ireland" *Éire-Ireland*, 55, 1, 2, 2020, 252–78.

9 www.iicsa.org.uk/news/two-thirds-child-sexual-abuse-survivors-didnt-tell-anyone-about-abuse-time.

10 *Royal Commission into Institutional Responses to Child Sexual Abuse* (Final Report, 2017, Vol 4, 9), ('*Royal Commission*').

11 P. Rush, "Jurisdictions of Sexual Assault: Reforming the Texts and Testimony of Rape" *Feminist Legal Studies* 19(1) 2011, 47–73.

12 Sinéad is an academic lawyer, Kate is a political scientist and Kim is a legal historian.

13 S. Subrahmanyan, "Connected Histories: Notes Towards a Reconfiguration of Early Modern Eurasia" *Modern Asian Studies* 31, 1997, 735–62.

14 Through their constitutions, and their adoption of international human rights laws, including the United Nations Convention on the Rights of the Child (UNCRC), and in the case of Ireland, and England and Wales, the European Convention on Human Rights (ECHR).

15 We note that Scotland and Northern Ireland have also experienced similar processes of discovery and reckoning with NRCSA and have instituted important public inquiries as well as other legal responses. We decided not to examine them here because they have their own sets of legal and political nuances and the scope of the book would have become unmanageably broad. Northern Ireland's Historical Institutional Abuse Inquiry, chaired by Sir Anthony Hart, reported in 2017 and was followed by the establishment of a Redress Board in 2019. An apology and memorial have yet to be delivered. In 2015, Scotland established a public inquiry into non-recent and recent abuse of children in care, chaired by Lady Anne Smith, www.childabuseinquiry.scot.

16 K. Gleeson and S. Ring, "Confronting the Past and Changing the Future? Public Inquiries into Institutional Child Abuse Inquiries, Ireland and Australia" *Griffith Law Review* 29(1), 2021, 109–33; IICSA, *The Roman Catholic Church Case Study: Archdiocese of Birmingham Investigation Report* (IICSA, 2019), www.iicsa.org.uk/reports-recommendations/publications/investigation/birmingham-archdiocese.

17 In the post-war period around 4,000 children were sent from the UK without their parents to other parts of the British Empire and Commonwealth through child migration programmes. Most went to Australia. These migration programmes were delivered by leading churches and charities, often with financial support from both states: G. Lynch, *Remembering Child Migration: Faith, Nation-Building and the Wounds of Charity* (London: Bloomsbury, 2015).

References

Balboni, J.M., *Clergy Sexual Abuse Litigation: Survivors Seeking Justice* (London: First Forum Press, 2011).

Doak, J., *Victims' Rights, Human Rights and Criminal Justice: Reconceiving the Role of Third Parties* (Oxford: Hart Publishing, 2008).

Gleeson, K. and Ring, S., "Confronting the Past and Changing the Future? Public Inquiries into Institutional Child Abuse Inquiries, Ireland and Australia" *Griffith Law Review* 29(1), 2021, 109–33.

IICSA, *The Roman Catholic Church Case Study: Archdiocese of Birmingham Investigation Report* (IICSA, 2019), www.iicsa.org.uk/reports-recommendations/publications/investigation/birmingham-archdiocese.

Lundy, P., "'I Just Want Justice': A Critical Analysis of the Historical Institutional Abuse Inquiry in Northern Ireland" *Éire-Ireland*, 55, 1, 2, 2020, 252–78.

Lynch, G., *Remembering Child Migration: Faith, Nation-Building and the Wounds of Charity* (London: Bloomsbury, 2015).
Lynch, G., *UK Child Migration to Australia, 1945-1970. A Study in Policy Failure* (Palgrave MacMillan, 2021).
Royal Commission into Institutional Responses to Child Sexual Abuse (Final Report, 2017), Vol. 4.
Rush, P., "Jurisdictions of Sexual Assault: Reforming the Texts and Testimony of Rape" *Feminist Legal Studies* 19(1), 2011, 47–73.
Subrahmanyan, S., "Connected Histories: Notes Towards a Reconfiguration of Early Modern Eurasia" *Modern Asian Studies* 31, 1997, 735–62.
Whittier, N., *The Politics of Child Sexual Abuse. Emotion, Social Movements, and the State* (Oxford: Oxford University Press, 2009).

Part I

The problem of non-recent child sexual abuse

2 The 'discovery' of non-recent child sexual abuse in England and Wales, Ireland and Australia

Introduction

This chapter introduces some of the key events, scandals and triggers that led to the public revelation and 'discovery' of non-recent child sexual abuse (NRCSA) and deeper political and professional understandings of NRCSA. Common to each country is the role of survivors in speaking out and holding the institutions of the state, religious organizations and the media to account. While international feminist activism in the 1970s and 1980s established the conditions for the revelations that were to follow, public awareness of child sexual abuse (CSA) and the ways in which NRCSA emerged as a distinct political and legal issue varied in each country.

The first section examines how NRCSA emerged as an issue of public concern in England and Wales. Over 100 years after William Stead's child sex trade exposé (see Chapter 3), the Home Office Consultation paper *Setting the Boundaries* that led to the Sexual Offences Act 2003[1] (SOA 2003) acknowledged that 'we understand much more now about sex abuse' but warned that the extent and nature of such offending which 'can take place within families, within institutions and within communities is only now coming to be realised in all its complexity and horror'.[2] The NRCSA narrative of England and Wales came to feature abuse perpetrated in care homes and residential schools (religious and non-religious), the sexual exploitation by well-known, and in their time 'much loved' celebrities from children's television and radio, national sports' coaches (youth football and swimming) and the scandal of unfounded allegations made against political elites in parliament and senior figures in the military and intelligence services.

The second section explains how in Ireland the first public discussions of NRCSA centred on sexual abuse in families, but in the mid-late 1990s the focus quickly shifted to abuse by swimming coaches, Catholic priests (and the cover-up by the Catholic Church's hierarchy) and abuse in industrial schools.

The third section explores how in Australia NRCSA first entered the public imagination through publicity surrounding investigations into other matters such as child migration, police corruption and redress for The Stolen Generations: First Nations children removed from their families. It was only in

DOI: 10.4324/9780429468162-3

2003 when the country's most senior ranking official, the Governor General, was embroiled in a scandal that NRCSA was forced onto the national agenda as an issue in and of its own right.

England and Wales

The Cleveland crisis highlighted the need for professionals to work together to protect children (see Chapter 3). Described at the time as 'the greatest child abuse crisis in Britain',[3] over five months two paediatricians at Middlesbrough hospital diagnosed 121 children as sexually abused using later-discredited anal dilation techniques. Social services determined that all these children should immediately be taken into care for their own protection. Protests by parents and others eventually led to a public inquiry chaired by Elizbeth Butler-Sloss, which reported in 1988. Her report was nuanced and complex. It found that CSA was a real and serious problem, that medical confidence in the anal dilation test in the absence of other evidence had been excessive and that decisions by social services to remove children had been unnecessarily hurried and had also produced a crisis in terms of the lack of resources to cope with the upsurge in cases.[4]

Television journalist Dame Esther Rantzen's Childwatch programme determined to give children that voice by launching the anonymous telephone counselling service *Childline* in 1986. Receiving 55,000 calls on the first night about all forms of abuse,[5] it opened eyes to the fact that children suffering sexual abuse 'didn't feel that anyone would believe them or understand or could help them'.[6] The subsequent Children Act 1989 created a blueprint for child protection prioritizing the welfare of the child. This was enhanced ten years later when the (long overdue) Youth Justice and Criminal Evidence Act 1999 finally removed many of the legal obstacles that made it difficult for child victims to testify in court (Chapter 3). Moral panics over 'satanic ritual abuse' in the Orkneys, Rochdale and Nottingham followed. In 1993, Jean La Fontaine was commissioned by the government to investigate such claims. The weight of official evidence and opinion led to a judgement that while the most extreme features of allegations of satanic abuse were a kind of group fantasy, this did not mean that no sexual abuse had occurred.[7] Important advances in knowledge about CSA were established by La Fontaine's inquiry and the evidence for ritual abuse and systems of organized child abuse became better understood.[8] While there appear to have been no successful convictions involving ritual abuse, La Fontaine has recently suggested in comparing early modern witchcraft with modern allegations that it is only a matter of time before such allegations will be forthcoming and that satanic ritual abuse could be the next big scandal.[9]

In the early years of the twenty-first century, radical feminists like Julie Burchill raised uncomfortable questions about the public outrage directed at allegations of homosexual CSA in the music industry (Jonathan King, Michael Jackson) but queried why no one was concerned about those involved with young girls such as Bill Wyman of the Rolling Stones who allegedly engaged in sexual acts with a 13-year-old girl in the 1980s.[10] Journalist and feminist Julie Bindel, like Burchill also writing for *The Times*, was the first to highlight the issue of contemporary child sexual exploitation involving the grooming and trafficking by gangs initially identified with Pakistani-heritage Muslim men.[11] This led directly to *The Times*' senior crime correspondent, Andrew Norfolk, claiming in 2011 to have uncovered a 'supposed "conspiracy of silence"[12] but which has now been accepted in a Home Office Report as racial stereotyping.[13] Although there is no credible evidence associating such abuse with one ethnic group, Norfolk's reportage enabled the wider acceptance and recognition of NRCSA through his numerous exclusives and covert investigations.

No safer than at home?

One of the most concerning features of the revelations of NRCSA in England and Wales is the large number of especially vulnerable children abused in non-familial settings, in so-called 'care' or residential homes managed by local authorities. Children found missing from home, who may have run away to avoid abusive parents or taken into care because they had been physically or sexually abused, orphaned or excluded from mainstream schooling due to personality traits or arrested for offending found themselves in even riskier situations, susceptible to abuse from professional child-carers and social workers employed to look after their welfare. The first major NRCSA prosecution was the 11-week trial in 1991 of Frank Beck (and two former colleagues) convicted of 29 charges of buggery, attempted buggery, rape, indecent and physical assaults committed between 1974 and 1986 on eight to 16-year-old boys and girls at local authority residential care homes Beck managed in Leicestershire. Beck, who appointed his cronies into jobs supervising children, led a paedophile ring of over a dozen men including Colin Fiddaman, a social worker and child protection officer who worked for the National Society for the Prevention of Cruelty to Children (NSPCC).[14] It is believed that more than 250 children were affected. By definition, the children abused were vulnerable individuals. Well-regarded by Leicestershire Social Services and in a position of authority, he could conceal his offending. Beck's horrific offending only came to light after a chance remark from a survivor. Despite 400 witness statements, evidence from dozens of survivors and 102 claims for compensation, 12 social workers were willing to testify to his good character highlighting his mercurial persona. Sentencing Beck to five life terms, Justice Jowitt declared, 'You are a man whose character combines considerable talent and very great evil...[this was] the grossest breach of trust imaginable'.[15] Beck died in prison three years later from a heart attack.

Beck cultivated powerful allies who protected him including the Labour MP for Leicester West, barrister, prolific author and President of the Jewish Board of Deputies, Lord Greville Janner QC. At Beck's trial, one of the witnesses, Paul Winston, named Janner as one of his abusers. Janner was interviewed by the police, but one of the investigators later stated that the investigation had been blocked 'by people more senior than me'.[16] Janner escaped prosecution after subsequent investigations in 2002 and 2006; it was only after the Savile scandal that a fourth investigation in 2013 convinced the Crown Prosecution Service (CPS) that there was sufficient evidence. In 2015 the CPS confirmed it had sufficient evidence to prosecute Janner for 22 charges of indecent assault and buggery between 1969 and 1988 involving nine boys from Beck's children's homes, but the Director of Public Prosecutions (DPP) declined to prosecute as Janner was suffering from Alzheimer's. He died a few months later.[17] A report the following year by retired judge Sir Richard Henriques concluded that the CPS had missed three opportunities to prosecute Janner for indecent assault and buggery. The response of institutions including the Leicestershire Police, the CPS, Leicestershire County Council and the Labour Party to allegations of sexual abuse against Janner forms the subject of an investigation by the IICSA (Chapter 10).

In June 1996 Peter Howarth, deputy head of Bryn Estyn residential care unit for children in Wrexham, Wales, was jailed for ten years. He was one of the four men convicted of committing similar offences to Beck during the 1970s and 1980s in children's homes in North Wales. Malcolm King, then chair of Clwyd County Council's social services committee, described 'children's homes as a gulag archipelago stretching across Britain – wonderful places for paedophiles but, for the children who suffered, places of unending nightmares'.[18] John Jillings, former director of Derbyshire Social Services, was appointed by Clwyd to conduct an inquiry. Clwyd refused to publish the 1996 report because of its implied criticism that local public figures and members of the North Wales Police were involved in the abuse and/or its cover-up. There was also concern about compensation claims. The report found that there had been a 'disturbing number of deaths and suicides' among former residents of children's homes in North Wales. It revealed how some had died after abusing drugs, solvents or alcohol.[19] Because of the attempts to hide the Jillings report, Parliament commissioned Sir Ronald Waterhouse to conduct a Tribunal of Inquiry, *Lost in Care*, which reviewed 9,500 social services files, 3,500 police and witness statements and made 72 recommendations to improve child safeguarding and ensure robust and independent procedures.[20] Ken Scott, one of Beck's appointees, was mentioned in the report underlining the ease with which abusers were able to secure jobs based on their connections. He was later sentenced to eight years for buggery and other offences against boys committed when working in Leicestershire between 1982 and 1985.

In November 2012 after survivor Steven Messham claimed on BBC *Newsnight* that the Waterhouse Inquiry had stalled, Operation Pallial was launched to reinvestigate the scandal. Keith Bristow, Director General of the National Crime Agency, assisted by a Strategic Coordinating Group, was appointed to prepare a report for the Chief Constable of North Wales to inform what action should be taken.[21] This revealed a further 140 allegations of 'significant and systematic' NRCSA at children's homes in North Wales over a much longer period than that identified by Waterhouse, from 1953 to 1995. By November 2017, 143 suspects had been identified, 9 convicted of a total of 75 offences, another 18 were charged and 41 believed to have died.[22] Few police forces were untouched by such offending, and the number of victims is astonishing. By 2000 there were nearly 100 inquiries investigating claims during the preceding 30 years including at least 22 large-scale inquiries across more than one council area or involving a number of institutions. By April 2003, 34 of the 43 forces in England and Wales were engaged in NRCSA investigations.[23] Police 'trawls' for witnesses were criticized in the press and by the Home Affairs Committee as an unregulated 'witch-hunt'.[24] Cheshire contacted 2,000 former care residents: 300 made allegations leading to the conviction of six care workers. Lancashire identified 11 suspects at seven residential care homes;[25] South Wales suspected more than 500.[26] Merseyside's Operation Care was one of the largest, investigating 84 care homes and organizations.[27] Cases are still coming to light. Police officers investigating Medomsley Youth Detention Centre, County Durham have uncovered 1,600 victims abused in the 1970s and 1980s. One suspect alone, Neville Husband convicted in 2003, is believed to have abused hundreds, raping young men on a daily basis. He died in 2010, but the Ministry of Justice paid £3.6 million settling 237 compensation claims for sexual abuse committed by him.[28] In 2019, five former prison officers in their 60s and 70s were convicted of physical abuse, but there were clear elements of sexual bullying, suggesting that prosecutors opted for the charge easiest to prove.[29] The IICSA began an investigation into how the scale of abuse continued for so long despite evidence of contemporaneous complaints to the police,[30] but in 2019 the IICSA determined that it would no longer investigate Medomsley.[31]

Clerical abuse

While care home scandals featured prominently in the public discourse, there were clear indications that other forms of NRCSA were also being uncovered despite attempts by the Roman Catholic and Anglican Churches to silence survivors abused by their clergy. In 1997 Catholic priest Michael Hill was one of the first clerics to be convicted of ten charges of NRCSA committed over 19 years against altar boys and other children. Sentenced to five years' imprisonment he was released after three. The Bishop of Arundel and Brighton, Cardinal Cormac Murphy-O'Connor, offered Hill counselling but two years later and despite protests from parents, was persuaded to reinstate him. Murphy-O'Connor failed to act on psychiatric reports that Hill had a 'psychosexual disorder' preferencing young males. Murphy-O'Connor moved him to Gatwick Airport as chaplain where he would have less contact with children, effectively laicising him. But in 2002 Hill betrayed that trust. Aged 68, he was convicted again of indecently assaulting three boys and sentenced to another five years' imprisonment. In a well-timed exposé, the media revealed that the church had paid 'hush money' to silence some of Hill's victims.[32] Murphy-O'Connor was now Archbishop of Westminster, head of the Roman Catholic Church in England and Wales. The scandal haunted his appointment in 2000, but the revelation that between 1995 and 1999, 21 Catholic priests were convicted of sexual offences compelled him to commission Lord Nolan to advise the church on safeguarding issues.[33] *A Programme for Action*, published in 2001, recommended the church issue guidelines on responding to the discovery of abuse and consider how these could be made compatible with canon law.[34] The Catholic Office for the Protection of Children and Vulnerable Adults was established as an independent advisory body. Within 18 months, 132 complaints were received alleging historical and current sexual abuse.[35] A list of 31 named Catholic priests convicted between 2008 and 2011 was published in *The Times*. An unknown number had received police cautions.[36] Dioceses endeavoured to settle claims, frustrating survivors who sought validation of their suffering through the public arena of the courts. Trustees attempted to defend the onslaught of claims by trying to avoid their vicarious liability under employment law, arguing unsuccessfully in one case at the Supreme Court that priests were not employees but independent representatives of God who had no employment contract (see Chapter 9).[37]

For years the Catholic Church was reluctant to admit condoning ongoing cover-ups at the highest levels to protect reputations. In 2005 it emerged that dozens of boys, some younger than ten, had been sexually abused between 1966 and 1995 at the prestigious Ampleforth College (Middlesbrough Diocese) where Cardinal Basil Hume was elected First Abbot in 1963. Hume resided there as a pupil aged ten and did not leave until appointed Archbishop as Murphy-O'Connor's predecessor in 1976. The police believed Hume knew what was occurring but the implicit references made shortly before his death 'I think about the relief my demise will bring to some people', came too late to hold him and others to account.[38] Richard Scorer, a legal expert advising survivors, suggested it unlikely the full extent of clerical abuse would be uncovered as Canon 490 of the Code of Canon Law requires each bishop to maintain a secret and secure document archive.[39] As with NRCSA in care homes, cases are still being uncovered. Underlining the geographical reach of clerical abuse, more than a dozen victims alleged (most recently in 2018) abused by Benedictine monks on remote Caldey Island off the Welsh coast with at least four men convicted.[40] Such examples are, of course, part of a global crisis that the Catholic Church continues to grapple with.[41]

Holding protestant clerics to account has proved even more problematic as, legally, Anglican parochial clergy are not employees but office holders. The Church can remove a cleric's practising licence but cannot defrock so abusers may continue to preach.[42] In March 2018, the Archbishop of Canterbury, Justin Welby, acknowledged that his church faced two years of shame and interrogation by the IICSA after he invited the Inquiry to investigate, 'as a matter of priority, the sexual abuse of children within the Anglican Church.[43] At the heart of the crisis is the church's collusion in closing ranks to protect Bishop Peter Ball.[44] Similar claims of a culture of lies, silencing and cover-ups have also been made in respect of the Methodist Church which issued a public apology in 2015 after an investigation uncovered 914 allegations of sexual abuse dating back to the 1950s[45] and in 2018 100 people made complaints about Jehovah's Witnesses.[46] The Salvation Army has also been implicated in NRCSA. At Preston Crown Court in 2018 three men (the eldest aged 88) were convicted of 23 offences committed in the 1970s/1980s at the Blackpool Salvation Army citadel including attempted rape and indecency with a child. They systematically abused the same girl starting from when she was aged 11.[47]

The popular and the powerful

In 2001, the popular music world was disturbed by the conviction of singer, record company founder and DJ Jonathan King for buggery and indecent assault committed on five boys aged 14 and 15 in the 1970s. King categorically denied such 'absurd allegations'. Sentencing him to seven years, Judge Paget said: 'This was a serious breach of trust. You used your fame and success to attract adolescent and impressionable boys. You then abused the trust they and their parents placed in you'.[48] King maintained his innocence on the basis he did not have full sexual intercourse with any of the boys and that they 'consented'. Interviewed in 2012, he claimed 'the only apology I have is to say that I was good at seduction… these were different times with different morals'.[49] Between 2012 and 2014 there was an unprecedented uncovering, and associated sensationalized media storm, of abuse by a number of well-known celebrities and popstars, some much loved by children in the 1970s and 1980s. This time there was a clear trigger: the fallout from the unprecedented revelations of children's TV presenter, Sir James Savile, after his death in 2011, aged 84. An ITV documentary, presented by former police officer and investigative journalist Mark Williams-Thomas, *Exposure: The other side of Jimmy Savile* aired on 3 October 2012, publicized claims from multiple women sexually assaulted or raped in the 1960s and 1970s. The allegations confirmed the suspicions of many who had tried to inform those in authority about Savile's actions. By mid-November 450 victims had come forward, 17 police forces recorded 199 crimes including 31 allegations of rape and Operation Yewtree became the largest ever inquiry into NRCSA.[50] The extent and prolific nature of Savile's abuse is impossible to articulate but is partly captured in the Joint Metropolitan Police and NSPCC report, *Giving Victims a Voice*: it occurred between 1955 and 2009 peaking 1966–1976, infiltrated all levels of society; hospitals, psychiatric institutions, children's homes, schools, the BBC, affected all ages from eight to 47, though most were 13 to 16, and was gender blind, involving initially 174 female and 40 male victims.[51] Five previous police investigations had been closed in dubious circumstances missing the opportunity of bringing Savile to trial. By 2014 the number of victims had increased to nearly 1,000, including 60 patients ranging from 5 to 75 years of age abused at Leeds General Infirmary where Savile was a fundraiser.[52] The increasing number of investigations forced the Secretary of State for Health to issue a public apology. The following year, Home Secretary Teresa May commissioned the first iteration of the IICSA (see Chapter 10).

Operation Yewtree's reach spread far beyond Savile's domain as other victims felt encouraged and empowered to report their experiences involving other childhood icons. Entertainer Rolf Harris was convicted in 2014 for 12 counts of indecent assault including offences against one of his daughter's friends aged 13–15 years. Born in Australia in 1930, Harris came to Britain in 1952. He made a successful career as a portrait artist, culminating in a commission to paint Queen Elizabeth' II's portrait for her 80th birthday. Australian women who were abused as children by Harris in the UK provided testimony in the English court case. Sentencing the 84-year-old to five years nine months, Sweeney J said, 'You have shown no remorse for your crimes at all. Your reputation now lies in ruins, you have been stripped of your honours but you have no one to blame but yourself.[53] Released after three years, he faced a further trial and retrial in 2017 on four counts of indecent assault, but neither jury was able to reach a verdict. In February 2019 Harris was reported walking into a primary school and waving at children in breach of the sex offender order imposed, indicating an enduring inability to transform his behaviour.[54] As well as Harris, presenter Stuart Hall, the Bay City Rollers' manager Tam Paton and band member Derek Longmuir, and public relations guru Max Clifford were all convicted of non-recent sexual crimes against children.

Not all investigations of high-profile men resulted in convictions, however. Acquittals following trials were secured by soap opera *Coronation Street* actors Michael Le Vell (charged with 12 serious child sexual offences on dates between 2001 and 2010) and William Roache (charged with two rapes and four indecent assaults involving complainants aged 16 and under, on dates between 1965 and 1971). In 2013 BBC radio presenter Paul Gambaccini was in the headlines when he was remanded on bail for sexual offences against two teenage boys in the early 1980s. He remained on bail without charge for 12 months before it was announced that no charges would be brought.[55] The controversy surrounding this case and others like it that received media attention[56] led to the introduction of a 28-day limit on pre-charge police bail.[57] But perhaps the most iniquitous breach of privacy was the alliance of South Yorkshire Police who tipped off the BBC in 2014 that they were going to search the home of the singer Sir Cliff Richard. The BBC sent a helicopter to film his home, reported the story as an exclusive and nominated it for the Royal Television Society's 'scoop of the year' award. Richard was never charged, but the BBC refused to apologize. Richard successfully sued the BBC and South Yorkshire Police and received substantial damages.[58] The case attracted criticism from all sides because of the competing interests of the freedom of the press versus the right of suspects to remain anonymous until charged.[59] Richard has called for changes to the law to protect the anonymity for persons suspected of sexual offences until they are actually charged with a crime.

Finally, in the post-Savile era, the world of sport has also been forced to face its demons. Police forces are investigating more than 1,000 NRCSA cases involving 250 football clubs and the Football Association commissioned Clive Sheldon QC to lead its own independent investigation into abuse of children between 1970 and 2005. The review identified 240 suspects and 692 survivors; it found 'significant institutional failings' by the Association.[60] Football's national league coach Barry Bennell was convicted at Liverpool Crown Court in 2018 for 50 offences committed against 12 junior players, aged eight–14, between 1979 and 1990. Survivors alleged that he abused some of them hundreds of times. Judge Clement Goldstone QC described him as the 'devil incarnate'.[61] Sentenced to 454 years, Bennell was imprisoned for the maximum period of 30 years. In March 2019 Premier League club Manchester City launched a compensation scheme to settle actions taken by victims of Bennell and another coach, John Broome, out of court without admission of liability. British Canoeing,[62] British Swimming, The British Rowing Association and Archery GB have all been forced to launch recent inquiries.[63] In November 2019, former Royal Ballet principal dancer Steven Beagley was sentenced to ten years after admitting eight charges of sexual offences committed against three girls aged between nine and 13 who were his dance pupils.[64]

Ireland

The public discovery of NRCSA in the 1990s followed decades of feminist activism on issues such as family planning, divorce, equal pay and interpersonal violence.[65] In 1984 the Director of the Dublin Rape Crisis Centre stated that the Centre was seeing many young women who needed to talk about childhood abuse that had gone on for years.[66] A pioneering study commissioned in 1987 for the national broadcaster, RTÉ and The Sanctuary Trust found that 6 per cent of adults in their sample reported having been sexually abused as children.[67] In 1989 therapists from the Dublin Rape Crisis Centre published *Surviving Sexual Abuse*, a handbook based on the centre's counselling models. Other feminists campaigned to reform the legal process.[68]

The first sustained engagement by the public with sexual violence against children came in 1992. The so-called 'X case' involved a 14-year-old girl who was suicidal and pregnant after being raped by a neighbour in a middle-class area of Dublin. A High Court ruling preventing her from leaving the country for an abortion caused a national outcry. Thousands of people marched in Dublin city centre in protest. Ultimately the Supreme Court allowed the girl to have an abortion in Ireland.[69] The case was a watershed moment, demonstrating that sexual violence against children could occur in every community and that it was a subject for public discussion.

Familial abuse

Although 'scandals' involving clerics and members of religious orders now dominate the public imagination, familial abuse was in fact pivotal to Ireland's 'discovery' of NRCSA. In October 1992, RTÉ aired the investigative documentary Silent Scream[70] featuring sisters Joyce, June and Paula Kavanagh who spoke about being sexually abused by their father in the 1950s and 1960s and their quest for criminal justice. Previous RTÉ programmes on child abuse had the interviewee's face hidden and voice distorted, but the sisters chose to speak to the camera. Kavanagh was convicted in 1990 and sentenced to seven years' imprisonment. The sisters were nominated for the Sunday Independent Irish Women of the Year. The programme was used as a training tool for professionals working with survivors. The programme won the United States National Women's Studies Association Award in 1994. In March 1993 a County Kilkenny father was sentenced to seven years having pleaded guilty to six charges of rape, incest and assault against his eldest daughter, Alison Cooper, from a total of 56 charges over the period 1976–1991. She became pregnant by her father and had a son at the age of 16. During the trial it emerged that health and social services had over 100 contacts with the family over 15 years. The case immediately attracted considerable public attention, with interest groups, journalists and politicians expressing outrage at the perceived lenience of the sentence and disbelief at how he could have acted with impunity for so long. Alison gave a powerful televised interview criticizing the response of the social services.[71] Following further widespread criticism of the state's role in the case, a non-statutory inquiry was ordered by Minister for Health Brendan Howlin.

The 1993 Kilkenny Incest Investigation, chaired by Catherine McGuinness, Senior Counsel,[72] was the first major inquiry into child abuse (of all kinds) in Ireland.[73] Its Report highlighted the deficiencies of the child protection systems and the professional activities of various practitioners. Like earlier British inquiries, including Cleveland, the investigating team went beyond their original brief and commented on 'the ambivalence of the community as a whole to this type of violence'.[74] It was unusual for its focus on the child protection system and for its recognition of the need for wider changes in attitudes to children, the family and domestic violence. The Inquiry (and the criminal trial of the abuser) received widespread media coverage and triggered increased awareness of abuse; one authoritative study found an increase of 10 per cent in the number of (general) child abuse referrals to social workers following the publicity.[75] The Inquiry's Report was the catalyst for the overhaul and expansion of the child protection services and changes to the criminal law (see Chapter 4). It was generally well received although there was some criticism of its decision not to hold any individual social workers, health professionals or gardaí (police) to account. The Kilkenny case's main impact was on social attitudes towards incest and a new public scrutiny of the inviolability of the family.[76] It paved the way for further inquiries into familial, institutional and clerical abuse.

In 1998 a civil liability suit attracted national and international media attention. It followed Joseph McColgan's conviction for 26 counts of physical and sexual assault of his children dating back to the mid-1970s. McColgan's children sued the Northwest Health Board and the family doctor Dr Desmond Moran in negligence. The case, which eventually settled, attracted much media attention[77] and inspired legislators to reform the time limits on civil claims (see Chapter 8). The report of the non-statutory Inquiry detailed the failure of the medical profession, social services management and society more broadly, to recognize and acknowledge CSA.[78]

Abuse in swimming

Throughout the early 1990s allegations against high-profile swimming coaches began to emerge. In April 1993 prominent swimming coach George Gibney sought to restrain his trial on 27 counts of indecency against young girls[79] and carnal knowledge of girls under the age of 15 on dates between 1967 and 1981. He was refused leave to apply for an injunction or order of prohibition preventing the trial. On appeal, the Supreme Court in a landmark judgment found that a fair trial was not possible because of the prejudicial effects of the passage of time on Gibney's defence.[80] The High Court later granted the application, finding that a fair trial was no longer possible, due to the passage of time.[81] In December 1994 a leading Sunday newspaper published sworn affidavits from four female swimmers who said they were abused by Gibney on various occasions dating back to the early 1970s. Later that month, Chalkie White told a national radio show that he was sexually assaulted by Gibney over three years in the 1960s. The Sunday Tribune continued to take an interest in Gibney's activities throughout the 1990s and he is the subject of a 2020 popular podcast series.[82] While Gibney's victims did not get justice, in 1998 Derry O'Rourke, a former national and Olympic swimming coach, pleaded guilty to 29 sample charges of unlawful carnal knowledge of girls under 15, sexual assault and indecent assault of young female swimmers between 1976 and 1992. He was sentenced to 107 years' imprisonment.[83] Minister for Sports Jim McDaid appointed a Senior Counsel to investigate child abuse in swimming. The private inquiry was far from the public tribunal requested by victims. Some victims and their allies boycotted the inquiry because they had no faith in it. Others felt let down because of its private and confidential nature and lack of powers of subpoena or discovery. The Report assigned pseudonyms to abusers. Its recommendations were optional.[84] The swimming scandal and the Report attracted significant media attention.[85] The editorial of *The Irish Times* identified the problem of the Irish Amateur Swimming Association's defensive approach and called for an independent social services inspectorate, along the lines of the one in Northern Ireland.[86] This was created on a non-statutory basis in 1999 and on a statutory basis under the Health Act 2007.

Abuse by Catholic priests and the role of the church hierarchy

The year 1994 was also a landmark year for revelations of clerical abuse. In June, Catholic priest Fr Brendan Smyth was jailed for four years by Belfast Crown Court for eight CSA offences committed in the period 1964–1988.[87] In October a UTV Counterpoint television documentary exposed the extent of his offending in Ireland, Northern Ireland and the United States, and the role of his congregation and certain members of the Catholic hierarchy in protecting him from civil justice.[88] A political crisis erupted when it emerged that an application for his extradition to Northern Ireland had been delayed for seven months. The Attorney General Harry Whelehan, by then President of the High Court, was forced to resign, as was Taoiseach Albert Reynolds. The Fianna Fáil-Labour coalition government collapsed.

Between 1994 and 1997 (when he was eventually convicted of 74 charges of sexual abuse of 20 young people over 36 years), Smyth's name was synonymous with the notion of the 'paedophile priest'. The iconic black and white close-up photograph of him leering into the camera as he left the Central Criminal Court in Dublin captured the drama of the national NRCSA crisis. Smyth died of a heart attack one month into his 12-year sentence. His notoriety was such that he was buried pre-dawn in the grounds of Kilnacrott Abbey, Co Cavan. A survivor of his abuse later successfully had the 'Rev' removed from his headstone.[89]

In 2010, the Smyth controversy enveloped the Catholic Primate of All Ireland, Seán Brady, when it became public that he had participated in a 1975 internal canon law investigation into Smyth. That process required victims to take an oath of silence. In 2012, the BBC's This World programme revealed that Cardinal Brady knew the names and addresses of those being abused by Smyth but did not ensure their safety.[90] Smyth went on to abuse many more children. In 2017 the Supreme Court granted an appeal allowing three of Smyth's victims to proceed a full hearing of their claim for damages in the High Court. They had settled a previous action in the late 1990s but sued the Bishop of Kilmore and Brady when they learned in 2012 that the Church authorities had been informed of Smyth's abuse of another child some years prior to their own abuse.[91]

Smyth's abuse formed the basis of a module of the Inquiry into Historical Institutional Abuse 1922–1995 in Northern Ireland. It is still not known how many children he abused.[92] His name has most recently surfaced in relation to a Garda investigation into the abuse of boys at a Dublin hostel.[93] The Smyth scandal had a deleterious effect on the Catholic Church's credibility and authority and rocked the political and legal establishments and led to a shift in public understanding of the enduring effects of sexual abuse on victims.

The role of survivor-activists

The actions of survivors in bringing civil suits and in breaking non-disclosure agreements associated with settlements have been an important part of Ireland's discovery of NRCSA. Andrew Madden was the first person to go public about the abuse he suffered as a child at the hands of a priest. In August 1994 The Sunday Times newspaper broke the story, but the details were very general. The article said compensation of £27,500 had been paid to a victim of clerical child abuse and the priest was still serving in a Dublin parish.[94] Following denials by Catholic leaders, in 1995 Madden revealed his identity and the documents outlining the transaction.[95] Madden's decision to go public led to other victims coming forward and to a Garda investigation. Father Ivan Payne was convicted in 1998 of the sexual abuse of Madden and eight other boys over a 20-year period.[96] This led to civil actions being initiated by other victims.[97] An Taoiseach Bertie Ahern refused Madden's request in 1998 for an independent inquiry into the Catholic Church's handling of CSA allegations against Catholic priests. It would take years of campaigning by Madden, Marie Collins (discussed next) and others, and a documentary exposing the cover-up of CSA in the Dublin Archdiocese[98] before the government agreed to establish an inquiry in 2002. This became a Commission of Investigation in the handling of abuse allegations by the Dublin Archdiocese chaired by Circuit Court judge Yvonne Murphy.[99]

Marie Collins played a pivotal role in Ireland's discovery and reckoning with NRCSA and CSA. In 1995 she reported to the Dublin archdiocese that she had been abused by Father Paul McGennis in 1960 when she was a patient at Our Lady's Hospital for Sick Children. This was her second time reporting. In 1985 she had told a local curate about her abuse who suggested it was probably her fault and offered absolution. In 1997, McGennis pleaded guilty to abusing Collins and was sentenced to 18 months. A few days later, he was sentenced to nine months imprisonment for indecently assaulting a girl in the late 1970s.[100] The newspaper coverage revealed that in 1960 the Archbishop of Dublin John Charles McQuaid had been told by gardaí that Scotland Yard had contacted them with Kodak transparencies of an indecent nature involving two children addressed to McGennis.[101] The Irish Times published Collins's letter detailing how in 1985 she had reported the abuse to her local priest in Dublin, who told her that she was to blame for the abuse and she was not to tell him the abuser's name.[102] In 2002 it emerged that Archbishop Desmond Connell had refused to co-operate with the criminal investigation and refused to provide gardaí with copies of admissions made by McGennis. This was contrary to the Irish bishops' own guidelines on CSA. Yet he maintained these had no authority in civil or canon law. Connell (now a Cardinal) issued an extensive public apology to Collins,[103] who went on to help the Irish bishops prepare revised child protection guidelines. In 2014 she was appointed by Pope Francis to the Vatican's Commission for the Protection of Minors but resigned in 2017 citing resistance to reform within the Curia. The Murphy Commission subsequently found that in 1960 Scotland Yard had told the Garda Commissioner about a film of indecent photographs of two girls owned by McGennis. Commissioner Costigan met Archbishop McQuaid and told him to take over the case because the gardaí 'could prove nothing'.

McQuaid met McGennis who admitted taking the photographs, but he did not put any measures in place to protect children from McGennis or other abusive priests.[104]

The heightened public awareness of clerical abuse led to more people seeking help from counselling and rape crisis centres and more people reporting to the Gardaí.[105] By mid-1998 31 Catholic priests and religious brothers had been convicted of NRCSA offences.[106] Faoiseamh, the helpline created by the Conference of Religious in Ireland and staffed by counsellors, experienced a significant increase in the numbers of people calling it, with over 3,000 people calling in 1998 alone.[107] As the decade drew to a close, the issue of clerical CSA was again at the top of the public agenda when Father Seán Fortune, whose case had been in the media since 1995, died by suicide in 1999 while awaiting trial on NRCSA charges. Survivors Colm O'Gorman and Paul Molloy gave media interviews about the impact of Fortune's abuse and the legal process.[108] O'Gorman founded the ground-breaking charity *One in Four* to support survivors of childhood sexual violence. In 2002 the BBC broadcast Suing the Pope presented a series of victim statements. Monica Fitzpatrick spoke publicly about her fears that her son Peter's death by suicide was linked to Fortune.[109] A wave of public anger and sympathy and the establishment of an official inquiry into abuse in the Ferns diocese followed.[110]

Abuse in industrial schools and reformatories

Although pioneering survivors had been drawing attention to the issue since the 1980s,[111] abuse of children in out of home 'care' entered the public discourse in earnest in 1992. The spark that would ignite decades of soul-searching and revelations about abuse was lit by Christine Buckley, the daughter of a Dublin woman and a Nigerian medical doctor who had been fostered out at three weeks old and at the age of four was placed in St Vincents' Industrial School, Goldenbridge, Dublin. Buckley's account of the abuse she suffered at Goldenbridge on the Gay Byrne Show on RTÉ Radio One on 8 November 1992 was the first time that abuse at Goldenbridge had been discussed in the public domain. Awareness of children's vulnerability to abuse and the failures of child protection services was further heightened by the publication of two investigations: the report into the death of 15-year-old Kelly Fitzgerald following sustained and grave neglect by her parents[112] and the report into abuse in the country's largest children's home, Madonna House in Dublin, run by the Daughters of Charity.[113] In February 1996, Christine Buckley was again in the spotlight with the broadcast of Louis Lentin's documentary *Dear Daughter*.[114] It exposed systematic brutal physical abuse in the Goldenbridge industrial school and provoked an outpouring of reaction from survivors and commentators. The intense public interest in these scandals and the anger on radio talk shows and in documentaries and newspapers breached the boundaries of silence about abuse and encouraged other people to share their experiences publicly. A steady increase in the numbers of former inmates of industrial schools initiating legal actions against the religious orders followed. The public attention also prompted care workers to voice concerns about long delays in concluding investigations into child abuse in residential centres.[115] Taoiseach John Bruton promised to provide a state-funded counselling and therapeutic service for abuse survivors which failed to materialize.[116]

In 1999, the state was forced to finally respond to the public outcry following the RTÉ television documentary States of Fear which exposed systematic abuse of children in the former industrial and reformatory school system.[117] In it, women and men survivors of mental, physical and emotional torture, neglect and sexual abuse in residential and industrial institutions spoke about their experiences. On 11 May 1999 prior to the airing of the third episode (which highlighted years of inaction and the previous government's suppression of details of the report into child abuse at Madonna House), Bruton's successor Bertie Ahern issued the first state apology for child abuse (see Chapter 10).

Public discourse on NRCSA since 2000

The increased public attention to NRCSA led to the establishment of the first comprehensive study of lifetime experiences of sexual offences in Ireland. *Sexual Abuse and Violence in Ireland* (2002) found that one in five women and one in six men reported experiencing contact sexual abuse in childhood.[118] Speaking at an event to mark the publication, the international child abuse expert David Finkelhor stated that Ireland had a particularly high rate of CSA when compared with other Western countries.[119]

Public discourse in the first two decades of the new millennium was dominated by the issue of NRCSA committed by members of religious orders and priests. The most significant event in this regard was the publication of the report of the Commission to Inquire into Child Abuse in 2009 (see Chapter 10). A series of investigations into the mishandling of reports into non-recent and contemporary abuse by the Catholic Church hierarchy, including the Ferns Report, the Murphy Report (both discussed earlier),[120] highlighted shocking institutional failings that would significantly undermine the Church's position in Irish society and would create the conditions for radical legal and policy changes (see Chapter 4).

More recently, forms of offending against children in organizations other than religious ones have begun to be examined. Child protection failures in foster care, the primary mode of contemporary state care, features regularly in media reports. In 2017, a Commission of Investigation chaired by Marjorie Farrelly SC was established to investigate sexual abuse against a girl with intellectual disabilities, given the pseudonym 'Grace', and 46 others who stayed at a foster home in Waterford. Despite concerns about abuse being raised as far back as 1993, children were not protected by the statutory authorities. Grace languished in the home for almost 14 years until 2009, after an original decision to remove her from the home was overturned. The Commission has found that there were repeated and systemic failings in the management of 'Grace's care'.[121] Its final report is due in 2022. In 2017 Grace settled a civil action against the state for €6.3 million.[122]

In 2018 a review at Scouting Ireland found that abuse of children between 1960s–1990s in its predecessor bodies the Catholic Boy Scouts of Ireland and the Scout Association of Ireland had been covered up. The number of victims has since risen to 356 alleged victims and 275 suspected abusers.[123] A review by child protection expert Ian Elliott published in 2020 concluded that past child abuse had been tolerated at the highest levels of the scouting bodies and that the crimes of known abusers had been covered up to protect the movement's reputation.[124] The Gardaí are currently undertaking 110 criminal investigations into former scout leaders.[125] Scouting Ireland is defending a number of civil actions.[126] It has created a fund of €2.5 million to cover legal actions by victims.[127] This is not likely to go far once legal fees are paid. In 2019, Tusla (the Child and Family Agency) raised concerns about safeguarding standards in Scouting Ireland due to the handling of several youth-on-youth abuse cases, suggesting that the lessons of the past have yet to be learned. A statutory inquiry into the abuse has not been ordered, with civil servants stating that such an inquiry could 'interfere with ongoing criminal investigations'.[128] This is somewhat surprising given the close collaboration of the police and the respective inquiries in Australia and England and Wales (see Chapter 10).

Australia

Setting the agenda: survivors coming forward

Much like Ireland and England and Wales, it was women coming forward in the 1970s who put sexual violence on the agenda in Australia. In the mid-1970s, rape crisis centres began to report contemporary accounts of incest among girls escaping violent families. The Australian Royal Commission on Human Relationships of 1974–1977 was also surprised to witness adults testifying about incest in their current families and, occasionally, their childhoods.[129] But it was phone-ins and surveys, such as those run by Australian Women Against Rape in 1978[130] and the Australian Women's Weekly magazine in 1979 that suggested the high prevalence of historical incest survivors.[131] The Australian Women's Liberation movement encouraged consciousness-raising as a strategy to enable women to view their personal experiences as collective and political, and to speak out about sexual and domestic violence. Government responses focused on prevention and punishment of contemporary crimes against children, and the problem of historical incest was neglected by the state. It was left to civil society, in the form of women's voluntary organizations such as the Incest Survivors Network, to establish counselling and support services for adults.[132]

State interest in protecting children in families was only ever minimal when compared with the police focus on 'paedophile rings' thought to operate locally and in the Asia-Pacific. Some authors suggest that the international political interest in 'organized paedophiles' operating outside of families and mostly targeting boys, which informed policing in the 1980s, was a form of transference and sublimation in reaction to feminist exposés of incest within the family.[133] Regardless, it is undoubtable that self-described 'paedophiles' were much more politically visible throughout this decade than in the past, and often at their own volition.

Following a number of arrests for child sex offences in Queensland, in 1985, the government established the Sturgess Inquiry into *Sexual Offences Involving Children and Related Matters*, which reported lurid details including prostitution and pornography.[134] By the mid-1980s CSA was a mainstream problem discussed routinely in the media. In 1986, the Sixth International Conference on Child Abuse and Neglect was held in Sydney attended by 1,600 delegates including American pioneer in the field, Roland Summit,[135] and curiously, Rolf Harris as MC. For the first time in its history, the conference was dominated by feminist representatives from the rape crisis and domestic violence sectors, and CSA 'erupted onto the international child protection stage'.[136] Contemporary crimes remained the focus of attention. This would gradually change once the media 'discovered' the story of child migrants.

In 1987 the Western Mail newspaper ran a series of exposés of the historical treatment of child migrants who had been residents of orphanages and other institutions run by the Christian Brothers and the Fairbridge Society.[137] From 1912 to 1969 approximately 7,000 mostly British children were forcibly expatriated to Australia in child migration schemes aimed to resettle the children of Empire.[138] Media reporting emphasized claims of 'horrific' physical and sexual abuse and the general failures of child migration, which some children experienced as 'robbing them of their identity'.[139] Australians gradually began to understand more about this 'dark and hidden' episode of their past.[140] A number of books were published about child migrants, and in 1992 the national broadcaster *ABC* screened the dramatic miniseries *The Leaving of Liverpool*, concerning two English children transported to Australia in the 1950s. The historical sexual and physical abuse of child migrants was now 'a scandal of immense proportions'.[141]

Government responses included a state parliamentary inquiry and the landmark national senate inquiry, *Lost Innocents. Righting the Record on Child Migration*, pursued in part through the advocacy of Senator Andrew Murray, a former child migrant who had been raised in orphanages in Rhodesia.[142] Due to 'the passage of time', no prosecutions were ever laid against the perpetrators of the child migrant scandals,[143] but it was the prosecution of Catholic clergy in Victoria that intensified the scandal of NRCSA associated with the Catholic Church in Australia.

Operation paradox: cracking open the past

In 1990 police across the country established 'Operation Paradox', an annual 'phone-in' to encourage victims and others with knowledge of child sex offences to self-report and disclose abuse. The national operation would come to shed light on decades of sex offending, especially within the Catholic Church. In response to the 1992 campaign, a number of Victorian men phoned the hotline to report their abuse in the 1970s by Gerald Ridsdale, Australia's so-called 'worst paedophile priest'.[144] After months of police investigations, in February 1993 Ridsdale was arrested for offences committed on 11 boys in the 1970s.[145] The trial remains controversial because Ridsdale was accompanied by then Auxiliary Bishop of Melbourne, George Pell, who was to become the Prefect of the Economy of the Holy See, and who was convicted in 2017 of multiple child sex offences before he successfully appealed his conviction.[146]

Following Ridsdale's 1993 trial, more adult victims came forward, and he was sentenced for crimes committed on another eight boys.[147] The survivors' support group Broken Rites maintains that since Ridsdale's first trial, thousands of survivors of Catholic clerical NRCSA have contacted it.[148] Ridsdale has since been convicted in numerous trials for offences on at least 65 boys and girls committed 'on a more or less continual basis' from 1961 to 1988.[149] In 1995 arrests were also made against Catholic priests in the Maitland-Newcastle diocese of New South Wales (NSW), following an investigation into Father Vincent Ryan, convicted of 53 offences committed against 31 children from 1972 to 1991.[150] By this time, the government and the media were preoccupied with the past and present activities of non-familial child sex offenders who, it would appear, had been protected by corrupt police for decades.

The Wood Royal Commission: focus on networks and police corruption

The Royal Commission into the NSW Police Service (the Wood Royal Commission) was established in 1994 to inquire into police corruption in the state, with the Police Commissioner forced to resign in response to its findings. Following the abandonment of a police investigation into alleged CSA at a Sydney preschool,[151] and a subsequent referral to the Independent Commission Against Corruption, the Terms of Reference (TOR) of the Commission were amended. Politicians who feared police cover-ups of organized abuse lobbied for the Commission to examine corruption in regard to 'paedophiles'. The new TOR included inquiring into 'the adequacy of investigations undertaken by the Police Service in relation to paedophiles or pederasts since 1983; however you may investigate any matters you deem necessary and relevant which may have occurred prior to 1983'.[152] This signalled the state's first dedicated investigation into historical child sex offences, with an explicit focus on men who have sex with male youths (pederasts) including in the period before men's homosexual sex was decriminalized in NSW (1984), when there was no legal age of consent for gay men or gay youths. Neither medical term—paedophile or pederast—was defined in the TOR.

The NSW government had conducted feminist-informed inquiries into 'child sexual assault' since 1984 (see Chapter 5), but the Commission dismissed these frameworks to instead focus on *sexual identities:* 'paedophiles' (assumed to be same-sex attracted men) and 'pederasts' (by definition, same-sex attracted men), thought to be operating in publicly-organized crime rings. This was despite the findings of a concurrent inquiry of the Australian parliament, that although there was some evidence of 'paedophile networks', there was 'no evidence to suggest that there were any paedophile groups in Australia that were "organised" in this sense' of organized crime.[153] In search of organized crime, the Commission dismissed the family as a site of investigation.[154] In doing so, it promulgated outdated medicalized beliefs about child sex offenders as either regressed (familial) or fixated (extrafamilial), with familial offenders portrayed as 'generally "triggered" into sexual behaviour with children by particular family or social stresses' and unlikely to reoffend once a disclosure was reported.[155] The so-called 'fixated' offenders were seen as much more dangerous.

The Commission's 'Paedophile Inquiry' ran for 365 days, hearing 630 witnesses and costing over $100 million.[156] Most of its initial work was directed by police informants, some of whom later retracted their allegations. The original informant on child sex offences, Colin Fisk, a self-described 'homosexual hebephile bordering on pederism [sic]', had been arrested in 1989 in a case of drug supply involving police corruption.[157] In 1993 Fisk appeared on television claiming to have been part of a network of organized paedophiles who were protected by the police. In exchange for immunity for drugs charges, Fisk cooperated with the Commission.[158] Despite his promise of delivering elite offenders, it was mainly working-class drug dealers including himself, and police officers, whom he put in prison.[159] Fisk's information did in part lead to the arrest and conviction of the most notorious child sex offender in Australia's history, his long-time friend, Robert 'Dolly' Dunn.[160] Dunn had been a Catholic high school science teacher since the 1970s and had been paying the police to avoid arrest for his abuse of boys and his amphetamine manufacture and supply since at least the 1980s.[161] He had fled to Honduras and was ambushed on camera by an Australian television crew, prompting his extradition. In 2001 Dunn was finally convicted of 27 counts of child sex offence committed between 1985 and 1992.[162]

The Wood Royal Commission signified the beginning of decades of prolonged investigations of churches for historical CSA. It examined a number of police investigations into allegations made against members of clergy of different denominations in NSW, concluding that:

> As a result of the impenetrability of these organisations and their lack of support for children in their care, and the failure of the police to effectively investigate those cases, arising out of deference, ignorance and a

> reluctance to challenge persons seemingly in positions of respect a very considerable amount of criminal conduct of the most serious kind has been left undetected and unpunished; and enormous harm has been done to generations of children.[163]

It would be another two decades before high-ranking religious leaders would be held to account in the Royal Commission into Institutional Responses to Child Sexual Abuse. No church leader has ever been convicted for the concealment of crime or for enabling child abuse in Australia.[164]

The relentless media response to the Wood Royal Commission ensured that historical child sex offences were at the fore of public attention for much of the 1990s, at least in NSW. The hitherto taboo subject of 'paedophile' activity was suddenly daily front-page news, with media outlets displaying a 'voyeuristic fascination'.[165] The community had little established frames of reference by which to assimilate and reconcile this onslaught of information that seemed to highlight the crimes of men perpetrated on boys in particular. Many feared vigilantism and a backlash against gay men at a time of great anxiety over HIV/AIDS in the mid-1990s when numerous killings of gay men went un-investigated and unsolved.[166] At the height of the media 'hysteria', the Australian Institute of Health and Welfare released a report confirming that 74 per cent of all reported cases of CSA involved girl victims and that in 80 per cent of these cases the abuse occurred within the family.[167] The Commission was dogged by allegations of homophobia and criticism of the tactics of providing immunity for drugs offences in exchange for information, sometimes decades old, on sex offences. It was also criticized for appearing to conflate crimes committed on children with those committed on youths for who, in the context of male homosexuality, there was no age of consent before it was set at 18 in 1984. The greatest criticisms concerned the Commission's association with murders and suicides, the most high-profile being the suicide of former Supreme Court Judge David Yeldham.

Using parliamentary privilege, in 1996 conservative Labor MP Franca Arena named Yeldham as a witness to the Wood Royal Commission.[168] He had been investigated for allegations dating back to the 1960s of indecent behaviour such as 'making a sexual advance' on a male youth, mostly in train station toilets, for which he had evaded arrest. After being named in parliament in association with paedophilia, Yeldham provided the Commission a statement in which he stated he was bisexual,[169] 'denied he was a paedophile' and 'admitted to sexual encounters over the years in public toilets with various persons, of whose ages he made no inquiries', but stated that he did not seek sex with youths under the age of 18.[170] He also stated he lived in fear of blackmail.[171] That afternoon 67-year-old Yeldham killed himself at home.[172] Outcomes such as Yeldham's suicide, vigilante murders committed on suspected child sex offenders[173] and an apparently skewed focus on the activities of gay men produced critiques of the Wood Royal Commission that influenced how future investigations were conducted. More generalized critiques, that the Commission provoked a 'sexual hysteria' and was likely to lead to civil liberties abuses in the form of public sex offender registers with the potential to pillory child sex offenders 'for the remainder of their lives even after they have completed their prison sentences',[174] would be less likely to be aired today. The shift in political and popular perceptions of NRCSA and the proper role of the state has since been profound.

The Stolen Generations: situating survivors and their trauma

The focus on NRCSA in children's institutions returned as the country was absorbing the recommendations of the Wood Royal Commission, but again it was only through an investigation into other matters that the state was confronted with the reality of systemic abuses. In 1997 the Australian Human Rights Commission released the much-awaited *Bringing Them Home (The Stolen Children Report)* documenting the practices and enduring effects of decades of policies of removing First Nations children from their families, to be placed in institutions or white households as indentured labourers.[175] The Report examined past and present laws and policies concerning First Nations children and child protection and made recommendations on redress for the Stolen Generations in accordance with the United Nations Van Boven Principles on Reparation of 1993. Over 500 First Nations Australians testified in person, and many more provided written statements to organizations such as the Aboriginal Legal Service.[176]

Although sexual abuse was not included in the TOR, it was soon clear that *Bringing Them Home* was performing an unprecedented documentation of NRCSA perpetrated on members of the Stolen Generations who had been placed in state care as children. Witnesses were not asked about their experiences of NRCSA, but many volunteered this evidence, leading the commissioners to conclude that 'children in every placement were vulnerable to sexual abuse and exploitation'.[177] Girls were much more at risk than boys in foster placements, but the ratios were similar within institutions. Almost one in ten men and just over one in ten women disclosed that they had been sexually abused in a children's institution.[178]

Whereas the Wood Royal Commission was intent on interrogating sex offenders and their accomplices about networks of organized crime, *Bringing Them Home* placed survivor testimony at the fore of investigations and reframed the state's interest in historical offences on children in terms of trauma, both localized and intergenerational. Australians were confronted with a class of 'survivors' for whom the devastating effects of past treatment were documented and evidenced. The first inquiry to include experiences of NRCSA explicitly in its TOR was the South Australian *Children in State Care Commission of Inquiry* established in 2004. By this stage, NRCSA had become a mainstream problem, precipitated by a constitutional crisis involving the Governor-General.

The governor-general: the question of responsibility

The scandal associated with Governor-General, Peter Hollingworth, came at the time when the Boston Catholic Archdiocese was negotiating its historic US $85 million settlement to 552 survivors of NRCSA. The 'worst scandal ever'[179] for the American Catholic Church ensured worldwide recognition of the need to hold senior Church personnel to account. It also coincided with the first Australian trial by which a survivor of Catholic clerical NRCSA attempted (and failed) to sue a Bishop as vicariously liable for abuse by his parish priest in the 1970s (see Chapter 9).[180] By the time Hollingworth stood down as Governor-General in 2003, questions of responsibility and liability were fundamental to how NRCSA was framed and understood.

The Australian Governor-General is a post authorized by the Australian Constitution to represent the Queen of Australia, which Australians have come to consider as their 'effective head of state'.[181] There could be no higher-level national scandal than one associated with the Governor-General. Hollingworth had been Anglican Archbishop of Brisbane for ten years before he was appointed in June 2001 on the recommendation of conservative Prime Minister John Howard who was immediately criticized for the 'bizarre choice' of a senior cleric of a religion representing around 13 per cent of the population.[182] Far greater controversy arose in 2001 on the resolution of a lawsuit brought against the Anglican Diocese of Brisbane by a woman who had been sexually abused as a student at Toowoomba Preparatory School in 1990.[183] Punitive damages were awarded against the Diocese for failing its duty of care, with Hollingworth 'deeply implicated' in his role as Archbishop.[184] Even more damning was the finding of a 2002 internal Anglican inquiry that Hollingworth had allowed a cleric with credible allegations against him to continue his ministry in the community in the 1990s.[185] Hollingworth appeared on television to explain his actions, but he appeared to minimize CSA.[186]

Hollingworth managed to remain as Governor-General until he stood down in 2003 on revelation that he was the subject of a lawsuit in the Supreme Court of Victoria claiming he had sexually assaulted a woman when she was a teenager, at an Anglican youth camp in the 1960s.[187] The suit was withdrawn after the plaintiff suicided.[188] Hollingworth returned to his role, only to finally resign in response to a sustained campaign by anti-child abuse campaigners, including an unprecedented Senate Motion calling for him to be sacked, and for the government to establish a Royal Commission into CSA.[189] This was the only time an Australian Governor-General has resigned.

The problem of NRCSA, its lingering effects on survivors and the failure to hold senior personnel to account for institutional abuses were all mainstream political issues by 2003 and further fuelled by the 2004 release of the first senate inquiry into abuse in out-of-home care, *Forgotten Australians*. By the time Independent Senator Nick Xenophon used parliamentary privilege in 2011 to name and identify a Catholic Monsignor as having committed sex crimes in the 1960s,[190] the issue was nationwide, with each Australian jurisdiction having endured one form or another of scandal, inquiry or multiple prosecutions for NRCSA involving both clerical and lay offenders.

Entertainment

Much like Ireland and in contrast to England, Australia's NRCSA crisis has not been strongly associated with media and entertainment personalities. The #MeToo movement has also been stymied in Australia, due in part to strict defamation laws and the lack of a constitutionally-protected right to free speech. There have, however, been a few significant prosecutions. Former children's television host Ric Marshall was convicted in 2012 aged 83, of multiple offences committed in the 1970s facilitated by his role on the *Super Duper Flying Fun Show*. The judge described him as having led a paedophile ring providing other 'profoundly perverted men' with access to boys.[191] In 2014, another television star Robert Hughes, who played the affable father on the then highest-rating sitcom *Hey Dad!* from 1987 to 1994, was charged with multiple child sex offences (see Chapter 7).[192] The most high-profile Australian media personality to have faced NRCSA allegations is, of course, Rolf Harris, discussed in the first section.

Incest

In 2012 the reality and trauma of historical and intergenerational incest was returned to the public consciousness through the discovery of an extended family of incestuous relations living as a quasi-cult in squalor in a bush camp in rural NSW. The 'Colt family case' involving up to 38 adults and children was so significant and troubling that the Children's Court made the unusual decision to identify the family in its ruling on the children's care orders in 2013.[193] All the women denied they had borne children to their relatives including their fathers, grandfathers and brothers, even though DNA testing revealed that they had. The mix of male and female, adult and child perpetrators, and the complete inability of the women to come to terms with the reality of their situation contributed to the shock among the community that the family could have sustained itself over four generations of incestuous relations. This was not a collective of adult survivors coming forward. Main testimonies were provided by the children. The women did not publicly identify as victims or survivors and indeed a number were implicated in the sexual abuse of children (including their own) and obstructing the course of justice. Non-recent incest has the potential to complicate straightforward narratives of victims and perpetrators, not because the damage is any less, but because of the particular traumatic effects associated with abuser-identification. In 2018 eight adult members of the family (men and women) were charged with incest, CSA offences, aggravated assault and perjury, 40 years after the first Australian incest survey, and only months following the summation of the

Australian Royal Commission into Institutional Responses to Child Sexual Abuse that declined to investigate the family (see Chapter 10).[194]

Conclusion

By the beginning of the twenty-first century the term 'historical child sexual abuse' had come to signify a distinct category of harm that merited dedicated legal responses.

In England and Wales NRCSA emerged as a political issue through multiple care-home scandals, many of which led to criminal investigations and prosecutions as well as high-profile inquiries. Since 2000 the stream of revelations relating to clerical abuse and the cover-ups in the Catholic Church, alongside the scandals involving prominent public figures in the world of entertainment and allegations of abuse relating to elite figures, created a very clear image in the public mind of NRCSA as a distinct problem in need of examination in the public legal forum of the IICSA.

In Ireland a combination of determined efforts by survivors, individually and collectively, to speak about their abuses forced politicians and the public to confront NRCSA. By complaining to the Gardaí, participating in television documentaries, taking legal actions, writing about their experiences and speaking in public, these survivors were agents of social change. Although the media and public focus on NRCSA originated in events involving abuse within the family, this issue was increasingly sidelined as NRCSA scandals in swimming, by priests and abuse in industrial schools and other forms of state care emerged. By the late 1990s it was clear that the state needed to effectively respond to NRCSA.

In Australia lobbying by mostly male child migrants for justice for the abuses they endured in orphanages and farm schools brought the problem of NRCSA to the attention of the media. While supposedly 'celibate' religious offenders were implicated in these crimes, much of the early framing of NRCSA was shaped by pre-occupations with unfounded and homophobic assumptions about the presumed connection between same-sex desire and paedophilia as an organized practice. Concerns about justice and care for survivors, their ongoing suffering and the complicity of institutions formed the focus of failed litigation and ultimately, government responses. It was only in 2003 when revelations concerning the Governor-General emerged that NRCSA was constituted as a distinct problem meriting a dedicated response, setting the scene for the establishment for the Royal Commission a decade later.

In each country as NRCSA began to crystallize as an issue, public discourse moved away from a focus on sexual violence within families. In each country NRCSA was entangled with the failure of those in the highest positions in a range of institutional settings to acknowledge and effectively manage allegations of abuse, and their refusal to accept their responsibilities to victims.

The horror and shock provoked by each country's reckoning with sexual violence against children in the past carried with it three potential broad resolutions: meaningful accountability of both abusers and organizations that should have protected children, including state authorities; redress and reparations for survivors; better protection of children from abuse reflecting the desire to create a definitive break with the abusive past. In Part II we explore to what extent the legal responses to NRCSA in each country achieved these objectives. In the next three chapters, we contextualize the legal and policy environment in which NRCSA claims emerged, by exploring how legal and policy frameworks developed in each country since the late Victorian period to the present.

Notes

1 Statutes are not italicized in England and Wales or in Ireland, but they are in Australia. We follow the conventions appropriate to each country.
2 Home Office, *Setting the Boundaries-Reforming the Law on Sex Offences* (London: Home Office, 2000), [1.1.5], [1.1.9].
3 S. Bell, *When Salem Came to the Boro: The True Story of the Cleveland Child Abuse Crisis* (London: Pan Books, 1988), 1.
4 E. Butler-Sloss, *Report of the Inquiry into Child Abuse in Cleveland 1987* (London: HMSO, 1988).
5 See J. Crane, *Child Protection in England, 1960-2000: Expertise, Experience and Emotion* (Basingstoke: Palgrave Macmillan, 2018), Ch. 3.
6 *BBC News*, 29 October 2011.
7 J. La Fontaine, *The Extent and Nature of Organised and Ritual Abuse: Research Findings* (London: HMSO, 1994).
8 A. Cooper, "A Short Psychosocial History of British Child Abuse and Protection: Case Studies in Problems of Mourning in the Public Sphere" *Journal of Social Work Practice* 28(3), 2014, 271–85, 277.
9 J. La Fontaine, "Witchcraft and Satanic Abuse" in D. Oldridge (ed.), *The Witchcraft Reader* (London: Routledge, 2019), Ch. 41.
10 J. Burchill, "You've Got the Cutest Little Babyface," *The Times*, 2 April 2005.
11 The *Times*, 30 September 2007.
12 *The Guardian*, 19 December 2020.
13 Home Office, *Group-Based Child Sexual Exploitation Characteristics of Offending* (London: Home Office, 2020).
14 He died by suicide before his trial.
15 *The Guardian*, 30 November 1991.
16 *The Times*, 21 December 2015.
17 Ibid.
18 *The Guardian*, 12 June 1996.
19 Completed in 1996, the local authority suppressed the report for 17 years. William Hague, Secretary of State for Wales, was unable to secure its disclosure. The Guardian and successive councils (Clwyd folded because of the scandal) forced its revelation in 2013 using freedom of information requests, even then it was heavily redacted. *The Guardian*, 8 July 2013.

20 Department of Health, *Lost in Care. Report of the Tribunal of Inquiry into the Abuse of Children in Care in the Former County Council Areas of Gwynedd and Clwyd since 1974* (London: HMSO, 2000).
21 Children's Commissioner for Wales, *Learning the Lessons: Operation Pallial* (Swansea: Children's Commissioner for Wales, January 2015).
22 www.wrexham.com/news/operation-pallial-five-years-on-investigation-phase-now-moving-towards-conclusion-140430.html.
23 *The Daily Telegraph*, 12 April 2003. The statistics cited are illustrative only as it is virtually impossible to accurately synthesize these from media and other reports given the magnitude of the problem.
24 *The Observer*, 26 November 2000; *The Guardian*, 7 November 2001; *The Daily Telegraph*, 12 April 2003.
25 *The Guardian*, 11 July 2000.
26 *The Observer*, 26 November 2000.
27 *The Independent,* 13 January 1995; *The Guardian,* 12 June 1996.
28 *BBC News*, 12 March 2019.
29 Ibid.
30 *The Guardian*, 28 January 2018.
31 See IICSA, *Children in Custodial Institutions Investigation* (IICSA, 2019).
32 *The Times,* 20 November 2002.
33 *The Guardian*, 21 November 2002.
34 M. Nolan, *Final Report of the Independent Review on Child Protection in the Catholic Church in England and Wales* (London: Catholic Bishops' Conference of England and Wales, 2001), 19.
35 *The Times,* 28 October 2003.
36 S. O'Neill, "Locked Archives that Guard the Catholic Church's Guilty Secrets," *The Times,* 17 January 2012.
37 *GE v Trustees Portsmouth Roman Catholic Diocesan Trust* [2012] EWCA Civ 938.
38 *The Guardian*, 18 November 2005.
39 O'Neill op. cit.; R. Scorer, "'Can I Sue the Pope?' Child Abuse Litigation against the Holy See" *Journal of Personal Injury Law* 2012, 25.
40 *The Guardian*, 12 December 2017, 2 February 2018.
41 *The Guardian*, 31 January 2018.
42 See Ecclesiastical Offices (Terms of Service) Regulations 2009: Regulation 33 applies Part X Employment Rights Act 1996 *as if,* and not *because*, clergy are employed. Also *Sharpe v Bishop of Worcester (in his Corporate Capacity)* [2015] EWCA Civ 399.
43 *The Guardian*, 2 March 2018; IICSA, *Investigation into the Anglican Church* (IICSA, 2020), < www.iicsa.org.uk/investigations/investigation-into-failings-by-the-anglican-church>.
44 M. Gibb, *An Abuse of Faith* (Online: Church of England, 2017), 2.
45 *The Independent*, 28 May 2015.
46 *The Guardian*, 8 March; 25 March 2018.
47 *Blackpool Gazette*, 22 March 2018.
48 *The Times*, 22 November 2001.
49 *The Independent*, 22 April 2012.
50 *The Telegraph*, 12 December 2012.
51 D. Gray and P. Watt, *Giving Victims a Voice* (London: MPS and NSPCC, 2013), 5.
52 *The Guardian*, 18 January 2014.

53 Judiciary of England and Wales, *R v Rolf Harris. Sentencing Remarks of Mr. Justice Sweeney* (United Kingdom, Courts and Tribunal Judiciary, 4 July 2014), www.judiciary.uk/wp-content/uploads/2014/07/sentencing-remarks-mr-j-sweeney-r-v-harris1.pdf.
54 *The Telegraph*, 6 February 2019.
55 See P. Gambaccini, *My Year under the Yewtree* (London: Biteback Publishing, 2015).
56 Prominent figures including comedians Jim Davidson, Freddie Starr and Jimmy Tarbuck were also investigated as part of Operation Yewtree and bailed for periods before being told that they would face no further action.
57 Senior police officers can apply for a three-month extension.
58 [2018] EWHC 1837 (Ch). Damages were assessed at £210,000, including £20,000 for the scoop nomination. Damages were apportioned 65:35 as between the BBC and South Yorkshire Police. Before the trial South Yorkshire Police agreed to pay Richard £400,000, plus costs. The BBC paid £2 million towards Richard's legal costs, *BBC News*, 4 September 2019.
59 *The Guardian*, 18 July 2018.
60 "Football's Child Sex Abuse Scandal: Sheldon Review Finds 'Institutional Failings'." *BBC News*, 17 March 2021, accessed 19 May 2021, www.bbc.com/sport/football/56418652. "Clive Sheldon QC's Report into Non-recent Child Sexual Abuse Allegations in Football" *The FA*, accessed 19 May 2021, www.thefa.com/news/2021/mar/17/clive-sheldon-qc-independent-commission-report-released-20210317.
61 *The Guardian*, 19 February 2018.
62 *The Telegraph,* 1 August 2017.
63 *The Sunday Times*, 3 September 2017.
64 *The Telegraph*, 1 November 2019.
65 See R. Sweetman, *On Our Backs. Sexual Attitudes in A Changing Ireland,* (London: Pan Books, 1979); L. Connolly and T. O'Toole, *Documenting Irish Feminism* (Dublin: The Woodfield Press, 2005).
66 S. McKay, *Without Fear. 25 Years of the Dublin Rape Crisis Centre* (Dublin: New Island Books, 2005), 81.
67 Cited in Law Reform Commission, *Consultation Paper on Child Sexual Abuse* (Dublin: Law Reform Commission, 1989), 2.
68 C. Fennell, "Criminal Law and the Criminal Justice System: Women as Victim" in A. Connolly (ed.), *Gender and the Law in Ireland* (Dublin: Oak Tree Press, 1993), 151.
69 *AG v X* [1992] 1 IR 1.
70 Doherty, M., *Silent Scream* (Dublin: RTÉ, 1992); Doherty, M., *Tuesday File* (Dublin: RTÉ, 1992).
71 *RTE News*, 2 March 1993.
72 South Eastern Health Board, 1993.
73 Prior to the Kilkenny Investigation, only two official investigations into the abuse or death of children in the care of the State were conducted. First, the Tribunal of Inquiry into the fire at St Joseph's Orphanage, Main Street, Cavan, 1943 where 35 children died. It only examined the causes of the fire. The second was a short press statement by the Minister for Health regarding the circumstances in which two children in the care of the Eastern Health Board died in 1982: H. Buckley, E. O'Sullivan, and C. Skehill, *Child Protection Services in Ireland. A Case Study* (Dublin: Oak Tree Press, 1997), 20, fn.2.

74 C. McGuinness, *Report of the Kilkenny Incest Investigation* (South Eastern Health Board, 1993), 89.
75 H. Buckley, "Child Protection Practice: An Ungovernable Enterprise?" *The Economic and Social Review* 30, 1999, 21–40, 24.
76 See G. Keane, *Male Rape: Overcoming Rape and Sexual Abuse* (documentary) (Irish Film Board and RTÉ) and C. Cleary, "Victim Confronting Past as he Seeks Healing from Child Sex Abuse by Uncle," *The Irish Times*, 29 February 1996.
77 *The Irish Times,* 10 December 1997; *The Irish Times*, 12 December 1997; *Irish Independent,* 17 January 1998.
78 M. Bruton, *West of Ireland Farmer Case: Report of Review Group* (Manorhamilton: North Western Health Board, 1998).
79 This is the phrase used in the Supreme Court's judgment—presumably this means indecent assault.
80 *GG v DPP* [1994] 1 IR 374.
81 (21 July 1994, unreported), High Court, *ex tempore*, Costello J.
82 M. Horgan, *Where Is George Gibney?* (BBC Sounds, 2020).
83 In 2000 and again in 2005 O'Rourke was convicted of further NRCSA offences. *The Irish Examiner*, 25 January 2005.
84 R. Murphy, *Report of the Independent Inquiry into Matters Related to Child Sexual Abuse in Swimming* (Dublin: Government Publications, 1998).
85 J. McCarthy, *Deep Deception. Ireland's Swimming Sandals* (2nd ed.) (Dublin: O'Brien Press, 2010).
86 *The Irish Times*, 18 June 1998.
87 He was convicted in Northern Ireland of eight more NRCSA offences in 1995.
88 C. Moore, *Suffer Little Children.* UTV Counterpoint.
89 *The Irish Times,* 8 April 2017.
90 *BBC News*, 2 May 2012.
91 *The Irish Times*, 23 March 2017.
92 See B. Boland and D. McIntyre, *A Young Boy. An Abusive Priest. A Buried Truth* (Dublin: O'Brien Press, 2014).
93 *The Irish Mirror,* 7 July 2019.
94 A. Madden, *Altar Boy* (Dublin: Penguin Ireland, 2003), 160–167.
95 Ibid.
96 Payne served four and a half years of a six-year prison sentence and was released in 2002.
97 *The Irish Tim*es, 24 June 1998.
98 Including documentary *Cardinal Secrets* (M. Raftery, *Cardinal Secrets* (Dublin: RTÉ Television, 2002).
99 Commission of Investigation, *Report in the Catholic Archdiocese of Dublin* (Dublin: Stationery Office, 2009).
100 *The Irish Times*, 28 June 1997. In 2011, McGennis received a two-year sentence for abusing a young girl parishioner in the early 1980s. *Irish Independent,* 30 July 2011.
101 *The Irish Times*, 4 July 1997.
102 M. Collins, Letters, *The Irish Times,* 4 July 1997.
103 *The Irish Times*, 15 April 2002.
104 [13.5]–[13.11].
105 *The Irish Times,* 2 December 1994.
106 *The Irish Times*, 24 June 1998.

107 *The Irish Times*, 25 September 1998.
108 A. O'Connor, *A Message From Heaven: The Life and Crimes of Father Sean Fortune* (Ireland: Mount Eagle, 2000).
109 *Irish Independent*, 29 March 2002.
110 F.D. Murphy, H. Buckley, and L. Joyce, *The Ferns Report* (Dublin: Government Publications, 2005).
111 For example, S. Bourke, "Daingean Days." *Limerick Post,* 6 June 2009. Rpt. from *Limerick Socialist*, 1982; M. Flynn, *Nothing to Say* (Dublin: Lilliput Press, 1983); P. Doyle, *The God Squad* (Ireland: Raven Arts Press, 1988).
112 Joint Committee on the Family. *Interim Report. Kelly – A Child is Dead* (Dublin: Government Stationery Office, 1996).
113 Department of Health and Children, *Report on the Inquiry into the Operation of Madonna House* (Dublin: Stationery Office, 1996).
114 L. Lentin, *Dear Daughter* (Dublin: RTÉ and The Irish Film Board, 1996).
115 *The Irish Times*, 24 February 1996.
116 Dictionary of Irish Biography, www.dib.ie/biography/buckley-christine-a10166.
117 M. Raftery, *States of Fear* (Dublin: RTÉ Television, 1999).
118 H. McGee et al., *Sexual Abuse and Violence in Ireland: A National Study of Irish Experiences, Beliefs and Attitudes Concerning Sexual Violence* (Dublin: Liffey Press, 2002).
119 *The Irish Times*, 20 April 2002.
120 And the Cloyne Report, *Commission of Investigation Report into Cloyne Archdiocese* (Dublin: Stationery Office, 2010).
121 Commission of Investigation (Certain matters relative to a disability service in the South East and related matters), *Substantive Interim Reports 1 and 2* (Dublin: Department of Health 2021), www.gov.ie/en/publication/856fd-farrelly-commission-of-investigation-substantive-interim-reports/.
122 *The Irish Times,* 27 April 2017.
123 *The Irish Times*, 8 March 2021.
124 I. Elliott, *Historical Sexual Abuse in Scouting. A Learning Review* (Ireland, 2020), www.scouts.ie/News/2020/Ian-Elliott-Learning-Review-Scouting-Ireland.pdf>.
125 Ibid.
126 *The Irish Times*, 28 July 2019; *The Irish Times*, 7 February 2021.
127 *The Irish Times,* 23 October 2019, 9.
128 *The Irish Times*, 10 August 2020.
129 M. Arrow, *The Seventies. The Personal, the Political and the Making of Modern Australia* (New South Wales: New South Publishing, 2019), 166.
130 N. Rehfeldt and P. Hetherington, "One Woman's Crusade: An Interview with Nancy Rehfeldt, Founder Member of the Incest Survivors' Association of Western Australia" in P. Hetherington (ed.), *Incest and the Community: Australian Perspectives* (WA: Optima Press, 1991), 139–47.
131 D. Scott and S. Swain, *Confronting Cruelty: Historical Perspectives on Child Protection in Australia* (Australia: Melbourne University Press, 2002), 156.
132 Rehfeldt and Hetherington, op. cit., 139–47.
133 S. Angelides. "The Emergence of the Paedophile in the Late Twentieth Century" *Australian Historical Studies* 36(126), 2005, 272–95.
134 D.G. Sturgess, *An Inquiry into Sexual Offences Involving Children and Related Matters* (Brisbane: Queensland Government Printer, 1985).

135 See, e.g., R.C. Summit, "The Child Sexual Abuse Accommodation Syndrome" *Child Abuse and Neglect* 7, 1983, 177–93.
136 Scott and Swain, op. cit., 151.
137 M. Porter, *Sex, Power & the Clergy* (Melbourne: Hardie Grant Bruce, 2003), 78–9.
138 Senate Standing Committees on Community Affairs, Parliament of Australia, *Lost Innocents: Righting the Record – Report on Child Migration* (Canberra: APH, 2001).
139 B.M. Coldrey, *Religious Life Without Integrity: The Sexual Abuse Crisis in the Catholic Church* (Melbourne: Tamanaraik Press, 2000).
140 Senator Andrew Murray cited in M. Rock, "Child Migration Schemes to Australia: A Dark and Hidden Chapter of Australia's History Revealed' *Australian Journal of Social Issues* 38(2), 2003, 149–67.
141 Porter, op. cit., 79.
142 Senate Standing Committees on Community Affairs, Parliament of Australia, op. cit.
143 Ibid., 219. Over 200 claimants pursued a lawsuit against the Christian Brothers, but the suit failed due to the strict Limitation Acts for civil law (see Chapter 8) and K. Gleeson, "Responsibility and Redress. Theorising Gender Justice in the Context of Catholic Clerical Child Sexual Abuse in Ireland and Australia" *University of New South Wales Law Journal* 39(2), 2016, 779–812.
144 V. Petraitis and C. O'Connor, *Rockspider: The Danger of Paedophiles-Untold Stories* (Sydney: ReadHowYouWant, 2012), 24–25.
145 Ibid.
146 *Pell v The Queen* [2020] HCA 12.
147 *R v Ridsdale* [1995] VSC 145 (4 April 1995).
148 *The Standard*, 10 November 2012.
149 *ABC News,* 31 August 2017.
150 *R v Ryan* (No.2) [2003] NSWCCA 35.
151 *Seabeach Kindergarten.*
152 J.R. Wood, *Royal Commission into the New South Wales Police Service: Final Report* (Sydney: Government of the State of New South Wales, 1997), 17.
153 Parliamentary Joint Committee on the National Crime Authority, *Organised Criminal Paedophile Activity* (Canberra: Commonwealth Parliament: 1995).
154 Wood, op. cit., 30.
155 A. Cossins, "A Reply to the NSW Royal Commission Inquiry into Pedophilia: Victim Report Studies and Child Sex Offender Profiles—A Bad Match?" *Australian & New Zealand Journal of Criminology* 32(1), 1999, 44–5.
156 C. Puplick, "The Source of All Our Discontents" in M. James (ed.), *Paedophilia: Policy and Prevention. Australian Institute of Criminology Research and Public Policy Series No. 12* (Canberra: Australian Institute of Criminology, 1997), 63.
157 Fisk, in Wood, op. cit., 17.
158 Ibid., 19.
159 Fisk, whose immunity only extended to drugs charges, was convicted in 1998 of 24 child sex offences dating back to the 1970s.
160 *R v Dunn* [2004] NSWCCA 346 at 112. He was released in 2009 but convicted in 2018 of more contemporary child sex offences and violating his release conditions. *ABC News*, 7 August 2018. Their associate Robert Bell was convicted in 1999 of 24 child sex offences committed from the 1970s to the 1990s.
161 Ibid., 18.

162 Ibid., 2. He died in prison in 2009.
163 Wood, op. cit., 236–37.
164 *R v Wilson* [2018] NSWDC 487.
165 Puplick, op. cit., 64.
166 *ABC News*, 28 May 2018.
167 In D. Buchanan, "Homosexual 'Pedophilia' and the NSW Police Royal Commission" in *Australian Institute of Criminology Conference, Pedophilia: Policy and Prevention* (Sydney: University of Sydney, 14 April 1997), 6.
168 Wood, op. cit., 21.
169 *The Independent*, 9 December 1996.
170 Wood, op. cit., 212.
171 Ibid.
172 *The Independent*, op. cit., 1996.
173 *ABC News*, 27 June 2018.
174 Puplick, op. cit., pp. 67–68.
175 Human Rights and Equal Opportunity Commission, *Bringing them Home: Report of the National Inquiry into the Separation of Aboriginal and Torres Strait Islander Children from their Families* (Canberra: HREOC, 1997).
176 Ibid.
177 Ibid., Ch.10.
178 Ibid.
179 *Fox News,* 9 September 2003.
180 *Ellis v Pell* [2006] NSWSC 109. The lower court trial ran from 2002–2003 (see Chapter 8).
181 G. Winterton, "Lessons from the Hollingworth Affair" *Monash University Law Review* 1, 2003, 2.
182 P. Kelly, *The March of the Patriots: The Struggle for Modern Australia* (Melbourne: Melbourne University Press, 2009), 518.
183 *S v The Corporation of the Synod of the Diocese of Brisbane* [2001] QSC 473.
184 B. Baird, "The Resignation of the Governor-General: Family Drama and National Reproduction" *Cultural Studies Review* 15(1), 2009, 65–87, 69.
185 Ibid.
186 He described a sexual relationship between a 14-year-old girl and an Anglican cleric who went on to become Bishop, as 'not sex abuse, there was no suggestion of rape or anything like that. Quite the contrary, my information is that it was rather the other way around'. Ibid.
187 *Sydney Morning Herald,* 24 May 2003.
188 Ibid.
189 *The Age,* 13 May 2003.
190 *ABC News*, 13 September 2011.
191 *ABC News*, 13 December 2012.
192 *Hughes v R* [2015] NSWCCA 330. In 2010, Hughes's co-star Sarah Monaghan appeared on television to report she had been sexually assaulted while working on the show as a six-year-old girl, although she did not name Hughes. A number of Hughes's other victims contacted Monaghan, and he was extradited from London and convicted of ten sexual offences against four girls under 16 years of age (see Chapter 7).
193 *DFaCS (NSW) and the Colt Children* [2013] NSWChC 5.
194 *ABC News*, 12 April 2018.

References

Angelides, S., "The Emergence of the Paedophile in the Late Twentieth Century" *Australian Historical Studies* 36(126), 2005, 272–95.

Arrow, M., *The Seventies. The Personal, the Political and the Making of Modern Australia* (Sydney: New South Publishing, 2019).

Baird, B., "The Resignation of the Governor-General: Family Drama and National Reproduction" *Cultural Studies Review* 15(1), 2009, 65–87.

Bell, S., *When Salem Came to the Boro: The True Story of the Cleveland Child Abuse Crisis* (London: Pan Books, 1988).

Boland, B. and McIntyre, D., *A Young Boy. An Abusive Priest. A Buried Truth* (Dublin: O'Brien Press, 2014).

Bourke, S., "Daingean Days." *Limerick Post,* 6 June 2009.

Bruton, M., *West of Ireland Farmer Case: Report of Review Group* (Manorhamilton: North Western Health Board, 1998).

Buchanan, D., "Homosexual 'Pedophilia' and the NSW Police Royal Commission" in *Australian Institute of Criminology Conference, Pedophilia: Policy and Prevention* (Sydney: University of Sydney, 14 April 1997), 6.

Buckley, H., O'Sullivan, E., and Skehill, S., *Child Protection Services in Ireland. A Case Study* (Dublin: Oak Tree Press, 1997).

Buckley, H., "Child Protection Practice: An Ungovernable Enterprise?" *The Economic and Social Review* 30 (1999), 21–40.

Burchill, J., "You've Got the Cutest Little Babyface," *The Times*, 2 April 2005.

Butler-Sloss, E., *Report of the Inquiry into Child Abuse in Cleveland 1987* (London: HMSO, 1988).

Children's Commissioner for Wales, *Learning the Lessons: Operation Pallial* (Swansea: Children's Commissioner for Wales, 2015).

Cleary, C., "Victim Confronting Past as he Seeks Healing from Child Sex Abuse by Uncle," *The Irish Times*, 29 February 1996.

Cloyne Report, *Commission of Investigation Report into Cloyne Archdiocese* (Dublin: Stationery Office, 2010)

Coldrey, B.M., *Religious Life without Integrity: The Sexual Abuse Crisis in the Catholic Church* (Melbourne: Tamanaraik Press, 2000).

Commission of Investigation, *Report in the Catholic Archdiocese of Dublin* (Dublin: Stationery Office, 2009).

Commission of Investigation (Certain matters relative to a disability service in the South Est and related matters), *Substantive Interim Reports 1 and 2* (Dublin: Department of Health 2021). www.gov.ie/en/publication/856fd-farrelly-commission-of-investigation-substantive-interim-reports/.

Connolly, L. and O'Toole, T., *Documenting Irish Feminism* (Dublin: The Woodfield Press, 2005).

Cooper, A., "A Short Psychosocial History of British Child Abuse and Protection: Case Studies in Problems of Mourning in the Public Sphere" *Journal of Social Work Practice* 28(3), 2014 271–85

Cossins, A., "A Reply to the NSW Royal Commission Inquiry into Pedophilia: Victim Report Studies and Child Sex Offender Profiles—A Bad Match?" *Australian & New Zealand Journal of Criminology* 32(1), 1999, 44–5.

Crane, J., *Child Protection in England, 1960-2000: Expertise, Experience and Emotion* (Basingstoke: Palgrave Macmillan, 2018).

Department of Health, *Lost in Care. Report of the Tribunal of Inquiry into the Abuse of Children in Care in the Former County Council Areas of Gwynedd and Clwyd since 1974* (London: HMSO, 2000).
Department of Health and Children, *Report on the Inquiry into the Operation of Madonna House* (Dublin: Stationery Office, 1996).
Doherty, M., *Silent Scream* (Dublin: RTÉ, 1992).
Doherty, M., *Tuesday File* (Dublin: RTÉ, 1992).
Doyle, P., *The God Squad* (Ireland: Raven Arts Press, 1988).
Elliott, I., *Historical Sexual Abuse in Scouting. A Learning Review* (Online, 2020), www.scouts.ie/News/2020/Ian-Elliott-Learning-Review-Scouting-Ireland.pdf
Fennell, C., "Criminal Law and the Criminal Justice System: Women as Victim" in A. Connolly (ed.), *Gender and the Law in Ireland* (Dublin: Oak Tree Press, 1993), 151.
Flynn, M., *Nothing to Say* (Dublin: Lilliput Press, 1983).
Gambaccini, P., *My Year under the Yewtree* (London: Biteback Publishing, 2015).
Gibb, M., *An Abuse of Faith* (London: Church of England, 2017).
Gleeson, K., "Responsibility and Redress. Theorising Gender Justice in the Context of Catholic Clerical Child Sexual Abuse in Ireland and Australia" *University of New South Wales Law Journal* 39(2), 2016, 779–812.
Gray, D. and Watt,P., *Giving Victims a Voice* (London: MPS and NSPCC, 2013).
Home Office, *Setting the Boundaries-Reforming the Law on Sex Offences* (London: Home Office, 2000).
Home Office, *Group-Based Child Sexual Exploitation Characteristics of Offending* (London: Home Office, 2020).
Horgan, M., *Where Is George Gibney?* (BBC Sounds, 2020).
Human Rights and Equal Opportunity Commission, *Bringing Them Home: Report of the National Inquiry into the Separation of Aboriginal and Torres Strait Islander Children from Their Families* (Canberra: HREOC, 1997).
IICSA, *Children in Custodial Institutions Investigation*,(United Kingdom: IICSA, 2019).
IICSA, *Investigation into the Anglican Church* (IICSA, 2020), www.iicsa.org.uk/investigations/investigation-into-failings-by-the-anglican-church.
Joint Committee on the Family. *Interim Report. Kelly – A Child is Dead* (Dublin: Government Stationery Office, 1996).
Keane, G., *Male Rape: Overcoming Rape and Sexual Abuse* (documentary) (Irish Film Board and RTÉ).
Kelly, P., *The March of the Patriots: The Struggle for Modern Australia* (Melbourne: Melbourne University Press, 2009).
La Fontaine, J., *The Extent and Nature of Organised and Ritual Abuse: Research Findings* (London: HMSO, 1994).
La Fontaine, J., "Witchcraft and Satanic Abuse" in D. Oldridge (ed.), *The Witchcraft Reader* (London: Routledge, 2019).
Law Reform Commission, *Consultation Paper on Child Sexual Abuse* (Dublin: Law Reform Commission, 1989).
Lentin, L., *Dear Daughter* (Dublin: RTÉ and The Irish Film Board, 1996).
Madden, A., *Altar Boy* (Dublin: Penguin Ireland, 2003), 160–167.
McCarthy, J., *Deep Deception. Ireland's Swimming Sandals* (2nd ed.) (Dublin: O'Brien Press, 2010).

McGee, H. et al., *Sexual Abuse and Violence in Ireland: A National Study of Irish Experiences, Beliefs and Attitudes Concerning Sexual Violence* (Dublin: Liffey Press, 2002).

McGuinness, C., *Report of the Kilkenny Incest Investigation* (South Eastern Health Board, 1993).

McKay, S., *Without Fear. 25 Years of the Dublin Rape Crisis Centre* (Dublin: New Island Books, 2005).

Moore, C., *Suffer Little Children.* UTV Counterpoint.

Murphy, F.D., Buckley, H., and Joyce, L., *The Ferns Report* (Dublin: Government Publications, 2005).

Murphy, R., *Report of the Independent Inquiry into Matters Related to Child Sexual Abuse in Swimming* (Dublin: Government Publications, 1998).

Nolan, M., *Final Report of the Independent Review on Child Protection in the Catholic Church in England and Wales* (London: Catholic Bishops' Conference of England and Wales, 2001).

O'Connor, A., *A Message from Heaven: The Life and Crimes of Father Sean Fortune* (Dingle Co Kerry: Mount Eagle, 2000).

O'Neill, S., "Locked Archives that Guard the Catholic Church's Guilty Secrets," *The Times,* 17 January 2012.

Parliamentary Joint Committee on the National Crime Authority, *Organised Criminal Paedophile Activity* (Canberra: Commonwealth Parliament, 1995).

Petraitis, V. and O'Connor, C., *Rockspider: The Danger of Paedophiles-Untold Stories* (Sydney: ReadHowYouWant, 2012).

Porter, M., *Sex, Power & the Clergy* (Melbourne: Hardie Grant Bruce, 2003).

Puplick, C., "The Source of All Our Discontents" in M. James (ed.), *Paedophilia: Policy and Prevention. Australian Institute of Criminology Research and Public Policy Series No. 12* (Canberra: Australian Institute of Criminology, 1997).

Raftery, M., *States of Fear* (Dublin: RTÉ Television, 1999).

Raftery, M., *Cardinal Secrets* (Dublin: RTÉ Television, 2002).

Rehfeldt, N. and Hetherington, P., "One Woman's Crusade: An Interview with Nancy Rehfeldt, Founder Member of the Incest Survivors' Association of Western Australia" in P. Hetherington (ed.), *Incest and the Community: Australian Perspectives* (Osborne Park: Optima Press, 1991).

Rock, M., "Child Migration Schemes to Australia: A Dark and Hidden Chapter of Australia's History Revealed" *Australian Journal of Social Issues* 38(2), 2003, 149–67.

Scorer, R., "'Can I Sue the Pope?' Child Abuse Litigation against the Holy See" *Journal of Personal Injury Law* 2012, 25.

Scott, D. and Swain, S., *Confronting Cruelty: Historical Perspectives on Child Protection in Australia* (Melbourne: Melbourne University Press, 2002).

Senate Standing Committees on Community Affairs, Parliament of Australia, *Lost Innocents: Righting the Record – Report on Child Migration* (Canberra: APH, 2001).

Sturgess, D.G., *An Inquiry into Sexual Offences Involving Children and Related Matters* (Brisbane: Queensland Government Printer, 1985).

Summit, R.C., "The Child Sexual Abuse Accommodation Syndrome" *Child Abuse and Neglect* 7, 1983, 177–93.

Sweetman, R., *On Our Backs. Sexual Attitudes in a Changing Ireland* (London: Pan Books, 1979).

Winterton, G., "Lessons from the Hollingworth Affair" *Monash University Law Review* 1, 2003.

Wood, J.R., *Royal Commission into the New South Wales Police Service: Final Report* (Sydney: Government of the State of New South Wales, 1997).

3 The evolution of legal and policy frameworks around child sex offences in England and Wales

Introduction

This chapter is the first of three exploring the evolution of each country's legal and policy frameworks around child sex offences from the late nineteenth century until the present. How child sexual abuse (CSA) has been recognized and understood by law and by society has been deeply contested terrain since the late nineteenth century. The repeated phases of advances in knowledge about sexual violence against children, and retreat from that knowledge, have been described as 'cycles of discovery and suppression'.[1] Each chapter first explores the doctrinal criminal law framework and the procedural hurdles to justice in the criminal trial courtroom, and the second section of each chapter examines the legal and political framework in each country around child protection and child welfare. This discussion contextualizes Part II's discussion of the legal responses to non-recent child sexual abuse (NRCSA). Each country's history of legal and policy frameworks around CSA shows that legal responses in the twentieth century were characterized by confusion and contradiction on how to frame it in the criminal law, a marked judicial and legislative resistance to making the criminal process receptive to child witnesses and a lack of coherence in child welfare policies.

The idea of CSA as we know it today, as a crime of violence rooted in relationships of unequal power and involving the negation of a child's rights to bodily autonomy, dignity and privacy, and which has devastating immediate and long-lasting psychological, physical and other effects on the victim, did not exist in law or policy until the closing decades of the twentieth century. This is not to say that the state or lawyers were not aware of sex crimes against children; the relevant offences for much of this period were rape, carnal knowledge, indecent assault, buggery and incest. Victorian rescue societies were also concerned with prostitution involving girls. These crimes had very little connection to how we understand CSA today; in particular, power was not part of the analysis of the dynamics of perpetration and the effects of sexual violence on children were understood in terms of the victim's damaged morality (loss of innocence) only.[2] In the Edwardian period, the idea that children

DOI: 10.4324/9780429468162-4

who had been abused, especially those who had been repeatedly abused, were no longer 'innocent' (and therefore a threat to the moral welfare of other children) was a serious problem for those who wanted to reframe the focus of the law and policy on abusers and the harm they caused.[3] Trauma discourse and medicalized understandings of trauma helped reframe the harm of CSA, as something that gave rise to serious consequences for the victim, and which should not be blamed on the victim.[4] It also allowed for a more sympathetic understanding of the effects of CSA into adulthood.

Scholars point to an ambivalence in how CSA victims were understood by law; they could be both victims of a terrible crime which was recognized as harmful, but also, *because of that very victimization*, they were seen as morally damaged and therefore not to be trusted as reliable witnesses and were treated as a threat to other children's moral welfare.[5] Reformers struggled throughout the Edwardian period to refocus legal and public debate on the abuser and the state's responsibility to punish him through the criminal law. This framing of the CSA victim as a moral threat who has lost their natural innocence, and is therefore a risk to other children and not to be fully trusted as a witness in legal proceedings, still influences understandings of CSA and CSE in policy and in policing and social work today.[6]

A key theme of all three chapters is the age of consent; the age below which it is ruled that a girl's consent to sex was not possible and any sexual acts performed with or on that female child were criminal. In England and Wales and Ireland, the age of consent for the offence of unlawful carnal knowledge of a girl was set at ten in 1828, raised to 12 in 1861 and to 13 in 1875.[7] In 1880, consent to indecent assault for both boys and girls was raised to 13.[8] However, boys were treated differently, with any sexual contact with boys being shaped by the criminalization of men's homosexual sex in 1885. This meant that boys over the age of consent were never really understood by the law as consenting to indecent acts, rather they were at risk of being tried as an accomplice to gross indecency.

The statutory age of consent has changed over the course of the past 200 years in response to changing public and political attitudes and conceptions of adult–child sexual relations and the recognition that boys and girls should be treated equally in law. The age of consent was an attempt to mark the sexual violation of girls as different to the crime of rape, which under the common law required an element of physical force.[9] Ideas of free choice that inform more recent interpretations of consent were not relevant. Therefore, although we use the phrase 'age of consent', we are aware that consent in the Victorian and Edwardian eras was unrelated to ideas of autonomy and agency.

The focus on an age of consent in legislative efforts to tackle sexual violence against girls became particularly pronounced in the late nineteenth and early twentieth centuries. While the age of consent facilitated prosecutions of carnal knowledge and indecent assault, political and public debates revealed contradictory understandings of the adolescent girl as either virtuous or dangerous; vulnerable to her own or men's desires or, if she was working class, as a prostitute who could blackmail respectable men (including legislators). In each country, issues of gender and sexuality were inseparable from goals of nation-building on the domestic and international stages. These conflicting anxieties around girls and their moral status precluded any sustained attention on the various contexts of children's sexual exploitation and the need for specific focus on sexual violence against boys.

This chapter explores the legal landscape in England and Wales from the nineteenth century to the present. We begin with England and Wales because legislative developments in criminal law also applied to Ireland until independence in 1922 and heavily influenced developments in the nineteenth century in Australia. The first section introduces the historiography and development of the law relating to the criminalization of sexual violence against children, starting with the foundational Criminal Law Amendment Act 1885 (CLAA 1885). The contrasting legislative protection and discriminatory consequences that the gender-specific offences of the Act created are examined, noting that these remained in effect until CSA was finally defined in law as late as the enactment of the Sexual Offences Act 2003 (SOA 2003). The second section explores the operation of the criminal justice process in applying the law to prosecutions with emphasis on the legal and practical barriers to obtaining evidence from children from the nineteenth century until the Criminal Justice Act 1991.

The third section considers the state's governance of child welfare and child protection, which has developed from the institutionalization of children at risk to consideration of the child's best interests as core to the work of law, social work and policing. This development occurred throughout the twentieth century, despite a sustained prioritization of institutional power above the rights and needs of children, a lack of clear inter-agency cooperation and contestation by some parents and media commentators of the proper role of professionals.

The criminal law

The CLAA 1885 was the first English statute to criminalize child prostitution and trafficking and increased the age of sexual protection, for girls only, from 13 to 16 years. Its application in England and Wales and in Ireland and its translation into similar legislation in Australia is crucial to understanding the apparent disinclination of subsequent parliaments to make even modest reforms in this area and is a contributory factor to some of the difficulties associated with the prosecution of NRCSA in each country in recent decades.

The age of consent from the CLAA 1885 to the Sexual Offences Act 1956

The original purpose of the CLAA 1885 was to 'make further provision for the protection of women and girls, the suppression of brothels and other purposes'. It was the culmination of some 15 years of agitation by feminists and social morality crusaders. The most prominent figure, Josephine Butler, campaigned against the double standard of the Contagious Diseases Acts under which any woman in various garrison towns could be arrested and medically examined on suspicion of prostitution. Despite the aim of the Acts ostensibly being to protect against the spread of venereal disease, men were exempt from prosecution. After the Acts were suspended in 1883, the focus of the campaigns shifted from rescuing the 'fallen prostitute' to ensuring that the 'incidence of the law be made to press equally on men and women alike'.[10] The threat posed to the institution of the family by male lust was linked to fears of a national decline at a time when the breakup of the United Kingdom (UK) was looming. Racism was also at the core of social purity campaigners' discourse; they denounced the 'savagery' of CSA amid concerns about national degeneration and racial depletion.[11] The moral climate was strongly in favour of the stricter regulation of sexual lives. William Stead's exposé of the ease with which young girls could be 'purchased' for sexual purposes finally convinced the House of Lords to pass the CLAA 1885. In a series of articles in the Pall Mall Gazette in summer 1885, his *Maiden Tribute to Modern Babylon*[12] exposed the presence of a heathen immorality at odds with England's professed modern Christian civilization. It caused such uproar that the government rushed through the Act while the articles were still appearing.

The Criminal Law Amendment Bill 1885 generated ferocious debates in parliament,[13] especially the defilement clauses extending the age threshold of sexual protection to 16. Some members of the Lords believed it was they who needed legal protection from young girls' 'immoral' advances and blackmail and insisted on the inclusion of a defence of reasonable belief that a girl was over 16.[14] Ss 4 and 5 criminalized the unlawful (outside the bonds of marriage) carnal knowledge of girls aged under 13 and 16, respectively.[15] A three-month time limit for prosecutions under s5 was introduced in 1885 attracting considerable criticism as many cases became time-barred. It was extended to 12 months in England and Wales by the Criminal Law (Amendment) Act 1922 (CLAA 1922) some 40 years later and was retained in 1956 effectively prohibiting many claims of NRCSA until it was removed in 2003. The CLAA 1922, in another political compromise, removed the universal defence of reasonable cause to believe a girl was under 16, limiting it to young men aged under 23. This so-called 'young man's defence' also survived the 1956 consolidation and was not abolished until 2003. The fallacy of such dispensation is underlined by the child grooming cases involving groups of young men aged between 18 and 23 in Rotherham, Oxford and Rochdale in the early twenty-first century.[16]

The emphasis on unlawful carnal knowledge contrasted with the lack of attention paid to other offences that could be used to prosecute abusers. The age of consent for indecent assault on boys and girls was left at 13 by the CLAA 1885. This had a particularly chilling effect on boys reporting, because of the effects of the Labouchère Amendment which criminalized 'gross indecency'[17] between males. This meant that any boy over 14[18] who attempted to report indecent assault by a male was running the risk of criminalization under the gross indecency provisions. The age of consent to indecent assault was finally raised to 16 in 1922, but the criminalization of gay sex continued to deter reporting by boy victims of CSA.

The Sexual Offences Act 1956 (SOA 1956) presented an opportunity to refine and update outmoded laws passed in the nineteenth century, but it disappointed.[19] The phenomenon of child sexual abuse was not yet universally acknowledged or understood, so there was little impetus for major reform. It was not until the 1960s that the developing sciences, including feminism, evolved more nuanced understandings about sexual violation relocating sexual discourse into the public sphere and purging longstanding social taboos.[20] Constituting one of the Consolidation Bills 1955–1956, the Act was mostly a tidying-up measure restating and repealing some existing statutes, particularly the CLAA 1885, but also the Punishment of Incest Act 1908 (POIA) and later Criminal Law Amendment Acts. The Chair of the Joint Select Committee advised the Lord Chancellor that without a full parliamentary debate, it would be inappropriate to propose 'any reforms that would increase criminal liability'.[21] The statute was primarily a consolidation of the CLAA 1885 with some modernization of its Victorian language.[22] For example, the offences of procuring 'any *girl* or woman to have unlawful carnal connexion' in ss 2, 3 and 4 CLAA 1885 were updated to procuring, by threats, false pretences or the administration of drugs, a woman to have 'unlawful sexual intercourse'. Although s48 notes that the erasure of 'girl' does not 'prevent the provision applying to any person to whom it would have applied' if it had been used, with hindsight such abstruse drafting implicitly downplays the seriousness of sexual violence against children. The CLAA 1885 provisions criminalizing unlawful carnal knowledge of girls aged under 13 and 16 were simply reproduced into ss 5 and 6 of the SOA 1956 with 'carnal knowledge' being replaced by 'unlawful sexual intercourse'. Another oversight in 1956 was the failure to consider any equivalent protection for boys; it would be 1994 before the crime of rape of a man was recognized in English law.[23] Under the 1956 Act sexual violence against boys could be charged as buggery or indecent assault but victim-shaming significantly restricted prosecutions.[24]

Indecent assault

The offence of 'indecent' assault potentially covered a wide range of illicit sexual touching and contact including penetration. However, as the two 1956 consolidations, s14 against females and s15 against males, were taken from the OAPA 1861, convictions necessitated proof of an assault or battery executed with hostile intent and in circumstances deemed to be indecent. The courts were unwilling to find indecent assault in situations where an adult asked a child to touch their genitals and the child did so.[25] In a display of wilful ignorance of the dynamics of sexual abuse, the courts deemed such acts to be indecent but not coercive and therefore not an assault.

While there are some historical examples of men charged with indecent assaults on boys, there are few involving female perpetrators.[26] In either context, boys under 16 were typically perceived as 'willing partners', condoned by the legal presumption that at 14 they were physically capable of sexual intercourse so implicitly possessed the mental capacity to 'consent'.[27] It is now acknowledged that women can be as sexually abusive as men, but this only became embedded in the public consciousness after 2003 when it became possible to convict them as principals for causing or encouraging sexual activity (including rape) committed by others.[28] The difficulties with defendants claiming that children had 'consented' to sexualized grooming was supposedly addressed in the Indecency with Children Act 1960 which created a single offence of 'inciting gross indecency with or towards a child under 14'.[29] It at least applied to both boys and girls, but the inclusion of 'gross' referenced the emphasis on the child's age not the *nature* of the assault. The derisory maximum sentence of two years or £100 fine was hardly a deterrent and appeals against conviction were won on the grounds that abusers who gained sexual pleasure from observation or encouragement had not done any physical act 'towards' a child.[30]

Incest

Pressure from the National Society for the Prevention of Cruelty to Children (NSPCC) and the National Vigilance Association helped pave the way for the introduction of the Punishment of Incest Act 1908 (POIA 1908). It coincided with the introduction of The Children Act 1908 which consolidated and extended previous child protection statutes. The main reason for the enactment of the POIA 1908 was not eugenics but the protection of children from sexual abuse by their parents.[31] As such it reflected a growing recognition of the different forms of CSA. Importantly, unlike other sexual crimes, the age of consent was irrelevant. Females under 16 were exempted from liability, but there was no equivalent exemption for males.[32] The Act made incest by a male or a female punishable by up to seven years' imprisonment, but in the case of incest by a male committed with a girl under 13, the punishment was life imprisonment.[33] The SOA 1956 reproduced the incest provisions in s10 and 11. Along with cruelty to children and wife-beating, incest was framed by reformers as a working-class crime, allowing activists and policymakers to separate incest from their conception of 'home' and the middle-class family. This would have particularly disastrous consequences for Irish working-class children (see Chapter 4).

Sexual Offences Act 2003

The law therefore presented a confused mix of generic and largely ineffective offences encompassing various anomalies depending on age, gender, nature of the abuse and relationship between the parties. The criminal law's limitations became increasingly evident[34] and were addressed by the SOA 2003 which introduced a series of gender-neutral offences that, apart from rape which necessitates penile penetration (s1), can be committed by and against males and females. The requirement of proving non-consent was eliminated for all child sex offences.[35] Ss 5–8 detail offences against children under 13 years including statutory rape, assault by penetration, sexual assault and causing a child to engage in sexual activity. Ss 9–15 address inappropriate sexual conduct including penetration with any child under 16 (s9) distinguishing adult culpability from those under 18 (through a reduced sentence) and providing a defence of reasonable belief that the child was in fact aged 16 or over. The statute criminalizes a range of behaviour including sexual touching, engaging in, inciting or facilitating sexual activity, grooming, prostitution and pornography. While these offences reflect the age thresholds set by the CLAA 1885, the 2003 Act also recognizes relational vulnerabilities by defining similar offences for those holding a position of trust in institutional and non-institutional settings where the young person is under 18, familial relationships (blood related, extended family and carers) and persons suffering from 'mental disorders'.

The 2003 Act therefore covers virtually all known forms of sexual abuse physically perpetrated against children after it came into force on 1 May 2004.[36] The relatively few appeals testing the substantive law suggest the provisions were largely well-conceived and carefully drafted. Claims of NRCSA committed *before* that date must be dealt with under the SOA 1956. But comparing offences under the SOA 1956 with those under the SOA 2003 'is fraught with difficulty; the ingredients of the offences are frequently not identical and consequently, care must be taken when embarking on such an exercise'.[37]

Prosecuting child sex offences in the twentieth century

Until recently, there was a huge gap in the historiography of child sex offences from the 1900s to the 1970s.[38] Research by Jackson, Delap and Bingham has started to fill in the detail, confirming that while its true incidence is unknowable, it has always been significantly under-reported. The media's role is crucial to understanding the prevailing public knowledge and societal attitudes about sexual offences, especially because court reports were officially censored so newspapers may be the only archival record.[39] Bingham classifies the twentieth century newspaper reportage into three phases: child sex offences 1918–1940 'briefly reported and discreetly placed'; their camouflage from the 1940s to the 1970s amongst wider debates on homosexuality and from the

1970s as 'new terms and conceptual approaches became available to define the problem of "child sexual abuse" the identification of the "paedophile" as a major threat'.[40] All three make uncovering the actuality of child sex offending extremely challenging.

During the nineteenth century the concept of 'childhood' came to be acknowledged as a developmental period distinguishable from the expectations of adulthood.[41] This informed early, often vociferous, twentieth century debates contesting the relics of Victorian *laissez-faire* attitudes over the responsibility of the state and the law for child welfare and protection. The 1925 Committee on Sexual Offences Against Young Persons wondered how to balance fair, impartial and public trials, with the needs of children 'who, on account of their immaturity, are unfit to be associated with the courts of justice, and for whom, on account of the nature of the wrongs they have suffered, publicity may be harmful in the extreme'.[42] Evidence was presented to the Committee that in a 'great number of trials…the guilty party escapes conviction'. From 1919–1923 of 286 persons charged with carnal knowledge of a girl under 13, 112 were acquitted, and for cases involving girls aged 13 to 16, 407 of 744 prosecutions failed.[43] The Committee expressed concerns about the strain on child witnesses, their courtroom experience and the legal difficulties of receiving and corroborating children's testimony. None of these would be effectively addressed until Judge Pigot's 1989 Report which compelled substantial changes to the law relating to the reception of children's evidence.[44]

The POIA 1908 was also illustrative of the tensions between the state and child-centred reformers. In the late nineteenth century, the NSPCC, feminists and purity campaigners had demanded legislation to prosecute fathers who abused their daughters but, as with the CLAA 1885, met similar resistance from a House of Lords fearful of passing a law that would bring such immoral cases 'into the light of day'.[45] It was believed that press reporting of incest trials would encourage others to commit similar offences. A compromise was reached whereby all prosecutions required the consent of the Director of Public Prosecutions and all trials be held *in camera* excluding the press and the public. While the aim of protecting the identity of child survivors was laudable, it prohibited the naming of any person charged under the POIA 1908. The subsequent dearth of reported prosecutions in newspapers reinforced the silence around incest as it appeared that none were in fact being committed. In the first five years post-1908, 56 offences were recorded by the police of which 88 per cent were prosecuted; the 1925 Committee expected the figure to be much higher.[46] The reporting restrictions were lifted by the CLAA 1922 (but they endured in Ireland until 1995; see Chapter 4), but throughout the twentieth century, there were no more than 200 prosecutions annually. Gibbens and Soothill believe that from the 1950s to the 1970s, only 50 per cent of incest cases reported to the police were prosecuted.[47] In 1987 184 men were proceeded against, but by 1997 this had dropped to just 25, suggesting that the 1908 Act was now obsolete.[48] The Criminal Law Revision Committee 1984[49] recommended that the word 'incest' be redacted from the law and replaced by 'unlawful familial sexual intercourse', but this would take another 20 years to secure.[50]

Legal barriers to justice

Courtroom barriers were both physical and metaphysical. In cases of abuse in the family, although the evidence of wives was made admissible in trials of their husbands in the Prevention of Cruelty to Children Act 1889, they were not compellable witnesses so the prosecution could not require a wife to testify against her husband. In Victorian and Edwardian courts, the sexual 'criminal'—the rapist or child abuser who was inspired by 'brutal lust'—was deemed to have little connection with the dutiful, hardworking middle-class family man.[51] Although sexual abuse was constructed as a shocking social problem, alleged abusers were often acquitted or sentenced to fines or minor terms of imprisonment.[52]

The lack of participation by women and by experienced professionals in sex abuse trials was heavily criticized by the 1925 Committee as was the need for complainants to continually repeat the 'sordid details' of the offence. There were insufficient female police officers to interview victims and take initial statements; policewomen's departments did not become universally established until the mid-twentieth century. At trial, women probation officers and women police officers were asked to leave the court when a child gave evidence as it was thought they should be protected from hearing testimony about immoral matters. While the Sex Disqualification (Removal) Act 1919 permitted women to become jurors, lawyers and eventually judges, it would take more than 50 years for the legal system to become more equitably gender calibrated. Courtrooms were unsuitable for children, waiting rooms were non-segregated, lengthy delays between disclosure and trial were typical and the child was in close physical proximity to the dock and jury box.[53] Such physical impediments and their impact on child victims would not be ameliorated until the 1990s/2000s.[54]

The 1925 Committee had also criticized the 'strain on child witnesses', but throughout the twentieth century there was a reluctance to acknowledge such stress exacerbated by uncompromising legal rules, age-inappropriate questioning and cross-examination, refusal to allow pre-trial counselling and the requirement that children give their evidence from memory. Another obstacle was authenticating the truth, typically with no visible signs of injury to convince jurors beyond all reasonable doubt that sexual violation had occurred. The reality of the incident and validity of a child's complaint were notoriously difficult to establish as indicated by the acquittal statistics above. In the adversarial courtroom, the judge acts as independent referee, the prosecution and defence must serve their own cause and the child victim has no legal representation or agency. Because of the nature of the allegation, a child's veracity depended on their credibility as a competent witness and the integrity of other independent, material evidence or testimony that could corroborate that narrative. Historically, the judiciary were fixated on the religious sanctity of the oath and supremacy of sworn evidence. The CLAA 1885 permitted the admission of unsworn testimony albeit requiring corroborating evidence, but even into the late twentieth century, some judges still associated truth with biblical understanding.[55] In *Hayes* 1977,[56] three boys aged 12, 11 and 9 alleged gross indecency and were interrogated by the trial judge about their understanding of God and Jesus. The Court of Appeal held the judge had discretion as to whether they could be sworn as a witness, but it was unnecessary that they must believe in divine sanctions. The decision was approved in 1983,[57] but in 1988, Exeter Crown Court Judge Willcock QC ordered the jury to dismiss two specimen charges of indecent assault against a 46-year-old man as 'it would be a waste of time' to ask the two girls aged ten and seven years to hold the New Testament and take the oath.[58] Such dissonance illustrates the unpredictability of the judiciary when dealing with child witnesses.

Reform of the legal system was spearheaded by law professors John Spencer and Diane Birch, Judge Thomas Pigot, the NSPCC, Children's Rights Centre and virtually every other professional body involved in child abuse cases, invigorated by the media and Childline. Law therefore found itself in conflict with other disciplines. Child psychiatrists, particularly in America, thought the law too sceptical towards children with cases dismissed or children so badgered or confused by defence lawyers that juries no longer regarded them as credible.[59] In the UK the courts started to accept diagnostic interpretations (using anatomically correct dolls, drawings, images, etc.) from interviews with children conducted by 'non-legal' child experts and behavioural scientists pioneered by Eileen Vizard, Arnon Bentovim and Marianne Tranter from Great Ormond Street Children's Hospital. The therapeutic value of such techniques risked crossing law's boundaries of fact and evidence contamination precipitating defence claims of 'coaching'. Law was compelled to adopt a more inclusionary approach recognizing expert opinion where supported by evidence of probative value. Experts could give evidence as to the child's psychiatric state but not opinion about whether they were telling the truth.[60] Judge Pigot's Advisory Group Report of 1989 had recommended that the competency requirement, that a judge must be satisfied that the child has sufficient intelligence to justify the reception of their unsworn testimony and understand the duty to tell the truth, be dispensed with.[61] This was achieved by s52 Criminal Justice Act 1991 permitting all children under 14 to give unsworn evidence[62] unless incapable of giving intelligible testimony. The corroboration warning, that legally a jury be warned of the dangers of convicting on the uncorroborated evidence of a child was removed by s34 Criminal Justice Act 1988 and practically because it was a sexual offence,[63] by s32 Criminal Justice and Public Order Act 1994. In 1990 a father was convicted on the unsworn evidence of his six-year-old daughter where the judge was satisfied she could give an account of what she experienced when she was aged five.[64] Ten years later, the Court of Appeal rejected an appeal against conviction from Steven

Barker for the anal rape of two-year-old C. Barker was convicted on C's testimony, aged four years at the time of the trial. The Court of Appeal agreed with the trial judge that C's testimony could be understood and so she was presumed to be a competent witness. Age is no longer determinative of the ability to give truthful and accurate evidence.[65] But it was not until 2014 that the Court of Appeal finally showed that the judiciary are not 'powerless' and can change questionable practices significantly if they wish. In *Lubemba*, Hallett LJ promoted a more interventionist judicial role through the use of 'ground rules' hearings where the defence must submit in writing questions they intend to introduce in cross-examination of child witnesses for judicial approval: 'It is now generally accepted that if justice is to be done to the vulnerable witness and also to the accused, a radical departure from the traditional style of advocacy will be necessary'.[66]

Judge Pigot also tackled the intimidating courtroom atmosphere. In 1987, he allowed a 13-year-old girl, one of five children to give evidence against three fathers, to sit behind a screen at the Central Criminal Court. He also permitted a social worker to sit next to them acknowledging, 'What is proposed is a radical departure from precedents and it is my duty to balance the advantages and disadvantages to ensure a fair trial'.[67] The men claimed, unsuccessfully, that they would be 'over-prejudiced in the eyes of the jury'[68] and appealed, again unsuccessfully, to the European Court of Human Rights.[69] From 1989, screens were superseded by video links largely unchallenged[70] and self-represented defendants were also prohibited from personally cross-examining children.[71] Ss23–39 of the Youth Justice and Criminal Evidence Act 1999 authorized special measures for vulnerable witnesses including the removal of wigs and gowns. The Act also confirmed the primacy of video-recording initial disclosures in response to the recommendations of Judge Pigot's advisory group report. But reform was agonistically slow and, apart from Pigot, the judiciary were hardly proactive. In 2004 the NSPCC-commissioned Report, *In Their Own Words*, followed five years later by *Measuring Up,* showed that the implementation of these improvements plus limits on delayed trials and waiting periods at court were far from systematically or automatically provided.[72] The 1999 Act also permitted the use of interlocutors and (s28) that evidence-in-chief and defence cross-examination could be video-recorded before the trial and outside the courtroom to avoid children attending and testifying in court. It took an indefensible 18 years for this to be implemented in 2017, almost a century after the 1925 Report flagged its concerns.

Inter-agency working in gathering child testimony

The extensive research on children's testimony demonstrates that from the age of three or so, child witnesses can be as reliable as adults.[73] However, the quality of a child witness' evidence can depend on the communication skills and expertise of the person who questions them.[74] It is law's responsibility to provide the 'bedrock of agency practice'.[75] For police and social workers, this was implemented in the *Memorandum of Good Practice* 1992[76] which introduced joint training and interviews. Practice changed significantly though the police tended to apply the Memorandum more rigidly, whereas social workers favoured a more child-centred approach and expressed frustration that once in court all the good work done by inter-agency teams was 'blown apart by the defence'.[77]

The Memorandum has now been superseded by the Achieving Best Evidence (ABE) protocol, and child witnesses are supported by Witness Care Units operationalizing the Witness Charter. Even so a government report in 2014 found in only ten out of 69 interviews were the specific needs of the child taken into account, video-recorded evidence was poor, inappropriate questioning techniques were used, interview rooms were unsuitable and better training was required.[78] The ABE protocol has meant that specialist child protection workers were replaced with 'child in need' teams, and the emphasis on joint working and joint training was lost. In a departure from previous guidance, this emphasis has led to a reversion to more traditional methods with the police resuming the lead, often without a social worker or a supportive adult present.[79]

Child welfare and child protection

The last two decades of the twentieth century witnessed a growth in specialist childcare provision with paediatricians, child psychiatrists and psychologists offering therapeutic treatment and assessing the effects of abuse on the individual. Leading experts such as paediatricians Dr Jane Wynne and Dr Christopher Hobbs developed more accurate means of identifying signs of sexual abuse and there was a heightened awareness amongst teachers, nursery nurses and other carers who became more alert to the possibility of disclosure. This resulted in a significant increase in referrals which consequently exposed the limitations of traditional police responses and interview strategies, highlighting the need for more effective inter-agency collaboration. While multi-disciplinary cooperation was nothing new, it was flagged up as one of the major steps forward of the 1980s in managing the increasing caseload of physical and sexual abuse.[80] Nevertheless, tensions between social workers and the police started to appear as the interventionist and positivistic emphasis of social work ideology clashed with the classically punitive principles of policing and need to secure evidence that would be admissible in court. Relationships between the two agencies had been criticized by the Committee of Inquiry into the death of Maria Colwell in 1974. They improved but subsequently social workers were condemned for failing to intervene in the deaths of Jasmine Beckford, Kimberley Carlisle and Tyra Henry in the mid-1980s. When Butler-Sloss LJ inquired into the complete breakdown of inter-agency trust that caused the Cleveland crisis, she acknowledged that the fervent interventions of social workers were a predictable over-compensation.[81]

The Cleveland crisis

Reprising early twentieth century debates, Stuart Bell MP described Cleveland as the greatest child abuse crisis 'Britain has ever faced. At its heart lay the fundamental question, who has ultimate power over children, the Family or the State?'[82] From January 1987 until March 1988, 545 complaints of sexual abuse were referred to Cleveland County Council.[83] In one six-week period, 197 children were taken into care, placing immense pressure on resources. The local magistracy was criticized 'for so many children needlessly and indiscriminately being removed from their families' at the behest of social workers.[84] Before the crisis there was a general measure of inter-agency understanding and respect. But by April 1987, when two cases were mishandled, followed by the admission of 23 children to Middlesbrough General Hospital over a bank holiday and a further 14 and 33 by mid-June, professional relations had deteriorated, and positions had become entrenched at senior operational levels. The police were highly suspicious of the diagnoses of Doctors Higgs and Wyatt and their controversial test of anal dilation insisting on the expertise of trusted police surgeons who knew how to obtain admissible forensic evidence. Relations irretrievably broke down when the Director of Cleveland Social Services ordered police surgeons to be excluded from medical examinations in favour of the consultant paediatricians. In response the Chief Constable advised his officers not to interview suspected perpetrators without a written statement from Dr Higgs or confirmation of medical examination from the police surgeon.

Protests by parents and others eventually led to a public inquiry chaired by Elizbeth Butler-Sloss, which reported in 1988. Butler-Sloss' report concluded that in a significant majority of the cases there were grounds to believe sexual abuse had taken place.[85] She did not attribute blame to one agency or individual concluding that all contributed to the eventual crisis. Journalist Bea Campbell called it a 'war of the sexes' caused by the masculinity of Cleveland police and their unwillingness to listen and learn from female social workers, doctors and victims.[86]

Moral panics over 'Satanic abuse' in the Orkneys, Rochdale and Nottingham followed. The weight of official evidence and opinion eventually settled on a judgement that the most extreme features of allegations of Satanic abuse were a kind of group fantasy;[87] but some important advances in knowledge about CSA were established and the evidence for ritual abuse and systems of organized child abuse became better understood.[88] Cleveland also embedded inter-agency co-operation and co-ordination formalized in the Department of Health and Social Security's official guidance, *Working Together* 1988 and Home Office Circular 52/1988 *The Investigation of Child Sexual Abuse*.

Another outcome of Cleveland was the Children Act 1989 hailed as 'the most comprehensive and far-reaching reform of child law which has come before parliament in living memory'.[89] The Act which brought together public and private law for the first time was informed by a review and subsequent

White Paper on childcare law and a Law Commission report on custody and guardianship. The 1989 Act centres on the idea that children are best cared for in their own families and every effort should be made to support that, where possible. It emphasizes that the child's welfare is paramount when making decisions about their upbringing and their wishes and feelings should be taken into account. Delays in making decisions are likely to have a negative impact. It also established the principle of 'parental responsibility' and sets out in detail what local authorities, courts and other agencies should do to protect the welfare of children. Under s47, local authorities have a duty to investigate if they suspect a child is at risk of significant harm, including physical and sexual abuse or treatment likely to damage a child's health or development. S17 charges councils with a duty to provide services for 'children in need' and their families. From the outset, there were concerns about funding especially when it came to prevention and wider support for families, services that have been particularly hard-hit by recent cuts. The proportion of local authority money allocated to early intervention has progressively decreased over the past decade, while the number of children subject to child protection plans has ballooned.[90]

Following Lord Laming's 2003 inquiry into the murder of Victoria Climbié[91] which identified a lack of priority given to safeguarding measures by local authorities, and to deficiencies in structures to detect and respond to child abuse, the Children Act 2004 was introduced. It places a duty on local authorities in England to make arrangements to promote co-operation with key partners and local agencies.

In 2008, there was a step change in the intensity of the cycle of crisis and reform after the death of Peter Connelly (Baby P) at the age of 17 months.[92] The story reached 'entirely new levels of irrationality' in terms of the scale of hostility directed at social workers. It was asserted in Parliament that thresholds for care proceedings were too high.[93] Reaction to Connolly's death led to reform on an unprecedented scale. The Munro review highlighted the need for politicians and other public figures to avoid 'knee-jerk reactions or conclusions' and for actions to be 'thoughtfully reviewed'.[94] The Children and Social Work Act 2017 amended the 2004 Act and aims to improve joint work at the local level to safeguard children and to improve decision-making and support for looked-after children and care leavers. *Working Together* has been updated in light of the legislative changes, most recently in 2018.[95]

Disclosure and disbelief: children as 'unreliable reporters'

As in Australia and Ireland, one of the fundamental reasons for the failure to report is that child victims found it hugely challenging to disclose their experiences.[96] The deep cultural suspicion of child reporters is illustrated by their experiences in boarding schools and in the Catholic Church. In 2017 the extent of NRCSA at public schools was revealed when journalist Alex Renton detailed his suffering at Ashdown House Boarding School in his autobiographical *Stiff Upper Lip*.[97] Ashdown was a small school with just 100 pupils, yet nearly half of the teaching staff were accused of sexual abuse at some stage. Parents complained about the assaults in 1975, but many were complicit believing that mistreatment was 'character-building' or that their son 'must have deserved it'. Forty years later teacher Martin Haigh was convicted and sentenced to 12 years imprisonment for indecent assaults and possession of child pornography. He admitted inciting the boys to masturbate but refused to acknowledge he had encouraged them to remove his trousers something he pompously declared would have 'undermined one's authority'. Renton's mother recalls the then-headmaster Billy Williamson telling her 'Little boys make things up' and nicknaming her son 'spoof' (the school liar).[98]

Renton's cathartic disclosure resulted in him receiving 425 unsolicited credible allegations involving 145 named schools. He believes that by 1989 there was official speculation of at least one case of NRCSA at 75 per cent of boarding schools hidden by a culture of silence and shame. Subsequent revelations included some highly prestigious institutions. Freedom of Information requests identified 404 allegations of sexual abuse reported to three-quarters of local councils in 2012–2017, one council responsible for 19 boarding schools had received 60 complaints. Renton cites Sherborne Prep and its 'charismatic headmaster' Robin Lindsay who groomed not only the boys but also the parents so that they would be willing to entrust their sons to him. When Dorset Police tried to establish a case in the 1990s, they were frustrated because many parents refused to let their sons be interviewed as they did not want any scandal tainting their potential acceptance into privileged public schools including Eton.[99]

The Catholic Church was also notorious in the way it engaged in and condoned conspiracies of silence. As with boarding schools, responsibility fell into the chasm between the accountability of senior leaders, including the Pope, and their scapegoating of the respective parish. In 2001, Pope John Paul II updated the list of canonical crimes to expressly include the sexual abuse of minors by clerics and crimes connected with solicitation in confession. This meant all such allegations should be automatically reported to the Congregation for the Doctrine of the Faith who would respond with relevant guidance in consultation with the Holy See. In response, in 2002 and also as a result of the Nolan report, *A Programme for Action*, the Catholic Office for the Protection of Children and Vulnerable Adults (COPCA) appointed child protection officers in every diocese. Yet six years later, Baroness Cumberlege's review of the Church's progress, *Safeguarding with Confidence,* criticized senior leaders' failure to proactively implement the recommendations.[100] The Prelate's successor, Pope Benedict XVI spoke in direct and lengthy terms about priests who 'twist the sacrament [of Holy Orders] into its antithesis, and under the mantle of the sacred profoundly wound human persons in their childhood, damaging them for a whole lifetime'.[101] But it was not until 2014 that Pope Francis issued a full apology on behalf of the Vatican.[102] While there have been proposals to introduce mandatory reporting, these have not gained traction largely because of disagreement over the extent of such a legal duty and appropriate sanctions although the Boarding Schools Association now require its members to report allegations of sexual abuse.

A Report for the Children's Commissioner[103] into child sexual exploitation in gangs and groups found that many interviewees described family sexual violence and their experiences never being acknowledged.[104] This prompted a further inquiry into CSA into the family. The 2014 Report found that the child protection system is far from child-centred, is concerned with meeting targets at the expense of listening to and protecting children and that the criminal justice system may subject victims of child sexual abuse to secondary victimization.[105] A further Report by the Children's Commissioner in 2015 found that only one in eight children who is sexually abused is identified by professionals. The majority of victims go unidentified because the police and social services are geared towards children self-referring or reporting abuse, although they rarely do so.[106] This clearly supports Kemp's argument that the true incidence of abuse is significantly higher that reported but is concealed under the surface.[107]

Family law and child protection

The family law system is too quick to assume that domestic violence affects only mothers and not children[108] and also that children are safe once a relationship is over. Women can find themselves in a catch-22, told by social services they must leave their abuser or risk their children being taken into care, but then disbelieved by a judge when that abuser applies for contact.[109]

Worryingly, in recent years, the discredited theory of 'parental alienation syndrome' has gained some traction. It was developed in the 1980s by psychiatrist Richard Gardner who thought CSA is not necessarily traumatic and that mothers who do not sexually fulfil their partners are to blame for fathers sexually abusing their daughters.[110] Gardner believed that many mothers who claim they have been abused are liars who poison their children against their partners. He asserted that it was even more damaging to children than sexual abuse. Despite its general rejection as unscientific, the construct of parental alienation syndrome continues to be used in legal settings as if it has an adequate foundation within science, clinical or forensic practice.[111] In family law courts, parental alienation is often used as a counter-allegation against mothers by fathers accused of abuse.[112] There is evidence of an increasing willingness by judges to transfer the residency of children from 'alienating' mothers to their fathers.[113] As a result, women have to think carefully about bringing abuse allegations to court even where there may be evidence in case they are accused of making false claims and lose custody as a result. This is particularly concerning in a context in which legal aid cuts are making it harder for courts to accurately assess risks to children.[114]

The 2020 Ministry of Justice Report *Assessing Risk of Harm to Children and Parents in Private Law Children Cases* was based on over 1,200 responses, roundtable and focus groups held with professionals, parents and children with experience of the family courts. Authored by three leading domestic violence and child abuse experts,[115] it found that although the Children Act 1989 requires the court to give paramount consideration to the welfare of the child, there were serious concerns about how domestic abuse and CSA was being dealt with in private law proceedings. The report found four structural barriers to identifying and addressing domestic abuse and CSA: the family court's pro-contact culture, resource constraints, the adversarial process and silo working. It explains how these barriers have operated systematically to minimize domestic abuse and to limit the effectiveness of previous reform efforts. The report found that court orders, whether agreed or determined by the court, often fail to protect children and adult victims from continuing abuse. It proposes a reform of the Child Arrangements programme, in particular in shifting from an adversarial to an investigative and problem-solving process. Features would include active investigation by the court to gain a comprehensive understanding of what is happening for the child, consultation with children, judicial continuity, joined-up working, follow-up by the court to ensure orders are safe and workable to avoid returns to court and the use of proceedings to continue abuse and control.

Conclusion

The period of NRCSA discovery in the late twentieth century is mirrored by the explosion in legal, social and philanthropic work on sexual violence against children in the late nineteenth and early twentieth century. The focus on adolescent girls and the age of consent in the Victorian period narrowed the focus of the criminal law so that public and legislative scrutiny and debate of the contexts and dynamics of sexual violence against children was neglected for much of the twentieth century. A particular blind spot was sexual violence against boys, and sexual violence (against both sexes) within the family and in institutional contexts (such as the Catholic Church, boarding schools and in care) were not addressed. The legal system itself compounded the silences around sexual violence by refusing to treat children as credible reporters of their experiences. The Cleveland crisis provoked a reckoning with these barriers to reporting and prompted greater inter-agency working.

Since the 1980s children's voices have been afforded greater credibility by social work and the legal system. However, the child protection system and the family law system are still operating in ways that minimize opportunities for children suffering or at risk of sexual violence in the family or in care or in the community from being taken seriously and their reports acted on.

In the next chapter we explore the evolution of criminal legal and child protection frameworks in Ireland.

Notes

1 E. Olafson et al., "Modern History of Child Sexual Abuse Awareness: Cycles of Discovery and Suppression" *Child Abuse and Neglect* 17, 1993, 7–24.

2 The roots of these frameworks lie in the nineteenth century when the romantic concept of the child as innately virtuous became increasing linked with ideas of the self and identity; P. Aries, *Centuries of Childhood: A Social History of Family Life* (New York: Vintage Books, 1962).

3 C. Smart, "Reconsidering the Recent History of Child Sexual Abuse, 1910–1960" *Journal of Social Policy* 29(1), 2000, 55–71, 56.

4 Ibid., 404.

5 Ibid., L. Jackson, *Child Sexual Abuse in Victorian England* (London: Routledge, 2000).

6 J. Kitzinger, "Defending Innocence: Ideologies of Childhood" *Feminist Review* 28, 1988, 77–87; A. Kosaraju, *Attrition in Cases Involving Crimes of Child Sexual Exploitation in England*, PhD Thesis (Canterbury: University of Kent, 2018).

7 S4 Offences Against the Person Act 1875.

8 s2 The Assault of Young Persons Act 1880.

9 William Blackstone described 'rape…or the carnal knowledge of a woman forcibly and against her will'. W. Blackstone, *Commentaries on the Law of England* (Oxford: Clarendon Press, 1765–1769), Vol. 4 Ch. 15, [3].

10 E. Hopkins, *England's Law for Women and Children* (London: Hatchards, 1883), 52.

11 Jackson, op. cit., 56–8.

12 W. Stead, "The Maiden Tribute to Modern Babylon," *Pall Mall Gazette*, 4 July 1885.

13 J. Kitzinger, *Framing Abuse: Media Influence and Public Understanding of Sexual Violence against Children* (London: Pluto, 2004).

14 See K. Stevenson, "Not Just the Ideas of a Few Enthusiasts: Early Twentieth Century Legal Activism and the Criminalization of Immorality" *Cultural and Social History Journal* 14(2), 2017, 1–18.

15 s4 was a felony punishable with life imprisonment and s5 was a misdemeanor punishable with two years' imprisonment; both sentences were replicated in 1956.

16 See A. Jay, *Independent Inquiry into CSE in Rotherham 1997-2013* (Rotherham: Rotherham Borough Council, 2014).

17 s11 CLAA 1885.

18 A legal presumption existed that boys under the age of 14 were not physically capable of sexual intercourse but became culpable from that age; see *R v Mason* (1968) 53 Cr.App.R. 12.

19 The 1956 Act only applied to England and Wales.

20 Olafson et al., op. cit.

21 Joint Select Committee, *Fourth Report on Consolidation Bills 1955-56, Report on Sexual Offences Bills* (London: HMSO, 1956), 1. Most of their deliberations centred on powers to search and arrest, not the substantive law.

22 Rape and indecent assault on females were reproduced from the Offences Against the Person Act 1861.

23 s142 Criminal Justice and Public Order Act 1994.

24 See K. Porter and J. Weeks (eds), *Between the Acts: Lives of Homosexual Men 1885-1967* (London: Routledge, 1991); M. Waites, *The Age of Consent: Young People, Sexuality and Citizenship* (Basingstoke: Palgrave, 2005), 80–6. The Labouchère

amendment of gross indecency, quietly inserted into the CLAA 1885, criminalized consensual homosexual activities.

25 *Fairclough v Whipp* [1951] 2 ALL ER 834; *DPP v Rogers* [1953] 1 WLR 1017.
26 *R v Mason* (1968) 53 Cr.App.R 12 is a rare example.
27 Ibid., 18.
28 s4 SOA 2003.
29 Later replaced by ss 9–13 SOA 2003.
30 *R v Francis* (1989) Cr.AppR.127; see also L. Jackson, "Child Sexual Abuse in England and Wales: Prosecution and Prevalence 1918–1970" *History and Policy* (2015), www.historyandpolicy.org/policy-papers/papers/child-sexual-abuse-in-england-and-wales-prosecution-and-prevalence-1918-197.
31 J. Temkin, *Rape and the Legal Process, 2nd ed.* (Oxford: Oxford University Press, 2002), 59.
32 s2.
33 The same as that for defilement of a girl under 13 (CLAA 1885 s4e). Interestingly, probably due to a drafting oversight, the punishment for attempted incest under the Act was two years for a man and seven years for woman. This was rectified in the SOA 1956.
34 Home Office, *Setting the Boundaries* (London: Home Office, 2000), ch.3.
35 K. Stevenson, et al., *The Sexual Offences Act 2003* (Oxford: Oxford University Press, 2004).
36 The Sexual Offences Act 2003 (Commencement) Order 2004. Since its enactment, the only form of sexual activity identified beyond its reach was upskirting; this has now been addressed by the Voyeurism (Offences) Act 2019.
37 L. Harris and D. Bunting, "Has the Approach to Sentencing Historical Offences Changed?" *Archbold Review* 4, 2015, 5–6.
38 Smart, 2000, op. cit.
39 K. Stevenson, "Outrageous Violations: Enabling Students to Interpret Nineteenth Century Newspaper Reports of Sexual Assault and Rape" *Law, Crime and History* 4(1), 2014, 36–61.
40 A. Bingham, " 'It Would be Better for the Newspapers to Call a Spade a Spade': The British Press and Child Sexual Abuse, c. 1918–90" *History Workshop Journal* 88, 2019, 89–110.
41 H. Hendrick, *Child Welfare England 1872-1989* (London: Routledge, 1994), 37.
42 Ibid.
43 Ibid., 11.
44 Home Office, *Report of the Home Office Advisory Committee on Video Recordings*, (London: HMSO 1989).
45 K. Stevenson, " 'These Are Cases Which It Is Inadvisable to Drag into the Light of Day': Disinterring the Crime of Incest in Early Twentieth Century England" *Crime History and Societies* 20(2), (2016), https://journals.openedition.org/chs/1669#quotation.
46 Ibid., 16.
47 T. Gibbens and K. Soothill, "Incest and Sexual Abuse of Children" in J. Hopkins (ed.), *Perspectives on Rape and Sexual Assault* (London: Harper and Row, 1984), 18.
48 Home Office, op. cit., [5.2.3].
49 Criminal Law Revision Committee, *Sexual Offences, 15th Report* (London: HMSO, 1984).

50 s64 SOA 2003.
51 Jackson, op. cit. 2000, 131 and ch 6.
52 Ibid.
53 Departmental Committee, *Report of the Departmental Committee on Sexual Offences Against Young Persons* Part V (1925).
54 Exceptionally in 1920, the Court of Appeal upheld a conviction where the trial judge had ordered the accused to sit on the stairs leading to the dock out of sight and sound of his daughter whilst she gave evidence. *R v Smellie* (1920) Cr.App.R. 128.
55 K. Stevenson, "'Children of a Very Tender Age Have Vicious Propensities': Child Witness Testimonies in Cases of Sexual Abuse" *Law, Crime and History* 7(1), 2017, 75–97.
56 *R v Hayes* [1977] 1 WLR 234.
57 *R v Campbell* [1983] Crim LR 174.
58 *The Times, 2* March, 1988.
59 B. Nurcombe, "The Child as Witness" *Journal of the American Academy of Child Psychiatry* 25(4), (1986), 473–80; C.C. Spencer, "Sexual Assault: The Second Victimization" in L. Crites and W. Hepperle (eds), *Women, The Courts and Equality* (California, IL: Sage, 1986), 68.
60 *Re S & B (Minors)* [1990] 2 FLR 489.
61 Home Office, 1989, op. cit.
62 Repealing s34 CJA 1988 which abolished s38 Children and Young Persons Act 1933.
63 *R v Graham* (1910) 4 Cr App R 218.
64 *R v B* [1990] Times LR 1 March.
65 *R v Barker* [2010] EWCA Crim 4.
66 *R v Lubemba* [2014] EWCA Crim 2064 [45].
67 *The Times,* 21 October 1987.
68 *R v* X Y Z [1990] 91 Cr. App. Rep. 96.
69 *Stanford v UK* (1994) Case No 50/1992/395/473.
70 G.M. Davies and E. Noon, *An Evaluation of the Live Link for Child Witnesses*, (London: HMSO, 1991).
71 s32 Criminal Justice Act 1988 as amended by s55 Criminal Justice Act 1991.
72 J. Plotnikoff and R. Woolfson, *In Their Own Words* (London: NSPCC, 2004) and *Measuring Up? Evaluating Implementation of Government Commitments to Young Witnesses in Criminal Proceedings* (London: NSPCC, 2009).
73 C. Peterson, "Reliability of Child Witnesses: A Decade of Research" *Canadian Journal of Police and Security Services* 5(3/4), 2007, 142–51.
74 J. Spencer and R. Flin, *The Evidence of Children* (London: Blackstone Press, 1990); J. Wood and S. Garven, "How Sexual Abuse Interviews Go Astray: Implications for Prosecutors, Police, and Child Protection Services" *Child Maltreatment* 5(2), 2000, 109–18.
75 E. Blyth and J. Milner, "The Process of Interagency Work" in *Violence Against Children Study Group, Taking Child Abuse Seriously* (London: Unwin Hyman, 1990), 200.
76 Department of Health and Social Security, *Memorandum of Good Practice on Video Recorded Interviews for Child Witnesses for Criminal Proceedings* (London: HMSO, 1992).

77 Social Services Inspectorate, *The Child, the Court, and the Video: A Study of the Implementation of the Memorandum of Good Practice* (London: Home Office, 1994).
78 Her Majesty's Crown Prosecution Service Inspectorate, Her Majesty's Inspectorate of Constabulary, *Achieving Best Evidence in Child Cases: A Joint Inspection* (London: HMSO, 2014).
79 S. Richardson and H. Bacon, "Introduction" in S. Richardson and H. Bacon (eds), *Child Sexual Abuse: Whose Problem? Reflections from Cleveland* (Bristol: Bristol University Press, 2018), 32–3.
80 C. Hallett and O. Stevenson, *Child Abuse: Aspects of Inter-professional Co-operation* (London: George Allen, 1980).
81 E. Butler-Sloss, *Report of the Inquiry into Child Abuse in Cleveland 1987*, (London: HMSO, 1988), [16].
82 S. Bell, *When Salem Came to the Boro: The True Story of the Cleveland Child Abuse Crisis* (London: Pan Books, 1988), 1.
83 B. Campbell, *Unofficial Secrets: Child Abuse: The Cleveland Case* (London: Virago, 1988), 4–5.
84 L. Blom-Cooper, "Legal Lessons from Cleveland" *New Law Journal* 15(88), 1988, 492.
85 Ibid.
86 Campbell, op. cit., 86.
87 J. La Fontaine, *The Extent and Nature of Organised and Ritual Abuse: Research Findings* (London: HMSO, 1994).
88 A. Cooper, "A Short Psychosocial History of British Child Abuse and Protection: Case Studies in Problems of Mourning in the Public Sphere" *Journal of Social Work Practice* 28(3), 2014, 271–85, 277.
89 HL Deb 06 December 1988, vol 502 cc487-54.
90 A. Elvin et al., "The Children Act 1989: 30 Years On" *Children and Young People Now* (2019), www.cypnow.co.uk/features/article/the-children-act-1989-30-years-on.
91 Department of Health and the Home Department, *The Victoria Climbié Inquiry, Report of an Inquiry by Lord Laming* (London: HMSO, 2003).
92 J. Warner, *The Emotional Politics of Social Work and Child Protection* (Bristol: Bristol University Press Policy Press, 2015), 3.
93 N. Parton and D. Berridge, "Child Protection in England" in N. Gilbert, N. Parton, and M. Skivenes (eds), *Child Protection Systems: International Trends and Orientations* (Oxford: Oxford University Press, 2011), 60–88.
94 E. Munro, *The Munro Review of Child Protection. Final Report: The Child's Journey* (London: Department for Education, 2011), 124.
95 HM Government, *Working Together to Safeguard Children. Statutory Framework: Legislation Relevant to Safeguarding and Promoting the Welfare of Children* (London: HMSO, 2018).
96 Joint interviewing of child witnesses in criminal cases is dealt with in Chapter 7.
97 A. Renton, *Stiff Upper Lip: Secrets, Crimes, and the Schooling of a Ruling Class* (London: Weidenfeld & Nicolson, 2017).
98 *The Times*, 27 June, 2018.
99 *The Sunday Times*, 18 February, 2018.
100 www.csas.uk.net/wp-content/uploads/2018/06/Safeguarding-with-Confidence-The-cumberlege-Commission-Report.pdf and see R. Scorer, *Betrayed: The English Catholic Church and the Sex Abuse Crisis* (London: Biteback Books, 2017).

101 Cited by W. Levada, "The Sexual Abuse of Minors: A Multi-faceted Response to the Challenge," in Toward Healing and Renewal: The 2012 Symposium on the Sexual Abuse of Minors Held at the Pontifical Gregorian University, 6 February 2012, www.vatican.va/roman_curia/congregations/cfaith/documents/rc_con_cfaith_doc_20120206_simposio-levada_en.html.

102 *BBC News*, 5 March 2014.

103 The Children's Commissioner for England is tasked with promoting and protecting children's rights, including those in or leaving care, living away from home or receiving social care services. The Commissioner may also provide advice and assistance to and represent children.

104 S. Berelowitz et al., *Office of the Children's Commissioner's Inquiry into Child Sexual Exploitation in Gangs and Groups Final Report* (London: Office of the Children's Commissioner, 2013).

105 M. Horvath et al., *"It's a Lonely Journey" A Rapid Evidence Assessment on Intrafamilial Child Sexual Abuse* (London: Office of the Children's Commissioner, 2014).

106 Office of the Children's Commissioner, *Protecting Children from Harm: A Critical Assessment of Child Sexual Abuse in the Family Network in England and Priorities for Action* (London: Office of the Children's Commissioner, 2015).

107 A. Kemp, *Abuse in Society: An Introduction* (Long Grove, IL: Waveland Press, 2017).

108 Women's Aid, *Child First: A Call to Action One Year On* (Bristol: Women's Aid, 2017).

109 S. Sodha, "The Idea that Family Courts Are Biased Against Men Is a Dangerous Fallacy," *The Guardian*, 5 March 2020.

110 "Overview of Dr Richard Gardner's Opinions on Pedophilia and Child Sexual Abuse." The Leadership Council. Last modified 2005, www.leadershipcouncil.org/1/pas/RAG.html.

111 W. O' Donohue et al., "Examining the Validity of Parental Alienation Syndrome" *Journal of Child Custody* 13, 2016, 113–25.

112 A. Barnett, "A Genealogy of Hostility: Parental Alienation in England and Wales" *Journal of Social Welfare and Family Law* 42(4), 2020, 1–12.

113 Ibid.

114 See *JY v RY* [2018] EWFC B16.

115 Professors Rosemary Hunter, University of Kent, Mandy Burton, University of Leicester and Liz Trinder, University of Exeter.

References

Aries, P., *Centuries of Childhood: A Social History of Family Life* (New York: Vintage Books, 1962).

Barnett, A., "A Genealogy of Hostility: Parental Alienation in England and Wales" *Journal of Social Welfare and Family Law* 42(4), 2020, 1–12.

Bell, S., *When Salem Came to the Boro: The True Story of the Cleveland Child Abuse Crisis* (London: Pan Books, 1988).

Berelowitz, S. et al., *Office of the Children's Commissioner's Inquiry into Child Sexual Exploitation in Gangs and Groups Final Report* (London: Office of the Children's Commissioner, 2013).

Bingham, A., "'It Would be Better for the Newspapers to Call a Spade a Spade': The British Press and Child Sexual Abuse, c. 1918–90" *History Workshop Journal* 88, 2019, 89–110.

Blackstone, W., *Commentaries on the Law of England* (Oxford: Clarendon Press, 1765–1769).

Blom-Cooper, L., "Legal Lessons from Cleveland" *New Law Journal* 15, 88, 1988, 492.

Blyth, E. and Milner, J., "The Process of Interagency Work" in *Violence Against Children Study Group, Taking Child Abuse Seriously* (London: Unwin Hyman, 1990), 200.

Butler-Sloss, E., *Report of the Inquiry into Child Abuse in Cleveland 1987* (London: HMSO, 1988).

Campbell, B., *Unofficial Secrets: Child Abuse: The Cleveland Case* (London: Virago, 1988).

Cooper, A., "A Short Psychosocial History of British Child Abuse and Protection: Case Studies in Problems of Mourning in the Public Sphere" *Journal of Social Work Practice* 28(3), 2014, 271–85.

Cumberlege Commission, *Safeguarding with Confidence – Keeping Children and Vulnerable Adults Safe in the Catholic Church* (London: The Incorporated Catholic Truth Society, 2007).

Davies, G. M. and Noon, E., *An Evaluation of the Live Link for Child Witnesses* (London: HMSO, 1991).

Department of Health and Social Security, *Memorandum of Good Practice on Video Recorded Interviews for Child Witnesses for Criminal Proceedings* (London: HMSO, 1992).

Department of Health and the Home Department, *The Victoria Climbié Inquiry, Report of an Inquiry by Lord Laming* (London: HMSO, 2003).

Departmental Committee, *Report of the Departmental Committee on Sexual Offences Against Young Persons* (1925).

Elvin, A. et al., "The Children Act 1989: 30 Years On" *Children and Young People Now* (2019), www.cypnow.co.uk/features/article/the-children-act-1989-30-years-on.

Gibbens, T. and Soothill, K., "Incest and Sexual Abuse of Children" in J. Hopkins (ed.), *Perspectives on Rape and Sexual Assault* (London: Harper and Row, 1984), 18.

Hallett, C. and Stevenson, O., *Child Abuse: Aspects of Inter-professional Co-operation* (London: George Allen, 1980).

Harris, L. and Bunting, D., "Has the Approach to Sentencing Historical Offences Changed?" *Archbold Review* 4, 2015, 5–6.

Hendrick, H., *Child Welfare England 1872-1989* (London: Routledge, 1994).

Her Majesty's Crown Prosecution Service Inspectorate, Her Majesty's Inspectorate of Constabulary, *Achieving Best Evidence in Child Cases: A Joint Inspection,* (London: HMSO, 2014).

HM Government, *Working Together to Safeguard Children. Statutory Framework: Legislation Relevant to Safeguarding and Promoting the Welfare of Children* (London: HMSO, 2018).

Home Office, *Report of the Home Office Advisory Committee on Video Recordings,* (London: HMSO, 1989).

Home Office, *Setting the Boundaries* (London: Home Office, 2000).

Hopkins, E., *England's Law for Women and Children* (London: Hatchards, 1883).

Horvath, M. et al., *"It's a Lonely Journey" A Rapid Evidence Assessment on Intrafamilial Child Sexual Abuse* (London: Office of the Children's Commissioner, 2014).

Jackson, L., *Child Sexual Abuse in Victorian England* (London: Routledge, 2000).

Jackson, L., "Child Sexual Abuse in England and Wales: Prosecution and Prevalence 1918-1970" *History and Policy* (2015), www.historyandpolicy.org/policy-papers/papers/child-sexual-abuse-in-england-and-wales-prosecution-and-prevalence-1918-197.

Jay, A. *Independent Inquiry into CSE in Rotherham 1997-2013* (Rotherham: Rotherham Borough Council, 2014).

Joint Select Committee, *Fourth Report on Consolidation Bills 1955-56, Report on Sexual Offences Bills* (London: HMSO, 1956).

Kemp, A., *Abuse in Society: An Introduction* (Long Grove, IL: Waveland Press, 2017).

Kitzinger, J., "Defending Innocence: Ideologies of Childhood" *Feminist Review* 28, 1988, 77–87.

Kitzinger, J., *Framing Abuse: Media Influence and Public Understanding of Sexual Violence Against Children* (London: Pluto, 2004).

Kosaraju. A., *Attrition in Cases Involving Crimes of Child Sexual Exploitation in England*, PhD Thesis (Canterbury: University of Kent, 2018).

La Fontaine, J., *The Extent and Nature of Organised and Ritual Abuse: Research Findings* (London: HMSO, 1994).

Levada, W., "The Sexual Abuse of Minors: A Multi-faceted Response to the Challenge," in Toward Healing and Renewal: The 2012 Symposium on the Sexual Abuse of Minors Held at the Pontifical Gregorian University, 6 February 2012, www.vatican.va/roman_curia/congregations/cfaith/documents/rc_con_cfaith_doc_20120206_simposio-levada_en.html.

Munro, E., *The Munro Review of Child Protection. Final Report: The Child's Journey* (London: Department for Education, 2011).

Nurcombe, B., "The Child as Witness" *Journal of the American Academy of Child Psychiatry* 25(4), 1986, 473–80.

O' Donohue, W., et al., "Examining the Validity of Parental Alienation Syndrome" *Journal of Child Custody* 13, 2016, 113–25.

Office of the Children's Commissioner, *Protecting Children from Harm: A Critical Assessment of Child Sexual Abuse in the Family Network in England and Priorities for Action* (London: Office of the Children's Commissioner, 2015).

Olafson E., et al., "Modern History of Child Sexual Abuse Awareness: Cycles of Discovery and Suppression" *Child Abuse and Neglect* 17, 1993, 7–24.

Parton, N. and Berridge, D., "Child Protection in England" in N. Gilbert, N. Parton, and M. Skivenes (eds), *Child Protection Systems: International Trends and Orientations* (Oxford: Oxford University Press, 2011), 60.

Peterson, C., "Reliability of Child Witnesses: A Decade of Research" *Canadian Journal of Police and Security Services* 5(3/4), 2007, 142–51.

Plotnikoff, J. and Woolfson, R., *In Their Own Words* (London: NSPCC, 2004) and *Measuring Up? Evaluating Implementation of Government Commitments to Young Witnesses in Criminal Proceedings* (London: NSPCC, 2009).

Porter, K. and Weeks J. (eds), *Between the Acts: Lives of Homosexual Men 1885-1967* (London: Routledge, 1991).

Renton, A., *Stiff Upper Lip: Secrets, Crimes, and the Schooling of a Ruling Class* (London: Weidenfeld & Nicolson, 2017).

Richardson, S. and Bacon, H. "Introduction" in S. Richardson and H. Bacon (eds), *Child Sexual Abuse: Whose Problem? Reflections from Cleveland* (Bristol: Bristol University Press, 2018), 32.

Scorer, R., *Betrayed: The English Catholic Church and the Sex Abuse Crisis* (London: Biteback Books, 2017).

Smart, C., "Reconsidering the Recent History of Child Sexual Abuse, 1910–1960" *Journal of Social Policy* 29(1), 2000, 55–71.

Social Services Inspectorate, *The Child, the Court, and the Video: A Study of the Implementation of the Memorandum of Good Practice* (London: Home Office, 1994).

Sodha, S., "The Idea that Family Courts Are Biased Against Men Is a Dangerous Fallacy." *The Guardian*, 5 March 2020.

Spencer, C.C., "Sexual Assault: The Second Victimization" in L. Crites and W. Hepperle (eds), *Women, The Courts and Equality* (California, IL: Sage, 1986), 68.

Spencer, J. and Flin, R., *The Evidence of Children* (London: Blackstone Press, 1990).

Stead, W., "The Maiden Tribute to Modern Babylon," *Pall Mall Gazette*, 4 July 1885.

Stevenson, K. et al., *The Sexual Offences Act 2003* (Oxford: Oxford University Press, 2004).

Stevenson, K., "Outrageous Violations: Enabling Students to Interpret Nineteenth Century Newspaper Reports of Sexual Assault and Rape" *Law, Crime and History* 4(1), 2014, 36–61.

Stevenson, K., "'These Are Cases Which It Is Inadvisable to Drag into the Light of Day': Disinterring the Crime of Incest in Early Twentieth Century England" *Crime History and Societies* 20(2), (2016), https://journals.openedition.org/chs/1669#quotation.

Stevenson, K., "Children of a Very Tender Age Have Vicious Propensities': Child Witness Testimonies in Cases of Sexual Abuse" *Law, Crime and History* 7(1), 2017, 75–97.

Stevenson, K., "Not Just the Ideas of a Few Enthusiasts: Early Twentieth Century Legal Activism and the Criminalization of Immorality" *Cultural and Social History Journal* 14(2), 2017, 1–18.

Temkin, J., *Rape and the Legal Process, 2nd ed.* (Oxford: Oxford University Press, 2002), 59.

Waites, M., *The Age of Consent: Young People, Sexuality and Citizenship* (Basingstoke: Palgrave, 2005).

Warner, J., *The Emotional Politics of Social Work and Child Protection* (Bristol: Bristol University Press Policy Press, 2015).

Women's Aid, *Child First: A Call to Action One Year On* (Bristol: Women's Aid, 2017).

Wood, J. and Garven, S., "How Sexual Abuse Interviews Go Astray: Implications for Prosecutors, Police, and Child Protection Services" *Child Maltreatment* 5(2), 2000, 109–18.

4 The evolution of legal and policy frameworks around child sex offences in Ireland

Introduction

The notion, often implied in Irish political leaders' apologies for non-recent child sexual abuse (NRCSA), that the seriousness of sexual violence against children was not fully appreciated by state actors until relatively recently is untrue. From the earliest years of the new nation, policy makers and parliamentarians, child welfare and criminal justice actors were keenly aware of the problem.[1] However, the needs of children vulnerable to sexual violence were subordinated to more pressing political agendas of creating an extraordinarily fertile but morally pure nation. The violence of the Easter Rising in 1916, a War of Independence from January 1919 to July 1921 and the Civil War from June 1922 to May 1923, produced a fragile new State keen to forge a new identity that was distinctly Irish. Gender and sexual morality were at the heart of this new identity, linked to broader international anxieties about modernity as a threat to the 'vitality of individual states'.[2] The heterosexual patriarchal family was the foundational unit of society and the rights of parents were jealously protected by the legal order. The limited reporting of prosecutions and official reports perpetuated the myth that sexual offending against children was unusual and committed by strangers. Policies and practices mandating unregulated reproduction, along with a lack of economic planning, led to an unmanageably large population of children living in poverty. The inviolability of the family did not apply to them; poor children were incarcerated in industrial schools which themselves became sites of objectification and sexual abuse. The revelations of NRCSA in the 1990s prompted a re-examination of policies on child welfare and protection but reform was hampered by an inflexible legal system and a culture committed to protecting the middle-class family before the child.

This chapter follows the structure of Chapter 3. The first section offers a historiography of the criminal law framework for sexual offences against children in Ireland in the twentieth century and the barriers to reporting and conviction. The second section examines the state's governance of child welfare and child protection, including the central role played by industrial schools throughout much of the twentieth century. These schools were sites

DOI: 10.4324/9780429468162-5

of widespread physical, emotional and sexual abuse of children. The chapter closes with an examination of how child welfare and protection policies and law, including family law, have developed from the mid-twentieth century to the present.

Criminal law

A morally pure nation

In 1929 the government introduced legislation restricting the reporting of certain details of judicial proceedings, the publication of which 'could be calculated to injure public morals' (s14). Although the Censorship of Publications Act 1929 did not expressly ban reporting of sexual crimes, its impact was to deepen the Irish press' existing propensity for self-censorship.[3] The sanitized image of Irish society portrayed by the national and regional press strengthened the state myth of a healthy nation with low levels of sexual immorality. The majority of sexual crimes brought to court were never reported by the press. When they were, the regional press went to great efforts to distance its communities from sexual crime and preserve the local area's reputation as respectable.[4] Sexual violence was portrayed as something inflicted on the Irish nation by the evils of colonization and a dangerous modernity spread by the cinema, dancehall, salacious newspapers and fiction. This presentation allowed regional press to draw a line between sexual offenders and the locals.[5] When sexual crime was reported in the press, vague references to the acts involved made it often impossible to discern the age, sex of the victim or circumstances of the crime. Press self-censorship continued for decades following the 1929 Act. In cases of incest the official silencing was further reinforced by the *in-camera* rule.[6] This rule meant that the proceedings were in private and the press could not report on them. As Chapter 3 noted, in England and Wales the rule reinforced the incest 'taboo', and the lack of reported cases created the misleading impression that it was a rare occurrence. It can reasonably be assumed that it had a similar effect in Ireland. Although England and Wales repealed the rule for incest cases in 1922, it persisted in Ireland until 1995.[7]

As in England and Wales much of criminal law reform in the early twentieth century focused on the age of consent and the crime of unlawful carnal knowledge, or defilement as it was also known. The CLAA 1885 applied unamended to Ireland until the enactment of the Criminal Law (Amendment) Act 1935. The CLAA 1935 followed the report of the Carrigan Committee set up to examine the 1880 and 1885 CLAAs and the 'problem of juvenile prostitution'. Chaired by prosecutor William Carrigan, the Committee's membership included a matron of the Dublin maternity hospital and a female poor law commissioner. The Committee held 17 sittings, heard from 29 witnesses and received memoranda and communications from numerous national and international sources. Its final report to the Minister for Justice in 1931 was an indictment of the new state, finding that 'gross offences are rife throughout the country'.[8]

The Committee detailed a 'degeneration in the standard of social conduct' which witnesses attributed to the loss of parental control and responsibility during the preceding period of upheaval and which had not been recovered since. The state's most senior policeman, Garda Commissioner General Eoin O'Duffy described the 'alarming amount of sexual crime increasing yearly, a feature of which was the large number of cases of criminal interference with girls and children from 16 years downwards, including many cases of children under 10 years'.[9] His evidence demonstrates that, contrary perhaps to popular belief, the police took sexual offences seriously, with high rates of prosecution of offences of unlawful carnal knowledge of girls and indecent assault against boys (which had very high rates of success in prosecution).[10] Although O'Duffy and other witnesses presented compelling evidence of a problem with offending against children, the Committee's focus was diluted by a concern with issues of sexual immorality generally. In a continuation of Victorian sensibilities but with a new Irish twist, sexual offences against children were considered together with sex outside marriage, prostitution and dancing in dance halls. The Committee was alarmed at the growing 'evil' of 'illegitimacy', which was deemed 'one of the principal causes of [..] crime and vice'.[11] Having reviewed the arguments of English social purity campaigners in favour of raising the age of protection, it noted that Irish girls were even more vulnerable than their English counterparts, who were 'accustomed to live in gregarious surroundings, which it may be said, instil in them instinct of "**canniness**" and self-discipline that the conditions of Irish agricultural life do not foster' (emphasis in original).[12] The Committee's Final Report to the Minister for Justice recommended raising the age of protection in respect of unlawful carnal knowledge of a girl to 18 years (at least) and that the crime should be 'absolutely prohibited', meaning that the defence of mistake as to age under the CLAA 1885 should be abolished.[13] It also recommended expanding the felony offence of unlawful carnal knowledge to cover girls up to 16 years. The Committee also addressed offending against boys and male teenagers, recommending repeal of the CLAA 1880 and the creation of a new law stating the consent of a person under 18 was no defence to a charge of indecent assault or gross indecency and that a young person should not be liable to be prosecuted or deemed to be an accomplice to any such offence.[14] It made other progressive recommendations around reform of the trial of sexual offences, which are discussed in the next section. Nevertheless, the Committee's overriding concern with sexual immorality and public manifestations of sexuality meant that serious attention was not paid to the contexts and dynamics of sexual offending against children. Sex crimes against children in families and in state-funded institutions like industrial schools were not explored whatsoever.

The Carrigan Report's description of a society rife with sexual immorality shocked the Minister for Justice and the Department, who thought it was exaggerated and 'too severe on men while overlooking the shortcomings of women and the highly coloured imaginations of children'.[15] The Minister suppressed the Report to preserve the image of independent Ireland as morally pure.[16] Rather than engaging in public debate about how to tackle sexual crime against women and children, a special committee of parliamentarians was convened to consider the Report in secret and consult with the Catholic hierarchy.[17] The result was the Criminal Law Amendment Act 1935. The CLAA 1935 followed a raft of legislation that sought to stem the tide of modernity and its influence on adolescents and young adults in particular, increasing censorship and regulating dance halls.[18] Its provisions reflected the government's concern with sexual immorality at the expense of adequate protection of children. It targeted the visibility of (recreational, extramarital) sex and sexuality, banning contraceptives (the ban lasted until 1973), increasing penalties for prostitution and creating new offences of brothel keeping and public indecency. In keeping with the Act's narrow focus on sexual immorality, the only significant reforms in the area of offending against children centred on unlawful carnal knowledge of girls. Although the Carrigan Committee had recommended raising the age of consent to 18, s2 CLAA 1935 criminalized unlawful carnal knowledge of a girl between 15 and 17.[19] To this day, 17 remains the age of consent. To appease concerns about blackmail of innocent men by 'predatory' girls, the Act also introduced a 12-month time bar on prosecutions under s2. It also raised from 13 to 15 the upper age at which unlawful carnal knowledge would be classed as a felony and carry a maximum sentence of life imprisonment.

The Carrigan Committee's recommendation to abolish the mistake of age defence was taken up. Along with the absence of a need for proof of force or non-consent, this made unlawful carnal knowledge a powerful tool for prosecuting sexual offending against girls (although proof of penetration was still needed). However, as discussed in the next section, the treatment of victims in criminal trials undermined this potential. Decades later, in 2006 the Supreme Court in the case of *CC v Ireland* declared the absence of a mistake of age defence for unlawful carnal knowledge of a girl unconstitutional.[20] This means that no prosecutions may now be brought under ss1 or 2 CLAA 1935 for crimes committed before 2006.

The *CC* case convulsed the country. Campaign groups, the public and politicians looked on aghast as convictions were overturned and prosecutions were dropped. The controversy led to a week of political turmoil which engulfed the minister for justice, the attorney general and the government. It prompted thousands of people to gather outside Leinster House, as well as in towns and cities across the country to call for legislative change and for better protection for victims. In response, the legislature introduced the Criminal Law (Sexual Offences) Act 2006. It replaced the offences under the CLAA 1935 of unlawful carnal knowledge with the broader gender-neutral offences of defilement of a child under 15 and under 17.[21] This was the first time a gender-neutral offence specifically addressing offending against children was introduced. It was some 16 years after a Law Reform Commission recommendation that an offence of CSA be created.[22] The Act also recognized the particular harms involved in abuse by a trusted adult; more serious punishment is provided for an offender who is a 'person in authority'; someone in a parental relationship or responsible for the education supervision or welfare of the victim. Despite the progressive tenor of these reforms, the use of the term 'defilement' mirrors the terminology used in the notes to the CLAAs 1885 and 1935 and reflects the remarkable persistence of Victorian attitudes linking sexual violence against children with notions of debasement and contamination. Consent is no defence to a charge of engaging in a sexual act with a child. Although there had been calls for a referendum to allow for strict liability in such cases,[23] the 2006 Act allowed a defence of honest mistake as to age, making prosecutions for such crimes extremely challenging. In 2017 the legislature finally amended the defence so that the defendant must show that they were reasonably mistaken as to the child's age. Girls under 17 have immunity from conviction (but only where they engaged in vaginal sexual intercourse).[24] This was challenged as unconstitutionally discriminatory against boys, but the Supreme Court has upheld the distinction because of the risk of pregnancy for girls.[25] This reasoning is questionable given that the legislation prohibits underage sex, not unprotected sex.[26]

The Criminal Law Sexual Offences Act 2017 created a new offence of abuse by a person in authority where the victim is aged between 17 and 18.[27] This is interesting because the age of consent is 17; the offence recognizes the power differential involved in such offending where a person is still legally a child. The Act also introduced child sexual exploitation offences, developing existing law on grooming, exploitation[28] and trafficking[29] and creating new offences relating to child sexual abuse imagery.[30]

Indecent assault, gross indecency and incest

As Chapter 3 noted, there were separate offences of indecent assault upon a female and indecent assault upon a male and each covered a wide range of behaviour. It was one of the most frequently prosecuted child sex offences because it did not require proof of penetration. In NRCSA cases, indecent assault is often charged. The CLAA 1935 set at 15 the age of consent to acts that could constitute indecent assault, and it remains there to this day (for the new gender-neutral offence of sexual assault, discussed below).[31] There is a defence of honest mistake as to age.[32] In contrast with national and international trends on the defendant's state of mind in respect of sexual acts, the belief need only be honest and genuine and not objectively reasonable. This means that it is especially difficult for prosecutors to convince the jury that the defendant is guilty.

In 1990 the offence of indecent assault was renamed the gender-neutral offence of sexual assault by the Criminal Law (Rape) (Amendment) Act 1990. A new offence of aggravated sexual assault (also gender neutral) was introduced. Another gender-neutral offence called 'rape under section 4' was introduced to cover sexual assaults involving some penetrative acts of the mouth and anus and vagina outside of penile penetration of the vagina.[33] Parliamentarians refused to recognize the realities of sexual violence and did not criminalize non-consensual penetration of the anus by an object. While such behaviour may still be charged as (aggravated) sexual assault, this was a missed opportunity to recognize the gravity of such violations.

Chapter 3 discussed the problem of courts being unwilling to find indecent assault were an adult invited a child to touch their genitals and the child did so. Judicial reluctance to criminalize such behaviour was also evident in Irish courts. Legislation to address the deficiency in indecent assault law was finally introduced in 2017,[34] almost 60 years after the issue was tackled in England and Wales.[35] Unfortunately this remedial legislation does not affect NRCSA prosecutions.

The criminalization of gross indecency between males in s11 CLAA 1885 also hampered Irish boys' ability to report abuse. S11 was finally repealed in Ireland by the Criminal Law (Sexual Offences) Act 1993.[36] The provision remains useful for prosecutors in NRCSA cases where it may be used to criminalize historical exploitative behaviour against boys.[37] The 1993 Act created an offence of gross indecency with an underage male, but this was abolished by the Criminal Law (Sexual Offences) Act 2006. This was regrettable since the offence covered sexual misconduct between males which did not come within the meaning of sexual assault, because the sexual assault element was not satisfied.[38] It may still be prosecuted in respect of conduct alleged between 1993 and 2006.

Sexual offending against children within the family has been gravely neglected by legislators throughout the twentieth century. The POIA 1908 is still the primary legislation on incest. The limited amendments to the Act have been piecemeal and have perpetuated existing inequalities. The CLAA 1935 extended the category of the most serious incest to cover female victims under 15 years. The 1935 Act further protected girls by raising their age of liability for incest from 16 to 17.[39] There was no such age exemption for boys. When the law was finally reformed the Criminal Law (Sexual Offences) Act 2017 continued this gendered inequality.[40] Although the CLAA 1922 in Britain reclassified incest as a felony, it was 1995 before incest by a male became a felony in Ireland. The maximum sentence for incest by a male was raised to life in the early 1990s.[41] The 1995 reforms were prompted by the Kilkenny incest case (Chapter 2), in which a man found guilty of incest and abuse of his daughter received a seven-year sentence, the maximum under the POIA 1908.[42] The reforms affected male offenders only. This caused controversy in 2009 when the first woman to be convicted of incest was sentenced by Roscommon Circuit Court to the maximum seven years.[43] In 2019 a ten-year sentence for incest committed by a male or incest committed by a female over 17 was introduced.[44] The legislation was passed without consideration of the power dynamics in familial CSA and whether a 17-year-old could in fact voluntarily agree to engage in sexual activity with their relative. Incest does not provide for offences arising in communities with extended family and kinship definitions and structures, for example, as is the case within Mincéir communities. There have been calls for the law on incest to be extended along the lines of the English SOA 2003 to any sexually exploitative conduct within the family, regardless of blood relationship.[45]

Criminalization of third parties

Finally, the legislature has also expanded criminal liability beyond the individual perpetrator. Under the Criminal Justice (Sexual Offences) Act 2006, a person who has authority or control over a child or an abuser and who intentionally or recklessly endangers a child by (a) causing or permitting them to be placed or left in a situation which creates a substantial risk of being seriously harmed or sexually abused, or (b) failing to take reasonable steps to protect a child from such a risk while knowing that the child is in such a situation.[46] The offence is punishable by a fine, or up to ten years' imprisonment or both. In an institutional setting, for example, a director or manager might have authority or control over child residents and over a staff member (or another resident) who has a record of abuse and who poses a risk to one or more children.[47] This is a progressive piece of criminal law whose potential is yet to be fully recognized.

We now turn to the challenges of prosecuting child sex offences.

Prosecuting child sex offences

Low rates of detection and prosecution

The 1931 Carrigan Report, discussed above, found that there was a very low prosecution rate of fewer than 15 per cent of crimes against children. The primary cultural barrier was shame; reporting sexual crime risked marking a child—or her family—out as tainted with immorality. The law itself was identified as a major barrier; Hanna Clarke, an NSPCC inspector noted that the law of evidence

> prevents reliability being placed on the evidence of young children between six and ten… Men that assaulted little girls under ten years appear to be well aware of the loophole of the inadmissibility of the uncorroborated evidence of their victims.[48]

Women and girls were viewed with extreme suspicion; one commentator described it as 'Every girl and woman witness against a man is guilty of perjury until proved innocent'.[49] This prejudicial assessment of female credibility was connected to stereotypes of the Irishman as saviour of Irish womanhood (and childhood) from the English aggressor. The true Irish male could not be both saviour and rapist.[50] The double standard around sexual violence against girls meant that victims who became pregnant were deemed immoral and were incarcerated in Magdalene Laundries. These were commercial laundries and places of detention run by religious orders with the state's cooperation. Women and girls were treated as 'penitents' who worked without payment for their 'redemption'.[51]

The Carrigan Report also highlighted 'the difficulty of proof, from the private nature of the offence, usually depending on the evidence of a single witness, the child, and the requirement of corroboration or the requirement that the Judge issue a corroboration warning'.[52] It recommended the abolition of the corroboration warning for all cases involving children.[53] It also made progressive recommendations around liberalizing the cross-admissibility of complainants' evidence in trials of child sex offences (see Chapter 7). Despite the CLAA 1935's rhetoric of protection, it did not reform these problematic aspects of evidence law and criminal procedure, leaving children at the mercy of a hostile legal process.

The police force's attitude to child sex crime was far from adequate. The 2009 Murphy Report on the handling of CSA allegations by the Archdiocese of Dublin found that in 1960 photographic film submitted for development by a priest based in a children's hospital was sent to Scotland Yard. A report was submitted to the Garda Commissioner, who passed the matter to the Archbishop and did not investigate (see Chapter 2). The Ferns Report (2005) identified 100 allegations against 21 priests in one diocese in Wexford over a 40-year period. The report concluded that nothing was done despite complaints of sexual abuse of children being made to the gardaí in the 1970s and 1980s. Gardaí did not even record the complaints. The testimony provided by survivors of all forms of NRCSA to the courts in criminal cases also shows that many reported to the gardaí, but their reports were ignored.[54]

Even when cases reached the courtroom, myths and stereotypical reasoning continued to distort justice. The problems identified by Carrigan around cross-examination of children and the use of corroboration warnings went unaddressed for decades. Complainants who failed to perform according to the norms of Irish femininity were seen as undeserving victims.[55] Juries were overwhelmingly male until well into the last quarter of the twentieth century.[56] The law's protection of the marital family meant that wives were not permitted to give evidence against their husbands[57] even in cases involving sexual abuse of their child until 1988.[58]

That same year the Irish Council for Civil Liberties (ICCL) Working Party on Child Sexual Abuse issued a landmark report that found that one in four girls and one in four boys had been sexually abused. Recognizing the invisibility of family violence, it stated that sexual abuse was being ignored because most cases take place within the family and the vast majority go unreported.[59] Many of the ICCL's proposed reforms of the legal system were echoed by the Law Reform Commission's 1990 Report on Child Sexual Abuse.[60] It decried the assumption that young children were unreliable and incompetent witnesses, stating the assumption was 'inimical to the constitutional rights of young citizens'.[61] The Commission recommended reforms on competency, abolition of the corroboration warning and the requirement of corroboration of unsworn evidence, the introduction of live-link evidence, screens and the admission of video-recorded interviews. It also recommended that gardaí should be involved in the early stages to facilitate the possibility of a prosecution, a more 'child friendly' court system, the introduction of a special panel of solicitors and specialist information and training for the judiciary.[62] This vision has yet to be fully realized.

Modernization of the law of evidence: The Criminal Evidence Act 1992

The Criminal Evidence Act 1992 (CEA 1992) was introduced to address the problems facing children giving evidence in a trial. It abolished the requirement under the Children Act 1908 that a child victim's evidence be corroborated before an accused could be convicted under that Act or under the CLAA 1885 or certain offences under the Offences Against the Person Act 1861.[63] It also abolished mandatory warnings to the jury about convicting on the uncorroborated evidence of a child.[64] The CEA 1992 finally made spouses not only competent but also compellable by the prosecution in child sex offence trials.[65] It also provided for the admission of a child's pre-recorded statements at trial.[66] This measure is vitally important for ensuring that jury see and hear the child's evidence as it was when (s)he reported, rather than years later when the trial is taking place. In a stark illustration of the state's lack of commitment to child sexual abuse prosecutions, this provision was not commenced until October 2008.[67] Although its use has now become routine, so too have defence challenges to the admissibility of pre-recorded statements, which often challenge the interviewer's adherence to the Garda Síochána Good Practice Guidelines on Specialist Interviews.[68] Unlike in England and Wales, pre-recorded cross-examination is not allowed, so children must undergo cross-examination by defence counsel at trial. Given the lengthy delays in trials coming to court, this negatively impacts children's ability to answer defence lawyers' questions, and ultimately on the jury's ability to make an accurate finding of fact.

The CEA 1992 also provided for the use of a television link and for the use of intermediaries. Intermediaries are professionals from the disciplines such as speech and language therapy or social work. They facilitate the taking of evidence from young children and children with disabilities. The Act provided for the use of intermediaries, but there are only two documented cases of their use.[69] In a further indication of the gap between law's rhetoric and the reality of its implementation, 30 years after the Act there is still no formalized scheme or Rules of Court to address these issues.

The 2015 EU Victims' Directive[70] forced Irish legislators to further reform trial procedure. Screens may be used to shield the victim[71] and lawyers and the judge are forbidden from wearing a wig or gown.[72] The judge may direct that the defendant shall not personally cross-examine the witness.[73] However, attitudes of some defence lawyers and trial judges remain an obstacle to meaningful improvement. In 2021 judges in the Court of Appeal expressed surprise that a child victim of sexual abuse and cruelty had been cross-examined by the defence barrister for six days.[74] Despite these reforms and increased specialization by police[75] and prosecutors,[76] rates of prosecution for reported child sexual abuse are extremely low.[77] A 2017 Garda Inspectorate study found that 66 per cent of all sexual offences reported to gardaí involved children.

59 per cent related to incidents that occurred more than a year before being reported. Fewer than 13 per cent of these were referred for prosecution, and only 32 per cent of these were prosecuted.[78]

In the next section, we explore the state's role in child welfare and protection throughout the twentieth century.

Child welfare and child protection

Reflecting Catholic social ideas,[79] Article 41 of the 1937 Constitution (which remains the fundamental law of the state) enshrined the heterosexual marital family as 'the necessary basis of social order and as indispensable to the welfare of the Nation and the State'. Article 42.5 empowered the state to intervene where parents 'failed in their duty towards their children', but the constitutional scheme and its interpretation by the courts created privileged parental rights, making it impossible to treat the child's rights as paramount, even where the child was being abused within the family.[80] The subordination of children was underscored by a legal order that left married women at the mercy of their husbands. Access to contraceptives was illegal, they had no legal right to the marital home until 1957,[81] could not claim an independent domicile and divorce was constitutionally prohibited until 1996. Mothers did not have equal legal status in the care of their children until 1964.[82]

The privileging of the married man's position as head of the family in law was matched with a strongly authoritarian approach to unmarried mothers and their children.[83] Mothers who gave birth outside of wedlock were stigmatized by family and community and were forced to enter a Mother and Baby Home, emigrate to England or give the child up for adoption. The state provided no economic support to unmarried mothers until 1973; children born outside of wedlock were legally 'illegitimate' until 1987.[84] For these children, along with children of working-class families, Mincéir children and children of mixed ethnicities,[85] and for many children with disabilities, the default was institutionalization in industrial schools or related institutions or adoption.

Industrial schools

Industrial schools were an important tool in the state's armoury for regulating the lives of working-class and single-parent families, who were perceived as a threat to the system of rural fundamentalism[86] and the morality/legitimacy of the nation. The first industrial school was certified in 1869, and by 1900 there were 70 schools with a capacity for almost 8,000 children, along with a small number of reformatories.[87] In 1924 there were more children in industrial schools in Ireland than in all the industrial schools across England, Scotland, Wales and Northern Ireland combined.[88] Approximately 42,000 children were incarcerated in industrial schools and reformatories from the

1930s to 1970s.[89] The largest industrial school for boys was Artane in Dublin where 776 children were detained in 1950. The largest industrial school for girls was Goldenbridge, also in Dublin, with 148 girls in 1950.[90] Industrial schools formed part of a larger network of interdependent institutions, including psychiatric hospitals, reformatory and industrial schools, mother and baby 'homes' and Magdalene Laundries. During the middle of the twentieth century, over 1 per cent of the population was involuntarily detained in one of these punitive institutions.[91] These institutions concealed citizens already marginalized by a number of interrelated social phenomena: poverty, illegitimacy, sexual abuse and infanticide.[92]

Why did Ireland embrace industrial schools and connected institutions so enthusiastically?[93] There is no straightforward answer but certainly property, patriarchal family structures and ideals of respectability were important. Unmarried mothers and their children posed a threat to the system of land inheritance. Female virginity was a valuable bargaining tool in marriage transactions. Children born out of wedlock could prevent marriage and present a threat to property.[94] In the newly independent state eager to construct an image of itself as morally pure, industrial schools were a way of disciplining children who threatened to the social order. Sex outside marriage was stigmatized, but reproduction within marriage was strongly encouraged. This, along with a dearth of necessary economic supports, led to high numbers of children living in poverty. For the Roman Catholic religious congregations who ran industrial schools and who committed large amounts of human and financial capital to them, the state capitation grant attached to each child, and the court-mandated weekly payments from parents, incentivized the maintenance of high numbers of inmates. Industrial schools also served a disciplinary function for the religious congregations themselves; members who stepped out of line were sent to industrial schools to work.

Children could be detained in industrial schools from infancy and generally remained until they were sixteen, when the state grant to the religious order that ran the industrial school expired. Girls significantly outnumbered boys in industrial schools, stayed longer and were more likely to be received into care for fear of 'moral waywardness'.[95] For women and girls, a continuum of containment existed whereby the child of an unmarried mother born in a mother and baby institution could be sent to an industrial school and after to a Magdalene Laundry. Sometimes one or more of these institutions would be on the same site.

Most children were sent to an industrial school by the Dublin Metropolitan Children's Court or the various District Courts under the framework of the Children Act 1908 which remained in force, with amendments (most notably by the Children Acts of 1929 and 1941), until 2001.[96] Ideas of neglect and delinquency were indistinguishable in this Act, which authorized the incarceration of children at risk alongside those convicted of criminal offences. In practice, Irish children were sent to industrial schools for being poor and were stigmatized as criminals.[97]

Under the most frequently used provision, s58(1) of the Children Act 1908,[98] children were sent to an industrial school for begging, lack of proper guardianship, being found destitute, for frequenting the company of a reputed thief or prostitute or for living in a house used for prostitution,[99] for having a parent who was 'unfit ('by reason of reputed criminal or drunken habits') or if a parent was serving a prison sentence. Fifty-nine per cent of survivors who gave evidence to the Commission to Inquire into Child Abuse (CICA)'s Confidential Committee (see Chapter 10) stated that their parents were married at the time of their incarceration.[100] By 1965 most committals to industrial schools involved a charge of lack of proper guardianship.[101] The ease with which District Court judges separated families and stripped parents of their rights without consideration of alternatives made a mockery of the constitutional rhetoric around protecting the family.

In a striking instance of victim-blaming, s58(1) also authorized the detention of any girl whose father had been convicted of a sexual offence against her.[102] Girls who had been sexual abused, and their friends, were often considered unsuitable for an industrial school and were sent to a reformatory school instead.[103]

The second largest category of those committed were children who had been involved in a criminal offence.[104] In addition, large numbers of children were sent to an industrial school for non-attendance at school.[105] In 1964, 66 children were sent to industrial schools for non-attendance, while in the same year in England, only 45 children were institutionalized for 'truancy', although England had 16 times the relevant age cohort.[106]

Despite the penal welfarist principles of the Children Act 1908, the operation of these institutions was mainly punitive. Head shaving, name changing, identifying children by number and flogging were used to punish and control. Although industrial schools, as recipients of grants for teachers, were required to provide a primary-level education, children often left not knowing even how to read the time. Children were treated as unpaid labourers, tasked with making items such as rosary beads, with the needs of the institution prioritized over those of the pupils.[107] Children endured an experience that was so stigmatizing that 'the removal from society, in many cases, was total'.[108] Links between the child and their family were often severed. Aftercare was minimal, and many emigrated to escape the stigma of having been an industrial school inmate.

The power of religious orders in charge of industrial schools was almost total. Although the state funded and was responsible for certifying and inspecting the industrial schools, there was a complete absence of effective oversight in deference to the cultural and political power of the Catholic Church.[109] The consequence of the lack of state oversight and deference to the religious congregations was that children were objectified, powerless and silenced. The CICA found that a climate of fear permeated most institutions, created by excessive and arbitrary punishment and that sexual abuse was endemic in boys' schools.[110] When they attempted to report sexual abuse, children were ignored or even blamed by institutional actors and punished severely.[111] Survivors' evidence presented to the courts and the CICA demonstrate that state officials, teachers, gardaí and parents actively silenced children who disclosed abuse.[112] For their part, Catholic authorities managed cases of sexual abuse by their members with a view to minimizing the risk of public disclosure and damage to the institution.[113]

The denial of children's constitutional rights to bodily integrity was enforced by the gardaí who returned escaped children to industrial schools and who deferred to Church authorities in their (mis)handling of reports.[114] Reports were made to school authorities, the Gardaí, the Department of Education, Health Boards, parish priests and others by children, their parents and relatives. Although protective action was sometimes taken, in other instances, reports were ignored, children were punished or pressure was brought to bear on the child and family to deny the complaint and/or to remain silent.[115]

The 1970 Report of the Kennedy Committee was a missed opportunity to reform Irish childcare policy and implementation. The Committee discovered a lack of funding, inspection and care in the industrial and reform school system. Rather than exposing the realities of life in the schools, the Committee's report focused on reform of the childcare system, calling for a shift to family-based services, repeal of the CA 1908, the unification and co-ordination of childcare services and the raising of the age of criminal responsibility.[116] The recommendations proved too controversial for policy makers and were only partially taken up. Some older schools closed but new ones replaced them, which were never adequately invested in or inspected.[117] In the meantime, children in state care continued to suffer abuse. Marginalized children were especially vulnerable. In 1985 New Hibernia magazine reported allegations of beatings and sexual abuse of boys at Trudder House, a state-funded residential home for Mincéir (Traveller) children sentenced by the criminal courts.[118] The criminal process was not formally involved until the mid-1990s when 19 young Mincéirí made allegations of sexual abuse against six people associated with the centre, including its Director, Duncan McInnes 'one of the most vicious paedophiles ever to work in an Irish childcare institution' and who later continued to be involved in childcare in Scotland.[119] Childcare worker Brendan Kelly received a seven-year prison sentence for two counts of attempted buggery of residents of the centre, but this was later overturned by the Court of Criminal Appeal in a landmark judgment (see Chapter 7). Sexual abuse and cover-ups at other residential centres for children were the focus of public anger and media attention throughout the mid-1990s.

Reformatory and industrial schools were eventually abolished by the Children Act 2001 but children in state care today continue to face a system that is not fit for purpose.[120] Mincéirí continue to experience over-representation in child protection and care statistics and experience ongoing racism and discrimination.[121] Homeless children are living in hotel rooms and children whose families are seeking asylum are housed in institutions where they must share accommodation with adults for years.[122]

CSA in the child protection framework

Echoing the growing academic and professional interest in child abuse internationally, Irish social workers and medics and counsellors became increasingly alert to the problem in the 1970s. Voluntary associations such as the Incest Crisis Service, the rape crisis centres and the Irish Association of Social Workers (IASW) were also key to the development of professional expertise. In 1975, a Department of Health Committee described a significant problem with 'non-accidental injury to children' and recommended procedures for dealing with such cases.[123] National child abuse guidelines followed in 1977,[124] but they made no mention of CSA.[125] Instead, practitioners led the way. The IASW organized a seminar in 1983 on incest.[126] The Director of the Dublin Rape Crisis Centre made public statements in 1984 about the increase in women seeking help for childhood abuse.[127] In 1987 the Department of Health issued revised guidelines that replaced 'non-accidental injury' with a broader concept of child abuse which included sexual abuse.[128] The guidelines are notable for making clear that all suspicions of child sexual abuse should be reported to the Gardaí, although there was no real guidance on how the relationship between the various agencies was to work.[129] In 1988, the Irish Council for Civil Liberties (ICCL) Working Party on Child Sexual Abuse reported, finding that one in four girls and one in four boys had been sexually abused. Recognizing the invisibility of family violence, it stated that sexual abuse was being ignored because most cases take place within the family and the vast majority go unreported.[130] It criticized the lack of training, the lack of integration of voluntary services with professional services and the assumption in official guidance that CSA could be dealt with adequately in the same way as non-accidental injury.[131]

The Child Care Act 1991

The 1991 Act introduced a new regime for dealing with children in need of care. It signalled a move away from a reactive child protection system and towards a preventative legal framework underpinned by the principles of best interests of the child and primacy of the family as the best place for children.[132] It clarified the role, duties and powers of the health boards and improved procedures to facilitate interagency cooperation between the Health Boards and the Gardaí.[133] One key change was the focus on risk-based approaches to child protection; it replaced the legal requirement to have 'evidence' of abuse or harm, to 'likely' risk of abuse or harm.

Shortly after the passage of the 1991 Act, the Report of the Kilkenny Incest Investigation chaired by lawyer Catherine McGuinness[134] had an impact comparable to the Maria Colwell inquiry in Britain. It found that the victim had more than 100 contacts with the authorities over a period of ten years before her father was arrested. The Report made important future-oriented recommendations, including constitutional reform to protect children's rights, effective resourcing of the child protection framework and the introduction of mandatory reporting. The further 'scandals' that followed (see Chapter 2) consolidated awareness of CSA. By 1995 there were 2,441 child sexual abuse notifications, up from 37 in 1983.[135]

Rules around the taking of children's evidence in child welfare proceedings were relaxed in 1997.[136] In 1998 legislation was introduced to provide immunity from civil liability to any person who reports child abuse 'reasonably and in good faith'. In 1996 the Catholic Bishops produced a framework for responding to child sexual abuse by priests and religious.[137] The Cloyne Inquiry would later find that it did not improve reporting of child sexual abuse to authorities. This was because the Vatican called the Framework 'merely a study document', effectively allowing bishops the freedom to ignore the new reporting procedures.[138]

In 1999 the Department of Health and Children published The Children First Guidelines.[139] These were a new framework for cooperation between the health board and the gardaí. The guidance went beyond identification and investigation to overall case management which included assessment, planning, intervention and review. Unlike previous guidelines, Children First was underpinned by a set of principles which included participation by parents/carers and children in conferences and the development of child protection plans and the national Child Protection Notification System which was to be managed by a multi-disciplinary group.[140] The Children First Guidelines were followed by guidance published by the Irish Sports Council and The Department of Education and Science, among others. Further state reforms aimed at clarifying the health boards' duties in relation to children in care, and reform of the juvenile justice system, were introduced by the Children Act 2001.[141]

The Children's Rights Referendum and mandatory reporting

Since the mid-2000s, the dominant official child welfare discourse has finally shifted towards being more child-centred, family oriented and accountable to the public.[142] Official reports into clerical and institutional child sexual abuse reveal repeated refusals over decades by Catholic Church authorities to address allegations of sexual abuse against priests in Wexford and Dublin were pivotal in bringing about this shift. The CICA report in 2009 (Chapter 10) highlighted the widespread nature of child sexual abuse in industrial schools. The tipping point was the report of the Commission of Investigation into a diocese in Cloyne, County Cork. Chaired by Judge Yvonne Murphy who had chaired the 2009 inquiry into the Dublin Archdiocese,[143] it examined how church and state authorities handled allegations of child sex crimes against 19 priests in the Cloyne diocese. It found that from 1996 to 2009, the diocese did not report nine complaints to the gardaí, including two cases where the alleged victim was still a minor at the time of the complaint. No complaints were reported to the relevant child protection authorities between 1996 and 2008.[144] The more recent nature of the allegations highlighted the lack of understanding and complete disregard for child protection and the dangers of leaving reporting requirements up to the church. This was contrary to the church's own 1996 guidelines, the year the country had been convulsed by the Brendan Smyth case (see Chapter 2). The allegations were not reported by the Bishop and the administrator of the diocese to the gardaí and there was evidence of active attempts to cover up allegations. The commission also noted that the primary duty of child protection rests with the state and that it was not convinced that the state's laws and guidelines were sufficiently strong and clear for this task. The government's response was to vehemently condemn the Catholic hierarchy (even engaging in a diplomatic standoff with the Vatican) and to commit to a constitutional amendment and a range of measures to strengthen child protection.[145]

The Children's Referendum inserted an explicit statement about children's rights into the Constitution. Article 42A asserts the interests of the child as paramount, broadens the possibility of use of adoption and emphasizes the importance of listening to the voice of the child. It removed the presumption that the best interests of children of married parents were presumed to be within the family. The change was vehemently opposed by conservatives, who saw it as a threat to parental rights. Only 33.5 per cent of the electorate voted, and it passed by only 57.4 per cent,[146] suggesting that despite the decades of revelations about sexual abuse, the Irish public still does not value children's rights.

Child protection was strengthened through the creation of a criminal offence of withholding information about an offence against a child,[147] which applies to all adults and a national vetting system of organizations involved in work or activities relating to children or vulnerable persons.[148] A new statutory Child and Family Agency called Tusla was established to support and promote the welfare and protection of children.[149]

The most important measure was the introduction of mandatory reporting. The Children First Act 2015 obliges a 'mandated person' to report child protection concerns whenever such a person

> knows, believes or has reasonable grounds to suspect, on the basis of information that he or she has received, acquired or becomes aware of in the course of his or her employment or profession' that a child is being, has been, or is at risk of being harmed.[150]

Mandated persons include social workers, medics, teachers, therapists, clergy and members of religious orders. There is no criminal penalty for violations of the mandatory reporting system. However, initial figures suggest there has been a significant increase in the number of reports made to the Irish authorities since the introduction of mandatory reporting.[151]

The legislative activity around CSA reporting contrasts with the lack of legislative or policy activity around investigations and therapy. There is no national therapeutic service for children; non-governmental organizations are heavily relied on but are not adequately funded. The Child Care Act 1991, which remains the key statute, has been identified by the Special Rapporteur as inadequate for investigating complaints of sexual abuse.[152] There is only one dedicated forensic examination unit for children under 14, so children must travel for hours of travel to be treated.[153] There remains considerable room for improvement in the quality of inter-agency collaboration between, Tusla, the Health Service Executive and An Garda Síochána. An independent audit found serious failures in recording, a dearth of child-protection training for gardaí, and poor and limited communication, co-operation and co-ordination between gardaí and Tusla. It also uncovered evidence of repeated removal of some children by gardaí from the same family circumstances, suggesting systemic failings.[154]

Childcare proceedings in the non-specialist District Court lack adequate capacity and resources, leading to delays in hearing cases and a reduction in the attention given to each case.[155] In 2016 the Law Reform Commission found that the law was too restrictive regarding the admission of out-of-court statements by children in childcare and family law proceedings, and recommended a presumption in favour of admissibility.[156] This has yet to be introduced.[157] There are also significant issues arising with regard to knowledge and understanding of child welfare and family relations within the legal system.[158]

Adults can refer experiences of abuse to the child protection system and there is a duty on social work services to assess the risk posed to any children.[159] Some child protection departments have large volumes of allegations of childhood sexual abuse made by adults which are not being investigated and the extent of risk to children is left unassessed.[160] This is a serious breach of statutory child protection obligations.[161] The system for assessing and managing adult disclosures of childhood sexual abuse has been criticized for lack of clear communication, delays in social work responses and failures of expertise and competence, compounded by a lack of a legislative framework underpinning retrospective disclosures.[162]

Family law

An inordinate preoccupation with adults' rights and interests has shaped legal doctrine and practice in this area to the detriment of children vulnerable to sexual abuse. Advocacy groups have highlighted that mothers reporting sexual violence against their children have had devastating experiences of the legal system. They point to a lack of specialization and a system working beyond capacity.[163] Interaction between the child protection/criminal court/family court systems is often problematic.[164] Data on numbers of cases involving child sexual abuse are not collected by Tusla or the Courts Service. Particular concerns have been expressed about the operation of the *in camera* rule in family law proceedings; the rule is operating in a way that means that a parent is not allowed to see the contents of crucial documents such as reports by experts.[165] The family courts also appear to be imposing confidentiality and non-disclosure clauses on parties, where the court rules that a child's disclosures of rape and sexual violence must not be reported to the police directly but must be mediated through appointed individuals or Tusla.[166]

Rape Crisis Network Ireland has also called for special measures to facilitate children and vulnerable witnesses in family law proceedings and increased availability of legal aid to increase effective access to the family court system.[167] A draft Bill aims to create a specialist family law court.[168] There are worrying signs of a lack of recognition of feminist analysis of gendered power among legal practitioners; in 2020, the *Irish Journal of Family Law* published articles describing the discredited parental alienation syndrome (see Chapter 3) as having 'widespread consensus among mental health and family law community experts' and calling for Ireland to 'lead the way in the field of parental alienation and child welfare'.[169]

Conclusion

Ireland's approach to CSA in the twentieth century was dominated by a legal system and political culture that understood victims as a threat to the state's image as morally pure. The CLAA 1935 was a significant missed opportunity; meaningful reform that could have targeted offending against all children, in families and by persons in authority over them in families, in industrial schools and elsewhere was subordinated to an official obsession with sexual immorality.

Detection and prosecution of sexual crime against children was low, and the hostile treatment of victims in the criminal courts meant that the rhetoric of the criminal law remained largely aspirational. Although the 1990s saw important changes to how children gave evidence, much of these changes were not implemented for another decade at least.

For most of the twentieth century, the state prioritized Catholic social teaching and nationalist ideals, along with nineteenth century discourses fusing welfare, criminal justice and discipline of the poor, over children's welfare. Children were institutionalized in high numbers, where they were objectified and abused. Adults in positions of responsibility refused to answer children's reports of sexual abuse. Following increased interest in sexual violence amongst professionals and greater public awareness of the problem following the activism of NRCSA survivors described in Chapter 2, child protection was finally reconceived in the twenty-first century. Mandatory reporting was a major step towards improving detection of sexual abuse and preventing institutional cover-ups. Children's rights were enshrined in the constitution. However, the rights of children in care and in families who are experiencing or are at risk of sexual violence continue to be violated as funding, statistical resources, interagency training and cooperation are still not prioritized, and where court proceedings fail to centre the child.

In the next chapter we explore Australia's treatment of child sex offending in the twentieth century and into the present.

Notes

1 Religious leaders were also aware of the problem; a 1926 circular issued by the Provincial of the Christian Brothers warned against having sexual relations with pupils. E. O'Sullivan, "This Otherwise Delicate Subject" in P. O'Mahony (ed), *Criminal Justice in Ireland* (Dublin: Institute of Public Administration, 2002), 176–202, 198.

2 L. Earner-Byrne, "Reinforcing the Family: The Role of Gender, Morality and Sexuality in Irish Welfare Policy, 1922–1944" *The History of the Family* 13(4), 2008, 360–9, 361.

3 Ibid., 139.

4 See L. Ryan, *Gender Identity and the Irish Press 1922-37* (Lewiston, NY: Edwin Mellen Press, 2002).

5 A. Keating, "Sexual Crime in the Irish Free State 1922-33: Its Nature, Extent and Reporting" *Irish Studies Review* 20(2), 2012, 135–55, 136.

6 s5 Punishment of Incest Act 1908.

7 Criminal Law (Incest Proceedings) Act 1995.

8 W. Carrigan, *Report of the Committee on the Criminal Law Amendment Acts (1880-85), and Juvenile Prostitution* (Dublin: Stationery Office, 1931.

9 Ibid., 14.

10 Finnane op cit., at 532, 533.

11 C10.

12 Recommendation No 1. Emphasis in original.

13 The English 'young man's defence' (under s2 Criminal Law Amendment Act 1922) did not apply to Ireland. See also D.M. Doyle, "Reasonable Belief and Unlawful Carnal Knowledge: A Historical Perspective" *Irish Jurist* 47(1), 2012, 49.

14 Recommendation Number 3.

15 F. Kennedy, "The Suppression of the Carrigan Report: A Historical Perspective on Child Abuse" *Studies* 89, 2000, 354–63, 358.

16 M. Finnane, "The Carrigan Committee of 1930-31 and the 'Moral Condition of the Saorstát'" *Irish Historical Studies* 32(2), 2001, 519.

17 S. McAvoy, "Sexual Crime and Irish Women's Campaign for a Criminal Law Amendment Act, 1912-35" in M.G. Valiulis (ed), *Gender and Power in Irish History* (Dublin, 2009), 84.

18 The Film Censorship Act 1923, Intoxicating Liquor Act 1927, Censorship of Publications Act 1929 and the Public Dance Halls Act 1935.

19 It attached a maximum sentence of ten years' imprisonment.

20 [2006] 4 IR 1. The decision does not affect people who had been convicted and sentenced under the provisions. *A v Governor of Arbour Hill Prison* [2006] 4 IR 88.

21 ss2, 3.

22 Ibid., [39].

23 Joint Committee on Child Protection, *Report* (Dublin: Houses of the Oireachtas, 2007).

24 s5 2006 Act.
25 *DM v Ireland* [2012] IESC 10.
26 T. O'Malley *Sexual Offences* (Dublin: Round Hall, 2nd edition, 2013), 132.
27 s3A of the 2006 Act as inserted by s18 of the 2017 Act.
28 Criminal Law (Sexual Offences) (Amendment) Act 2007, ss6 and 241 the Children Act 2001.
29 Criminal Law (Human Trafficking) Act 2008.
30 Criminal Law (Sexual Offences) Act 2017 ss11–14.
31 s 14 CLAA 1935
32 *P.G. v Ireland* [2006] 4 IR 1.
33 S2 Criminal Law (Rape) Act 1981 placed the common law offence of rape on a statutory basis. Rape can only be committed by a man on a woman. The CrimInal Law (Rape)(Amendment) Act 1990 also abolished the common law presumption that a boy under 14 could not commit a penetrative act. The age of criminal responsibility was lowered to ten years for rape, rape under section 4 and aggravated sexual assault.
34 s4.
35 Indecency with Children Act 1960.
36 S14 Criminal Law (Sexual Offences) Act 1993.
37 *P v Judges of the Circuit Court and Ors* [2019] IESC 26. The Supreme Court has held that charges for buggery cannot be brought in relation to penetrative abuse perpetrated on boys before 1993. This is because it is a common law offence and nothing in the 1993 Act provided for historical prosecutions: see *DPP v Devins* [2012] IESC 7. As O'Malley notes, the alternative charge of indecent or sexual assault can be used. T. O'Malley op. cit., 123.
38 Ibid., 138.
39 s12(c) CLAA 1935.
40 s28
41 Criminal Law (Incest Proceedings) Act 1995.
42 *People (DPP) v X* Central Criminal Court, 1 March 1993.
43 *The Irish Times*, 23 January 2009.
44 Criminal Law (Sexual Offences) (Amendment) Act 2019.
45 See O'Malley op. cit., [7–17].
46 s176(2).
47 O'Malley op. cit., [5–34].
48 Ibid., 142.
49 M.E. Duggan, the Honorary Secretary of the Watching the Courts Committee cited in Keating op cit. at 143.
50 Ibid., 144.
51 M. Luddy, *Prostitution and Irish Society 1800-1940* (Cambridge: Cambridge University Press, 2007); C. McGettrick, K. O'Donnell, M. O'Rourke, J.M. Smith, and M. Steed, *Ireland and the Magdalene Laundries. A Campaign for Justice* (London: I.B. Tauris, 2021).
52 Carrigan Report op. cit., 14.
53 Ibid., Recommendation Number 8.
54 S. Ring, "The Victim of Historical Child Sexual Abuse in the Irish Courts 1999-2006" *Social and Legal Studies* 26(5), 2017, 562–80.
55 L. Weinstein, "Unlawful Carnal Knowledge of Teenage Girls: Performing Femininity and the Myth of Absolute Liability" *Éire-Ireland* 49(1 &2), 2014, 69–71.

56 In the years 1927–1975, only two women served on juries in criminal cases: *de Búrca and Anderson v Attorney General* [1976] IR 38. The Juries Act 1927 forced women to have to opt-in to jury service, and where they did so, they were often objected to.
57 And vice versa.
58 *People (DPP) v JT* (1988) 3 *Frewen* 141.
59 *Report of the Child Sexual Abuse Working Party* (Dublin: Irish Council for Civil Liberties, 1988).
60 Law Reform Commission, *Child Sexual Abuse* (LRC 32–1990).
61 Ibid., [7.02].
62 Ibid.
63 S28 (1) CEA 1992.
64 S 28(2).
65 S22 (1)(b). In 1985 the Law Reform Commission had recommended this change and the abolition of any rule making a spouse of an accused incompetent to testify against their spouse. Law Reform Commission, Report on Competence and Compellability of Spouses as Witnesses (LRC 13–1985).
66 s16(1)(b).
67 The first trial in which a pre-recording was admitted as evidence-in-chief was not until 2010: Rape Crisis Network Ireland, *Hearing Every Voice: Towards a New Strategy on Vulnerable Witnesses in Legal Proceedings* (Dublin: RCNI, 2018), www.rcni.ie/wp-content/uploads/210807-Rape-Crisis-Network-Ireland-Hearing-Every-Voice-Report-3.pdf, 10.
68 Ibid.
69 Ibid., 11.
70 Directive 2012/29/EU of the European Parliament and of the Council of 25 October 2012 establishing minimum standards on the rights, support and protection of victims of crime, and replacing Council Framework Decision 2001/220/JHA.
71 Criminal Law (Victims of Crime) Act 2017 s19.
72 s30 CL(Vof C)A 2017.
73 s36 Criminal Law (Sexual Offences) Act 2017. Victims of crimes are also conferred with rights to information throughout the investigation and any criminal proceedings, and the right to request a review of a decision not to prosecute. s9 Criminal Law (Victims of Crime) Act 2017.
74 RTÉ News, 11 January 2021.
75 An Garda Síochána, "Divisional Protective Services Units Now Operational Nationwide," 21 September 2020, available at www.garda.ie/en/about-us/our-departments/office-of-corporate-communications/press-releases/2020/september/an-garda-siochana-divisional-protective-services-units-now-operational-nationwide-.html.
76 A new Sexual Offences Unit is being created in the Office of the DPP: Annual Report 2019, 5, www.dppireland.ie/app/uploads/2020/10/AR-2019-eng.pdf.
77 Garda Inspectorate, *Responding to Child Sexual Abuse* (Dublin: Garda Inspectorate 2017), 18.
78 Ibid., 22.
79 J.H. Whyte, *Church and State in Modern Ireland 1923–1979* (Dublin: Gill and Macmillan, 1980).

80 Kilkenny incest Inquiry at 30; U. Kilkelly and C. O'Mahony, "The Proposed Children's Rights Amendment: Running to Stand Still?" *Irish Journal of Family Law* 10(2), 2007, 19–25.
81 Married Women's Status Act 1957.
82 The Guardianship of Infants Act 1964.
83 Social Welfare Act 1986.
84 Status of Children Act 1987.
85 The Association of Mixed-Race Irish, *Shadow Report to the UN Committee on the Elimination of Racial Discrimination: A Response to Ireland's Combined 5th Periodic Report* (2019), <https://tbinternet.ohchr.org/Treaties/CERD/Shared%20Documents/IRL/INT_CERD_NGO_IRL_37383_E.pdf>.
86 D. Hannan and P. Commins, "The Significance of Small-Scale Landholders in Ireland's Socio-Economic Transition" in J.H. Goldthorpe and C.T. Whelan (eds), *The Development of Industrial Society in Ireland* (Oxford: The British Academy, 1992), 79.
87 E. O'Sullivan and I. O'Donnell, 'Introduction' in E. O Sullivan and I. O'Donnell (eds), *Coercive Confinement in Post-Independence Ireland* (Manchester: Manchester University Press 2012), 22.
88 The 1936 Cussen Report noted that the state's reliance on these institutions deviated sharply from international trends but did not recommend a policy change. Commission of Inquiry into the Reformatory and Industrial School System 1934–1936, *Report* (Dublin: Stationery Office, 1936).
89 Statement of Chairperson, 25 November 2019, www.childabusecommission.ie.
90 Central Statistics Office, *That Was Then, This Is Now: Change in Ireland, 1949-1999* (Dublin: Stationery Office, 2000), 51.
91 O'Sullivan and O'Donnell op. cit., Figure 1.2.
92 Smith et al. op. cit.
93 In England and Wales, the Children and Young Person's Act 1933 renamed industrial and reformatory schools 'Approved Schools', which were run by voluntary children's societies and overseen by the Home Office. Children could be sent to them by courts. The IICSA noted that the accounts from adult NRCSA survivors of CSA who were detained in approved schools were among the worst the Inquiry has heard. IICSA, *Sexual Abuse of Children in Custodial Institutions: 2009-2017 Investigation Report* (2019), v.
94 M. O'Callaghan, *British High Politics and a Nationalist Ireland: Criminality, Land and the Law under Forster and Balfour* (Cork: Cork University Press, 1994), 6.
95 O'Sullivan op. cit. 2002, 195.
96 At least 80 per cent of admissions to the industrial schools were from the courts: CICA 2009 at [3.46].
97 Commission to Inquire into Child Abuse (CICA), *Final Report. Volumes I–V.* (Dublin: Government Publications, 2009), [3.24]. 67 per cent of survivors who gave evidence to the CICA Confidential Committee reported that their parents were unskilled. Ibid., [3.08].
98 CICA op. cit., Vol I, Ch 3 [3.05]. The grounds for committal were expanded and changed slightly by Children Acts in 1929, 1941, 1949 and 1957 and the Employment of Children Act 1903. Another gateway was the health authorities, under the Health Acts. See J. Barnes, *Irish Industrial Schools, 1868-1908: Origins and Development* (Dublin: Irish Academic Press 1989), and CICA, op. cit., Vol 1, Ch 3.

99 (f) and (g).

100 CICA op. cit., Vol III, Ch 3 at [3.05].

101 S.-A. Buckley, *The Cruelty Man. Child Welfare, the NSPCC and the State in Ireland, 1889-1956* (Manchester: Manchester University Press, 2013), 118. NSPCC inspectors were key to maintenance of the system. The first Irish branch of the NSPCC was founded in Dublin in 1889, with other branches across the country following soon after. The NSPCC was succeeded by the Irish Society for the Prevention of Cruelty to Children in 1956.

102 s58(1)(e).

103 St Anne's Reformatory School in Kilmacud, County Dublin: CICA op. cit., 2009, Vol 1, Ch 3 at [10].

104 CICA op. cit., Vol I Ch 3 at [2.09]. S 57 as amended by s9 Children Act 1941.

105 Under the School Attendance Act 1926, if their parent was convicted of a second offence of failing to send a child under 14 years.

106 CICA op. cit., 2009. In England, industrial schools and reformatories were replaced by approved schools.

107 Commission of Inquiry into the Reformatory and Industrial School 1934-1936 op. cit.; and CICA, op. cit., Ch 1.

108 O'Sullivan and O'Donnell op. cit., 6.

109 S.-A. Buckley and C. McGregor, "Interrogating Institutionalization and Child Welfare: The Irish Case, 1939-1991" *European Journal of Social Work* 22, 2019, 1062–72.

110 CICA op. cit., Executive Summary.

111 CICA, [4:654].

112 Ring op. cit.

113 CICA Executive Summary and Murphy Report op cit.

114 Commission to Inquire into Child Abuse op cit.

115 Ibid., Executive Summary.

116 E. Kennedy, *Reformatory and Industrial Schools System Report* (Dublin: Stationery Office 1970). The raising of the age of criminal responsibility to 12 (with certain exceptions) and the ending of the role of the Department of Education in the administration of residential childcare were not achieved until 2006 and 2007, respectively.

117 A. Keating, "A Contested Legacy The Kennedy Committee Revisited" *Irish Studies Review* 22(3), 2014, 304–20.

118 *Sunday Independent*, 31 October 1999.

119 *Irish Independent*, 10 March 1998.

120 J. Power, "'Serious' Child Abuse Allegations Repeatedly Not Investigated" *The Irish Times*, 24 January 2020; C. O'Mahony, "No Hashtags and Street Protests Over Abuse of Children in Care" *The Irish Times*, 30 April 2018.

121 European Commission Against Racism and Intolerance (2019) *Report on Ireland* 2019, available at < https://rm.coe.int/fifth-report-on-ireland/168094c575>.

122 R. Dunbar et al., *Direct Provision's Impact on Children: A Human Rights Analysis* (Galway: Irish Centre for Human Rights, 2020).

123 E. O'Sullivan, "Residential Child Welfare in Ireland, 1965–2008: An Outline of Policy, Legislation and Practice: A Paper Prepared for the Commission to Inquire into Child Abuse" CICA op cit 245–430.

124 Memorandum on Non-Accidental Injury to Children. Later editions followed in 1980 and 1983.

125 H. Buckley, "Child Abuse Guidelines In Ireland: For Whose Protection?" in H. Ferguson and T. McNamara (eds) *Protecting Irish Children: Investigation, protection and welfare*, (Dublin: IPA, 1996), 37.
126 Ibid.
127 S. McKay, *Without Fear. 25 Years of the Dublin Rape Crisis Centre* (Dublin: New Island Books, 2005): 81.
128 Department of Health, *Guidelines on Procedures for the Identification, Investigation and Management of Child Abuse* (Stationery Office 1987).
129 Ombudsman for Children, *A report based on an investigation into the implementation of Children First: National Guidelines for the Protection and Welfare of Children* (Stationery Office 2010) 88.
130 *Report of the Child Sexual Abuse Working Party* (Dublin: ICCL, 1988).
131 Many of the ICCL's reforms were echoed by the Law Reform Commission's 1990 report . Law Reform Commission. *Child Sexual Abuse.* (LRC 32–1990).
132 McGregor op. cit., 773.
133 Department of Health (1995) *Notification of Suspected Cases of Child Abuse between the Gardai and the Health Boards* (Dublin: Stationery Office, 1995).
134 C. McGuinness, *Report of the Kilkenny Incest Investigation* (South Eastern Health Board, 1993).
135 H. Buckley, C. Skehill and E. O'Sullivan, *Child Protection Practices in Ireland* (Dublin: Oak Tree Press, 1997), Figure 1.2.
136 Children Act 1997, Part III.
137 Irish Catholic Bishops' Advisory Committee on Child Sexual Abuse by Priests and Religious. *Child Sexual Abuse: Framework for a Church Response* (Dublin: Veritas, 1996).
138 Cloyne Report, [1.18].
139 Children First: National Guidelines for the Protection and Welfare of Children.
140 O'Sullivan op. cit., 260.
141 The Education (Welfare) Act 2000 reformed the law on school attendance.
142 McGregor op. cit., 776
143 Commission of Investigation into the Dublin Archdiocese, *The Cloyne Report* (Department of Justice and Equality, 2011).
144 At para 1.21.
145 Joint statement by the Minister for Justice, Equality and Defence, Mr. Alan Shatter, T.D., and the Minister for Children and Youth Affairs, Ms. Frances Fitzgerald, T.D., on the publication of the Commission of Investigation Report into the Catholic Diocese of Cloyne www.justice.ie/en/JELR/Pages/Cloyne-Joint-Statement, accessed 10 August 2021.
146 *The Irish Times*, 11 November 2012.
147 s2.
148 The National Vetting Bureau (Children and Vulnerable Persons) Act 2012 established.
149 s82(2) Child and Family Agency Act 2013. The name is derived from the Irish for First or New Day. The agency's primary functions, set out in s8 of the Act, are to support and promote the development, welfare and protection of children, to support families and to offer a range of services in respect of domestic, sexual or gender-based violence.
150 S14(1).

151 C. Hanly, "The Reporting of Child Abuse and Neglect in Ireland in an International Context" *International Journal of Law, Policy and the Family* 34(2), 2020, 145–67.

152 C. O'Mahony, *Annual Report of the Special Rapporteur on Child Protection* (2020), www.gov.ie/en/collection/51fc67-special-rapporteur-on-child-protection-reports/, 2.6 See also the National Vetting Bureau (Children and Vulnerable Persons) Act 2012.

153 Visit to Ireland: Report of the Special Rapporteur on the sale and sexual exploitation of children, including child prostitution, child pornography and other child sexual abuse material, UN Doc No A/HRC/40/51/Add.2, 15 November 2019 at [12], https://undocs.org/A/HRC/40/51/Add.2.

154 G. Shannon, *Audit of the Exercise by An Garda Síochána of the Provisions of Section 12 of the Child Care Act 1991* (Dublin: An Garda Síochána, 2017).

155 Coulter op. cit., 1, and Special Rapporteur on the sale and sexual exploitation of children op. cit., [66].

156 Law Reform Commission Report 2016–2.78–2.83. The Children Act 1997, s23.

157 A Review of the 1991 Act is underway: www.gov.ie/en/publication/97d109-review-of-the-child-care-act-1991/.

158 C. Coulter, *Final Report of the Child Care Law Reporting Project* (Dublin: Child Care Law Reporting Project, 2015). C. Coulter, *An Examination of Lengthy, Contested and Complex Child Protection Cases in the District Court* (Dublin: Child Care Law Reporting Project, 2018).

159 J. Mooney, "Adult Disclosures of Childhood Sexual Abuse and Section 3 of the Child Care Act 1991: Past Offences, Current Risk" *Child Care in Practice* 24(3), 2018, 245–57. 8.

160 HIQA 2015, 2016a, 2016b, 2017.

161 Mooney, 2018, op. cit.

162 J. Mooney, "How Adults Tell: A Study of Adults' Experiences of Disclosure to Child Protection Social Work Services" *Child Abuse Review* 30(3), 2021, 193–209.

163 *Irish Times*, 19 December 2020.

164 The Children Living with Domestic and Sexual Violence Group, "Submission to the Family Justice Oversight Group Consultation February 2021," www.rcni.ie/wp-content/uploads/Joint-CLwDSV-Sub-to-the-Family-Justice-OG-FINAL.pdf.

165 See RCNI, "Submission to the Joint Oireachtas Committee on Justice and Equality on the Family Law Courts" (2019), www.rcni.ie/wp-content/uploads/RCNI-Family-Law-Courts-Submission-to-JOCJE-Final-April-2019.pdf, p. 3.

166 Ibid., 3.

167 RCNI, "Submission to the Family Justice Oversight Group Consultation Topics - Phase 1," 3 (2021), www.rcni.ie/wp-content/uploads/RCNI-Family-Justice-Oversight-Group-Submission-February-2021-FINAL-1.pdf.

168 Family Court Bill, General Scheme (September 2020), www.justice.ie/en/JELR/Family%20Court%20Bill%20General%20Scheme.pdf/Files/Family%20Court%20Bill%20General%20Scheme.pdf.

169 B. O'Sullivan and B. Guildea, "*Clinical and Legal Aspects of Parental Alienation*" *Irish Journal of Family Law* 23(4), 2020, 101–8.

References

Barnes, J. *Irish Industrial Schools, 1868-1908: Origins and Development* (Dublin: Irish Academic Press, 1989).

Bishops' Advisory Committee on Child Sexual Abuse by Priests and Religious, *Child Sexual Abuse: Framework for a Church Response* (Dublin: Veritas, 1996).

Buckley, H., "Child Abuse Guidelines in Ireland: For Whose Protection?" in H. Ferguson and T. McNamara (eds), *Protecting Irish Children: Investigation, Protection and Welfare* (Dublin: IPA, 1996), 37.

Buckley, H., Skehill, C., and O'Sullivan, E., *Child Protection Practices in Ireland* (Dublin: Oak Tree Press, 1997).

Buckley, S.-A., *The Cruelty Man. Child Welfare, the NSPCC and the State in Ireland, 1889-1956* (Manchester: Manchester University Press, 2013).

Buckley, S.-A. and McGregor, C., "Interrogating Institutionalization and Child Welfare: The Irish Case, 1939-1991" *European Journal of Social Work* 22, 2019, 1062–72.

Carrigan, W., *Report of the Committee on the Criminal Law Amendment Acts (1880-85), and Juvenile Prostitution* (Dublin: Stationery Office, 1931).

Central Statistics Office, *That Was Then, This Is Now: Change in Ireland, 1949-1999* (Dublin: Stationery Office, 2000).

Commission to Inquire into Child Abuse, *Final Report* (Dublin: Stationery Office, 2009).

Commission of Inquiry into the Reformatory and Industrial School 1934-1936, *Report* (Dublin: Stationery Office, 1936).

Commission of Investigation into Cloyne Archdiocese, *Report* (Dublin: Department of Justice and Equality, 2010).

Commission of Investigation into the Dublin Archdiocese, *The Cloyne Report* (Department of Justice and Equality, 2011)

Coulter, C., *Final Report of the Child Care Law Reporting Project* (Dublin: Child Care Law Reporting Project, 2015).

Coulter, C., *An Examination of Lengthy, Contested and Complex Child Protection Cases in the District Court* (Dublin: Child Care Law Reporting Project, 2018).

Department of Health, *Guidelines on Procedures for the Identification, Investigation and Management of Child Abuse* (Dublin: Stationery Office, 1987).

Department of Health, *Notification of Suspected Cases of Child Abuse between the Gardai and the Health Boards* (Dublin: Stationery Office, 1995).

Doyle, D.M., "Reasonable Belief and Unlawful Carnal Knowledge: A Historical Perspective" *Irish Jurist* 47(1), 2012, 49.

Dunbar, R. et al., *Direct Provision's Impact on Children: A Human Rights Analysis* (Galway: Irish Centre for Human Rights, 2020).

Earner-Byrne, L., "Reinforcing the Family: The Role of Gender, Morality and Sexuality in Irish Welfare Policy, 1922–1944" *The History of the Family* 13(4), 2008, 360–69.

European Commission Against Racism and Intolerance, *Report on Ireland* 2019, https://rm.coe.int/fifth-report-on-ireland/168094c575.

Finnane, M., "The Carrigan Committee of 1930-31 and the 'Moral Condition of the Saorstát'" *Irish Historical Studies* 32(2), 2001, 519–36.

Garda Inspectorate, *Responding to Child Sexual Abuse* (Dublin: Garda Inspectorate, 2017).

Hanly, C., "The Reporting of Child Abuse and Neglect in Ireland in an International Context" *International Journal of Law, Policy and the Family* 34(2), 2020, 145–67.

Hannan, D. and Commins, P., "The Significance of Small-Scale Landholders in Ireland's Socio-Economic Transition" in J.H. Goldthorpe and C.T. Whelan (eds), *The Development of Industrial Society in Ireland* (Oxford: The British Academy, 1992), 79.

IICSA, *Sexual Abuse of Children in Custodial Institutions: 2009-2017 Investigation Report* (2019).

Joint Committee on Child Protection, *Report* (Dublin: Houses of the Oireachtas, 2007).

Keating, A., "Sexual Crime in the Irish Free State 1922-33: Its Nature, Extent and Reporting" *Irish Studies Review* 20(2), 2012, 135–55.

Keating, A., "A Contested Legacy The Kennedy Committee Revisited" *Irish Studies Review* 22, 2014, 304–20.

Kennedy, E., *Reformatory and Industrial Schools System Report* (Dublin: Stationery Office, 1970).

Kennedy, F., "The Suppression of the Carrigan Report: A Historical Perspective on Child Abuse" *Studies* 89, 2000, 354–63.

Kilkelly, U. and O'Mahony, C., "The Proposed Children's Rights Amendment: Running to Stand Still?" *Irish Journal of Family Law* 10(2), 2007, 19–25.

Law Reform Commission, *Report on Competence and Compellability of Spouses as Witnesses* (LRC 13–1985).

Law Reform Commission, *Child Sexual Abuse* (LRC 32–1990).

Luddy, M., *Prostitution and Irish Society 1800–1940* (Cambridge: Cambridge University Press, 2007).

McAvoy, S., "Sexual Crime and Irish Women's Campaign for a Criminal Law Amendment Act, 1912-35" in M.G. Valiulis (ed), *Gender and Power in Irish History* (Dublin: Irish Academic Press, 2009), 84.

McGettrick, C., O'Donnell, K.; O'Rourke, M.; Smith, J.M., and Steed, M., *Ireland and the Magdalene Laundries. A Campaign for Justice* (London: I.B. Tauris, 2021).

McGuinness, C., *Report of the Kilkenny Incest Investigation* (South Eastern Health Board, 1993).

McKay, S., *Without Fear. 25 Years of the Dublin Rape Crisis Centre* (Dublin: New Island Books, 2005).

Mooney, J. "Adult Disclosures of Childhood Sexual Abuse and Section 3 of the Child Care Act 1991: Past Offences, Current Risk" *Child Care in Practice* 24(3), 2018, 245–57.

Mooney, J., "How Adults Tell: A Study of Adults' Experiences of Disclosure to Child Protection Social Work Services" *Child Abuse Review* 30(3), 2021, 193–209.

O'Callaghan, M., *British High Politics and a Nationalist Ireland: Criminality, Land and the Law under Forster and Balfour* (Cork: Cork University Press, 1994).

O'Mahony, C. "No Hashtags and Street Protests Over Abuse of Children in Care" *The Irish Times*, 30 April 2018.

O'Mahony, C., *Annual Report of the Special Rapporteur on Child Protection* (Dublin, 2020), www.gov.ie/en/publication/cfbc8-special-rapporteur-on-child-protection-13th-report/.

O'Malley, T., *Sexual Offences* (Dublin: Round Hall, 2nd edition 2013).

O'Sullivan, B. and Guildea, B., "Clinical and Legal Aspects of Parental Alienation" *Irish Journal of Family Law* 23(4), 2020, 101–8.

O'Sullivan, E., "This Otherwise Delicate Subject" in P. O'Mahony (ed), *Criminal Justice in Ireland* (Dublin: Institute of Public Administration, 2002), 176.

O'Sullivan, E., "Residential Child Welfare in Ireland, 1965–2008: An Outline of Policy, Legislation and Practice: A Paper Prepared for the Commission to Inquire into Child Abuse" *CICA* 2009, 245–430.

O'Sullivan, E. and O'Donnell, I., "Introduction" in E.O Sullivan and I. O'Donnell (eds), *Coercive Confinement in Post-Independence Ireland* (Manchester: Manchester University Press, 2012), 1.

Power, J., "'Serious' Child Abuse Allegations Repeatedly Not Investigated" *The Irish Times*, 24 January 2020.

RCNI, *Hearing Every Voice. Towards a New Strategy on Vulnerable Witnesses in Legal Proceedings* (Dublin: RCNI, 2018).

RCNI, "Submission to the Joint Oireachtas Committee on Justice and Equality on the Family Law Courts" (2019), www.rcni.ie/wp-content/uploads/RCNI-Family-Law-Courts-Submission-to-JOCJE-Final-April-2019.pdf

RCNI, "Submission to the Family Justice Oversight Group Consultation Topics - Phase 1," 3 (2021), www.rcni.ie/wp-content/uploads/RCNI-Family-Justice-Oversight-Group-Submission-February-2021-FINAL-1.pdf

Report of the Child Sexual Abuse Working Party (Dublin: Irish Council for Civil Liberties, 1988).

Ring, S., "The Victim of Historical Child Sexual Abuse in the Irish Courts 1999-2006" *Social and Legal Studies* 26(5), 2017, 562–80.

Ryan, L., *Gender Identity and the Irish Press 1922-37* (Lewiston, NY: Edwin Mellen Press, 2002).

Shannon, G., *Audit of the Exercise by An Garda Síochána of the Provisions of Section 12 of the Child Care Act 1991* (Dublin: An Garda Síochána, 2017).

The Association of Mixed-Race Irish, *Shadow Report to the UN Committee on the Elimination of Racial Discrimination: A Response to Ireland's Combined 5th Periodic Report* (2019), https://tbinternet.ohchr.org/Treaties/CERD/Shared%20Documents/IRL/INT_CERD_NGO_IRL_37383_E.pdf>.

Weinstein, L., "Unlawful Carnal Knowledge of Teenage Girls: Performing Femininity and the Myth of Absolute Liability" *Éire-Ireland*, 49(1 & 2), 2014, Spring/Summer, 69–71.

Whyte, J.H. *Church and State in Modern Ireland 1923–1979* (Dublin: Gill and Macmillan, 1980).

5 The evolution of legal and policy frameworks around child sex offences in Australia

Introduction

This final chapter of Part I traces the development of criminal justice and child welfare and child protection frameworks for child sexual abuse (CSA) in the federation of the Commonwealth of Australia and the colonies that preceded it. The first section traces the evolution of criminal laws addressing the age of consent.[1] As was the case in Ireland and England and Wales, the focus on the age of consent detracted from understandings of the multiple forms of offending against children. The second section examines legal and procedural barriers to the prosecution of child sex offences in the twentieth century. Many of these mirror the situation described in the previous two chapters. The third section explores the penal welfarism of the state that was felt most keenly by First Nations children and their families. Turning to child protection laws and policies that developed from the mid-twentieth century, the chapter then examines the position of children in the care of state institutions. Finally, the chapter briefly considers how the Australian family law system has treated reports of CSA in families, and the challenges facing mothers seeking to protect their children. The conclusion reflects on the themes drawn out in Part I.

The criminal law

In the colonies that were to become Australia, there was a flurry of legislating age of consent provisions around the time of the Criminal Law Amendment Act 1885 (CLAA 1885) of England and Wales. Some colonies passed laws that preceded the CLAA 1885, and each drafted legislation influenced by local conditions including ideas about children's labour and education and colonial priorities associated with the so-called 'criminal classes' and prostitution.[2] Much as in England, Stead's 'Maiden Tribute' series was received with great sensationalized interest when it arrived in the colonial ports in August 1885.[3] Local purity and feminist campaigners had already had some success in raising the age of consent. New South Wales (NSW) was the first colony to raise the age, with the *Criminal Law Amendment Act 1883 (NSW)*. The law

DOI: 10 4324/9780429468162-6

restated the death penalty for rape and the maximum penalty for indecent assault (five years' penal servitude) while extending carnal knowledge to girls under the age of 14 (previously 12). The notion that girls in NSW reached puberty earlier than their English counterparts was used as one justification for why the 'protection of the law should be thrown around them'.[4] Western Australia and Queensland followed suit with the *Criminal Law Amendment Act 1892 (WA)* and the *Criminal Code Act 1899 (Qld)*. South Australia and Victoria raised the age of consent to 16 with the *Criminal Law Act 1885 (SA)* and the *Crimes Act 1891 (Vic)*. Some colonies also introduced measures protecting children from procurement and prohibiting sexual relations between female students and male teachers.[5] The reforms were not as helpful as campaigners might have hoped. Girls' complaints were still not taken as seriously as women's complaints of rape, prosecution of which required evidence of the victim's resistance. Conviction rates for adolescent carnal knowledge complaints were even lower than those for adolescent rape complaints and the sentences were minimal.[6]

On federation of the Commonwealth of Australia in 1901, each state consolidated its criminal laws with a Crimes Act or Criminal Code.[7] In the early twentieth century, NSW Western Australia and Tasmania raised the age of consent to 16, while Queensland raised it to 17 and Victoria to 18. South Australia had already raised the age of consent to 17 in 1899. Much as in England, there was concern about men being netted in the new legislation, which was discussed in terms of the 'age of protection' more than the 'age of consent' and driven by a preoccupation with prostitution.[8]

Incest

The prohibition on incest was another example of the colonies pre-empting English law. South Australia criminalized incest in 1876 with the *Criminal Law Consolidation Act*. Unlike the POIA 1908 in England and Wales and Ireland, incest was made a felony.[9] From 1891 to 1924, each other jurisdiction enacted similar provisions[10] with NSW, one of the first states to raise the age of consent, one of the last states to act on incest.[11] Australian parliaments were able to pass anti-incest provisions because they included them in consolidating legislation addressing other crimes, rather than the stand-alone legislation attempted repeatedly in England.[12] Whereas the age of consent debates garnered great public interest, incest attracted much less public attention and political resistance. Incest was mainly understood as a problem of poverty and overcrowding.

As was the case in Ireland and in England and Wales, all the early sex offence legislation was gendered and heteronormatively biased. Same-sex offences were not considered to be 'natural' ecclesiastical offences like the offences of fornication and adultery that were associated with incest and carnal knowledge. In all the colonies, male same-sex offences committed on boys were addressed by anti-buggery and anti-gross indecency provisions that precluded the possibility of consent. Consensual homosexual sex between men was subject to the same provisions and was therefore wholly illegal until the last quarter of the twentieth century.

Modernization of the criminal law

When compared internationally, Australian second-wave feminists had great influence on reform of sexual offences, with rape law reform commencing in South Australia in 1976. The most radical and influential reform was the *Crimes (Sexual Assault) Amendment Act 1981* of NSW, bringing the common law offences of rape and carnal knowledge into statute as the newly termed 'sexual assault', applicable to both women and men as victims and perpetrators. Informed by international feminist models, the language of 'assault' aimed to emphasize the physical violence and abuse of power, rather than sexual motive, inherent to rape.[13] Gender-neutrality aimed to remedy 'artificial' distinctions between victims and counter the homophobia that had prevented the acknowledgement of male rape as a crime distinct from men's consensual gay sex.[14] The 1981 Act paved the way for the modernization of child sex offences, for the most part moving away from antiquated ideas of 'carnal knowledge' to a focus on violence.

Buoyed by their influence in rape law reform, feminists pressured the NSW government to stage the first Australian inquiry into child sexual assault, the 1984 Child Sexual Assault Task Force, which aimed to heighten child abuse notifications and improve intergovernmental cooperation in service delivery and justice responses. The Task Force radically identified 'child sexual assault' as a problem of patriarchal power inflicted on both girls and boys, rather than a problem of morality or 'carnal knowledge'. Its primary legislative outcome was the *Crimes (Child Assault) Amendment Act 1985 (NSW)* that pre-empted the UNCRC 1989 by four years when it named 'child sexual assault' in statute.[15] The Act replaced common law carnal knowledge offences with a new suite of child sexual assault offences protecting girls and boys equally.[16] Modern definitions of sexual intercourse including oral and digital penetration that were introduced in the 1981 Act were retained in child sex offences. The new category of assault by a 'person in authority' was also introduced, defined as 'the person is in the care, or under the supervision or authority, of the other person'.[17] Although the 1985 Act was nationally influential in shaping discourse about CSA, the other states and territories failed to introduce a dedicated child sexual assault law. For example, when Victoria (again) modernized sexual offences, including offences against children, it did so by way of the general *Crimes (Sexual Offences) Act 1991 (Vic)*,[18] whereas Queensland retained the language of carnal knowledge and incest in the *Criminal Law Amendment Act 1997 (Qld)*. The final factor contributing to the modernization of child sex offences was the decriminalization of men's homosexual sex, performed around the country from 1972 to 1997, and accompanying advances in the equal treatment of LGBTI youth, which finally allowed for offences against boys to be treated as truly equal to offences against girls. The next part explores how this criminal law framework translated to the criminal processes over time.

Prosecuting child sex offences in the twentieth century

A great myth about CSA is that it was rarely prosecuted or taken seriously by the courts. Although historical crime data are inconclusive, it is evident that in the first half of the twentieth century, prosecutions were commonplace, with conviction rates similar to rates for sex crimes today. One estimate based on trials and newspaper reports in three jurisdictions suggests there might have been more than 15,000 prosecutions for child sex offences across Australia from 1900 to 1950,[19] when the population rose from 3,774,000 to 8,307,000 non-Indigenous inhabitants.[20] Offenders were typically known to victims, and many offenders were family members. Offences by strangers were rare. Christian Brothers were prosecuted and convicted at least from 1919,[21] but compared to today, there is much less evidence of the prosecution of religious leaders.[22] Most cases concerned carnal knowledge and incest committed on girls, which did not require proof of non-consent or force as required in rape trials.[23]

Offences against boys were also prosecuted, such as buggery and gross indecency, which again did not require proof of non-consent. In one study of all same-sex offences tried between 1920 and 1939 in NSW and Queensland, cases involving boys accounted for 56 per cent and 77 per cent in each jurisdiction, respectively.[24] One-quarter of the complainants in NSW and a third in Queensland were boys under 12.[25] Serious offences committed in public were most likely to 'face the full force of law'.[26] Despite the criminal prohibition on homosexual sex, and the fact that occasionally children were prosecuted for 'participating' in sex acts with men, 'the courts were generally more concerned with protecting young males than prosecuting them'.[27]

In all trials in this period, conviction was more common than acquittal. Evidence of penetration was significant in sentencing, as was the age of the victim. Capital punishment seems never to have been enforced and otherwise severe penalties were typically reserved for incest committed by fathers. It is clear that in the first half of the twentieth century, some judges understood incest committed on girls as a particularly grave abuse of power.[28] Severe penalties were also awarded for offences committed on very young children and 'unnatural offences' committed on boys.[29] Many 'less serious' (non-penetrative) offences appear to have been addressed with non-custodial sentences.[30]

By the middle of the twentieth century, motivations for policing sexual contact with children had changed. One study of sex offences tried at the NSW higher courts throughout the 1950s indicates that in a decade overly concerned with sexual morality, acts of carnal knowledge with girls and homosexual offences committed on boys were principal concerns. Arrests for carnal knowledge quadrupled throughout the decade, reaching 16 arrests per 100,000 people in 1959, suggesting a preoccupation with the sexual lives of the new identity of 'the teenager'.[31] Children constituted two-thirds of all sex trial complainants.[32] For trials concerning children under 13, 75 per cent involved offences committed on girls, 21 per cent on boys and 3 per cent on both sexes.[33] Twenty-seven per cent of all sex offence trials concerned offences committed on girls by family members, with fathers and step-fathers the most likely defendants.[34] These familial cases had a conviction rate of 75 per cent.[35] Contrary to the first half of the twentieth century, offences by men unknown to children were commonly prosecuted.[36] There is little evidence of awareness of institutional CSA, except in a few cases involving teachers.[37] Again, as in the earlier period, cases with younger complainants had the highest conviction rates. Guilty pleas were entered more frequently in relation to offences on boys than girls. It is evident that courts understood the moral harm done to boys as graver than that done to girls,[38] in a period when all homosexuality was understood as an 'illness' that could be contracted, and psychological understandings of the trauma of sexual abuse were only nascent.

Finally, a study of all child sex offences tried in the NSW courts in 1982 found that 69 per cent of complainants were girls, with boys constituting 31 per cent. The majority of complainants were 12 years old or younger.[39] Most offenders were an acquaintance (39 per cent), family member (23 per cent) or 'authority figure' (12 per cent) in the child's life. Thirteen per cent of offenders were strangers.[40] In total, 363 counts were laid against 191 individuals, 70 per cent of whom pleaded guilty to all charges. In summary, in 82 per cent of the 235 cases in which a defendant was charged with at least once count of child sexual abuse, the defendant was convicted. However, only 73 offenders received custodial sentences. The remaining 120 convicted offenders received non-custodial sentences.[41]

Although disparate and piecemeal, all of this data from the twentieth century suggest at least a contradiction of the common mythology that the state did not take CSA seriously in the past. However, sentencing remarks from courts of different states in the 1980s indicate that even in a decade of great legal reforms and feminist activism, some judges held archaic views, including that children 'consented' to sex; that child sexual abuse was 'not violent'; that one offender (the victim's teacher) was 'a weakling who succumbed to his eroticism'; that child victims were 'promiscuous' and that some offenders did not understand that what they were doing was wrong.[42]

A problem with any discussion of historical CSA in Australia is the lack of data concerning Indigenous victims, which means that all of the above should be read with care. Until the 1970s and 1980s, First Nations Australians were governed by a suite of racist paternalistic legislation that shaped how their sexual agency was perceived and treated, including the right to marry.[43] For example, the relevant Queensland law provided a defence to carnal knowledge that an Aboriginal girl had reached puberty (regardless of her age).[44] First

Nations Australians, who lived on church-run Missions and reserves, or in out-of-home care, faced particular difficulties speaking out about any forms of exploitation or abuse as discussed below.[45]

Disclosing abuse

Much like today, offences that reached the courts reflected only a very small proportion of incidents of child sexual abuse. Throughout the twentieth century, if a child did disclose, the most common person confided in was a family member, often their mother.[46] For children abused in institutions, data from the Royal Commission into Institutional Responses to Child Sexual Abuse (the Royal Commission) (see Chapter 10) show that many children did disclose at the time of or soon after an offence, but for others, a lack of sex education and explicit sexual conversation within families and society meant it was not obvious that what was done to them was sexual abuse.[47] Very young children did not have the language to describe their assaults.[48] The idea that children were the property of adults, and 'should be seen and not heard', was extremely influential.[49] First Nations children disclosed abuse less readily than non-Indigenous children.[50] For one-fifth of survivors who were Aboriginal or Torres Strait Islander, their disclosure to the Royal Commission was the first time they had told anyone about their abuse.[51] Girls have historically disclosed abuse more readily than boys who faced homophobic stigma if abused by men, and shame and incredulity if abused by women.[52] Of the 1,200 survivors who had never disclosed their abuse in institutions until appearing before the Royal Commission, 75 per cent were men.[53]

All children were least likely to disclose abuse if the offender was a family member, out of fear of reprisal and the impact on the family.[54] For some First Nations children, extended families and close communities may have made familial abuse seem all but impossible to disclose. Children in closed religious communities faced similar obstacles to speaking out.[55] Children abused in church institutions often faced the extra burden of comprehending their abuse in terms of the offender's supposed 'celibacy', and some were terrified of God or the church/synagogue should they report their abuse by a priest or religious leader. Many religious offenders ingratiated themselves with families and communities as a process of grooming children, making disclosure even more troubling or overwhelming for the child.[56] Children who were institutionalized in orphanages or other forms of out-of-home care (discussed below) rarely had family and social networks to turn to. Many were punished if they complained of abuse within an institution. Children with disabilities were particularly vulnerable to abuse and often at the mercy of carers with whom they may have had complex relationships centred on their bodily and emotional needs.[57] Discerning who was trustworthy in this environment was not necessarily straightforward.[58] Along with gender and race, class and dis/ability have played significant roles in determining children's access to justice and protection in Australia.

Groundbreaking surveys of the 1980s revealed that even in the time of women's liberation and modern rape law reform, mothers faced significant challenges when their children disclosed abuse within the family. 37 per cent of women who volunteered to participate in an anonymous incest survey (so were open to discussing their child's abuse) had not reported the offence to the police.[59] Fears of traumatic legal processes and the severity of criminal punishment of family members were primary reasons for declining to involve the police.[60] In reality, however, many reports that were made to the police were never acted on. A further 40 per cent of respondents to the survey did report to the police, but this did not result in prosecution.[61]

The first CSA and rape survey of Aboriginal women and children in 1985, conducted confidentially by the Adelaide Rape Crisis Centre, found that when the perpetrator was an Aboriginal man, 84 per cent of all cases of CSA were not reported to the police or any government authority.[62] This was mainly due to a fear of the perpetrator and a fear of not being believed.[63] When the offender was not Aboriginal, government authorities were contacted in 54 per cent of cases.[64] The enduring colonial legacies of child removal and destruction of Indigenous cultures and communities made First Nations children especially vulnerable to sexual abuse. These legacies continue to foster distrust in the arms of the state charged with child protection and criminal justice.[65] A desire to keep communities intact and perhaps address sexual abuse with restorative, not criminal, approaches, has also informed some First Nations Australians' objections to involving the coercive, punitive state.[66]

Any woman's reluctance to report CSA, especially her own child's, must be viewed through the prisms of gender and power and the intergenerational trauma of abuse. Historically, a woman confronted with a child's disclosure faced great shame and the potential breakup of her family and community, religious or otherwise. The standard response to family violence has long been to remove the victims rather than the perpetrator. Before the establishment of the Single Mother's Benefit in 1973, followed by the Family Court and no-fault divorce in 1976, reporting abuse may have proved socially and economically diabolical for the entire family. The strength of the patriarchal norms that allowed abuse to proliferate in many communities and families shaped all members of those relationships, not only the perpetrators. This entrenched power dynamic made a full understanding of sexual abuse challenging. It is also likely that a significant number of women (and men) receiving children's disclosures were abuse survivors themselves, who may never have disclosed their own abuse or received justice, therapy or even compassion and understanding. Conversely, at the time of emerging awareness of CSA in the 1970s and 1980s, many feminists did not trust the state or endorse the carceral regime of criminal justice. Individual objections to involving the state in CSA were, and remain, complex and multifaceted.[67]

Reporting to the police

For those children and adults who did seek to involve the police, the response was unpredictable and potentially dangerous. Children and even adults who reported CSA in the 1950s and 1960s were often dismissed. Some were physically assaulted by police.[68] The low status of state wards made them particularly vulnerable. Girls who 'escaped' from training schools in the 1960s to report their abuse were told by police that there was nothing to be done, as 'it's a government institution and you have been made a ward of the state', and they were returned to their abusers by police.[69] Others were told to keep quiet and not speak of the abuse, out of respect for the idea that care workers and religious institutions were beyond reproach. Children who were disempowered by institutionalization faced extraordinary barriers when attempting to report to the police, especially if the offender was a powerful community figure such as a priest or doctor.[70] Children's reports of abuse increased in the 1970s and 1980s, but there was little consistency in police responses. Children in institutions continued to be viewed fundamentally as 'troublemakers'.[71] Boys faced extreme discrimination in that they could be treated as accomplices to crimes of men's homosexual sex if they reported abuse.[72]

Most police were not equipped to deal with child complainants in this context. Many cases did not proceed because of police mishandling of interviews and evidence, in police stations that did not have adequate resources such as private interviewing rooms, and where police often delayed their reports to the prosecutor or preferred to 'dump' the matter on child protection agencies.[73] Specialist police units addressing CSA including reforms to interviewing procedures were not introduced until the 1990s, when most states enacted multi-disciplinary team-based responses to child abuse, including police, child protection and health agencies participating in joint interviewing and case review. The power relationships that allowed abuse to proliferate in institutions such as churches and the family were also influential among individual police and within police cultures. Policing was always a male preserve. Even in the mid-1990s, women constituted only 14 per cent of sworn police officers.[74]

Even if individual police officers did believe and act on children's allegations, police cultures were often infused with corruption.[75] The Royal Commission exposed the obstructive police cultures particularly in regional communities, where police, judges, lawmakers, politicians and religious personnel tend to be drawn from the same hierarchical, homosocial institutions and networks. First Nations children who lived with over-policing, disproportionate rates of family break-up and incarceration, and over-regulation of their lives were perhaps the least likely of all to seek and receive police assistance.

Barriers in the courtroom

The law's distrust of children's evidence, which created obstacles for child victims of sexual abuse in England and Wales and in Ireland, was replicated in

Australia. The common law on children's testimony was incorporated in the Australian colonies and the country that followed. As in Ireland and England and Wales, children could give evidence only if they were able to swear an oath by demonstrating an adequate understanding of its Christian meaning, a requirement believed to have prevented the prosecution of many sex offences because children 'frequently failed the oath test'.[76] The 'accumulated wisdom' of the Australian courts was that children were essentially 'prone to fantasy, suggestible and inherently unreliable',[77] although it is evident that judges applied and interpreted tests for their intelligence and religious knowledge with great variation. Age appears to have been mostly irrelevant. In some cases, seven-year-olds were deemed competent. In other cases, 14-year-olds were deemed incompetent.[78] In place of an oath, children could be permitted to give affirmations or declarations, but this rule was also applied inconsistently. Children with cognitive impairments were often construed as inherently incompetent witnesses. If a child did swear an oath, it was usually accepted that they were being truthful and evidence corroborating their testimony was not mandatory.

Australian colonies introduced laws comparable to the English CLAA 1885.[79] The Victorian Act allowed children's unsworn testimony to be received in cases of rape, carnal knowledge and indecent assaults on girls, and adopted the English requirement for corroborative evidence implicating the accused.[80] Tasmania and Western Australia enacted similar provisions concerning corroboration. Queensland instead continued to require children to swear an oath. South Australia allowed for unsworn testimony and did not introduce corroboration requirements until 1955, instead retaining the common law approach.[81] In the twentieth century further special provisions were introduced to govern children's evidence. For example, the *Child Welfare Act 1939 (NSW)* and the *Community Welfare Act 1982 (NSW)* provided that children could give evidence without an oath if they were of sufficient intelligence and understood the duty to speak the truth, but their evidence still required material corroboration 'by some other material evidence in support thereof implicating the accused'.[82] Provisions were also made to hear the unsworn evidence of children 'of tender years' in regard to carnal knowledge, buggery and indecent assault if, in the opinion of the court, the child was of 'sufficient intelligence to justify the reception of the evidence, and understands the duty of speaking the truth', again with corroboration.[83] The corroboration requirement has been identified as one of the most significant obstacles to justice for CSA, even when the police and prosecutor were committed to proceeding with a case.[84] As with England and Wales and Ireland, when children were deemed incompetent to swear on an oath, they were essentially barred from realizing justice.

The 1980s and 1990s were a key period of change in laws governing children's evidence, with the most significant changes introduced as a result of the 1980s feminist reforms of NSW. The *Crimes (Child Assault) Amendment Act 1985 (NSW)* allows a child who does not understand the meaning of an oath to give evidence if the court was 'satisfied that the child is intelligent enough to justify the reception of that evidence, and understands the duty of telling the truth'.[85] The Act also abolished the corroboration requirement, thereby placing children's evidence on a par with that of adults, and included child sex offences in the range of offences for which a judge was no longer required to warn the jury against inferences from a delay in complaint. It made a spouse a compellable witness in the trial of a husband or wife in respect of child sexual assault. A prohibition on publishing information identifying child victims was also introduced, along with provisions for evidence to be provided by closed-circuit television. Other states eventually followed suit, and the *Uniform Evidence Act 1995* (UEA) adopted by most jurisdictions replaced all corroboration requirements with a discretionary approach to jury directions focused on the needs of the specific case.

Despite the statutory reforms of the 1980s and 1990s, in determining whether or not a child's evidence is admissible, judges have typically relied on their own accumulated 'observations and assumptions about human behaviour'.[86] When compared internationally, Australian courts have 'resisted applying research in psychology, instead acting on the basis that human behaviour is directly observable'[87] and that 'common sense' should prevail over the use of expert psychological evidence.[88] Until recently, the admission of expert testimony in cases involving CSA was rare, and in its absence, jurors have been vulnerable to interpreting a child's 'counterintuitive' behaviours (such as delay in reporting or staying in contact with the offender) as indications of their unreliability.[89] When courts did accept psychological evidence, it was sometimes used to discredit child witnesses.[90]

Historically, if children's evidence was admissible, child victims were not spared the rigours of cross-examination, even in cases of sexual abuse. In fact, such cases often gave rise to particularly egregious interrogations centred on Freudian myths of fantasy and seduction or the child's alleged immorality including their sexual history. Prior to the feminist 'rape shield' reforms of the 1970s that were meant to prohibit the admission of evidence of a complainant's sexual reputation or sexual history,[91] cross-examination of children was essentially a 'free for all' with few questions ruled out.[92] If an accused was unrepresented, he could directly question the child.[93] Children were often overlooked in the early procedural reforms of sexual assault laws. In Victoria in the 1980s under the *Rape Offences (Proceedings) Act 1976 (Vic)*, complainants could no longer be questioned about their sexual history in trials for 'rape, attempted rape or assault with attempt to rape', but this did not extend to incest trials (which could involve children).[94] In NSW it took the *Crimes (Child Assault) Amendment Act 1985 (NSW)* to extend these types of protections explicitly to children, following their inclusion in the general sexual assault reforms in 1981.

The veracity of children's memories was typically targeted by defence lawyers attempting to undermine their credibility and create doubt in the minds of judges and juries.[95] The trauma of cross-examination, especially in cases without substantial medical evidence, was such that it probably played a part in police declining to investigate CSA, and prosecutors declining to pursue trials.[96] Even in cases with medical evidence, children were not spared: evidence of penetration could easily be construed as evidence of immoral or bad character and a motive for false allegations, because 'someone else had done it to her, hadn't they?'[97] First Nations children whose first language was not English and who may have attended less formal schooling than non-Indigenous children faced even greater challenges in the adversarial court system, which relies on oral testimony premised on intellectual understandings of Christianity and its precepts.[98]

The final section explores the historical position of children in the care of the state, especially in residential institutions, and the development of child protection law and policies in Australia, including how the family law system has responded to children at risk of sexual violence at home.

Child welfare and child protection

Children in the care of the state: a brief history of institutionalization

Australia's federal political system and its history as a settler-colonial state are strongly implicated in failures in the regulation of children's institutions where so much sexual violence is documented to have taken place. Ideologies informing the colonial project and the uneven development and population of the colonies directed the nature and number of residential institutions that persisted throughout the country until partial deinstitutionalization in the late twentieth century. These enduring historical legacies directed the involvement of religious and charitable bodies in child welfare and the state's capacity to inspect and regulate institutions and their care of children.

In the mid-nineteenth century, migration and urbanization associated with gold rushes heightened interest in children's welfare. A mix of non-denominational 'subscriber charities' such as Barnardo's and The Benevolent Society was imported from England and embedded alongside religious organizations in the child welfare landscape. At least 40 institutions started as orphanages: many Catholic, representing the Irish convict population, and some Protestant.[99] These early examples established a hybrid system of private and public funding and control that would influence Australian welfare for centuries to come, playing out differently in each state.[100] Rather than orphans (of whom there were not many), families were targeted for reformation, and it was children of deserted women and widows who were most vulnerable to institutionalization in the colonies preoccupied with governing the so-called 'criminal classes'.[101]

State involvement in children's institutions commenced in earnest in the 1850s on the realization of the failings of orphanages and asylums run by the benevolent societies. A government inquiry into the 'Conditions of the Working Classes' recommended the introduction of juvenile reformatories modelled on European institutions, which ultimately developed into the juvenile justice system, separate from orphanages and other forms of care, representing a form of 'penal welfarism' blending ideals of punishment and welfare.[102] Between 1864 and 1874, each colony passed industrial schools legislation as *de facto* 'juvenile poor laws', ostensibly to address 'neglected children' in families and train them through religious instruction and hard labour. At least 26 industrial schools were founded, run by religious bodies such as the Catholic Church and the Salvation Army and the state.[103]

Reformatories were established from 1864, with boys mainly referred formally by the courts, and girls referred informally on recommendation of family members and local clergy if there were suspicions about their sexual morality.[104] Girls were also sent to work in Magdalene laundries with 'indefinite sentences' imposed by the community.[105] Up until the 1880s, a significant number of children were incarcerated in adult prisons, including some under the age of ten. It was the twentieth century before children's criminal proceedings were separated from adults by way of legislation such as the *Neglected Children and Juvenile Offenders Act 1905 (NSW)*, which solidified the objectives of penal welfarism by combining protection with punishment.[106]

In the last decades of the nineteenth century, colonial governments finally appointed inspectors and superintendents to report on charitable bodies receiving government subsidies, including for running institutions.[107] By the mid-1870s, government inquiries in NSW had determined that children were not being trained properly in institutions and advocated for 'the family principle' to guide children's placements, much like the foster care situation that was promoted first in South Australia. A period of deinstitutionalization followed, which informed the two-tier system in Australia of foster care and institutions that characterized the twentieth century.[108]

Indigenous institutions

Child protection was explicitly and essentially racialized in Australia, with First Nations children treated differently from their European counterparts. Colonial institutions such as the Parramatta Native Institute[109] were inspired by English missionaries to assimilate local First Nations children into the working class through religious and industrial training.[110] Between one in three and one in ten First Nations children are estimated to have been removed from their families between 1910 and the 1970s, either sent to institutions or to work in white households and farms.[111] First Nations children had always been placed in the mainstream (and denominational) institutions, but those states and territories with significant surviving populations also created Aboriginal-specific institutions, at least 98 in total.[112] The most infamous were the church-run Missions established in the early nineteenth century to accommodate orphans, which came to accommodate the children of adults living on the Mission. Government-run Aboriginal Reserves performed similar functions.

Mission dormitories became 'the schools and home that were central to the child-removal policy introduced in the 19th century and spreading across the country in the 20th century'.[113] Although Missions were authorized by legislation, the churches were rarely held accountable to the state for their treatment of children. Missions were typically the most isolated of all institutions, with little contact with the rural settler and urban populations that might have advocated on behalf of the children. Missionaries who staffed these reserves considered themselves accountable to a diverse array of powers including God, their church and the missionary societies that paid their wages.[114] Most of their conduct was beyond the scrutiny of mainstream society or the law.

Oversight of institutions

As early as the 1880s, physical conditions for children in institutions, including corporeal punishment, were condemned,[115] but overriding concerns about 'order and economy' marginalized opportunities for government inquiries to examine the quality of care.[116] State differences persisted, with philanthropic bodies having different degrees of influence in each jurisdiction. Legislation passed in the first half of the twentieth century generally aimed to refine and consolidate existing regimes and clarify the ambit of state oversight through laws such as the *Destitute Children's Society Act 1901 (NSW)* and the *Children's Welfare Act 1926 (Vic)*.[117] However, the new legislation did little to encourage regular inspection and supervision of institutions. The twentieth century legacy of Australian colonial institutions persisting with relative autonomy amid inconsistent and piecemeal regulation serves as a reminder of 'the power of groups such as the churches, and the powerlessness of women, children and young people and poor families'.[118] The result of this power was 'an extraordinarily complex and diverse mix of out-of-home "care" for children'[119] in which accountability was barely enforced. For the many non-government institutions, 'lines of responsibility were loose and often blurred'.[120] While the state did have formal legislative power to inspect the institutions of churches and other charities, many governments found they had 'limited bargaining power' when in need of places for children, especially as the definition of who could be made a ward of the state broadened throughout the twentieth century.[121] Fully self-funded charities continued to operate with the least scrutiny of all, with little attention paid to the conduct of those individuals who believed they had a 'calling' to 'care' for children.[122]

In the first half of the twentieth century, ideas of neglect and delinquency remained fused such as in the *Child Welfare Act 1939 (NSW)*, which mandated the incarceration of children at risk alongside those convicted of criminal offences.[123] The principle of the 'best interests of the child' was finally enshrined in a series of *Children's Welfare Acts* of the 1950s which gradually displaced the centrality of 'criminality' or 'immorality' in determining children's fates. Regardless, it was the 1960s and even the 1970s before all governments had child welfare departments in place and still many laws appeared to remain 'locked into the past'.[124] The twentieth century regime 'seemed to imbue governments and managers of children's homes with wide discretionary powers' over children.[125] Laws and policies were 'often skewed towards the needs of people in power, judgmental and punitive towards children and young people and not overly stringent on what on what they required of adults charged with the care and protection of children'.[126] It was the 1980s before the discriminatory *Aborigines Protection Acts* governing First Nations Australians were finally overturned on the basis of racial equality, modern Children's Courts were established and child protection legislation was enacted including the principle that First Nations children in need of care should be placed with family or kinship/community members. The first government inquiry to examine CSA in institutional contexts came as late as 1992 with the Western Australian Duty of Care Inquiry into foster care.[127]

Child protection policies and laws

Historically, child welfare including the children's court was governed by a regime modelled on British 'child saving' endeavours as embodied in the original legislation: the *Neglected Children and Juvenile Offenders Act 1905 (NSW)*, which consolidated the penal welfare regime combining protection and punishment of children. The welfare state established in Australia from the 1940s provided a new regime of government services other than criminal justice that would come to be tasked with 'child protection'. By the early 1980s, these systems were under review led by the groundbreaking Victorian Child Welfare Practice and Legislation Review Committee established in 1982 with the main outcome the *Children and Young Persons Act 1989 (Vic)*. In 1984, both South Australia and Victoria established child sexual abuse task forces, reporting in 1986. The New South Wales initiative discussed above was the first to result in substantial child protection reforms addressing sexual abuse in the form of the *Children (Care and Protection) Act 1987 (NSW)*.[128] In all states, from the early twentieth century, Children's Courts were provided to hear cases involving juvenile offenders and children at risk. The *Children (Care and Protection) Act 1987 (NSW)* was introduced together with the *Community Welfare Act 1987 (NSW)* and the *Children's Court Act 1987* (NSW) to allow proceedings to be initiated in the new Children's Court to protect children by removing them from abusive situations in families and institutions, including foster care. The *Children (Care and Protection) Act 1987 (NSW)* extended mandatory notification provisions to child sexual abuse for prescribed professions such as social workers, teachers and medical practitioners. By 1999 each state and territory had passed a new child protection act mandating the removal and placement of children at risk.

Child protection services were completely unprepared and under-resourced for the surge of CSA notifications that accompanied heightened attention paid to all child sex offences in the 1980s. In NSW Wales, for example, in

1977 before the introduction of mandatory reporting, 800 notifications were made to the Department of Youth and Community Services about children at risk.[129] In 1984 with mandatory reporting extended to the medical profession for sexual and physical abuse, 12,000 notifications were made.[130] In this climate, despite the influence of feminist frameworks over law reform and reporting procedures, in practice, their impact was limited. Political opposition to extending mandatory notification in the 1990s was explicitly couched in terms of resources.[131] And, even though the law had been reformed to reflect feminist principles, child protection practices often remained influenced by therapeutic concepts of mother-blaming, reinvigorated in the late 1980s by an international anti-feminist backlash, partly in response to the spike in CSA notifications and controversy over therapeutic and legal techniques focused on repressed memories.[132]

Family law and the denial of CSA in the family

While child abuse allegations are now 'core business' of Australian family law,[133] throughout the best part of the twentieth century, this branch of law failed to recognize the harm of CSA and adequately protect children within their families. The notion that the family is a 'private space' permeates family law even when children's welfare is at stake.[134] Feminist campaigns to have family violence viewed as a public issue were central to the evolution of family law, the political significance of which tends to swing on a pendulum informed by conservative and feminist ideologies. Family law decisions continue to be troubled by the anti-feminist politicization of CSA commencing in the 1980s and the incoherent, piecemeal fabric of Australia's child protection landscape, ultimately the product of federalism. The 'volatile' nature of family law and the 'plethora' of laws and regulations for children's welfare in different Australian jurisdictions undermine the potential for nationally standardized child protection.[135] The political and ideological significance of family law has made this arena unpredictable and unreliable as a form of child protection. Australian Family law is undeniably implicated in the historical denial and mismanagement of CSA within the family.

While for the most part private rights were considered a matter for the states, marriage was understood as a question of legal status requiring national uniformity.[136] In 1959, the *Matrimonial Causes Act (Cth)* was introduced, aiming to make uniform existing state-based divorce provisions[137] with no major changes in law.[138] But in an effort to provide a more compassionate response to litigants, the Act came to include a controversial new ground for divorce: irretrievable breakdown of marriage demonstrated by a period of five years' separation.[139] This provision marked the genesis of modern Australian no-fault divorce enacted by the *Family Law Act 1975 (Cth)*. Between 1986 and 1990, all states except Western Australia[140] referred their powers to the Commonwealth in respect of custody, maintenance of and access to ex-nuptial children, thereby consolidating federal control of this arena but not the associated realms of child protection, welfare and adoption, which remain the province of states and territories.[141] The outcome of this process is a convoluted and inconsistent maze of state and territory-based child protection systems with little legal relationship to family law.

The Family Law Act 1975 (Cth) was archetypal of the Whitlam Labor government and complemented ideals of feminism and the social democratic state informing the 1973 introduction of the Supporting Mother's Benefit for single mothers. It established the Family Court as a 'helping court' staffed by 'men and women of compassion who have a deep understanding of the subtleties of human conduct and marital relationships',[142] with judges and welfare officers working 'closely with other social security agencies in the community'.[143] In this system, children became the focus of custody settlements[144]; however, the removal of fault from divorce proceedings meant that a spouse's violent behaviour was generally not mentioned or was disregarded when determining parenting potential.[145] The *Family Law Reform Act 1995 (Cth)* was the first to identify child sexual abuse as a factor to be considered in assessing the best interests of the child,[146] and it emphasized parental 'responsibilities' (not 'rights') as well as children's 'rights of contact with both parents'.[147] The paradoxical aims of protecting children from violence and safeguarding their contact with both parents have made for a highly contested family law arena.[148]

Matters of child abuse occurring within the family have essentially necessitated a two-court solution in Australia: the Children's Courts in the states and territories and the Family Court at the federal level.[149] How CSA was identified in each realm differed substantially, especially when all the different children's court's jurisdictions are considered. The thresholds for intervening in matters of child protection differed between states[150] and between the state-based children's court and the federal Family Court.[151]

Women making allegations of CSA in Family Court proceedings were particularly vulnerable to the anti-feminist backlash promulgated in response to the dramatic spike in child sexual abuse notifications. The notion that children and adults make false allegations of sexual abuse was widely propagated in the 1980s and 1990s, coalescing in Australia in an organized backlash against no-fault divorce, the so-called 'social engineering' of the Family Court and the introduction of the Commonwealth Child Support system in 1988.[152] The lack of a criminal fact-finding process in the Family Court, and the reliance on medical discourses that historically pathologized women, have allowed allegations of CSA to be portrayed as the vexatious and vengeful outcomes of divorce. Psychiatrists of the 1980s in particular diagnosed women as prone to making false allegations due to their 'delusions or hysteria, or as involved in over-enmeshed and anxious relationships with their children', or due to their desire for revenge aimed at their husbands.[153] The now widely discredited Parental Alienation

Syndrome and the related Sexual Allegations in Divorce Syndrome which peaked in the 1990s were almost exclusively attributed to women in divorce proceedings.[154]

Conclusion

The criminal law on child sexual abuse in Australia has developed in a piecemeal way associated with the different histories of the colonies, from initial concern about European girls' age of consent, to feminist-inspired reforms that viewed 'child sexual assault' as a violent crime that is the product of patriarchy enacted on both girls and boys. These reforms, commencing in Australia in the mid-1980s, came decades before the new offences in England and Wales and in Ireland at the beginning of the twenty-first century. However, the varied progress made in the Australian states and territories was often undermined by social and legal barriers to disclosure and reporting and having testimony given appropriate weight at trial. It was also compounded by obstacles to delivering child protection through under-resourced government departments that remained influenced by archaic therapeutic understandings of the causes and effects of CSA. Legal frameworks governing child welfare were deeply gendered and racialized until feminist activism led to more neutral child-centred reforms in child protection and family law. Even so, the system remains informed by these colonial legacies today. The enshrining of a 'pro-contact culture' in family law since the mid-1990s has also put mothers trying to protect their children from abusive fathers in an impossible bind as they negotiate the two systems.[155]

Several themes emerge from the examination in this chapter and the preceding two, of the various legal and policy frameworks in each country. First, since at least the early twentieth century, the state in each jurisdiction has been aware of CSA and taken it seriously, by detecting and prosecuting sexual offences against children, albeit with different children receiving different levels of care based on their race, class and gender. Although governments spent considerable time and energy developing laws and policies aimed at different sexual offences against children, these were often concerned with notions of sexual morality rather than individual harms done to rights-bearing children. This focus on morality meant that child victims of sexual violence were stigmatized as impure and a threat to the moral welfare of the state, society and even the family. Second, a focus on the age of consent in criminal law hampered the development of specialist and contextualized understandings of CSA. Cloaked in the language of protection, much of each country's historical legal focus was on the minimum 'consensual' threshold above which men and boys could engage in sexual intercourse with girls. The narrowness of focus undermined our abilities to witness and comprehend the depth of offending against boys, the breadth of locations in which CSA occurs and the ways in which offenders gain access to children. Third, criminal prosecutions have been hampered by enduring Victorian attitudes about children's evidence as unreliable, and in Ireland, public awareness was stymied by censorship or conservative media reporting. Norms of morality and stigmatization were reflected in the state's, especially the criminal law's, hostile and suspicious treatment of any child who reported being abused. Norms of respectability and deference to community and religious leaders meant that children were silenced by their own family members and by teachers and other adults with responsibility for their care, including the police who had the ultimate power to proceed with investigations. Fourth, while reforms in the final decades of the twentieth century and into the twenty-first century promised to improve the criminal trial process somewhat for child victims, implementation of these was often piecemeal and problems persist around obtaining a child's testimony. Fifth, child protection policies have improved significantly over the course of the past century and a half, albeit at a slower pace in Ireland than in England and Wales and Australia. In each country, a child is recognized as a rights holder and entitled to protection by the state. However, serious issues around funding and implementation and monitoring of policies persist, particularly for children abused in foster care or state residential care and within the family. Court systems have yet to integrate child-centred approaches into their work.

The law displayed a certain ambivalence towards the phenomenon of CSA; for most of the past century, it was strictly prohibited and punished severely, but only in some situations, and only where the criminal process deemed the victim legitimate on its terms. When reform came, amidst fanfare and rhetoric about children as rights holders, it was partial and inadequately funded.

Part I has set the scene for Part II's examination of the four primary legal responses to NRCSA: criminal trials, civil lawsuits, and commissions of inquiry and state reparations. As we explore these responses, we ask whether the same ambivalence is evident in the state responses as is in this historiography.

Notes

1 The achievement of Responsible Government in the colonies in the mid-nineteenth century and the *Colonial Laws Validity Act 1865* provided heightened independence for colonial parliaments. Certain English initiatives associated with sexual regulation, such as the Contagious Diseases Acts, were rejected by all colonies except Queensland. In another significant act of independence, Queensland, Western Australia and Tasmania implemented criminal codes, whereas attempts to codify the law of England and Wales foundered in the nineteenth century never to be revived.

2 R. Phillips, *Sex, Politics and Empire* (Manchester: Manchester University Press, 2006), 57–82.

3 L. Finch, "The Nineteenth Century Identification of Incest as a Working-Class Crime: Implications for Analysis" in P. Hetherington (ed), *Incest and the Community: Australian Perspectives* (WA: Optima Press, 1991), 22.

4 Cohen cited in G.D. Wood, *A History of Criminal Law in New South Wales: The Colonial Period, 1788-1900* (Sydney: Federation Press, 2002), 348.
5 *Crimes Act 1900* (NSW) s43.
6 J. Bavin-Mizzi, "Understandings of Justice: Australian Rape and Carnal Knowledge Cases 1876–1924" in D. Kirkby (ed), *Sex, Power and Justice: Historical Perspectives of Law in Australia* (Oxford: Oxford University Press, 1992), 70–71.
7 In the colonies that were to become Australia, 'the law' developed from English common law enforced on the First Peoples and overriding existing Indigenous customary laws and traditions. Today, the Australian legal system involves a 'complex web of relationships and methods of dispute resolution' at multiple levels of the federated state. Criminal law remains primarily the domain of individual states (the former colonies) and the territories, although the Australian Parliament has made laws such as the *Criminal Code Act 1995 (Cth)* to meet international treaty obligations and address matters governed by Commonwealth including trafficking, child sex offences committed by Australians abroad and some child pornography (child exploitation material) offences. If there is inconsistency between a state or territory law and a Commonwealth law, the latter will prevail. The High Court of Australia is the highest court in the land and is available to appeal on matters arising from all jurisdictions. P. Vines, *Law and Justice in Australia: Foundations of the Legal System* (Oxford: Oxford University Press, 2013).
8 *R v Skinner* [1913] 16 CLR 338.
9 s73.
10 The Northern Territory was governed by South Australian legislation until 1983. In 1900, The Australian Capital Territory introduced the *Crimes Act 1900*, based on the New South Wales Crimes Act.
11 *Crimes Act 1900* (NSW) s78a-f.
12 Finch op. cit., 23.
13 J. Scutt, *Rape Law Reform: A Collection of Conference Papers* (Canberra: Australian Institute of Criminology, 1980), 56.
14 Ibid.
15 In NSW today, child sexual abuse is governed by various sections of *the Crimes Act* (such as s 66A, Sexual intercourse—child under 10) and child protection legislation (such as s227, *Children and Young Persons (Care and Protection) Act 1998 No 157*).
16 Except in respect of the age of consent, which remained 16 for girls and which had been set at 18 for boys in 1984, when homosexual sex was finally decriminalized.
17 *Crimes (Child Assault) Amendment 1985* s.61A(c).
18 This followed the *Crimes (Sexual Offences) Act 1980* which had already dismissed the language of 'carnal knowledge' in favour of 'sexual offences against young persons'.
19 M. Finnane and Y. Smaal, "Some Questions of History: Prosecuting and Punishing Child Sexual Assault" in Y. Smaal, A. Kaladelfos, and M. Finnane (eds), *The Sexual Abuse of Children. Recognition and Redress* (Melbourne: Monash University Press, 2016), 11.
20 The Australian census did not count Aboriginal and Torres Strait Islander peoples until 1971. Australian Bureau of Statistics, *Australian Historical Population Statistics, 2014*, www.abs.gov.au/ausstats/abs@.nsf/Latestproducts/3105.0.65.001Main%20Features12014?opendocument&tabname=Summary&prodno=3105.0.65.001&issue=2014&num=&view=.

21 Australian Royal Commission into Institutional Responses to Child Sexual Abuse, *Criminal Justice Report Executive Summary and Parts I-III*, 2017, 260.
22 Finnane and Smaal op. cit., 7–19.
23 Finnane and Smaal op. cit., 9.
24 Y. Smaal and M. Finnane, "Flappers and Felons: Rethinking the Criminal Law and Homosex in Interwar Australia, 1920-1939" in S. Brady (ed), *From Sodomy Laws to Same-Sex Marriage: International Perspectives Since 1789* (London: Bloomsbury, 2019), 83–95.
25 Ibid.
26 Ibid.
27 Ibid.
28 I.W. Heath, *Incest. A Crime Against Children* (Victoria: Government Printing Office, 1985), 4.
29 Finnane and Smaal op. cit., 2016, 14–15.
30 Ibid., 7–19.
31 L. Featherstone and A. Kaladelfos, *Sex Crimes in the Fifties* (Melbourne: Melbourne University Press, 2016), 6.
32 Ibid., 11.
33 Ibid., 78.
34 Ibid., 105.
35 Ibid., 106.
36 Ibid., 80.
37 Ibid., 81–82.
38 Ibid., 80.
39 J. Cashmore and M. Horsky, *Child Sexual Assault: The Court Response* (Sydney: NSW Bureau of Crime Statistics and Research, 1998), 13.
40 Ibid., 18
41 Ibid., 59.
42 A. Freiberg, H. Donnelly, and K. Gelb, *Sentencing for Child Sexual Abuse in Institutional Contexts* (Royal Commission into Institutional Responses to Child Sexual Abuse, 2015), 95.
43 The *Aborigines Protection Acts* enacted in the nineteenth century and reinforced in the early twentieth century.
44 Finnane and Smaal op. cit., 2016, 16.
45 For example, see Australian Royal Commission into Institutional Responses to Child Sexual Abuse, *Report of Case Study No. 17. The Response of the Australian Indigenous Ministries, the Australian and Northern Territory Governments and the Northern Territory Police Force and Prosecuting Authorities to Allegations of Child Sexual Abuse Which Occurred at the Retta Dixon Home,* 2015.
46 Australian Royal Commission into Institutional Responses to Child Sexual Abuse, *Final Report Volume 4: Identifying and Disclosing Child Sexual Abuse,* 2017, 102.
47 Ibid.
48 Ibid., 106.
49 Royal Commission, *Criminal Justice Report Executive Summary and Parts I-III,* p. 262.
50 Ibid., 33.
51 Australian Royal Commission into Institutional Responses to Child Sexual Abuse, *Final Report Volume 5: Private Sessions*, 2017, 159.
52 Royal Commission, *Final Report Volume 4,* 99.

53 Ibid., 39.
54 Ibid., 41.
55 Ibid., 43.
56 V. Waller, *Submission to the Inquiry into the Handling of Child Abuse by Religious and Other Non-Government Organisations* (2012), www.parliament.vic.gov.au/images/stories/committees/fcdc/inquiries/57th/Child_Abuse_Inquiry/Submissions/Waller_Legal.pdf.
57 Royal Commission, *Final Report Volume 4,* 38.
58 Ibid.
59 Mulligan, *Mothers Speak Out on Child Sexual Abuse,* 12.
60 Ibid.
61 Ibid.
62 E. Carter and J. Allen., *Aboriginal Women Speak Out about Rape and Child Sexual Abuse: A Report of an Adelaide Survey, October 1985-May 1986 Conducted in the Aboriginal Community* (Adelaide Rape Crisis Centre Incorporated, 1987), 17.
63 Ibid.
64 Ibid.
65 Australian Royal Commission into Institutional Responses to Child Sexual Abuse, *A Brief Guide to the Final Report: Aboriginal and Torres Strait Islander Communities*, 2017, 1–12.
66 H. McGlade, "Justice as Healing: Developing Aboriginal Justice Models to Address Child Sexual Assault," *Indigenous Law Bulletin* 7(1), 2007, 10–13.
67 Mulligan op. cit.
68 Ibid.
69 Ibid., 263.
70 Royal Commission op. cit., 265.
71 Ibid.
72 D. Andrews, MP. Victorian Parliamentary Debates, *Hansard*, 24 May 2016, www.premier.vic.gov.au/apology-to-those-convicted-under-unjust-laws-against-homosexual-acts/.
73 Independent Commission Against Corruption, *Interim Report on Investigation into Alleged Police Protection of Paedophiles* (ICAC, 1994), 9–12.
74 V. Wilkinson and I. Froyland, "Women in Policing" *Trends and Issues in Crime and Criminal Justice No.58* (Canberra: Australian Institute of Criminology, 1996), <https://aic.gov.au/publications/tandi/tandi58>.
75 T. Fitzgerald, *Commission of Inquiry into Possible Illegal Activities and Associated Police Misconduct,* 1989.
76 R. Blewer, "Testing the Law and Testing a Child's Evidence: Nineteenth-Century Corroboration Reforms and Child Witness Testimony" *Australian Historical Studies* 5(3), 2020, 267.
77 M. Harris and G. Urbas, "Children's Unsworn Evidence: Historical Developments and Contemporary Issues" *UNSW Law Journal* 40, 2017, 1392.
78 Ibid., 1399.
79 *Criminal Law Amendment Act 1885 (Imp); Criminal Law and Evidence Amendment Act 1891 (NSW); Crimes Act 1891 (Vic); Criminal Law Amendment Act 1892 (WA), Prevention of Cruelty to, and Better Protection of, Children Act 1895 (Tas).*
80 Blewer op. cit., 272.
81 Ibid.
82 Harris and Urbas op. cit., 1392.

83 *NSW Crimes Act 1900* s418.
84 Blewer op. cit.
85 L. Hewitt and Department of the Premier and Cabinet, *Child Sexual Assault Discussion Paper* (Melbourne: 1986), 149.
86 Royal Commission, *Criminal Justice Report. Summary and Parts i-iii*, 230.
87 Ibid.
88 Ibid.
89 J. Goodman-Delahunty, A. Cossins, and K. O'Brien, "A Comparison of Expert Evidence and Judicial Directions to Counter Misconceptions in Child Sexual Abuse Trials" *Australian & New Zealand Journal of Criminology* 44(2), 2011, 196–217, 198.
90 This is what happened in the Seabeach kindergarten case which set in train the chain of events that led to the Wood Royal Commission: S.E. Hatty, "Of Nightmares and Monsters: Around Child Abuse in Australia" *International Journal of Law and Psychiatry* 1991, 255–67.
91 For example, *Evidence Act Amendment Act 1976 (No. 145) (WA); Evidence Act (No. 3) 1976 (Tas); Evidence Act Amendment Act 1976 (No.84) (SA); Rape Offences (Proceedings) Act 1976 (Vic)*; *Crimes Act 1914* (Cth) ss 15YB–15YC; *Criminal Procedure Act 1986* (NSW) s 293; *Evidence Act 2001* (Tas) s 194M; *Evidence (Miscellaneous Provisions) Act 1991* (ACT) ss 48–53. Non-uniform Evidence Act jurisdictions: *Evidence Act 1929* (SA) s 34I; *Evidence Act 1958* (Vic) s 37A; *Criminal Law (Sexual Offences) Act 1978* (Qld) s 4; *Evidence Act 1906* (WA) ss 36A–36BC; *Sexual Offences (Evidence and Procedure) Act 1983* (NT) s 4. There is evidence that rape shield laws do not always prevent the admission of such evidence.
92 R. Zajac, N. Westera, and A. Kaladelfos, "The 'Good Old Days' of Courtroom Questioning: Changes in the Format of Child Cross-Examination Questions Over 60 Years" *Child Maltreatment* 23(2), 2018, 186–95.
93 R. Zajac, N. Westera, and A. Kaladelfos, "A Historical Comparison of Australian Lawyers' Strategies for Cross-Examining Child Sexual Abuse Complainants" *Child Abuse & Neglect* 72, 2017, 236–46, 237.
94 Heath op. cit., 20.
95 Ibid.
96 Scott and Swain op. cit., 155.
97 Ibid.
98 A. Cossins, "Prosecuting Child Sexual Assault Cases: To Specialise or Not, That Is the Question" *Current Issues in Criminal Justice* 18, 2006, 299–317, 335.
99 Ibid., p. 8.
100 S. Swain, "Institutional Abuse: A Long History" *Journal of Australian Studies* 42(2), 2018, 153–63, 154.
101 S. Swain, *History of Institutions Providing Out-Of-Home Residential Care for Children*. Royal Commission into Institutional Responses to Child Sexual Abuse, Australian Catholic University (Sydney: Royal Commission into Institutional Responses to Child Sexual Abuse, 2014), 6. Other institutions such as farm schools and children's homes were also established in the nineteenth century and persisted well into the twentieth. Notably, the one colony not founded by British convicts had the least enthusiasm for children's institutions. Reflecting its Protestantism, South Australia promoted English Evangelical 'boarding out' for the children 'here under the Southern Cross' whose 'parent is the State'. D. Scott,

"'Here Under the Southern Cross....' Reflections on Child Welfare Reform in Australia" *Developing Practice: The Child, Youth and Family Work Journal* 26, 2010, 4–6.

102 Ibid., 15, 1.

103 Swain op. cit., 2014, 6.

104 Swain and Musgrove op. cit., 10.

105 Ibid., p. 9.

106 Carrington op. cit., 25.

107 Community Affairs References Committee op. cit., 23.

108 Carrington op. cit., 18.

109 Established in 1823.

110 E. Grant, "The Incarceration of Aboriginal Women and Children" in P. Ashton and J. Wilson (eds), *Silent System: Forgotten Australians and the Institutionalisation of Women and Children* (Melbourne: Australian Scholarly Publishing, 2014), 43–58, 45.

111 Human Rights and Equal Opportunity Commission, *Bringing Them Home: Report of the National Inquiry into the Separation of Aboriginal and Torres Strait Islander Children from their Families* (Sydney: HREOC, 1997).

112 S. Swain, *History of Australian Inquiries Reviewing Institutions Providing Care for Children* (Sydney: Royal Commission into Institutional Responses to Child Sexual Abuse, 2014), 27.

113 Ibid.

114 C. McLisky, "Managing Mission Life, 1869–1886" in L. Boucher and L. Russell (eds), *Settler Colonial Governance in Nineteenth-Century Victoria* (Canberra: ANU e Press, 2015), 118.

115 Community Affairs References Committee op. cit., 20.

116 Swain, History of Australian Inquiries, 7.

117 S. Swain, *History of Child Protection Legislation* (Sydney: Royal Commission into Institutional Responses to Child Sexual Abuse, 2014), 63.

118 Community Affairs References Committee op. cit., 19.

119 Swain, History of Australian Inquiries Reviewing Institutions, 28.

120 Ibid.

121 Community Affairs References Committee op. cit., 26.

122 Swain, History of Australian Inquiries, 28.

123 Carrington op. cit., 28.

124 Swain, History of Australian Inquiries, 28.

125 Community Affairs References Committee op. cit., 32.

126 Ibid.

127 Swain, History of Australian Inquiries, 30.

128 It replaced the *Child Welfare Act 1939* (NSW).

129 Hewitt and Department of the Premier and Cabinet op cit., 64.

130 Ibid.

131 J. Breckenridge, "Subjugation and Silence: The Role of the Professions in Silencing Victims of Sexual and Domestic Violence" in J. Breckenridge and L. Laing (eds), *Innovative Responses to Sexual and Domestic Violence* (Sydney: Allen & Unwin, 1999), 6, 25.

132 A. Cossins, "Recovered Memories of Child Sexual Abuse: The Science and the Ideology," in Breckenridge and Laing, (eds), *Innovative Responses to Sexual and Domestic Violence* (Sydney: Allen & Unwin, 1999), 103.

133 P. Parkinson, "Family Law and Parent-Child Contact: Assessing the Risk of Sexual Abuse" *Melbourne University Law Review* 23, 1999, 345–71, 347.

134 R. Croucher, "Challenges for Responding to Family Violence in a Federal System" in A. Hayes and D. Higgins (eds), *Families, Policy and the Law: Selected Essays on Contemporary Issues for Australia* (Melbourne: Australian Institute of Family Studies, 2007), 207.

135 Family Law Council, *The Best Interests of the Child? The Interaction of Public and Private Law in Australia, Discussion Paper 2* (Barton: Family Law Council, 2000), 3.

136 Croucher op. cit., 208.

137 In the colonies, divorce was governed by various domestic iterations of the English *Matrimonial Causes Act 1857* enacted between 1858 and 1873, providing for divorce by judicial decree on the grounds of fault, such as such as adultery, desertion, drunkenness, bigamy, imprisonment and habitual cruelty which could be evidenced (for men) by a wife's persistent refusal to have sex. Adultery was the most common cause, and children were not acknowledged as victims of cruelty. Their interests were absent in legislation. G. Lehmann, "The Divorce Explosion" *Quadrant* 189, 1983, 27, 49.

138 Curiously, this statute preceded a national marriage act by two years: *Marriage Act 1961* (Cth).

139 G. Barwick, *A Radical Tory: Garfield Barwick's Reflections and Recollections* (Leichhardt: Federation Press, 1995), 127.

140 Western Australia established a Family Court in the 1970s.

141 As a form of 'referral power', s51(xii) of the Australian Constitution provides that the powers of the Australian parliament include those 'making powers for the peace, order and good government of the Commonwealth with respect to marriage, divorce and matrimonial causes; and in relation thereto, parental rights and the custody and guardianship of infants'.

142 H. Finlay, *To Have But Not to Hold: A History of Attitudes to Marriage and Divorce in Australia 1858-1975* (Sydney: Federation Press, 2005), 379.

143 Ibid.

144 While under the *Matrimonial Causes Act 1959* children's interests were meant to be of 'paramount consideration', the legal focus on fault meant that the moral character and conduct of each spouse informed custody rulings. In practice, 'children took very much a back seat and the system paid little regard to their welfare'.

145 S. Swain, *Born in Hope. The Early Years of the Family Court* (Sydney: New South Press, 2012), 102.

146 That is, 'sexual assault, of the child which is an offence under a law, written or unwritten, in force in the State or Territory in which the act constituting the assault occurs' *Family Law Reform Act 1995* (Cth) s.60D(1). See M. Harrison and R. Graycar, "The Family Law Reform Act: Metamorphis or More of the Same?" *Australian Journal of Family Law* 11(3), 1997, 327–42.

147 *Family Law Reform Act 1995* (Cth) s60B(1). This was in deference to the UNCRC 1989.

148 W. Foote, *Child Sexual Abuse Allegations in the Family Court*, PhD Thesis (Sydney: University of Sydney, 2006), 62.

149 The introduction of the Federal Circuit Court (formerly the Federal Magistrates Court) to address less complex family law disputes in 1999 might mean that

three courts are in fact involved. In 2021, the Family Court as it had existed was abolished to be merged with the Federal Circuit Court. It remains to be seen what this will mean for child abuse assessments in divorce proceedings.

150 For example, from 'significant harm' in Victoria, to 'in need of care and protection' in New South Wales and 'at risk' in South Australia: Family Law Council, op. cit., 349–50.

151 In family law, the threshold is that contact between a parent and child should be denied where it would expose the child to 'unacceptable risk' of abuse. Ibid.

152 K. Gleeson, "A Voice for the Injured. Bettina Arndt and Australian Family Law" *Australian Feminist Studies* 28(78), 2013, 375–97.

153 Foote op. cit., 127–28.

154 Ibid., 106.

155 The Family Law Council recommends that a referral be granted so that federal Family Courts can have concurrent jurisdiction with state and territory courts 'to deal with all matters relating to children'; in Croucher op. cit., 211. States are, however, typically reluctant to refer their powers to the Commonwealth.

References

Barwick, G., *A Radical Tory: Garfield Barwick's Reflections and Recollections.* (Leichhardt: Federation Press, 1995).

Bavin-Mizzi, J., "Understandings of Justice: Australian Rape and Carnal Knowledge Cases 1876–1924" in D. Kirkby (ed), *Sex, Power and Justice: Historical Perspectives of Law in Australia* (Oxford: Oxford University Press, 1992).

Blewer, R., "Testing the Law and Testing a Child's Evidence: Nineteenth-Century Corroboration Reforms and Child Witness Testimony" *Australian Historical Studies* 5(3), 2020, 266–81.

Breckenridge, J., "Subjugation and Silence: The Role of the Professions in Silencing Victims of Sexual and Domestic Violence" in J. Breckenridge and L. Laing (eds), *Innovative Responses to Sexual and Domestic Violence* (Sydney: Allen & Unwin, 1999), 6.

Carter, E. and Allen, J., *Aboriginal Women Speak Out about Rape and Child Sexual Abuse: A Report of an Adelaide Survey, October 1985-May 1986 Conducted in the Aboriginal Community* (Adelaide Rape Crisis Centre Incorporated, 1987).

Cashmore, J. and Horsky, M., *Child Sexual Assault: The Court Response* (NSW Bureau of Crime Statistics and Research, 1998).

Cossins, A., "Recovered Memories of Child Sexual Abuse: The Science and the Ideology" in J. Breckenridge and L. Laing (eds), *Innovative Responses to Sexual and Domestic Violence* (Sydney: Allen & Unwin, 1999), 103.

Cossins, A., "Prosecuting Child Sexual Assault Cases: To Specialise or Not, That is The Question" *Current Issues in Criminal Justice* 18, 2006, 299–317.

Croucher, R., "Challenges for Responding to Family Violence in a Federal System" in A. Hayes and D. Higgins (eds), *Families, Policy and the Law: Selected Essays on Contemporary Issues for Australia* (Melbourne: Australian Institute of Family Studies, 2007), 207.

Family Law Council, *The Best Interests of the Child? The Interaction of Public and Private Law in Australia, Discussion Paper 2* (Barton: Family Law Council, 2000).

Featherstone, L. and Kaladelfos, A., *Sex Crimes in the Fifties* (Melbourne: Melbourne University Press, 2016).

Finch, L., "The Nineteenth Century Identification of Incest as a Working-Class Crime: Implications for Analysis" in P. Hetherington (ed), *Incest and the Community: Australian Perspectives* (WA: Optima Press, 1991), 22.

Finlay, H., *To Have but Not to Hold: A History of Attitudes to Marriage and Divorce in Australia 1858-1975* (Sydney: Federation Press, 2005).

Finnane, M. and Smaal, Y., "Some Questions of History: Prosecuting and Punishing Child Sexual Assault" in Y. Smaal, A. Kaladelfos, and M. Finnane (eds), *The Sexual Abuse of Children. Recognition and Redress* (Melbourne: Monash University Press, 2016), 11.

Fitzgerald, T., *Commission of Inquiry into Possible Illegal Activities and Associated Police Misconduct* (Brisbane, 1989).

Foote, W., *Child Sexual Abuse Allegations in the Family Court*, PhD Thesis (Sydney: University of Sydney, 2006).

Freiberg, A., Donnelly, H., and Gelb, K., *Sentencing for Child Sexual Abuse in Institutional Contexts* (Royal Commission into Institutional Responses to Child Sexual Abuse, 2015).

Gleeson, K., "A Voice for the Injured. Bettina Arndt and Australian Family Law" *Australian Feminist Studies* 28(78), 2013, 375–97.

Goodman-Delahunty, J., Cossins, A., and O'Brien, K., "A Comparison of Expert Evidence and Judicial Directions to Counter Misconceptions in Child Sexual Abuse Trials" *Australian & New Zealand Journal of Criminology* 44(2), 2011, 196–217.

Grant, E., "The Incarceration of Aboriginal Women and Children" in P. Ashton and J. Wilson (eds), *Silent System: Forgotten Australians and the Institutionalisation of Women and Children* (Melbourne: Australian Scholarly Publishing, 2014), 43–58.

Harris, M. and Urbas, G., "Children's Unsworn Evidence: Historical Developments and Contemporary Issues" *UNSW Law Journal* 40, 2017, 1392.

Harrison, M. and Graycar, R., "The Family Law Reform Act: Metamorphis or More of the Same?' *Australian Journal of Family Law* 11(3), 1997, 327–42.

Hatty, S.E., "Of Nightmares and Monsters: Around Child Abuse in Australia" *International Journal of Law and Psychiatry* 1991, 255–67.

Heath, I.W., *Incest. A Crime against Children* (Victoria: Government Printing Office, 1985).

Hewitt, L. and Department of the Premier and Cabinet, *Child Sexual Assault Discussion Paper* (Melbourne: 1986).

Human Rights and Equal Opportunity Commission, *Bringing Them Home: Report of the National Inquiry into the Separation of Aboriginal and Torres Strait Islander Children from Their Families* (Sydney: HREOC, 1997).

Independent Commission against Corruption, *Interim Report on Investigation into Alleged Police Protection of Paedophiles* (ICAC, 1994).

Lehmann, G., "The Divorce Explosion" *Quadrant* 189, 1983, 27.

McGlade, H., "Justice as Healing: Developing Aboriginal Justice Models to Address Child Sexual Assault" *Indigenous Law Bulletin* 7(1), 2007, 10–13.

McLisky, C., "Managing Mission Life, 1869–1886" in L. Boucher and L. Russell (eds), *Settler Colonial Governance in Nineteenth-Century Victoria* (Canberra: ANU Press, 2015), 118.

Parkinson, P. "Family Law and Parent-Child Contact: Assessing the Risk of Sexual Abuse" *Melbourne University Law Review* 23, 1999, 345–71.

Phillips, R., *Sex, Politics and Empire* (Manchester: Manchester University Press, 2006).

Royal Commission into Institutional Responses to Child Sexual Abuse, *Report of Case Study No. 17. The Response of the Australian Indigenous Ministries, the Australian and Northern Territory Governments and the Northern Territory Police Force and Prosecuting Authorities to Allegations of Child Sexual Abuse Which Occurred at the Retta Dixon Home* (2015).

Royal Commission into Institutional Responses to Child Sexual Abuse, *Criminal Justice Report Executive Summary and Parts I-III* (2017).

Royal Commission into Institutional Responses to Child Sexual Abuse, *Final Report* (Canberra, 2017).

Scott, D., "'Here Under the Southern Cross....' Reflections on Child Welfare Reform in Australia" *Developing Practice: The Child, Youth and Family Work Journal* 26, 2010, 4–6.

Scutt, J., *Rape Law Reform: A Collection of Conference Papers* (Canberra: Australian Institute of Criminology, 1980).

Smaal, Y. and Finnane, M., "Flappers and Felons: Rethinking the Criminal Law and Homosex in Interwar Australia, 1920-1939" in S. Brady (ed), *From Sodomy Laws to Same-Sex Marriage: International Perspectives Since 1789* (London: Bloomsbury, 2019), 83–95.

Swain, S., *Born in Hope. The Early Years of the Family Court* (Sydney: New South Press, 2012).

Swain, S., *History of Australian Inquiries Reviewing Institutions Providing Care for Children* (Sydney: Royal Commission into Institutional Responses to Child Sexual Abuse, 2014), 27.

Swain, S., *History of Child Protection Legislation* (Sydney: Royal Commission into Institutional Responses to Child Sexual Abuse, 2014).

Swain, S., *History of Institutions Providing Out-Of-Home Residential Care for Children* (Sydney: Royal Commission into Institutional Responses to Child Sexual Abuse, 2014).

Swain, S., "Institutional Abuse: A Long History" *Journal of Australian Studies* 42(2), 2018, 153–63.

Vines, P., *Law and Justice in Australia: Foundations of the Legal System* (Oxford: Oxford University Press, 2013).

Waller, V., *Submission to the Inquiry into the Handling of Child Abuse by Religious and Other Non-Government Organisations* (2012), www.parliament.vic.gov.au/images/stories/committees/fcdc/inquiries/57th/Child_Abuse_Inquiry/Submissions/Waller_Legal.pdf.

Wilkinson, V. and Froyland, I., "Women in Policing" *Trends and Issues in Crime and Criminal Justice No.58* (Canberra: Australian Institute of Criminology, 1996).

Wood, G.D., *A History of Criminal Law in New South Wales: The Colonial Period, 1788–1900* (Sydney: Federation Press, 2002).

Zajac, R., Westera, N., and Kaladelfos, A., "A Historical Comparison of Australian Lawyers' Strategies for Cross-Examining Child Sexual Abuse Complainants" *Child Abuse & Neglect* 72, 2017, 236–46.

Zajac, R., Westera, N., and Kaladelfos, A., "The 'Good Old Days' of Courtroom Questioning: Changes in the Format of Child Cross-Examination Questions Over 60 Years" *Child Maltreatment* 23(2), 2018, 186–95.

Part II

Legal responses to non-recent child sexual abuse

6 Introduction to Part II

Legal responses to non-recent child sexual abuse

Introduction

In Part II of this book, we explore the various legal responses to adult survivors of non-recent child sexual abuse (NRCSA) who seek justice: criminal prosecutions, civil lawsuits; public inquiries and state reparations. In this introductory chapter we consider what justice might mean for survivors who engage with the legal responses explored in the following chapters. We are not definitive about this; we acknowledge that each survivor will have a different and personal conception of justice. We also examine the available literature on why survivors have delayed in engaging with law. This is an important question because 'delay' in reporting to the police or bringing a civil action has posed (and continues to pose) a significant barrier to justice for many survivors. The courts and parliaments in each country have struggled to incorporate these reasons into their civil and criminal legal responses to NRCSA. The passage of time also plays a role in public inquiries and reparations, as governments and state actors may seek to use such state responses to demarcate the boundary between the abusive past and the supposedly progressive present. In the final section, we explain that trauma discourse, by which we mean both medical/psychological diagnostic categories and broader cultural ideas of trauma, has provided a key framework through which survivors' claims for justice can be comprehended by legislators, courts, jurors, public inquiries and redress boards.

Possible meanings of justice for NRCSA survivors

One important conceptualization of perceptions of justice shared by some survivors of sexual violence, 'kaleidoscopic justice', offers a fruitful way of thinking about NRCSA survivors and ideas of justice.[1] Developed by legal scholars Clare McGlynn and Nicole Westmarland, kaleidoscopic justice is a lived, ongoing, evolving experience and process rather than an end.[2] Kaleidoscopic justice is a pluralistic conception of justice that spans six broad themes: justice as consequences, recognition, dignity, voice, prevention and connectedness. *Justice as consequences* is related to accountability and involves

DOI: 10.4324/9780429468162-8

meaningful consequences for perpetrators that can take a variety of forms, including and beyond conventional criminal justice processes.[3] Kaleidoscopic justice also involves 'recognition' as central to a survivor's sense of justice, encompassing 'acknowledgement of the significance and nature of the harm, and an attempt to remedy the injury to self-respect'.[4] It must be experienced by survivors with *dignity* by treating them with respect and ensuring that trial procedures are sensitive to their needs. Beyond this, it involves actors in the legal system and the community affording survivors their full social standing.[5] Closely related to recognition is the idea of *justice as voice*. This encompasses more than simply being consulted or telling one's story but relates to the idea that the survivor is someone whose perspectives are heard in a meaningful sense and acted on. Crucially, this is a way of securing recognition of harm and of bringing about social and cultural change and is related to a further theme, *justice as prevention*. This involves ideas of social and transformation.[6] Finally, *justice as connectedness* is about redressing a survivor's shattered sense of belonging; it is about 'society's material expression of empathy, support and dignity, with the aim of enabling a victim-survivor to regain a sense of belonging and connection with society and feel a sense of justice.'[7]

These six themes resonate with the findings of studies examining what justice means from the perspective of NRCSA survivors. Research by advocacy groups indicates that a key goal for survivors is to be believed.[8] NRCSA survivors who have engaged with state inquiries also speak of changing the present and the future, and making CSA visible in order to prevent other children being harmed.[9] Marie Keenan's research with Irish survivors shows that some victims report their experiences to the police to prevent others being abused.[10] Keenan also demonstrates that reporting to the police may be a means of unburdening one's self of a perceived responsibility to deal with the abuse and the abuser.[11] Shirley Jülich's research with NRCSA survivors in New Zealand found that a common theme was a desire to 'tell their story in a safe forum' and address underlying causes of offending, and while they wanted to de-emphasize punishment, survivors still wanted consequences for the perpetrator.[12] Procedural justice, which refers to the procedures and processes used by a legal institution in making a decision, has been identified by Anne-Marie McAlinden and Bronwyn Naylor as the 'optimal mode of redress for victims of historical institutional abuse'.[13] Psychologist Tom Tyler's work shows that the key factor shaping people's willingness to accept the decisions of legal authorities is the fairness of the procedures used.[14] In fact, perceptions of procedural justice[15] are more important in shaping people's acceptance of legal decisions than their evaluation of the fairness of the actual decisions made by authorities. The following are the core elements of procedural justice: that the decision-making is viewed as neutral, consistent, rule-based and without bias; that people are treated with dignity and respect with their rights acknowledged and that they have an opportunity to participate in the situation by explaining their perspective and indicating their views about how problems should be resolved.[16] We argue that procedural justice can also be part of treating survivors as valued knowers who deserve to have their knowledge of the past and of sexual violence listened to, taken seriously and acted upon. This aligns with the kaleidoscopic justice aim of *justice as voice*. When survivors are not afforded the status of knower, an epistemic injustice is perpetrated—a concept referring to unjust treatment around issues of knowledge, understanding and participation in communicative practices.[17] Máiréad Enright and Sinéad Ring have written of how survivors of historical institutional abuse experience epistemic injustice in their encounters with the Irish state.[18]

Kathleen Daly examined the 'justice interests' of victims of historical institutional abuse in civil litigation, public inquiries and redress schemes in Australia and Canada and identified the following elements: victim participation in the design of justice responses, victim voice, validation, vindication and offender accountability.[19] In her work on the Historical Institutional Abuse Inquiry in Northern Ireland, Patricia Lundy has identified 12 complementary survivor justice needs: voice, acknowledgement, authoritative historical record, vindication (including validation), apology, redress (monetary/symbolic), rehabilitation measures, intergenerational needs, access to records, offender accountability and taking responsibility, and prosecution.[20]

Reflecting on this important and evolving body of international scholarship, we suggest that NRCSA survivors have diverse and evolving perceptions of justice. Justice for survivors is not linear, and is not an outcome, but an ongoing lived experience. We can also state that survivors require **accountability**, in the sense of publicly holding the abuser, the abusive organization or the state to account for their wrongdoing, and ensuring that consequences follow. Survivors also require **recognition** in the sense of recognizing the significance of the harm of the sexual violence (through the imposition of a sanction or damages or award of redress). And they require personal recognition, as full legal subjects (**citizenship**), and full members of the community (**belonging**), who deserve respect and dignity, including through their knowledge of injustice being taken seriously and acted on by the legal system and society. We return to these insights as we consider each form of legal response in the chapters that follow. When analyzing state responses to historical institutional sexual abuse in Chapters 10 and 11, we also consider the transitional justice goals of accountability, truth-telling, non-repetition and reparations, each of which resonates with the accounts of justice as accountability and recognition presented here.

We now turn to the issue of survivors' reasons for their delayed reporting of NRCSA.

Reasons for the interval between the abuse and the decision to seek a legal response

As we noted in the Introduction, what sets NRCSA apart from many other forms of interpersonal violence is the significant interval between the abuse and the survivor's decision to seek a legal response in the form of reporting to the police, initiating civil proceedings or claiming for redress. The criminal and civil law in all three countries has traditionally viewed any delay in reporting a crime or in bringing a claim for damages or redress (especially a delay after a person has reached adulthood) as inherently suspicious and indicative of weakened credibility. However, research conducted with survivors over the past 40 years has shown that there are very good reasons why survivors take a long time before deciding to engage with the law.

The 'delay' in coming to law must be understood in the broader context of the barriers to disclosure. It is estimated that almost 30 per cent of CSA survivors never tell anyone at all,[21] and of those who do, most do not disclose their abuse until adulthood.[22] The Australian Royal Commission found that on average, an NRCSA survivor has taken 23.9 years to tell someone about the abuse.[23] Research conducted for the IICSA found that over 80 per cent of NRCSA survivors did not disclose at the time of the abuse[24] and that the average time between first CSA victimization and contact with a support service was 19 years. In Ireland, survivors reporting childhood sexual victimization to Rape Crisis Centres in 2020 had waited an average of 33 years to come forward.[25] Male survivors are more likely to delay reporting CSA than females.[26] In this section, we consider factors that inhibit children from disclosing CSA and factors inhibiting adult survivors from disclosing NRCSA. It is important to explore both sets of barriers because the factors that inhibit children disclosing at the time of abuse may endure into adulthood.

First is the victim's relationship with the abuser. Recent research indicates that the most common form of CSA may be that perpetrated by a family member, and that it may be the hardest to uncover and the most damaging to victims.[27] International research suggests that fathers and step-fathers are the most common offenders and girls are most likely to be victims.[28] Other research indicates that sibling sexual abuse is vastly underreported and that it might be the most common form of intra-familial CSA.[29] Intra-familial CSA tends to involve multiple incidences and is usually perpetrated for more than one year.[30] When the abuser is a parent or primary caregiver, the abuse shatters the child's fundamental assumptions about the world and reporting puts the attachment and care from caregivers at risk.[31] Myths about CSA being rare and only committed by strangers can lead victims of intra-familial abuse to think they will not be believed. Victims of intra-familial abuse are the least likely of all CSA victims to disclose their abuse at the time, if at all.[32] Non-disclosure and delays increase the most when the perpetrator is a parent.[33]

Another barrier is the child's lack of understanding of their experiences as abuse. Many children cannot understand and verbalize their experiences.[34] For children with disabilities, these issues are exacerbated.[35] They are at greater risk of sexual abuse than other children[36] and are also more likely to delay or not disclose at all.[37]

Many children comply with the abuser's demand for silence because of secrecy pacts, violence and threats.[38] For others, shame, self-blame and fear of stigmatization and serious consequences for themselves or others (their siblings, their parents, even the perpetrator) can inhibit disclosure.[39] Furthermore, demographic characteristics such as age and gender appear to play a significant role in non-disclosure by children, with younger victims and males being significantly less likely to tell anyone about their abuse.[40]

Perhaps the most important barrier of all is the attitude of adults to reports of CSA. Many adults have entrenched beliefs that prevent them from facing the reality of children's vulnerability to sexual violence.[41] As Roland Summit noted in 1983, 'the child victim encounters an adult world which gives grudging acknowledgment to an abstract concept of child sexual abuse but which challenges and represses the child who presents a specific complaint of victimization'.[42] For people abused in the mid-late twentieth century, this adult world was one where speaking about sexual violence was taboo. As Chapters 2, 3 and 4 explored, in each of the three jurisdictions considered in this book, there was a deep cultural and societal silence around CSA which was perpetuated by a legal infrastructure that was partial in its scope and often hostile in its treatment of victims. The legal system was a primary deterrent to reporting, so perpetrators went undetected and could offend with impunity. Within social work and medicine, CSA was perhaps understood within a narrow frame of pathology or deviance, but not as a widespread social problem. Children had little social power, and their rights and welfare came a distant second to those of adults.

This culture of silencing meant that even if a child did seek help at the time, they were often not listened to. The evidence presented to the Irish courts by victims in the period 1999–2006 shows that many children did in fact disclose abuse to their parents, or family members, or teachers, but they were not listened to and nothing was done.[43] In Australia, one of Robert Hughes' (see Chapter 5) victims reported him to police in the late 1980s and again in the 1990s but was apparently told nothing could be done.[44] There are countless more stories like these that characterize the late twentieth century for victims of CSA.

Institutional barriers can also pose formidable obstacles to the disclosure of CSA. Institutions that are isolated from the broader community and function as closed communities and that have violent cultures or where physical punishment and sexual abuse are pervasive, can starkly inhibit disclosure.[45] Disclosure is greatly inhibited where institutions do not act to protect children. For example, the IICSA in England and Wales found that staff in Lambeth Council's children's homes 'demonstrated a callous disregard for the vulnerable children they were paid to look after' and failed to act when they knew about sexual abuse, leading to further perpetuation of that abuse.[46] Disclosure is inhibited where the institution prioritizes its reputation over the care of children. As the many inquiries in Ireland into NRCSA by clerics have evidenced,[47] members of the Catholic Church hierarchy silenced children and their families, and refused to refer information to the gardaí. The IICSA made similar findings regarding the historical response of the Catholic Church in England and Wales to allegations and concerns about CSA.[48] The

Australian Royal Commission described how the authority and power of perpetrators within institutions and the community as well as the authority of the institutions themselves were barriers to disclosure.[49]

The IICSA has found that in some religious organizations and settings in particular, there are significant barriers to reporting including: victim-blaming; lack of discussion of sex and sexuality; abuse of power by religious leaders; preponderance of men in senior positions; mistrust of external agencies and misuse of ideas of forgiveness to pressure children not to report or to justify failures by religious leaders to take appropriate action.[50]

These factors explain in part why children could not disclose at the time of their abuse. The reasons why adults delay disclosure are, somewhat surprisingly, under-researched, although it stands to reason that many of the factors discussed in relation to children endure well into adulthood. The limited existing scholarship suggests that adult survivors face intrapersonal, interpersonal and sociocultural barriers.[51] Intrapersonal barriers include factors that are also experienced in childhood, such as feelings of stigma and self-blame and guilt, as well as uncertainty about how to address the subject. Survivors may also fear others' reactions to their disclosure; a recurring theme is the fear of not being believed.[52] Some survivors may be afraid that disclosure will cost them their relationship with their partner or their family of origin, or cost them their career or mental well-being. Others, particularly survivors of institutional abuse, may not want their own children to be tainted with shame and stigma on account of their experiences.[53] Some survivors indicate a lack of clarity around their memories or having memories which they perceive to have been unavailable for years.[54] Gender stereotypes also play a role; for men, disclosure of sexual abuse may be in conflict with social expectations and stereotypes so that men may encounter even more shame, self-blame and identity issues than women.[55] Previous negative experiences of disclosure during childhood may also impact future decisions to disclose.

Of course, being ready to talk about abuse to someone else, such as a counsellor or friend, is very different to being ready to seek a legal response in the form of making a complaint to the police or a claim for damages or redress. Reaching a decision as an adult survivor to engage with the law can take even longer as survivors consider the many factors outside their control once they enter into legal proceedings. These include, but are not limited to, the impact on the survivor, their family and community of a drawn-out and upsetting criminal prosecution; financial risks associated with civil litigation and the prospect of being dismissed or humiliated by official actors through engagement with state redress processes. In a rare example of research into redress processes, Daly scrutinized 19 major cases of institutional abuse of children in Australia and Canada and found that it took government and church authorities on average 37 years from gaining official knowledge of a problem of abuse to introducing a sustained response.[56]

For one or all of these varied and overlapping reasons, many survivors of CSA, even once they reached adulthood, still cannot contemplate making a complaint to the police, suing for damages or claiming for redress. For many, it was not until the media spotlight on CSA in the 1980s (England and Wales and Australia) and the 1990s (Ireland) that they began reckoning with what had happened to them. Often this led to seeking counselling, which in turn helped survivors better understand their childhood suffering and realize that the medical, psychological and social difficulties of their adulthood were caused by their childhood abuse. Even then, this process of understanding and turning that understanding into legal action can take years as survivors negotiate concerns about the impact it might have on their families. For others, disclosure was motivated by a life event that brought the experience of abuse to the surface, such as the birth of a child, the death of a parent or a relationship breakdown, or the realization that they were in mental distress.

In engaging with legal responses, survivors are demanding that the law (at least) acknowledge the legitimacy of their complaint by holding a trial, or settlement conference, despite the lengthy 'delay' involved. Evolving understandings of trauma have provided new frameworks for understanding why survivors take time to come to law. These are considered next.

Trauma discourse

Trauma discourse, by which we mean both medical/psychological diagnostic categories and broader cultural ideas of trauma, has provided a key framework through which survivors' claims for justice can be comprehended by legislators, courts, jurors and the general public. Trauma's political power has heavily shaped how survivors' experiences of NRCSA have been understood and received by law. Psychological trauma involves feelings of 'intense fear, helplessness, loss of control, and threat of annihilation'.[57] Understandings of trauma have evolved over the course of the past 150 years. In the late nineteenth century, psychiatrists Sigmund Freud and Josef Breuer developed the idea that neuroses (phobias, hysterical paralysis and pains, some forms of paranoia and so on) had their origins in deeply traumatic experiences, including sexual abuse, which had occurred in the patient's past but which were later forgotten.[58] Although Freud subsequently abandoned this theory,[59] the idea of psychological trauma was resurrected in the US by Vietnam War veterans and feminist allies. Together, they succeeded in having post-traumatic stress disorder (PTSD) included in the diagnostic manual used by psychiatrists and clinicians in 1980.[60]

The explosion in research on the previously ignored subject of sexual assault from the 1970s led to new insights and a new language for articulating the harms of sexual violence. Work with CSA survivors[61] demonstrated the traumatic effects on children and their life-long effects on adult survivors of childhood sexual abuse.[62] Psychiatrist Judith Herman reported on her clinical research with female victims of domestic and sexual violence, including CSA, proposing a new diagnosis called Complex PTSD (CPTSD). The symptoms of CPTSD are now expressed in the International Classification of Diseases as: re-experience of the threat (the abuse), avoidance of traumatic reminders, heightened sense of threat, emotion regulation difficulties, relationship difficulties and negative self-concept (such as beliefs about the self as a failure).[63] PTSD and CPTSD, sometimes referred to as Rape Trauma Syndrome, explain that many victims of sexual violence will not discuss their abuse with others for many years because of feelings of shame, self-blame, fear of stigma and a fear of not being believed.[64] Today, both diagnostic categories of PTSD and CPTSD help to explain why an adult survivor of childhood sexual abuse may not bring proceedings until many years later.

Although PTSD and CPTSD may help courts, legislators and jurors understand why survivors could not come forward sooner, it carries risks of excluding certain survivors or forms of victimhood. Survivors may not have been traumatized in a strictly psychological sense, but they may have not sought a justice response sooner because they were afraid of being disbelieved by a hostile legal system, or society, or were afraid of the immense toll it would take on their family. They may have, understandably, tried to put the past behind them before coming to the realization that they also wanted to seek justice. Gender and race play a significant role in how survivors are received and responded to. It is also important to remember that many survivors are resilient and despite their suffering live rewarding lives, and most do not suffer from debilitating psychiatric problems. What is certain is that non-disclosure or partial disclosure is a normal part of the experience of someone who has been abused as a child.[65] It is not pathological.

On a broader cultural level, the idea of trauma has helped legitimize experiences of past victimization. 'Trauma' has come to signify the lasting impacts of a deeply upsetting event. It is a powerful way of articulating impacts of terrible events (a crime, natural disaster, war, terrorism, colonial dispossession) on a person or on a collective that lasts far beyond the time of the traumatic/originating event. In part due to the work of survivors, discourses of trauma in the media, in political speech, and even in everyday speech are now normalized. The idea of trauma 'is thus becoming established as a commonplace of the contemporary world, a shared truth'.[66] In parallel, women and men speaking out about sexual harassment and sexual violence in the near and distant past, on social media and in other public fora, have helped further legitimize experience as a form of knowledge. Both cultural developments have helped shift societal attitudes around the enduring nature of some harms, especially harms caused by sexual violence.

Conclusion

This introduction has set out the three key ideas in approaching the chapters in Part II: survivors' perceptions of justice, reasons why survivors delay disclosing and seeking a legal response and the role of trauma discourse in making the courts, legislators and jurors more receptive to survivors' demands of justice. The remaining chapters in this Part will explore the legal responses to NRCSA in each case study. We begin with the original legal response to sexual violence: criminal trials.

Notes

1 An extensive literature exists on justice for sexual violence survivors. For a review, see P. Lundy, "'I Just Want Justice': A Critical Analysis of the Historical Institutional Abuse Inquiry in Northern Ireland" *Éire-Ireland* 55(1 & 2), 2020, 252–78.
2 C. McGlynn and N. Westmarland, "Kaleidoscopic Justice: Sexual Violence and Victim-Survivors' Perceptions of Justice" *Social & Legal Studies* 28(2), 2019, 179–201,186.
3 Ibid., 9.
4 Ibid., 189.
5 This is our understanding of dignity as we read McGlynn and Westmarland. Ibid., 190–91.
6 Ibid., 194.
7 Ibid.
8 Reclaiming Self, *Ryan Report Follow-Up. Submission to the United Nations Committee against Torture Session 61* (Reclaiming Self, 2017), https://tbinternet.ohchr.org/Treaties/CAT/Shared%20Documents/IRL/INT_CAT_CSS_IRL_27959_E.pdf; J. Brown, D. McKenna, and E. O'Kennedy, *Only a Witness: The Experiences of Clients of One in Four in the Criminal Justice System* (Dublin: One in Four, 2016).
9 Testimony to Oireachtas Joint Committee on Retention of Records Bill, http://jfmresearch.com/retention-of-records-bill-2019/. herewing are the RCC, if appropriate.esn.ils are correct as set in this reference/
10 M. Keenan, *Sexual Trauma and Abuse: Restorative and Transformative Possibilities?* (Dublin: University College Dublin, 2014), 59, 61.
11 Ibid., 61.
12 S. Jülich, "Views of Justice Among Survivors of Historical Child Sexual Abuse: Implications for Restorative Justice in New Zealand" *Theoretical Criminology* 10(1), 2006, 125–38.
13 A.-M. McAlinden and B. Naylor, "Reframing Public Inquiries as 'Procedural Justice' for Victims of Institutional Child Abuse: Towards a Hybrid Model of Justice" *Sydney Law Review* 383, 2016, 277–308, 285. See also K. Daly, *Redressing Institutional Abuse of Children* (Basingstoke: Palgrave MacMillan, 2014), 117.
14 T.R. Tyler, *Why People Obey the Law, 2nd ed.* (Princeton: Princeton University Press, 2006); T.R. Tyler, "Procedural Justice, Legitimacy and the Effective Rule of Law" *Crime and Justice* 30, 2003, 283–357.
15 And perceptions of motive-based trust.
16 Tyler op. cit., 2003, 300–1.
17 I.J. Kidd et al., *The Routledge Handbook of Epistemic Injustice* (Abingdon: Routledge, 2017), 1.
18 M. Enright and S. Ring, "State Responses to Historical Institutional Abuse: Shame, Sovereignty and Epistemic Injustice" *Éire-Ireland* 55(1 & 2), 2020, 68–99.
19 K. Daly op. cit.

20 This study involved survivors of both sexual and non-sexual historical institutional abuse.

21 J.E. Halvorsen et al., "'To Say It Out Loud Is To Kill Your Own Childhood'" An Exploration of the First Person Perspective of Barriers to Disclosing Child Sexual Abuse" *Children and Youth Services Review* 113, 2020, 104999, 5.

22 R. McElvaney, "Disclosure of Child Sexual Abuse: Delays, Non-disclosure and Partial Disclosure. What the Research Tells Us and Implications for Practice" *Child Abuse Review* 24, 2015, 159–69. Lemaigre et al put this figure at 60–70 per cent. C. Lemaigre et al, 'Barriers and facilitators to disclosing sexual abuse in childhood and adolescence: A systematic review' *Child Abuse and Neglect* 70, 2017, 38–52.

23 Royal Commission into Institutional Responses to Child Sexual Abuse, *Final Report*, Volume 4, 9. 20.6 years for females and 25.6 years for males.

24 IICSA, *Truth Project Dashboard June 2016-December 2020* (2021), www.iicsa.org.uk/document/truth-project-dashboard-august-2021, 6.

25 Rape Crisis Network Ireland, *National Rape Crisis Statistics and Annual Report 2020* (2021), www.rcni.ie/wp-content/uploads/RCNI-Rape-Crisis-Statistics-2020-FINAL.pdf.

26 J. Cashmore et al., *The Impact of Delayed Reporting on the Prosecution and Outcomes of Child Sexual Abuse Cases* (Royal Commission into Institutional Responses to Child Sexual Abuse, 2016), 192.

27 M. Stoltenborgh et al., "A Global Perspective on Child Sexual Abuse: Meta-Analysis of Prevalence Around the World" *Child Maltreatment* 16(2), 2011, 79–101; J. Benedet and I. Grant, "Breaking the Silence on Father-Daughter Sexual Abuse of Adolescent Girls: A Case Law Study" *Canadian Journal of Women and the Law* 32(2), 2020, 239–87.

28 M.C. Seto et al., "The Puzzle of Intrafamilial Child Sexual Abuse: A Meta-analysis Comparing Intrafamilial and Extrafamilial Offenders with Child Victims" *Clinical Psychology Review* 39, 2015, 42–57.

29 D. Finkelhor, 1980; M. Ballantine, "Sibling Incest Dynamics: Therapeutic Themes and Clinical Challenges" *Clinical Social Work Journal* 40, 2012, 56–65.

30 D.G. Fischer and W.L. McDonald, "Characteristics of Intrafamilial and Extrafamilial Child Sexual Abuse" *Child Abuse & Neglect* 22(9), 1998, 915–29.

31 Halvorsen et al. op. cit.

32 T.B. Goodman-Brown et al., "Why Children Tell: A Model of Children's Disclosure of Sexual Abuse" *Child Abuse and Neglect* 27(5), 2003, 525–40.

33 Ibid.

34 B.A. Van der Kolk, *The Body Keeps the Score. The Brain, Mind, and Body in the Healing of Trauma* (New York: Penguin Books, 2005).

35 Office of the Children's Commissioner for England, 2017.

36 L. Jones et al., "Prevalence and Risk of Violence Against Children With Disabilities: A Systematic Review and Meta-analysis of Observational Studies" *The Lancet* 380(9845), (2012), 899–907.

37 I. Hershkowitz et al., "Exploring the Disclosure of Child Sexual Abuse with Alleged Victims and Their Parents" *Child Abuse and Neglect* 31(2), 2007, 111–23.

38 P. Schaeffer et al., "Children's Disclosures of Sexual Abuse: Learning from Direct Inquiry" *Child Abuse and Neglect* 35(5), 2011, 343–52.

39 S.E. Morrison et al., "Children's Disclosure of Sexual Abuse: A Systematic Review of Qualitative Research Exploring Barriers and Facilitators" *Journal of Child Sexual Abuse* 27(2), 2018, 176–94.
40 R. Alaggia and S. Kirshenbaum, "Speaking the Unspeakable: Exploring the Impact of Family Dynamics on Child Sexual Abuse Disclosures" *Families in Society*, 86(2), 2005, 227–34; L. Sas and A. Cunningham, *Tipping the Balance to Tell the Secret: The Public Discovery of Child Sexual Abuse* (London, ON: London Court Clinic, 1995).
41 R.C Summit, "The Child Sexual Abuse Accommodation Syndrome" *Child Abuse and Neglect* 7(2), 1983, 177–93.
42 Ibid., 178.
43 S. Ring, "The Victim of Historical Child Sexual Abuse in the Irish Courts 1999–2006" *Social and Legal Studies* 26(5), 2017, 562–80.
44 *Sydney Morning Herald,* 11 May 2014.
45 Royal Commission op. cit., 12.
46 IICSA, *Children in the Care of Lambeth Council Investigation Report* (2021), www.iicsa.org.uk/reports-recommendations/publications/investigation/lambeth-council,32 and 181.
47 See Chapter 4.
48 IICSA, *The Roman Catholic Church Investigation Report* (IICSA, 2020), www.iicsa.org.uk/document/roman-catholic-church-investigation-report-november-2020.
49 Royal Commission, 16.
50 IICSA, *Child Protection in Religious Organisations and Settings: Investigation Report* (2021), www.iicsa.org.uk/document/child-protection-religious-organisations-and-settings-investigation-report-september-2021, 7.
51 D. Tener and S.B Murphy, "Adult Disclosure of Child Sexual Abuse: A Literature Review" *Trauma Violence and Abuse* 16(4), 2015, 391–400, 395–96.
52 R. Alaggia, "Many Ways of Telling: Expanding Conceptualizations of Child Sexual Abuse Disclosure" *Child Abuse & Neglect* 28, 2004, 1213–27.
53 B. Walshe and C. O'Connell, *Consultations with Survivors Institutional Abuse on Themes and Issues to be Addressed by a Survivor Led Consultation Group,* (Dublin: Government Publications, 2019), 9, https://assets.gov.ie/26386/0e067451b0024081b4353b1ba4177841.pdf.
54 See J. Freyd, *Betrayal Trauma: The Logic of Forgetting Childhood Abuse* (Cambridge, MA: Harvard University Press, 1996).
55 Halvorsen et al. op. cit., 7.
56 Daly op. cit., 105.
57 B.J Sadock et al., *Comprehensive Textbook on Psychiatry, 10th edition* (Lippincott Williams and Wilkins, 2017).
58 S. Freud and J. Breuer, *Studies on Hysteria* (1895) (trans. N. Luckhurst) (London: Penguin, 2004).
59 But Freud and many psychoanalysts did continue to take CSA seriously: C. Smart, "Reconsidering the Recent History of Child Sexual Abuse, 1910–1960" *Journal of Social Policy* 29(1), 2000, 55–71.
60 American Psychiatric Association (ed.) *Diagnostic and Statistical Manual, 5th ed.* (Arlington, VA: American Psychiatric Association Publishing, 2013).
61 J.L. Herman and L. Hirschman, "Father-Daughter Incest" *Signs: Journal of Women in Culture and Society* 2, 1977, 735–56; D. Finkelhor and A. Browne, "The Traumatic Impact of Child Sexual Abuse: An Update" *American Journal*

of Orthopsychiatry 55, 1985, 530–41; also see D. Finkelhor and A. Browne, "Initial and Long-Term Effects: A Conceptual Framework" in D. Finkelhor (ed), *Sourcebook on Child Sexual Abuse* (Beverly Hills, CA: Sage, 1986).

62 J.L. Herman, *Trauma and Recovery* (New York: Basic Books, 1992).

63 World Health Organization, *International Classification of Diseases 11th Revision*, (2019), https://icd.who.int/en; A. Maercker et al., "Proposals for Mental Disorders Specifically Associated with Stress in the International Classification of Diseases-11" *The Lancet* 381(9878), 2013, 1683–5.

64 F. Raitt and S. Zeedyk, *The Implicit Relation of Psychology and Law. Women and Syndrome Evidence* (London: Routledge, 2000).

65 McElvaney op. cit.

66 D. Fassin and R. Rechtman, *The Empire of Trauma: An Inquiry into the Condition of Victimhood* (trans. R. Gomme) (Princeton: Princeton University Press: 2009), 2.

References

Alaggia, R., "Many Ways of Telling: Expanding Conceptualizations of Child Sexual Abuse Disclosure" *Child Abuse and Neglect* 28, 2004, 1213–27.

Alaggia, R. and Kirshenbaum, S., "Speaking the Unspeakable: Exploring the Impact of Family Dynamics on Child Sexual Abuse Disclosures" *Families in Society* 86(2), 2005, 227–34.

American Psychiatric Association (ed.) *Diagnostic and Statistical Manual, 5th ed.* (Arlington, VA: American Psychiatric Association Publishing, 2013).

Ballantine, M., "Sibling Incest Dynamics: Therapeutic Themes and Clinical Challenges" *Clinical Social Work Journal* 40, 2012, 56–65.

Brown, J.D., McKenna, D., and O'Kennedy, E., *Only a Witness: The Experiences of Clients of One in Four in the Criminal Justice System* (Dublin: One in Four, 2016).

Cashmore, J. et al., *The Impact of Delayed Reporting on the Prosecution and Outcomes of Child Sexual Abuse Cases* (Royal Commission into Institutional Responses to Child Sexual Abuse, 2016).

Daly, K. *Redressing Institutional Abuse of Children* (Basingstoke: Palgrave MacMillan, 2014).

Enright, M. and Ring, S., "State Responses to Historical Institutional Abuse: Shame, Sovereignty and Epistemic Injustice" *Éire-Ireland* 55(1,2), 2020, 68–99.

Fassin, D. and Rechtman, R., *The Empire of Trauma: An Inquiry into the Condition of Victimhood* (trans. R. Gomme) (Princeton: Princeton University Press, 2009).

Finkelhor D. and Browne, A., "The Traumatic Impact of Child Sexual Abuse: An Update" *American Journal of Orthopsychiatry* 55, 1985, 530–54.

Finkelhor, D. and Browne, A., "Initial and Long-Term Effects: A Conceptual Framework" in D. Finkelhor (ed), *Sourcebook on Child Sexual Abuse* (Beverly Hills, CA: Sage, 1986).

Fischer, D.G. and McDonald, W.L. "Characteristics of Intrafamilial and Extrafamilial Child Sexual Abuse" *Child Abuse & Neglect* 22(9), 1998, 915–29.

Freud, S. and Breuer, J., *Studies on Hysteria* (1895) (trans. N. Luckhurst) (London: Penguin, 2004).

Freyd, J., *Betrayal Trauma: The Logic of Forgetting Childhood Abuse* (Cambridge, MA: Harvard University Press, 1996).

Goodman-Brown, T.B. et al., "Why Children Tell: A Model of Children's Disclosure of Sexual Abuse" *Child Abuse and Neglect* 27(5), 2003, 525–40.

Halvorsen, J.E. et al., "'To Say It Out Loud Is To Kill Your Own Childhood'. An Exploration of the First Person Perspective of Barriers to Disclosing Child Sexual Abuse" *Children and Youth Services Review* 113, 2020, 104999, 5.

Herman, J.L. and Hirschman, L., "Father-Daughter Incest" *Signs: Journal of Women in Culture and Society* 2 (1977), 735–56.

Herman, J.L., *Trauma and Recovery* (New York: Basic Books, 1992).

Hershkowitz, I. et al., "Exploring the Disclosure of Child Sexual Abuse with Alleged Victims and Their Parents" *Child Abuse and Neglect* 31(2), 2007, 111–23.

IICSA, *The Roman Catholic Church Investigation Report* (2020), www.iicsa.org.uk/document/roman-catholic-church-investigation-report-november-2020.

IICSA, *Children in the care of Lambeth Council* (2021), www.iicsa.org.uk/reports-recommendations/publications/investigation/lambeth-council.

IICSA, *Child Protection in Religious Organisations and Settings: Investigation Report* (2021), www.iicsa.org.uk/document/child-protection-religious-organisations-and-settings-investigation-report-september-2021

IICSA, *Truth Project Dashboard June 2016-December 2020* (2021), www.iicsa.org.uk/document/truth-project-dashboard-august-2021.

Jones, L. et al., "Prevalence and Risk of Violence against Children with Disabilities: A Systematic Review and Meta-analysis of Observational Studies" *The Lancet* 380(9845), 2012, 899–907.

Jülich, S. "Views of Justice among Survivors of Historical Child Sexual Abuse: Implications for Restorative Justice in New Zealand" *Theoretical Criminology* 10(1), 2006, 125–38.

Keenan, M. *Sexual Trauma and Abuse: Restorative and Transformative Possibilities?* (Dublin: University College Dublin, 2014).

Kidd, I.J. et al., *The Routledge Handbook of Epistemic Injustice* (Abingdon: Routledge, 2017), 1.

Lundy, P.,"'I Just Want Justice': A Critical Analysis of the Historical Institutional Abuse Inquiry in Northern Ireland" *Éire-Ireland* 55, 1, 2, 2020, 252–78.

Maercker, A. et al., "Proposals for Mental Disorders Specifically Associated with Stress in the International Classification of Diseases-11" *The Lancet* 381 (9878), 2013, 1683–5.

McAlinden A.-M. and Naylor, B. "Reframing Public Inquiries as 'Procedural Justice' for Victims of Institutional Child Abuse: Towards a Hybrid Model of Justice" *Sydney Law Review* 38(3), 2016, 277–308.

McElvaney, R., "Disclosure of Child Sexual Abuse: Delays, Non-disclosure and Partial Disclosure. What the Research Tells Us and Implications for Practice" *Child Abuse Review* 24, 2015, 159–69.

McGlynn, C. and Westmarland, N., "Kaleidoscopic Justice: Sexual Violence and Victim-Survivors' Perceptions of Justice" *Social & Legal Studies* 28(2), 2019, 179–201.

Morrison, S.E. et al., "Children's Disclosure of Sexual Abuse: A Systematic Review of Qualitative Research Exploring Barriers and Facilitators" *Journal of Child Sexual Abuse*, 27(2), 2018, 176–94.

Office of the Children's Commissioner for England, 2017.

Raitt, F. and Zeedyk, S., *The Implicit Relation of Psychology and Law. Women and Syndrome Evidence* (London: Routledge, 2000).

Rape Crisis Network Ireland, *National Rape Crisis Statistics and Annual Report 2020,* (2021), www.rcni.ie/wp-content/uploads/RCNI-Rape-Crisis-Statistics-2020-FINAL.pdf.

Reclaiming Self, *Ryan Report Follow-Up. Submission to the United Nations Committee against Torture Session 61.* Reclaiming Self, 2017, https://tbinternet.ohchr.org/Treaties/CAT/Shared%20Documents/IRL/INT_CAT_CSS_IRL_27959_E.pdf.

Ring, S., "The Victim of Historical Child Sexual Abuse in the Irish Courts 1999–2006" *Social and Legal Studies* 26(5), 2017, 562–80.

Royal Commission into Institutional Responses to Child Sexual Abuse, *Final Report*, Volume 4, 9.

Sadock, B.J. et al., *Comprehensive Textbook on Psychiatry, 10th Edition* (Lippincott Williams and Wilkins, 2017).

Sas, L. and Cunningham, A. *Tipping the Balance to Tell the Secret: The Public Discovery of Child Sexual Abuse* (London, ON: London Court Clinic, 1995).

Schaeffer, P. et al., "Children's Disclosures of Sexual Abuse: Learning from Direct Inquiry" *Child Abuse and Neglect* 35(5), 2011, 343–52.

Seto, M.C. et al., "The Puzzle of Intrafamilial Child Sexual Abuse: A Meta-analysis Comparing Intrafamilial and Extrafamilial Offenders with Child Victims" *Clinical Psychology Review* 39, 2015, 42–57.

Smart, C., "Reconsidering the Recent History of Child Sexual Abuse, 1910-1960" *Journal of Social Policy* 29(1), 2000, 55–71.

Stoltenborgh, M. et al., "A Global Perspective on Child Sexual Abuse: Meta-Analysis of Prevalence around the World" *Child Maltreatment* 16(2), 2011, 79–101.

Summit, R.C., "The Child Sexual Abuse Accommodation Syndrome" *Child Abuse and Neglect* 7(2), 1983, 177–93.

Tener, D. and Murphy, S.B., "Adult Disclosure of Child Sexual Abuse: A Literature Review" *Trauma Violence and Abuse* 16(4), 2015, 391–400.

Tyler, T.R. "Procedural Justice, Legitimacy and the Effective Rule of Law" *Crime and Justice* 30, 2003, 283–357.

Tyler, T.R. *Why People Obey the Law, 2nd ed.* (Princeton: Princeton University Press, 2006).

Van der Kolk, B.A., *The Body Keeps the Score. The Brain, Mind, and Body in the Healing of Trauma* (New York: Penguin Books, 2005).

Walshe, B. and O'Connell, C., *Consultations with Survivors Institutional Abuse on Themes and Issues to be Addressed by a Survivor Led Consultation Group* (Dublin: Government Publications, July 2019), 9, https://assets.gov.ie/26386/0e067451b0024081b4353b1ba4177841.pdf.

World Health Organization, *International Classification of Diseases 11th Revision*, (2019), https://icd.who.int/en.

7 The criminal trial

Introduction

Criminal justice is the ultimate expression of a society's condemnation of unacceptable behaviours. In a liberal democracy, the criminal trial represents the power of the state to determine the truth of allegations about past events and to hold the defendant accountable, blameworthy and liable to punishment for harming the victim and violating agreed public norms in the form of criminal law. Criminal prosecutions are arguably the most important form of legal response to non-recent child sexual abuse (NRCSA) in terms of what they offer victims and what they mean for the public recognition of the wrongfulness of abuse, but NRCSA prosecutions pose great challenges to the criminal processes' ability to judge the past accurately and fairly. Most of these challenges flow from the impact of the 'delayed' reporting, specifically the interval of time between the alleged sexual abuse and the report to the police, discussed in Chapter 6. Until the 1980s in Australia, and the 1990s in England and Wales and in Ireland, although there was no statutory rule against prosecuting 'historical' crimes,[1] delay in reporting any crime was generally understood to mean that the defendant could not receive a fair trial and the prosecution should not proceed. The belief that criminal trials were incapable of adjudicating events in the distant past without exposing defendants to the risk of unfair conviction was slowly beginning to be eroded in the closing decades of the twentieth century, as (albeit rare) prosecutions were taken in England and Wales against aged defendants for murders committed during the Holocaust.[2] More significantly, in each of the three countries an important shift was taking place in the status of victims in criminal proceedings. Through the panoply of procedural and cultural changes discussed in Chapters 3–5 the victim of crime was transforming from being a mere witness for the prosecution, to a juridical subject of significance with a range of rights and interests in the criminal trial.[3] Despite these developments, however, the criminal law in each country was not yet ready for the advent of NRCSA prosecutions.

Survivors reporting NRCSA to the police in the late twentieth century were calling into question a core tenet of criminal procedure that held that some crimes, especially sexual crimes committed in secret, were simply too old to

DOI: 10.4324/9780429468162-9

prosecute. After decades of legal hostility to children reporting sexual violence against them, adult survivors were asking to finally be taken seriously as full subjects of the criminal law, for the harms they suffered to be recognized and for their abusers to be held accountable through a trial. Maintaining the status quo would have meant that no NRCSA prosecution would ever have reached a jury, thus continuing the effective amnesty from criminal accountability enjoyed by those who violated children. NRCSA prosecutions also present(ed) a further distinctive challenge; how should courts and juries treat the evidence of multiple adults who testified to having been abused as children by the same individual? This is a particularly pertinent question in prosecutions for NRCSA within families and in state-funded schools or children's homes and raises issues about how a jury should, if at all, take into account the evidence of one victim when considering the defendant's guilt in respect of a charge relating to another victim. This is a controversial question since the law is generally concerned about jurors being unduly influenced by the fact of multiple victims in such trials.

This chapter examines what criminal law, through the medium of the criminal trial,[4] offers NRCSA survivors reporting today and how this has changed since the early days of reports of NRCSA in the 1990s as courts and legislatures in each country have responded to the problem posed by delayed reporting and multiple victims. We ask whether the criminal law's historical suspicion of child victims of sexual offences, described in Chapters 3, 4 and 5, has been transcended, or whether traces of it persist in how the courts deal with issues of delay and multiple victims. For reasons of space we do not explore other important issues that arise in NRCSA prosecutions, including attrition,[5] the drafting of indictments,[6] the decision to prosecute,[7] timely disclosure, directions to the jury on the possibility that a witness may be honestly mistaken, the role of expert psychological evidence in NRCSA trials, the treatment of witnesses, the admissibility of evidence relating to the defendant's character and sentencing for NRCSA offences.

This chapter begins with an exploration of the reasons why survivors of childhood sexual abuse 'delay' reporting the crime to the police. We then examine the evidential and practical issues that can arise in NRCSA trials in the light of each country's experience. It is apparent that courts in each are seeking to deliver accountability for NRCSA while remaining vigilant about the judge's duty to ensure a fair trial. But there are also variations. For example, in Ireland, applications to halt a trial because of the effects of time have featured prominently in the jurisprudence.[8] In England and Wales and Australia, 'delay' has received much less judicial analysis. Conversely, the issue of cross-admissibility of multiple victims' evidence has received more extensive judicial treatment in England and Wales, and Australia, than in Ireland. The chapter concludes with comparative observations on how each country has dealt with the evidential challenges posed by the passage of time in NRCSA prosecutions.

In this chapter, we use the term victim instead of complainant because victim better reflects the position of the person who has reported an NRCSA crime against them and who has called on the state, through the prosecution, to act[9] and is in keeping with current legal approaches.[10] In using 'victim', we are not assuming that the defendant is guilty.

Why have NRCSA survivors delayed reporting?

As discussed in the Introduction to this Part, survivors delay disclosing the abuse to another person for a number of reasons. Together these have often meant that making a complaint to the police and seeking justice in the criminal courts was all but impossible. Until the advent of NRCSA cases, the criminal law in each of the three countries refused to allow criminal prosecutions for alleged crimes where there was any significant delay in reporting the crime to the police. This was because of concerns about fairness to the defendant. However, it completely ignored the reality of much sexual crime and certainly failed to appreciate the multiple reasons why an NRCSA victim might delay reporting. As Chapters 3, 4 and 5 explored, the criminal process in each country was particularly suspicious of complainants of sexual assaults and children's testimony.

In reporting childhood sexual abuse to the police, the survivor is seeking justice and is seeking to be believed and validated.[11] Reporting to the police may also be motivated by other factors, including ensuring the safety of victims and preventing future abuse; punishing the offender; providing emotional processing and coping for the victim.[12] Major barriers to reporting are other people's negative perceptions (such as being blamed or judged) and the reporting process itself and emotional distress.[13]

The evidential and practical challenges of NRCSA trials

Unlike tort law (see Chapter 8), criminal law does not generally impose statutory limitation periods beyond which a prosecution is time-barred. Where a limitation period is legislated for, this is usually for non-serious crimes (summary offences/misdemeanours) and not serious crimes (indictable offences/felonies). For sexual offences against children, the law historically provided for limitation periods but only for certain offences, usually those involving adolescent girls. The CLAA 1885 introduced a three-month time limit for prosecutions for unlawful carnal knowledge of girls aged between 13 and 16. In England and Wales this was extended to 12 months by the Criminal Law (Amendment) Act 1922 and was retained in the Sexual Offences Act 1956.[14] In Ireland a 12-month time limit for prosecutions for unlawful carnal knowledge of a girl aged between 15 and 17 years[15] was introduced by the CL(A)A 1935. This was finally repealed in 2006.[16] In Australia the law's historical suspicion of victims was even greater; indecent assault, carnal knowledge and incest were often bound by a limitation period of three months in the first half of the twentieth century and then, one to three years.[17] The rationale was that the time limit would 'prevent the possibility of a victim blackmailing an innocent man'.[18] Apart from these very important exceptions, which illustrate law's preoccupation with unlawful carnal knowledge rather than victimization of children, most other crimes of a sexual nature involving children did not engage any statutory time limit. Accordingly, NRCSA prosecutions do not generally involve any statutory time limit. Instead, to claim that their trial would be unfair, defendants must argue that their fundamental right to a fair trial is irreparably threatened by the effects of the delay in reporting.

In a criminal prosecution the defendant is entitled to certain robust legal protections to shield them from the state's enormous power. These include the right to due process and the protection of liberty, which are expressed in precepts such as the presumption of innocence, the burden and standard of proof,[19] and in constitutional[20] and human rights law.[21] The interval of time between the alleged abuse and trial presents significant challenges to the defendant's ability to raise an effective defence. Certain evidence or witnesses may no longer be available. Witnesses' memories may have decayed. Documentary evidence such as institutional records and real evidence, such as the bed on which a person was sexually assaulted, may be destroyed or lost. Locations such as schools or homes may have been demolished. The defendant can argue that the trial should be halted because of unfair prejudice to their case flowing from the effects of delay.[22] It can be very challenging for a judge to assess the value of a piece of missing evidence. Over the course of the past three decades, courts in each country have shifted from assuming that any missing evidence will inevitably mean the defendant is unfairly prejudiced, to becoming more willing to engage with the evidence and the alleged facts and closely examine defendants' claims of unfair prejudice.

Prosecutors also face significant evidential challenges because of delay. Victims may struggle to remember important details and there may be a paucity of other evidence to support the prosecution's case. Defence lawyers may try to portray the victim as unreliable or lying, vengeful or pathologically damaged.[23] These tactics play into widespread rape myths and misconceptions about how a victim of sexual assault is likely to behave, both during and after the assault, and can lead jurors to form an unjustifiably negative view of their credibility.[24] Appellate courts are increasingly alert to such risks of unfairness to the prosecution and changes in guidance for trial judges and juries reflect a broader understanding of the public interest in a fair trial, including the interests of the victim and the need for the jury to function as an impartial tribunal.

Trials involving multiple alleged victims

In some NRCSA cases more than one person alleges that the same defendant abused them. The prosecution may wish to try the charges together because the offending forms part of a pattern of offending and separate trials would fail to give the jury the full picture. Joined trials also reduce the burden on individual victims having to wait for the trial of the charges relating to them. If the charges are tried together in one conjoined trial, particular issues arise. Evidence of multiple alleged victims can aid in prosecution, but it is subject to exclusionary rules. The established approach in all three countries is generally as follows: evidence of multiple victims may be cross-admissible because of the *unlikelihood of a coincidence* that separate, independent people have made similar, but untrue, allegations against the defendant. This is called '*coincidence*'. Alternatively, evidence of multiple victims may go to *propensity* (or *tendency*): the jury may be asked to consider whether the accused has a particular propensity to commit sexual offences against children (in the context of the alleged offending). The distinction between propensity and coincidence reasoning has been criticized as artificial and unhelpful by scholar David Hamer.[25] This criticism is borne out by the experiences of the courts in each country in struggling to coherently approach cross-admissibility in NRCSA cases involving multiple victims.

When admitting the evidence of multiple victims, concerns arise about the risk of unfair prejudice to the defendant. Courts may be worried that jurors will convict without fully considering the question of guilt in respect of each charge; or jurors may (wrongly) reason that the number of victims *alone* means the accused is guilty. Or, jurors may (un)consciously decide the defendant is a 'bad type' and less deserving of the presumption of innocence, thereby convicting without properly evaluating the prosecution's case. Courts are concerned that judicial directions will not safeguard against these problematic forms of reasoning. In some cases, there may be a risk of innocent contamination of evidence, because of the victims' association with each other, or even the risk of collusion and fabrication.[26] Courts have struggled to clarify when such evidence should be cross-admissible and how to direct the jury on how the evidence may be used in deciding on guilt on individual charges.

In the rest of this chapter we consider how the courts in each country have treated arguments of unfairness by defendants in NRCSA cases and how they have dealt with cross-admissibility of witness testimony in trials involving multiple victims.

England and Wales

Defendants' applications for stays of prosecutions

Defendants in NRCSA prosecutions can claim that the proceedings ought to be stayed as an abuse of process. To succeed in this application, they must show that due to the delay, they would suffer serious prejudice to the extent that no fair trial could be possible.[27] A trial judge's decision to grant or refuse a stay is discretionary.[28] The grounds for requesting the stay may be relied upon on appeal in alleging that the conviction is unsafe.[29] During the early days of NRCSA coming before the courts, applications for stays were readily granted, even when no specific prejudice to the defence had been shown.[30] In 2009 the Court of Appeal set out a more restrictive approach to such applications. Kenneth MacKreth (a former detective constable and criminology graduate) was 86 years old when convicted of 23 counts of indecent assault and 10 of rape against 12- to 16-year-old girls. The offences took place when he was managing a Liverpool City Authority care home for young people in the 1970s. MacKreth requested a stay because some social services' documentation was no longer available and certain witnesses had not been produced in an earlier trial in 1977. This was rejected and he was convicted.[31] On appeal, counsel submitted that six previous Court of Appeal decisions concerning NRCSA since 2000 required a more generous application of the law towards those charged with NRCSA offences.[32] The case was championed by the Historical Abuse Appeal Panel, a group of specialist lawyers representing appellants convicted of NRCSA offences. Rix LJ concluded that the cases did not espouse any new principle and that 'mere speculation about what missing documentation might show' does not necessitate the staying of such trials or that any subsequent 'conviction must be recognised as unsafe'.[33] Missing documentation could be significant but only when linked to live issues. The evidence was 'formidable and convincing', and there was an unusual amount of documentation still surviving and no evidence of contamination or collusion amongst the witnesses.[34] In 2011, the Court of Appeal issued a landmark decision in *R v SF*[35] clarifying that a stay should be the exception, not the rule, and should only be granted for serious prejudice to the defence that cannot be addressed by the judge's power to regulate the admissibility of evidence and to give appropriate judicial directions on the issue of delay. The presence or absence of explanation or justification for the delay is a matter for the jury to consider in assessing the victim's credibility. It has no relevance to an abuse of process argument, unless, unusually, it impacts on the question of whether there can be a fair trial. The Court of Appeal also held that ordinarily an application for a stay should be at the outset of the trial and before the evidence is heard.[36] The Court of Appeal disapproved of the practice that had developed[37] of deferring the ruling until relevant evidence had been heard.

An application for a stay on the grounds of delay can still be successful. In 2016 the judge at Exeter Crown Court stayed proceedings against a 97-year-old former headmaster for 50 offences dating from the 1950s to the 1970s. The judge was concerned that lost documents, the age of the defendant, his associated mental health problems, need for audio amplification equipment as he was 90 per cent deaf, his limited memory recall and that of the victims could all potentially prejudice a fair trial.[38] However, successful applications are now rare. There are numerous examples of trials relating to events dating back to the 1960s and even the 1950s with defendants aged 70 or more,[39] including one at Birmingham Crown Court in December 2016 where a

101-year-old former lorry driver was convicted of a total of 30 charges dating back to the period 1974–1983.[40]

The issue of missing documents is frequently raised in applications for stays and appeals against conviction. However, the courts will carefully examine such arguments. In *R v H*,[41] the Court of Appeal dismissed the appellant's claim that his trial for abusing two sisters aged 7 and 11 some 25 years previously should not have gone ahead because some documents, dating back to the 1980s, originally held by schools and social services were no longer available. Conversely, in *Joynson,* the conviction of a care worker charged with abusing boys at a boarding school for special needs children was deemed not safe because of the delay and discrepancies in some of the evidence.[42] Despite concerns in some quarters,[43] successful appeals against conviction based on such arguments are very much the exception rather than the rule. In the 2020 case of *H*, involving the head of a children's care home in Norwich in the 1970s and 1980s, the court noted that there were regrettable errors and shortcomings in the process of disclosure. The conviction was upheld because defence counsel had been able to effectively cross-examine the victim and the missing documentation was neither decisive nor strongly supportive evidence on a specific issue in the case.[44]

These cases evidence an important shift in approach from one that accepted defence assertions of unfairness caused by delay and stopped prosecutions from proceeding, to one that is weighted in favour of allowing the trial to take place. Only a clear demonstration of prejudice to the fair trial will suffice to justify a stay in exceptional circumstances. This shift is indicative of a new commitment on the part of the courts to holding alleged NRCSA abusers to account by allowing trials to proceed. It points to a new judicial understanding that a person's 'delay' in reporting childhood sexual abuse is entirely consistent with having been abused and is not a reason in itself to query their credibility or to prevent accountability through a trial process.

Judicial directions on delayed reporting

The Court of Appeal has made it clear that trial judges must be careful to direct on the disadvantage to the defendant arising from the delay in complaint. Judges should point out the difficulties facing a defendant in challenging allegations, the effect of fading memories, loss of evidence (and that it may be unclear what has been lost) and a summary of the main elements of prejudice identified during the trial.[45] Directions are crucial to the safety of any conviction in cases where evidence may be missing or destroyed. In *PR*,[46] evidence gathered by the police in 2002 that would have been relevant to the defence case had been accidentally destroyed by water damage. The Court of Appeal upheld the trial judge's refusal of a stay and the conviction, because the trial judge gave an 'impeccable' direction to the jury on the need to take the prejudice caused by the loss of materials into account when considering whether the prosecution has been able to prove guilt beyond a reasonable doubt.

As well as warning about the prejudice to the defendant's case caused by the delay, the trial judge must also issue a separate direction to the jury on the reasons why victims in NRCSA cases may delay reporting.[47] This should inform the jury that victims of sexual offences may not report crimes immediately through a sense of shame or humiliation and that the fact that a complaint is unsupported by other evidence is not of itself an indication that the evidence is untrue.[48] Such directions are now routinely given and the Crown Court Compendium provides examples to help judges.[49] Judges may rely on their experience of trying cases to warn juries of the risks of using stereotypical assumptions to inform their decision-making.[50]

Trials involving multiple victims

A trial may involve offences against different victims if the offences are founded on the same facts, or form, or are part of a series of offences of the same or a similar character.[51] Evidence of multiple victims may go to propensity, or it may be relevant because of the unlikelihood that a series of independent witnesses should make similar complaints.[52] For each individual count, the other victims' evidence on the other counts must be treated as bad character evidence and must satisfy the requirements of the Criminal Justice Act 2003 (CJA 2003).[53] At one time, it was thought that multiple complaints could only be taken as mutually supportive if they were not just similar but 'strikingly similar'. But even before the CJA 2003 came into force, the need for striking similarity had been weakened by the House of Lords judgment in *DPP v P*[54] and is now obsolete. Evidence of other allegations is admissible if its probative value outweighs its prejudicial effect.

In *R v Freeman and Crawford*,[55] the Court of Appeal reviewed the case law before clarifying that the correct approach is for trial judges to direct juries to look at the totality of the evidence 'in the round'. In determining guilt in respect of any count, the jury should be told it is entitled to have regard to the evidence relating to any other count, if that evidence is relevant and admissible.[56] So in some cases, the jury may use the evidence in relation to the other count(s) to help it to decide on the defendant's guilt in respect of the count that it is considering.[57] In *Richards*, the Court of Appeal held that a propensity approach (in addition to the absence of coincidence) was appropriate regarding an issue of whether the appellant had a sexual interest in boys and where propensity evidence post-dated the alleged offences.[58] In some rare cases, it may be appropriate to direct the jury that the evidence that is cross-admissible is capable of being used for both propensity-type reasoning and to rebut the argument of coincidence.[59]

A high-profile case from 2019 illustrates the systemic nature of some NRCSA offending and the importance of cross-admissible evidence in trials involving multiple victims. Robert Higgins, a very successful youth football coach, was convicted of 45 offences of indecent assault against 23 victims between 1971 and 1996 while working at two major English clubs. The trial came after former professional footballer Andy Woodward gave interviews in 2016 to The Guardian Newspaper and the BBC Victoria Derbyshire Show where he talked about the abuse he endured as a trainee. The NSPCC set up a dedicated helpline for anyone who had encountered CSA in a sport environment. Higgins' name was repeatedly mentioned by former players. At trial, the jury heard how he used his notoriety and power from his coaching role to gain victims' trust and to exploit the trust of their parents. When some of the boys challenged Higgins, he told them if they spoke up no-one would believe them and their future as footballers would be in jeopardy. The prosecution was able to demonstrate a systematic and pervasive pattern of behaviour by Higgins. Each victim gave a similar account of him touching their legs and/or groins while driving them to or from a match and abusing them at his home. Most victims did not know each other or had not spoken for years since their footballing days so the DPP argued there could be no suggestion of collusion.[60] Higgins was sentenced to 24 years and 3 months.

Until the mid-1990s there was reasonably clear authority that if there is a real risk of collusion between victims, the evidence should be excluded. In 1995, the House of Lords overruled these cases in *R v H*.[61] It involved sexual offences against a daughter and a stepdaughter between whom, the parties agreed, there existed a risk of collusion. The Lords ruled that contamination is not a factor in determining admissibility unless it is so blatant as to render the evidence totally unworthy of belief. Otherwise, the issue of contamination should be left to the jury. If the evidence is admitted and it becomes clear collusion was present, or the question is raised by the defence, the judge must make appropriate directions to the jury. This approach was criticized by leading evidence lawyers for underplaying the dangers of admitting contaminated evidence[62] but it endures albeit with some development. Where evidence may have been innocently contaminated, but there is no threat to the safety of any conviction, the judge will be expected to deliver a suitable direction to the jury. This should mention the risk of accidental contamination, as well as deliberate collusion.[63] If the judge considers that there has been significant concoction, collaboration or inadvertent contamination that threatens the safety of any eventual conviction, the trial judge must stop the trial and direct an acquittal or order a retrial.[64]

Ireland

For most of the twentieth century, child sex offences[65] were not a regular feature of the Irish criminal courts. In the mid-late 1990s, as greater public attention was afforded to the issue of NRCSA, the numbers of adults reporting to the gardaí rose. This produced a rich body of jurisprudence involving judicial exploration of a broader range of NRCSA than that examined by the Commission to Inquire into Child Abuse (CICA) (see Chapter 10) and is important to survivors, scholars and the public as an (imperfect) archive of 'historical' child sexual abuse and survivors' attempts to obtain justice. The prosecutions involved priests and Christian Brothers,[66] as well as fathers, uncles, brothers, neighbours, teachers, coaches, farm labourers and school bus drivers.[67]

Defendants' applications to halt the trial on the grounds of delay

The defendant's right to a fair trial is expressly protected in the Constitution, and the courts have robustly protected this right.[68] The courts traditionally took a very strict approach to the issue of 'delay'; in a 1992 case, an interval of one year precluded the prosecution of a child's complaint.[69] Faced with increasing numbers of cases, and then the 'torrent'[70] of NRCSA cases from the late 1990s onwards, the courts were forced to reckon with the fact that 'delayed' reporting is not unusual, but in fact typical of CSA, and that victims' fear should not confer abusers with effective immunity from prosecution. Until recently, the primary avenue for NRCSA defendants seeking to halt their trial was a pre-trial application to the High Court for an order prohibiting the trial (or the proceedings)[71] or injuncting the DPP from continuing with the prosecution.

The reviewing court must decide whether there is a real and serious risk of an unfair trial due to the lapse in time between the alleged abuse and the initiation of proceedings. There is a right of appeal from a decision of the High Court to the Supreme Court. This contrasts with equivalent procedures in England and Wales and in Australia where there is limited opportunity to appeal pre-trial.[72] Such applications add years to an already fraught and slow criminal process, heightening the stress involved for the parties and exacerbating evidential issues. In recent years, the courts have moved away from hearing pre-trial applications and instead have stressed that the passage of time and its effects are best dealt with by the trial judge instead of a reviewing court. This brings Ireland into line with the practice in England and Wales and in Australia. However, unlike in the comparator countries, Irish defendants are still permitted to apply pre-trial for prohibition and may appeal from any refusal, forcing victims to endure an agonizing wait to see if the trial proper may get underway.

In the cases decided between the early 1990s and 2006, courts hearing prohibition applications focussed on the accused's role in (allegedly) causing the delay. The court would inquire into the victim's reasons for not reporting sooner. The 'reasonableness' of the delay was crucial and centred on an evolving psycho-legal concept of 'dominion': the relationship of domination between the abuser and the victim that prevented contemporaneous reporting to the police.[73] If dominion was found to have existed (following extensive psychological assessments and the reception into evidence of victims' affidavits explaining why they could not report sooner), the delay was 'reasonable' and therefore excusable and the trial would be allowed to take place. Dominion was found in most cases and was used by the courts to effectively circumvent law's established approach to historic crimes and ensured instead that sexual violence committed against children in the past did not go unprosecuted. Thus, the judicial development of 'dominion' was a significant and progressive moment for Irish law's engagement with the problem of historical violence against children. However, the dominion jurisprudence was also deeply problematic from the perspective of both defendants and victims. The focus on the victim's reasons for delayed reporting distracted the court's focus from the core question of whether the trial could be fair, thereby diluting defendant's due process rights.[74] The law's construction of victims as dominated, silenced and passive, meant that certain victims, often those who displayed agency in adulthood, were discounted from being considered legitimate victims. Furthermore, evidence that victims reported to parents or teachers at the time of the abuse was entirely marginalized and sidelined by the focus on a psychological paralysis expressed through the psycho-legal concept of dominion.[75]

In the 2006 case of *SH v DPP*,[76] the Supreme Court ended the focus on the victim's reasons for the delay and instead restored the judicial spotlight to where it belonged—whether the defendant has shown that there is a real or serious risk that, by reason of the delay, they will not obtain a fair trial. The test also provides for prohibition in exceptional circumstances, where it would be unfair or unjust to put them on trial. Trials may also be halted due to 'wholly exceptional circumstances' such as the defendant's severe ill health, cognitive impairment or learning disability.[77] This is fact-dependent, with many examples of cases involving defendants of advanced age and complaints dating back many decades being allowed to proceed.[78]

Defendants are expected to engage with the facts and show that the missing witness or evidence could have been of assistance to the defence.[79] In *PH v DPP*,[80] the applicant was a former teacher charged with 16 counts of indecent assault involving nine victims some 50 years earlier. He claimed prejudice arising from the death of a number of witnesses he would have wished to call and the absence of the roll books of classes he taught. He claimed that the witnesses would have supported his claims that he had frequent visitors in the classroom and that the layout of the classroom was different to that described by the victims. The decision to allow the trial to go ahead was upheld on appeal. In *AT v DPP*,[81] the Court of Appeal was unwilling to prohibit a trial despite the absence of many potential witnesses, because there was no reason to believe that the absent witnesses were aware of the alleged abuse and because there was scope for testing the credibility and reliability of the victim's testimony through other avenues.

In recent years, the superior courts have shown a clear preference for arguments of unfairness to be dealt with by the trial judge following an application at the close of the prosecution case or the close of the evidence, rather than a pre-trial reviewing court working primarily off affidavits.[82] As noted earlier, the move from pre-trial applications to the High Court, to applications to the trial judge during the trial brings Ireland closer to the approach taken to delay in England and Wales and Australia. Yet, there remains a significant gap; unlike in England and Wales, where the trial judge should usually make the assessment at the outset of the case, in Ireland, the assessment is to be made after the evidence has been heard.

In 2019 the Supreme Court clarified the approach to be taken by trial judges. In *CC*, the appellant had been found guilty of raping and indecently assaulting his niece some 44 years earlier. The defence argued that the unfairness primarily stemmed from the absence of one witness. The Court set down the principle that the trial judge must assess whether a trial is fair and just in light of the lapse of time and whether the accused had thereby been deprived of a realistic opportunity of a useful line of defence.[83] Clarke CJ described how a trial judge should assess prejudice to the defence.[84] First, the judge must consider the prosecution case at trial, and then the judge must consider 'whatever evidence is available as to the testimony which might have been given but which is said to be no longer available'. This exercise will generally involve considering the available evidence about what might have been said by the missing witness or what might have been contained in missing physical evidence, such as documents or objects. Clarke CJ noted that this exercise 'must necessarily be speculative at least to some extent'.[85] If satisfied that there was a real prospect that the evidence concerned could have been tendered, the judge must assess its materiality to the prosecution's case. Finally, the judge must reach an assessment of whether 'the absence of the missing evidence has deprived the accused of a realistic opportunity of an obviously useful line of defence'.[86]

In the 2020 case of *X*, the Court of Appeal refused an injunction of the prosecution of the appellant in respect of 105 charges of indecent assault against a younger relative over the course of 12 years.[87] There was a delay of 37 years, but the defendant was not elderly and was capable of remembering highly relevant issues when interviewed by gardaí. Donnelly J found that the defendant's complaint was a mere assertion of prejudice and noted that 'Following on from [*CC*], those who wish to challenge their prosecution on the grounds of delay may be well advised to think twice before proceeding to judicial review'.[88]

The Supreme Court's return in *CC* to the trial process as the appropriate venue to determine questions of fairness avoids the crystal ball gazing involved in many prohibition applications[89] which rely on 'affidavits professionally drafted and speculation as to what might transpire at a trial'.[90] It better reflects the trial judge's unique competence to determine issues of fairness having heard the evidence and taking into account factors such as the presumption of innocence and the ability to make evidential rulings and give appropriate warnings and directions to the jury. It is a nuanced approach that recognizes both the importance of the constitutional guarantee of due process to the defendant, and the need to fully scrutinize and contextualize defence arguments in light of the importance of NRCSA prosecutions for victims and for the public more generally. The challenges facing trial judges should not be underestimated; in *CC* itself, two of the five Supreme Court judges thought the unavailability of a witness meant that the trial should have been halted. Nevertheless, the *CC* approach is a welcome confirmation that the courts recognize the significance of NRCSA trials for individual victims and the importance of making sure that defence arguments are fully scrutinized so that only cases which truly would be unfair to try are halted before they reach the trial.

Judicial directions on delay

The Court of Appeal has made it clear that trial judges must direct on the issue of delay in NRCSA cases and that failure to do so may result in a finding on appeal that the conviction is unsafe.[91] The lengthy warning given to the jury by Haugh J. in *RB* is often cited as a useful explanation of the difficulties facing a defendant in an NRCSA trial and has been reproduced in various appellate judgments.[92] Running to 100 lines, the *RB* direction warns of the dangers of a credibility contest, particularly when there is a lack of detail in the complaints due to the delay. The warning should be tailored to the specific case before the jury.[93] The appellate courts have jealously protected fairness to the accused, even in circumstances where the need was not necessarily apparent; in the 2020 case of *TG*,[94] the Court of Appeal to the jury held that a warning's impact was fatally undermined by a judge's comments that the prosecution case was not lacking in detail.

In addition to a (effectively mandatory) delay warning, trial judges may also give a discretionary warning on corroboration. Although a corroboration warning is no longer mandatory in sexual offences trials (see Chapter 4), there is a continued judicial attachment to giving them.[95] It is far from clear that they are only rarely given in NRCSA trials,[96] which is worrying because so-called 'delay warnings' also refer to credibility issues relating to the victim's evidence. There is a risk that the trial judge's directions to the jury in a NRCSA trial will unduly focus on the victim's credibility.

In a welcome attempt to recalibrate the scales of justice, Supreme Court judge Peter Charleton has canvassed the possibility of a limited warning by the trial judge to highlight that the legitimate reasons why a victim's account in a sexual offence trial may not be as fulsome as a juror might expect. The warning would highlight that victims are at a disadvantage in reciting the details of what they claim has occurred to them and that in every case a witness is likely to have made errors in prior statements which can be compounded by embarrassment.[97] This would bring Irish law more into alignment with developments in Australia and England and Wales.

Trials involving multiple victims

Sexual abuse of multiple children by teachers, priest or those in positions of authority feature regularly in the Irish criminal courts.[98] While the joinder of multiple victims on an indictment will strengthen the prosecution case, it also raises a number of difficult and technical issues for the run of the trial and the charge to the jury.[99] Defence counsel may make an application to sever the indictment so that the accused will only face allegation(s) made by a single victim in a number of trials.[100]

Arguments about the cross-admissibility of victims' evidence tend to focus on the idea that the offending may be part of a 'system' of offending. It can be used to show a pattern of offending and to rebut defences of innocent explanation, accident or denial. Trial judges must assess whether the probative value of the evidence outweighs its prejudicial effect on the defence case. This was the House of Lords' test in *P*[101] which was incorporated into Irish law in the NRCSA cases *B*[102] and *BK*.[103] In *BK*, the accused had been convicted on several counts of attempted buggery and indecent assault against three former residents of Trudder House, a home for Mincéir children (see Chapter 4). BK appealed arguing that each of the counts should have been tried separately because they related to different boys, trying them together effectively provided corroboration where there was none. The Court of Criminal Appeal held that evidence that the defendant acted in a certain way on one occasion is not admissible *per se* for the purpose of showing that he acted in the same way on another occasion. There would have to be some further 'nexus' between the two occasions to permit evidence of one to be admitted as proof on the other. That nexus could be satisfied where the manner in which a particular act was done on one occasion suggests that it was also done on another occasion by the same person and with the same intent.[104] Such evidence is admissible because of the inherent improbability of several persons making up exactly similar stories and because it shows a practice which would rebut accident, innocent explanation or denial.[105]

Since *BK*, the courts have continued to use the probative versus prejudicial balancing test, but similarities between allegations remain important in assessing probative value. These may relate to the location, timing and the manner in which the offences were allegedly perpetrated[106] or similarities in how the victims were groomed.[107] Similarity is not as strictly policed as it was before 2000. The superior courts are trusting trial judges to make decisions on cross-admissibility and to direct the jury accordingly.

In *ST*,[108] the defendant Christian Brother was accused of abusing 17 boys at a school in Limerick during the years 1978–1981. He was convicted of abusing six boys. The Court of Criminal Appeal upheld the trial judge's decision to allow the complaints to be tried together; the offence took place at the school; the offences were perpetrated in the same manner; the appellant's status as a Christian Brother and teacher meant he would have had absolute authority and control over the location. The judge also noted that ST was not indiscreet about his behaviour and that the fact that pupils from three consecutive year groups involved was highly probative in itself and weighed against any possibility of collusion. In *SL*,[109] the three victims were in the same degree of relationship to the appellant and were all girls; they all lived in the same farmhouse; they were all approximately the same age at the time of being abused; the familial and neighbour relationship between the two families created or assisted the opportunity to abuse. The single most striking similarity was the nature of the abuse perpetrated and the way in which it was carried out.

In *AR*, the Court of Appeal upheld a joint trial on the basis that both victims were sisters and the appellant's neighbours and babysat his children. Most of the offending occurred in the appellant's house; both referred to his habit of laughing in a menacing fashion.[110] In *MS*,[111] a retired surgeon was charged with indecently assaulting his male patients. The charges dated back some 26–52 years. Upholding his convictions in relation to three victims, the Court held that the degree of similarity was very significant in that all victims were teenage boys at the time of the abuse, all attended MS for medical treatment and all allegations involved the touching of each boy's genitals.

Defendants may argue that evidence is not cross-admissible because there is some collusion, accidental contamination or some form of copy-cat complaint. The courts acknowledge that the risk of collusion is almost always present in sexual offence cases where siblings or close friends are involved. There are also particular issues that arise in relation to where a group of victims has emerged from a counselling group or where they share the same solicitor or where there has been a campaign to find other victims. However, important differences in the detail of allegations may weigh against any suggestion of collusion[112] and the trial may be allowed to proceed. As with their counterparts in England and Wales, the approach taken by the superior courts in Ireland is that juries are robust and can take direction from a trial judge.[113]

Jury directions in cases involving multiple victims

Evidence of multiple victims may also have a corroborative effect. The judge must determine and instruct the jury on how to understand and use particular evidence. It is then for the jury to decide as a matter of fact whether the evidence is actually corroborative in the circumstances of the particular case.[114] In *CC*,[115] the appellant was a religious brother who taught in a primary school in the west of Ireland in the 1960s and 1970s. The trial involved 35 indecent assault charges against four victims. O'Donnell J in the Court of Criminal Appeal (the preecessor of the Court of Appeal) stated that if a jury concluded in relation to any one victim that the case was compelling and they were satisfied beyond a reasonable doubt of the accused's guilt in relation to such evidence, then they could consider that it was more likely that the account given by another victim of a similar incident was true. He stressed that it is also possible for a jury not to be satisfied to the criminal standard on the individual evidence relating to any single victim or incidence, but nevertheless to reach that point of being satisfied to the criminal standard by virtue of the range of offences, their interconnection and the unlikelihood that the evidence is the product of collusion or chance.[116] In this situation, the reliance on the evidence of other victims is much greater and should be specifically addressed in the judge's direction.[117] *CC* represents a welcome recognition of the jury's ability to reason about the facts and to appreciate the dynamics of CSA.

Australia

Over the past two decades, there have been significant reforms to the ways NRCSA offences are prosecuted. These vary between jurisdictions, and it is difficult to determine the exact effects of each reform. But, by way of comparison, a 'historical' complaint lodged by an adult in New South Wales (NSW) is much more likely to result in conviction than a contemporary complaint lodged on behalf of a child.[118] In South Australia, the opposite is the case.[119] In both jurisdictions, serious historical offences (such as sexual assault) are more likely to result in conviction than less serious historical offences (such as indecent assault).[120]

Statutes of limitations and applications for stays of prosecution

As noted earlier, Australia had more statutes of limitation that impacted investigation and prosecution of historical child sex offences than England and Wales or Ireland. The removal of limitation periods for all sex offences commenced in South Australia in 1985,[121] but national progress was inconsistent. It was 1992 before NSW enacted similar provisions addressing carnal knowledge and indecent assault committed on children aged 14 or 15 (which had limitation periods of 12 months).[122] The problem with this suite of reforms was that they were not retrospective.[123] For some years, the situation was politically justified in NSW with the reasoning that the limitation period's impact was 'ameliorated by the fact it was limited to carnal knowledge and indecent assault offences and in most cases complaints of this nature involved other offending that was not caught by the limitation', such as sexual assault(s).[124] We now understand that much child sex offending has involved only non-penetrative offences and that historical conceptions of sexual assault or rape overlooked oral penetration, all of which are now known to cause significant trauma and harm to children. Once the problem of NRCSA became better understood in the twenty-first century, most jurisdictions enacted further reforms to allow for the retrospective abolition of statutes of limitations for all sex offences.[125] In 2018, NSW introduced a reform to retrospectively remove the carnal knowledge and indecent assault limitation period that prevented many survivors from seeking justice, in the *Criminal Legislation Amendment (Child Sexual Abuse) Act 2018 (NSW)*.[126]

Defendants' applications for stays for abuse of process

Courts have the power to stay proceedings on the ground that the trial would be an abuse of the court's process. This is like the remedy in England and Wales. In *Jago,*[127] the High Court of Australia ruled that a stay should only be granted if the defendant's right to a fair trial has been prejudiced, which cannot be presumed simply from delay. The defendant must demonstrate that the effect of the delay is such that they cannot obtain a fair trial. In considering an application for a stay, the court should take into account factors such as length of delay; the prosecution's reasons for delay; the accused's responsibility for and past attitude to delay; potential prejudice to the accused and the public interest in the disposition of charges of serious offences and convicting those guilty of crime.[128] The courts have generally avoided examining justifiability of the delay when considering the issue of prejudice to the accused.[129] Since the development of judicial directions on delay in the twenty-first century, discussed below, it is unusual that evidential prejudice to the defendant—called forensic disadvantage in Australia—would be considered sufficient to grant a stay.[130]

Judicial directions to the jury

NRCSA prosecutions have generated a significant body of case law addressing the consequences of the passage of time between the alleged abuse and the report to the police in the form of damage to the victim's credibility and 'forensic disadvantage' to the accused. Much of this precedent appears to favour the accused, although some reforms have addressed both parties 'more even-handedly'.[131] Since the 1980s most NRCSA trials required what is known as the *Longman* warning on forensic disadvantage, named after the 1989 High Court case *Longman v R,* in which complaints of CSA were made 20 years after the alleged offences. *Longman* requires that the jury be advised that, because of the passage of time, 'it would be 'dangerous to convict' on the victim's evidence alone unless the jury is satisfied of its truth and accuracy, having scrutinized the victim's evidence with great care'.[132] The reasoning is that the accused is prejudiced because they have lost the 'means of testing the victim's allegations which would have been open to him [or her] had there been no delay'.[133] *Longman,* which is given even in cases where there is corroboration of the victim's evidence,[134] is criticized for suggesting an 'irrebuttable presumption that the delay *has* prevented the accused from adequately testing and meeting the victim's evidence'[135] irrespective of whether the accused has in fact been prejudiced. The warning is said to focus on the evidence of the victim, rather than the forensic disadvantage suffered by the defendant, and it appears to connect the delay in complaint with credibility.[136] Increasingly, *Longman* is also criticized for providing juries with guidance that is contrary to modern understandings of the ways in which sexual abuse, especially CSA, comes to light, and for perpetuating outdated understandings of memory and evidence.[137]

Out of fear that the *Longman* warning could suggest to juries that delay *inevitably* creates a forensic disadvantage,[138] most jurisdictions have introduced statutory provisions to partially mitigate it. Most have incorporated the relevant provision of the *Uniform Evidence Act (UEA) 1995*, which was introduced to standardize evidence procedures and rules in criminal trials across the country.[139] Unlike *Longman,* which focussed on the credibility of the victim's evidence, s165B of the UEA focusses on the disadvantage to the accused:[140] if the court is

> satisfied that the defendant has suffered a significant forensic disadvantage because of the consequences of delay, the court must inform the jury of the nature of that disadvantage and the need to take that disadvantage into account when considering the evidence.[141]

Significant forensic disadvantage cannot be established by the mere fact of delay,[142] but it might be established, for example, by the fact that any potential witnesses have died or are not able to be located, or if potential evidence has been lost or is otherwise unavailable.[143] The judge 'must not in any way suggest to the jury that it would be dangerous to convict or unsafe to convict the defendant solely because of the delay or the forensic disadvantage suffered because of the consequences of the delay'.[144]

Victoria is the only jurisdiction to have introduced a stand-alone act to simplify jury directions to allow trials to be conducted fairly and more efficiently. The Jury Directions Act 2015 (Vic) represents a radical departure from the approach taken to jury directions in England and Wales, Ireland and the rest of Australia[145] and has been positively received by trial judges in Victoria.[146] The Act prohibits any suggestion that, because of delay, it would be dangerous or unsafe to convict, or that the victim's evidence should be scrutinized with great care.[147] It prohibits statements and suggestions that victims of sexual offences or victims who delay in reporting (or who do not report) are, as a class, not credible or reliable.[148] The Act also requires judges to explain to the jury that people may react differently to sexual offences, that some people may complain immediately while others may not, and that delay in making a complaint in respect of sexual offences is a common occurrence.[149]

Victoria and New South Wales also provide for a jury direction to be given if the trial judge considers, having heard submissions, that there is a difference in the victim's accounts of the offence charged that is relevant to their credibility or reliability. The judge must inform the jury that such differences in a victim's account may be relevant to their assessment of credibility and reliability, but they must also inform the jury that experience shows that trauma may affect how people recall events, and it is common for there to be differences in accounts of a sexual offence.[150] This is a welcome balancing of the competing goals of fairness to the defendant and recognition of the effects of NRCSA on victims.

Despite the reforms mitigating *Longman* and modernizing jury directions, procedural convention remains affected by the common law. Following the 1996 High Court decision in *Crofts*, in most states and territories, if a judge gives a statutory warning about good reason for delay, they must also *consider* advising the jury that 'delay in complaint may be taken into account in evaluating the evidence of the victim and in determining whether or not to believe the victim'.[151] The interplay between the common law and statute remains highly complex, especially when all the different state and territory jurisdictions are taken into account.[152]

Trials involving multiple victims

The Royal Commission into Institutional Responses to Child Sexual Abuse identified prosecutions for NRCSA involving multiple victims as 'one of the most significant issues',[153] implicated in a number of unjustified acquittals. It recommended greater use of joint trials and cross-admissibility of evidence from different victims.[154] As in England and Wales and Ireland, the cross-admissibility of victims' evidence in a joint trial is highly contested, and the law is exceptionally complex.[155] In the UEA jurisdictions,[156] coincidence evidence and propensity (or 'tendency') evidence are governed by identical admissibility tests: evidence may be admitted if the court believes it will have significant probative value[157] which 'substantially' outweighs any prejudicial effect on the defendant. This test is performed by a judge, and it has resulted in significantly different thresholds for admissibility in different UEA jurisdictions.[158] Queensland is the only state where the common law continues to apply in this area, and the test for admissibility is even stricter there, where each form of evidence is allowed only when 'there is no rational view of the evidence that is consistent with the innocence of the accused' (the *Pfennig* test).[159]

The High Court's decision in *R v Hoch*[160] imposed a high threshold for admissibility where there is a possibility of collusion between victims: the judge should definitively exclude the possibility of collusion before evidence can be deemed cross-admissible. The Royal Commission found numerous examples of trials of NRCSA where joint trials were rejected in the past where a defendant (such as a schoolteacher or religious leader) was accused by multiple victims.[161] More recently, as in Ireland and England and Wales, the trend has been to move away from focussing on the possibility of collusion, (innocent) contamination or concoction between victims in any admissibility decision. In 2015, the NSW Supreme Court found that these issues are matters for the jury rather than the judge to decide, and in 2020, this was enacted in legislation.[162] This is a welcome reassertion of the jury's role as factfinder.

Focus on tendency evidence: Hughes v R

Judicial consideration of tendency (propensity) evidence has featured far more prominently in Australian case law than in Ireland or England and Wales. Today, many, if not most, Australian NRCSA trials will involve applications for either tendency or coincidence evidence or both.[163] The Royal Commission was highly critical of the law in this area, finding that there have been unjust outcomes in the form of unwarranted acquittals because of the exclusion of such evidence and that concerns about a high risk of unfair prejudice to the accused posed by such evidence were misplaced.[164] The complex considerations involved and the special nature of the federated Australian criminal justice system were brought to bear in the 2017 appeal of Robert Hughes, the TV star of the long-running sitcom *HeyDad!* (see Chapter 5). In 2014, Hughes was convicted of ten child sex offences including aggravated indecent assault and digital penetration of five girls, committed over 20 years earlier.[165] His appeals to the NSW Court of Criminal Appeal and the High Court of Australia concerned the probative value of evidence used to establish his tendencies to have 'a sexual interest in female children under 16 years of age' and use 'his social and familial relationships…to obtain access to female children under 16 years of age so that he could engage in sexual activities with them'.[166] The core question on appeal concerned the test of admissibility of various forms of sexual behaviours with three other girls, based on the evidence of women who were not victims at trial but who testified that Hughes had sexually touched or indecently exposed himself to them when they were children. This evidence was introduced to establish that Hughes repeatedly perpetrated CSA in the vicinity of other adults where there was a risk of him being detected. Hughes argued that the tendency evidence did not involve conduct that was sufficiently similar to the charges at hand to prove any relevant tendency. He relied on the Victorian Supreme Court's decision in *Velkoski v The Queen* that tendency evidence must possess 'sufficient common or similar features with the conduct in the charge in issue so as to demonstrate a pattern that cogently increases the likelihood of the occurrence of that conduct'.[167] The NSW Court of Criminal Appeal rejected the Victorian authority and thus the High Court was concerned with adjudicating the rulings of each state court, which differ substantially on this issue. The High Court favoured the NSW authority over the Victorian authority, but only by a slim margin. Hughes's appeal was dismissed with the ruling that the evidence admitted had significant probative value: the fact that Hughes expressed his 'sexual interest in underage girls in a variety of ways did not deprive proof of the tendency of its significant probative value'.[168]

Although *Hughes* resulted in conviction and a lengthy prison sentence, and appears to be of benefit to the prosecution of NRCSA, the Royal Commission criticized the ruling for not going far enough to characterize the aberrant or deviant nature of CSA.[169] It criticized the Court's finding that it was Hughes's tendency to commit child sexual abuse in particularly risky ways (in close proximity of other adults) that was deemed evidence of a tendency to a certain state of mind, rather than his sexual interest in girls. Feminist academics have also criticized the Court's reliance on subjective, lay interpretations of the psychology of child sex offenders, rather than the Diagnostic and Statistical Manual of Mental Disorders (DSM) which identifies all adult sexual interest in children as a mental disorder.[170] In a case like *Hughes*, they argue, what tendency evidence might be attempting to ascertain is an unprofessional 'diagnosis' of offending that is formulated within a society that apparently tolerates a great deal of sexual exploitation. The use of the DSM definition in the courts, if it were adopted, might make the question of the significant probative value of tendency evidence about child sex offences a much more straightforward and objective assessment.[171]

Reforms to the admissibility test

In 2020 NSW introduced legislation to reduce the threshold for adducing coincidence and tendency evidence from one requiring that that the probative value '*substantially* outweighs *any prejudicial effect* it may have on the defendant' to one requiring that the probative value '*outweighs the danger* of unfair prejudice to the defendant'.[172] This is a significant change to the admissibility threshold and arguably better reflects the empirical evidence on sexual offending against children, which suggests that general similarities, such as age and gender of the victim and his or her relationship with the offender may provide high comparative propensities and thus high probative value.[173]

NSW has also responded to the criticisms of *Hughes* by introducing a new provision that tendency evidence relating to the defendant's sexual interest in children (regardless of whether s/he has acted on it) is presumed to have significant probative value.[174] While the court retains discretion to decide that the evidence does not have such value,[175] the exercise of this discretion is limited. The Act sets out seven factors that are not to be taken into account by the court in exercising its discretion, including lapse of time, differences between the tendency evidence and the act(s) alleged in terms of the nature of the interest or act, or the circumstances in which each occurred and the personal characteristics (such as age, sex or gender) of the subject of the sexual interest or alleged act.[176] Victoria, Tasmania, the Australian Capital Territory and the Northern Territory have all agreed to implement similar amendments.[177] These reforms are an important example of lawmakers recognizing the probative value of evidence of a sexual interest in children. Most people are very unlikely to have such an interest or commit CSA. The likelihood of committing sexual abuse increases considerably for a person who is shown to have committed sexual abuse on another occasion,[178] and arguably the same is true for a person who is shown to have a sexual interest in children.

Conclusion

In reporting the crimes against them to the police, survivors in each country have rightly demanded that the criminal justice system deliver accountability and recognition. For survivors and their families, and for wider society, criminal prosecutions of NRCSA are an essential component of justice. NRCSA cases have forced prosecutors, the judiciary and in the case of Australia, legislators, to re-evaluate previously established rules and assumptions about victims, defendants and about the court process and the roles of judges and juries within it. The notion that some cases may be simply too old to try has been discarded in recognition of the overwhelming need for victims and the public to have abusers held to account and not benefit from the very domination that facilitated the abuse in the first place. In Ireland the courts struggled for a decade with protracted and retraumatizing pre-trial inquiries into the victim's reasons for delayed reporting. The courts used the notion of dominion to allow cases to proceed, but also created a hierarchy of victims and marginalized evidence relating to active silencing by adults when children in the past tried to report. The shift towards focussing on fairness arguments only is welcome and reflects a new commitment to taking NRCSA cases seriously. Similar approaches are seen in England and Wales and Australia, where the trial judge must make the assessment as to whether to stay the proceedings. There is now in all three countries a strong working presumption that the trial process is equipped to deal with the problems posed by delay. This shift is reflective of increased understanding of the importance of accountability and the effects of trauma on CSA victims.

The shift from automatic exclusion to greater trust in the judge's ability to evaluate any prejudice to the accused reflects a judicial recognition of the dynamics of CSA and is linked to a greater trust in the jury's ability to reason about the evidence in accordance with proper judicial directions. Courts have recalibrated evidential and procedural rules to better reflect the nature of much sexual offending against children. Courts (and parliaments) are increasingly confident that instead of excluding important evidence, the jury can consider evidence fairly and in a way that reflects the judge's directions. However, there is a lack of clarity in each country on the guidance given to trial judges on the interaction of delay warnings and corroboration warnings. In each country,[179] there is a clear risk that juries will be directed towards delay and scrutinizing (with the exception of Victoria in Australia) victims' credibility to an unnecessary degree, while not receiving adequate (or in the case of Ireland, any) direction on the real and legitimate reasons for that delay. This creates a situation in which survivors risk engaging with a trial in which the psychologically harmful effects of CSA, the societal denial of CSA and the legal system's historical suspicion of victims of sexual violence are all ignored by the judge and the jury.

The common law on the cross-admissibility of evidence of multiple victims is unnecessarily complex, and this has restricted a full consideration by courts of the probative value of such evidence. In Australia legislators have responded with statutory reforms aimed at relaxing the admissibility test for evidence of multiple victims, but this remains inconsistent across the country. The reforms aimed at increasing the admissibility of tendency evidence of a sexual interest in children is an example of a legislative initiative that reflects the reality that sexual interest in children is unusual and is highly probative. It is a progressive legal response to NRCSA that lawmakers in Ireland and in England and Wales would do well to study. However, gaps in knowledge about sex offending against children are hampering further legal reform. Further research by scholars and practitioners of law and of psychology is needed to identify the logical inferences that may be made by a jury in NRCSA trials. Questions that might arise include: are there particular *facts* (not stereotypical assumptions) about people who abuse children *in general* that may influence how a juror can or should reason about the evidence of multiple victims?[180] Could increased use of expert evidence on the likelihood of reoffending help? Without research into these key areas, it will be difficult for legislators to coherently reform this area.

In short then, the criminal law has shown itself to be ambivalent about NRCSA cases. While delayed reporting is no longer a reason to stop a trial from proceeding, courts in all three countries have a long way to go to improve guidance for judges and juries on how to treat evidence of delay and evidence of multiple victims. The next two chapters explore another key avenue for accountability and justice for NRCSA survivors, one that may be more attractive to survivors for a range of reasons: civil litigation.

Notes

1 Exceptions to this are explored below.

2 In England and Wales, the War Crimes Act 1991 allowed the prosecution and conviction of a man in 1997 on two sample counts of murder in Belorussia in 1942: *R v Sawoniuk* (2000) 2 Cr App R 220 (CA).

3 S. Kilcommins, "The Victim in Law; The Emergence of a New Juridical Subject in the Crime Conflict" *Criminal Law and Practice Review* 2(1), 2018, 53–68.

4 Each jurisdiction operates the common law adversarial criminal trial, in which the prosecution and the defence present competing narratives about past events. The judge rules on questions of law and procedure such as whether the prospective trial will be fair, the admissibility of evidence, whether a particular defence can be raised and directs the jury on how to reason about the evidence. The jury is the factfinder. It must reason about the evidence in light of the judge's directions and make the decision as to guilt or innocence.

5 Attrition in NRCSA cases is vastly understudied. For a rare example, see K. Chenier, et al., "'Cold Feet': The Attrition of Historic Child Sexual Abuse Cases Reported to the Police in a Northern Canadian Territory" *Child Abuse and Neglect* 2021, 105206, doi: 10.1016/j.chiabu.2021.105206.

6 See *R v Walker and Coatman* [2017] EWCA Crim 392.

7 CPS, *Child Sexual Abuse: Guidelines on Prosecuting Cases of Child Sexual Abuse* (2018), <https://www.cps.gov.uk/legal-guidance/child-sexual-abuse-guidelines-prosecuting-cases-child-sexual-abuse>; *CPS Guidance on Rape and Sexual Offences* (2021), <https://www.cps.gov.uk/legal-guidance/rape-and-sexual-offences-overview-and-index-2021-updated-guidance>.

8 S. Ring "The Victim of Historical Child Sexual Abuse in teh IRish Courts 1999–2006' *Social and Legal Studies* 26(5), 562–80.

9 S. Mulla 'Facing Victims: Forensics, Visual Technologies, and Sexual Assault Examination' Medical Anthropology: *Cross Cultural Studies in Health and Illness* 30(3), 2011, 271–94.

10 Such as the EU Victims' Directive which treats anyone who reports a crime to the police/gardaí as a victim.

11 J.D. Brown, et al., *Only a Witness. The Experiences of Clients of One in Four in the Criminal Justice System* (Dublin: One in Four, 2016).

12 Ibid.

13 G.M. Winters, et al., "Why Do Child Sexual Abuse Victims Not Tell Anyone about Their Abuse? An Exploration of Factors that Prevent and Promote Disclosure" *Behavioral Sciences and the Law* 38(6), 2020, 568–611, 601.

14 s6(1) to deal with this problem in NRCSA prosecutions decades later, it became common practice to charge such offences as indecent assault on a female under s14 SOA 1956. The House of Lords applied the brakes in 2004 in *R v J* [2004] UKHL 42.

15 And a 12-month limitation period for unlawful carnal knowledge of a female with an intellectual disability: s4. This was repealed by s14 Criminal Law (Sexual Offences) Act 1993.

16 see s8 Criminal Law (Sexual Offences) Act 2006 and Schedule.

17 For example, s78 *Crimes Act 1900 (NSW):* No prosecution in respect of any offence under ss 71, 72 or 76 shall, if the girl in question was at the time of the alleged offence over the age of 14 years and under the age of 16 years, be commenced after the expiration of 12 months from the time of the alleged offence.

18 P. Collins, MP, *Criminal Legislation (Amendment) Bill 1992 Second Reading*. Hansard 25 February 1992, <https://www.parliament.nsw.gov.au/Hansard/Pages/HansardResult.aspx#/docid/HANSARD-1323879322-89251>.

19 P. Roberts, "Theorising Procedural Tradition: Subjects, Objects and Values in Criminal Adjudication" in R.A. Duff, et al. (eds), *The Trial on Trial. Volume Two. Judgment and Calling to Account* (Oxford: Hart, 2006).

20 s80 Australian Constitution; Article 38.1 Constitution of Ireland.

21 European Convention on Human Rights Act 2003 (Ireland); Human Rights Act 1998 (England and Wales); International Covenant on Civil and Political Rights, Article 14 which binds all three countries.

22 In each jurisdiction, an elderly defendant may also argue, separately, that they cannot face trial because they are unfit to plead due to their ill-health or reduced cognitive capacity. One high-profile example of this was the Australian trial involving former Marist Brother, Kostka Chute and his abuse of children in his role of high school teacher in the 1970s and 1980s. In 2019, he faced 16 charges of NRCSA offences committed between 1979 and 1986 after he had already served six years in prison for similar offences committed earlier. Chute's lawyers successfully argued that the 87-year-old was not fit to participate in the trial due to his Parkinson's disease and dementia. Despite the impossibility of a trial, a special hearing was held in front of a judge 'to determine the evidence about the charges'. Mossop J accepted that 14 of the 16 counts had occurred beyond a reasonable doubt, providing some form of accountability, but this is not equivalent to a conviction. Chute continues to reside in a nursing home. *ABC News*, 28 March 2019.

23 These were formally expressed in the legal concepts of corroboration and the doctrine of recent complaint.

24 *Australian Law Reform Commission, Family Violence—A National Legal Response,* para.26.38; J. Goodman-Delahunty, et al., "What Australian Jurors Know and Do Not Know about Evidence of Child Sexual Abuse" *Criminal Law Journal* 41, 2017, 86; A. Cossins, "The Future of Joint Trials of Sex Offences After Hughes: Resolving Judicial Fears and Jurisdictional Tensions with Evidence-Based Decision-Making" *Melbourne University Law Review* 41(3), 2018, 2–18.

25 D. Hamer, "Submission to The Royal Commission into Institutional Responses to Child Sexual Abuse," October 28, 2016, available at <https://www.childabuseroyalcommission.gov.au/sites/default/files/file-list/Consultation%20Paper%20-%20Criminal%20Justice%20-%20Submission%20-%2055%20Prof%20David%20Hamer.pdf>.

26 See K. Pezdek, et al., "Interviewing Witnesses: The Effect of Forced Confabulation on Event Memory" *Law and Human Behaviour* 31(5), 2007, 463–78.

27 *R v S (SP)* [2006] EWCA Crim 756; *AG's Reference No.1 of 1990* [1992] QBD 630.

28 The prosecution can appeal a stay. *K., B. and A.* [2007] EWCA Crim 971.

29 *AG's Reference (No. 1 of 1990)* [1992] Q.B. 630.

30 *R v Telford JJ ex parte Badhan* [1991] 2 QB 78; *R v JAK* 1992] Crim LR 31.

31 After serving a five-year sentence, MacKreth sought leave to appeal his conviction but died a week later. His daughter was then authorized to continue the application.

32 [2009] EWCA Crim 1849.

33 Ibid., [39].

34 Ibid., [62]. MacKreth also claimed the jury had not been informed that the motivation for some victims was likely to have been to obtain compensation. The Court dismissed this also on the basis that jurors would have presumed that survivors would have been eligible.

35 [2011] EWCA Crim 1844. See *R v D* [2013 EWCA Crim 1592.

36 *R v F(S)* [2011] EWCA Crim 1844.

37 Since *Smolinski* [2004] EWCA Crim 1270.

38 R. Jory and S. Jones, "The Aged Accused," *Counsel*, November, 2016, <https://www.counselmagazine.co.uk/articles/the-aged-accused>.

39 Bizarrely, in 2016, the DPP was forced to remind Chief Constables not to present 'CPS lawyers with endless files of evidence on dead suspects', highlighting Operation Hydrant's identification of 286 deceased individuals. *The Independent,* 13 May 2016.

40 *The Daily Mail*, 9 May 2016.

41 [2011] EWCA Crim 74 [26].

42 *R v Joynson* [2008] EWCA Crim 304 [30].

43 N. Hickman, "Logic and Experience" *Criminal Law Review* 8, 2020, 6.

44 *R v H* [2020] EWCA Crim 1247.

45 *R v PS* [2013] EWCA Crim 992, [35].

46 [2019] EWCA Crim 1225. See also *R v RD* [2013] EWCA Crim 1592.

47 *R v D* [2008] EWCA Crim 2557.

48 *Breeze* [2009] EWCA Crim 255. Criminal Procedure Rules r .25.14.

49 Crown Court Compendium (London: Judicial College, 2020), <https://www.judiciary.uk/publications/crown-court-compendium-published/>.

50 See *R v Miller* [2011] Crim LR 79; *GJB v The Queen* [2011] EWCA Crim 867. F. Gerry and C. Sjolin, "Rape Trauma Direction" (2017), counselmagazine.co.uk, <https://www.counselmagazine.co.uk/articles/rapetrauma-direction> (accessed 21 September 2020). If such evidence is given, appropriate directions must be given. Complaints may have been made at some point earlier in time to a friend or a family member or a teacher. There may be records of such complaints. This hearsay evidence may be adduced to establish consistency or inconsistency, to rebut a suggestion of recent fabrication or to refresh a memory. Changes to the rules of evidence in 2003 have relaxed the requirements around the admissibility of this evidence. s120 Criminal Justice Act 2003.

51 Rule 3.21(4)(a) Criminal Procedure Rules 2020.

52 *R v H* [2011] EWCA Crim 2344.

53 s101(1)(d). See D. Ormerod, et al., "Bad Character Provisions and Their Application to Sexual Offences" in P. Radcliffe et al. (eds), *Witness Testimony in Sexual Cases* (Oxford: Oxford University Press, 2016), 89.

54 *DPP v P(P)* [1991] 2 AC 447.

55 [2008] EWCA Crim 1863.

56 Although the jury should be warned, it has to reach a verdict on each count separately.

57 R. Munday, *Evidence* (Oxford: Oxford University Press, 2017), [7.89].

58 *R v Richards* [2018] EWCA Crim 2374.

59 Crown Court Compendium op. cit., [13.9].

60 https://www.cps.gov.uk/wessex/news/ex-youth-football-CofAch-jailed-over-24-years-abusing-boys

61 *R v H* (1995) 2 AC 596.

62 C. Tapper, "The Erosion of *Boardman v DPP*" *New Law Journal* 145(6708), 1995, 1223 and *New Law Journal* 145(6709), 1995, 1263; A. Keane, "Is There a Weakness in the Current Law on 'Similar Fact Evidence'?", Memorandum 32, House of Commons Home Affairs Committee, *The Conduct of Investigations into Past Cases of Abuse in Children's Homes,* Fourth Report of Session (2001–2002), H.C. 836, October 31, 2, 2002, 66–7.

63 *R v NH* [2011] EWCA Crim 730.

64 s107 CJA 2003.

65 There is no specific offence of child sexual abuse in Irish law despite the recommendation of the Law Reform Commission to this effect. See Chapter 4.

66 A worldwide Catholic male religious congregation founded in Ireland by Edmund Rice in 1802. Their curriculum, which included an explicitly Catholic and patriotic emphasis, shaped Ireland's national identity pre- and post-Independence.

67 The prosecutions are not connected to the work of the CICA; unlike the Royal Commission or the IICSA, it did not generally engage in police referrals (see Chapter 10).

68 Article 38.1 Constitution of Ireland; *The State (Healy) v Donoghue* [1976] 1 IR 325; *The State (O'Connell) v Fawsitt* [1986] IR 362.

69 *People (DPP) v Synott* (29 May 1992, unreported), Court of Criminal Appeal.

70 G. Hogan and G. Whyte, *Kelly: The Irish Constitution, 4th ed.* (Dublin: Butterworths, 2003), 1155.

71 Prohibition applications are made by judicial review to the High Court.

72 Supreme Court [Senior Courts] Act 1981, s19(3); *R v DPP ex p Kebilene* [2002] 2 AC 326.

73 *PO'C v DPP* [1999] 2 IR 25.

74 S. Ring, "Beyond the Reach of Justice? Victim Delay in Historic Child Sexual Abuse Cases and the Right to a Fair Trial" *Judicial Studies Institute Journal* 2, 2009, 162–203.

75 Ring op. cit., 2017.

76 [2006] 3 I.R. 575.

77 *PT v DPP* [2008] 1 IR 701. Trials may also be halted due to the 'totality of the circumstances': *JM v DPP* [2004] IESC 47, and *DD v DPP* [2008] IESC 47; *JD v DPP* [2009] IEHC 48; *PT v DPP* [2008] 1 I.R. 78; *MC v DPP* [2011] IEHC 378 at para 6.7.

78 [2021] IEHC 564; *MS v DPP* [2015] IEHC 84; *PH v DPP* [2018] IEHC 329.

79 *SO'C v DPP* [2014] IECH 65

80 [2018] IEHC 329.
81 *AT v DPP* [2020] IECA 6.
82 *NS v DPP* [2019] IEHC 671; *Nash v DPP* [2015] IESC 32. *RB v DPP* [2019] IECA 48.
83 *DPP v C.C.* [2019] IESC 94. See also *SB v DPP* [2006] IESC 67.
84 Clarke C.J., [9.2]–[9.5]. McMenamin J. and O'Malley J. and O'Donnell J. agreed on this approach.
85 [9.2].
86 at [9.4].
87 *X v DPP* [2020] IECA 4.
88 Ibid., [40].
89 G. McLoughlin-Burke, "The Effect of Delay in Cases of Historic Child Sexual Abuse" *Irish Criminal Law Journal* 29(2), 2019, 260.
90 CC 2019 op. cit., [44] (O'Donnell J.).
91 *People (DPP) v EC* [2006] IECCA 69.
92 *People (DPP) v RB* (12 February 2003, unreported), Court of Criminal Appeal. Approved in *DPP v Walsh* [2010] IECCA 80; *People (DPP) v PJ* [2003] 3 IR 550; *People (DPP) v CC* [2006] 4 IR 287; *DW v DPP* [2003] IESC 54.
93 *DPP v TG* 2020 at [30]; *The People (DPP) v MS* [2019] IECA 120.
94 *DPP v TG* [2020] IECA 26.
95 S. Leahy, "The Corroboration Warning in Sexual Offence Trials: Final Vestige of the Historic Suspicion of Sexual Offence Victims or a Necessary Protection for Defendants?" *International Journal of Evidence and Proof* 18(1), 2014, 41–64.
96 See *DPP v TOD* [2017] IECA 160.
97 P. Charleton and S. Byrne, "Sexual Violence Witnesses and Suspects: A Debating Document" *Irish Journal of Legal Studies* 1, 2010, 1–25, 13, 24.
98 A.-M. Lawlor, "Joint Trials Involving Multiple Victims in Sexual Cases" 18th Annual national prosecutors Conference, 26 November 2017, Dublin Castle, <https://www.dppireland.ie/app/uploads/2017/11/PAPER_-_Anne-Marie_Lawlor.pdf>. In O'Malley's study published in 2013, the majority of cases involved more than one victim. T. O'Malley, *Sexual Offences. Law Policy and Punishment, 2nd Edition* (Dublin: Round Hall, 2013). 2013), [26–09].
99 Ibid.
100 s6(3) Criminal Justice (Administration) Act 1924.
101 *DPP v P(P)* [1991] 2 AC 447.
102 *B v DPP* [1997] 3 IR 140.
103 *People (DPP) v BK* [2000] 2 IR 199; followed in *People (DPP) v Nevin* [2003] 3 IR 321.
104 *People (DPP) v BK* [2000] 2 IR 199, 203 (Barron J).
105 Ibid., 211.
106 *DPP v DO'S* [2004] IECCA 23.
107 *People (DPP) v EC* [2007] 1 IR 749.
108 *DPP v ST* [2017] IECA 73.
109 *People (DPP) v SL* [2020] IECA 129. See also *NR v DPP* [2018] IECA 20.
110 *People (DPP) v AR* [2019] IECA 229.
111 *The People (DPP) v MS* [2019] IECA 120.
112 *DPP v McG* [2012] IECA 98.
113 *DPP v JMcG* [2020] IECA 160; *People (DPP) v LG* [2003] 2 IR 517.
114 *People (DPP) v McCurdy* [2012] IECCA 76; *DPP v M(L)* [2015] IECA 82.

115 *DPP v CC (No 2)* [2012] IECCA 86.
116 Ibid., [38].
117 *CC* 2019.
118 J. Cashmore et al., *The Impact of Delayed Reporting on the Prosecution and Outcomes of Child Sexual Abuse Cases* (Australian Royal Commission Into Institutional Responses to Child Sexual Abuse, 2016), 20.
119 Ibid.
120 Ibid.
121 *Criminal Law Consolidation Act Amendment Act 1985 (SA).*
122 *Criminal Legislation (Amendment) Act 1992* (NSW) sch 1, cl 5. See Royal Commission into Institutional Responses to Child Sexual Abuse, *Criminal Justice Report Parts III-VI*, 2017, 122–23.
123 *R v RL (No 2)* [2016] NSWDC 182. See Royal Commission, *Criminal Justice Report Parts III-VI*, 127–28.
124 Ibid., p. 127.
125 *Criminal Law Consolidation Act (Abolition of Time Limit for Prosecution of Certain Sexual Offences) Amendment Act* 2003, (SA), providing (s72A) that 'any immunity from prosecution arising from the time limit imposed by the former [section of the Act] is abolished'. In 2014, Victoria introduced similar provisions. *Crimes Amendment (Sexual Offences and Other Matters) Act 2014* (Vic).
126 NSW Government, "New Legislation to Strengthen Child Sexual Abuse Laws. Factsheet for Service Providers" *Media Release,* December 2018, <https://www.justice.nsw.gov.au/Documents/Media%20Releases/2018/new-legilsation-strengthen-child-sexual-abuse-laws-factheet-serivce-providers.pdf>.
127 *Jago v District Court (NSW)* (1989) 168 CLR 23; *Glossop* [2001] NSWCCA 165.
128 *Jago* [60–1] (Deane J).
129 See P. Lewis, *Delayed Prosecution for Childhood Sexual Abuse* (Oxford: Oxford University Press, 2006), 64.
130 D. Dalton, "The Importance of the Pre-trial Application and the Vagaries in the Subsequent Appeal Process," 19 February 2014, <Public Defenders.nsw.gov.au>.
131 D. Hamer, "Trying Delays: Forensic Disadvantage in Child Sexual Assault Trials" *Criminal Law Review* 9, 2010, 671–93.
132 *Longman v The Queen* (1989) 168 CLR 79.
133 Australian Law Reform Commission, *Family Violence-A National Legal Response* (Canberra: Commonwealth of Australia, 2010), 1317.
134 A. Cossins, "Time Out for Longman: Myths, Science and the Common Law" *Melbourne Law Review* 34(1), 2010, 69–105.
135 *R v BWT* (2002) 54 NSWLR 241.Original emphasis.
136 Australian Law Reform Commission op. cit., 1317–18.
137 Ibid.
138 A. Cossins, "The Future of Joint Trials of Sex Offences after *Hughes*: Resolving Judicial Fears and Jurisdictional Tensions with Evidence-Based Decision-Making" *Melbourne University Law Review* 41(3), 2018, 1121– 59.
139 Western Australia and Queensland do not subscribe to the Uniform Evidence Act (UEA), although Queensland adopts some of its provisions. The *Longman* warning is still used in WA: *State of Western Australia v JGB* [2020] WADC 100. Queensland mitigates it with amendments based on the UAE: s 132BA *Criminal Code (Child Sexual Offences Reform) and Other Legislation Amendment Act 2020* (QLD). See also s 34CB *Evidence Act 1929* (SA); s165b (2) *Evidence Amendment*

Act (2007) No. 46 (NSW); *Evidence Amendment Act* (No 46) 2010 (TAS); *Evidence Act* 2008 (Vic); s165(b) *Evidence (National Uniform legislation) Act 2011 (NT)*.The UEA also includes model amendments in the *Evidence Amendment (Professional Confidential Relationship Privilege) Bill* and amendments in the *Uniform Evidence Law (Tendency and Coincidence) Model Provisions 2019* agreed to by the Council of Attorneys-General on 29 November 2019, <https://www.pcc.gov.au/uniform/2019/Evidence_Model_Bill_Nov-2019.pdf>.

140 *GG v The Queen* (2010) 79 NSWLR 194, 53.

141 S165B(2). The judge need not comply with (2) if there are good reasons for not doing so: (3).

142 s165B(6).

143 S165B(7).

144 *W v R* [2014] NSWCCA 110, 125.

145 C. Maxwell and G. Byrne, “Making Trials Work for Juries: Pathways to Simplification” *Criminal Law Review* 11, 2020, 1034–56; M. Weinberg, “Jury Direction – An Antipodean Experiment” *Amicus Curiae* 2016(107), 2019, 2–8.

146 Maxwell and Byrne op. cit., 1034–56.

147 s51(2).

148 s51(1).

149 S52, *Jury Direction Act 2015 (Vic)*.

150 S54D *Jury Direction Act 2015 (Vic) and s293A Criminal Procedure Act 1986 (NSW)*.

151 Australian Law Reform Commission, op. cit., 1324; *Crofts v The Queen* (1996) 186 CLR 427.

152 S54 *Jury Directions Act 2015* (Vic) abolishes the rule in *Croft*.

153 Royal Commission, Criminal Justice Report Parts III-VI, 411.

154 Joint trials are run at the court’s discretion. The threshold for ordering joint trials is the ‘cross-admissibility’ of different victims’ evidence, when considering the importance of not subjecting the accused to prejudice. Trials for all sex offences are held to a particularly high standard because the possibility of prejudice is viewed as extreme. *De Jesus v R* [1986] HCA 65.

155 T. Gartelmann and C. Berrigan, “Tendency, Coincidence and Joint Trials” in Public Defenders Conference, March 17, (2018), 2, <http://www.publicdefenders.nsw.gov.au/Documents/Tendency%20Coincidence%20and%20Joint%20Trials%20-%20Gartelmann.pdf>.

156 See Chapter 5.

157 Uniform Evidence Law, ss97, 98.

158 See Cossins op cit.

159 Royal Commission, *Criminal Justice Report Parts III-VI* p.418. *Pfennig v R* [1995] HCA 7, confirmed in *Phillips v The Queen* [2006] 225 CLR 303.

160 [1988] 165 292.

161 See, for example, the case of Father Dennis Maguire: *R v John Dennis Maguire* [2015] NSWDC No. 2013/295587, discussed in Royal Commission into Institutional Responses to Child Sexual Abuse, *Criminal Justice Report Parts III-VI*, (2017) 432–34.

162 s94(5) Evidence Act 1995, as inserted by Evidence Amendment (Tendency and Coincidence) Act 2020 No 8 (NSW).

163 P. McGrath, “Tendency and Coincidence Evidence.” Tendency and Coincidence Evidence NSW Legal Aid Conference, July 2017.

164 Royal Commission, Criminal Justice Report Parts III-VI, 652–66.
165 *Hughes v R* [2015] NSWCCA 330.
166 *Hughes v The Queen* [2017] HCA 20 14 June 2017 S226/2016, 3.
167 *Velkoski v The Queen* (2014) 45 VR 680, 3.
168 *Hughes v The Queen*, 63.
169 Royal Commission, Criminal Justice Report Parts III-VI, 652–66.
170 Cossins (2018) op. cit.
171 Ibid.
172 s101(2) *Evidence Act 1995* as amended by the *Evidence Amendment (Tendency and Coincidence) Act 2020 (NSW)*. The Act also clarifies that coincidence evidence concerning two victims of a single perpetrator is capable of being adduced by way of the normal process for adducing coincidence evidence in s98.
173 D. Hamer, "Proof of Serial Child Sexual Abuse" in T. Crofts and A. Loughnan (eds), *Criminalisation and Criminal Responsibility in Australia* (Oxford: Oxford University Press, 2015), 242, 255–57.
174 s97A *Evidence Act 1995* as amended by s2 Evidence Amendment (Tendency and Coincidence) Act 2020 (NSW).
175 s 97A(4).
176 s97A *Evidence Act 1995* as amended by s2 of the 2020 Act.
177 Hamer welcomes the relaxation of admissibility but also notes that the admissibility test should be further simplified. See D. Hamer, "Propensity Evidence Reform," *Queensland Legal Yearbook 2019* (Brisbane: Supreme Court Library Queensland, 2020), 102–24.
178 See discussion of previous offences by Hamer, Ibid., 118–19.
179 But see reforms in Victoria and NSW.
180 For example, see New South Wales legislation.

References

Australian Law Reform Commission, *Family Violence-A National Legal Response* (Canberra: Commonwealth of Australia, 2010).

Brown, J.D., et al., *Only a Witness. The Experiences of Clients of One in Four in the Criminal Justice System* (Dublin: One in Four, 2016).

Cashmore, J. et al., *The Impact of Delayed Reporting on the Prosecution and Outcomes of Child Sexual Abuse Cases* (Australian Royal Commission Into Institutional Responses to Child Sexual Abuse, 2016).

Charleton, P. and Byrne, S., "Sexual Violence Witnesses and Suspects: A Debating Document" *Irish Journal of Legal Studies* 1, 2010, 1–25.

Chenier, K., et al., "'Cold Feet': The Attrition of Historic Child Sexual Abuse Cases Reported to the Police in a Northern Canadian Territory" *Child Abuse and Neglect* 2021, 105206, doi: 10.1016/j.chiabu.2021.105206.

Cossins, A., "Time Out for Longman: Myths, Science and the Common Law" *Melbourne Law Review* 34(1), 2010, 69–105.

Cossins, A., "The Future of Joint Trials of Sex Offences After Hughes: Resolving Judicial Fears and Jurisdictional Tensions with Evidence-Based Decision-Making" *Melbourne University Law Review* 41(3), 2018, 2–18; 1121–59.

Crown Court Compendium (London: Judicial College, 2020), <https://www.judiciary.uk/publications/crown-court-compendium-published/>

Gartelmann, T. and Berrigan, C., "Tendency, Coincidence and Joint Trials" in Public Defenders Conference, March 17, (2018), 2, <http://www.publicdefenders.nsw.gov.au/Documents/Tendency%20Coincidence%20and%20Joint%20Trials%20-%20Gartelmann.pdf>

Gerry, F. and Sjolin, C., "Rape Trauma Direction" (2017), counselmagazine.co.uk, <https://www.counselmagazine.co.uk/articles/rapetrauma-direction>

Goodman-Delahunty, J., et al., "What Australian Jurors Know and Do Not Know about Evidence of Child Sexual Abuse" *Criminal Law Journal* 41, 2017, 86.

Hamer, D., "Trying Delays: Forensic Disadvantage in Child Sexual Assault Trials" *Criminal Law Review* 9, 2010, 671–93.

Hamer, D., "Proof of Serial Child Sexual Abuse" in T. Crofts and A. Loughnan (eds), *Criminalisation and Criminal Responsibility in Australia* (Oxford: Oxford University Press, 2015) 242, 255–57.

Hamer, D. "Submission to The Royal Commission into Institutional Responses to Child Sexual Abuse," October 28, 2016, www.childabuseroyalcommission.gov.au/sites/default/files/file-list/Consultation%20Paper%20-%20Criminal%20Justice%20-%20Submission%20-%2055%20Prof%20David%20Hamer.pdf

Hamer, D., "Propensity Evidence Reform," *Queensland Legal Yearbook 2019* (Brisbane: Supreme Court Library Queensland, 2020), 102–24.

Hickman, N., "Logic and Experience" *Criminal Law Review* 8, 2020, 6.

Hogan, G. and Whyte, G., *Kelly: The Irish Constitution, 4th ed.* (Dublin: Butterworths, 2003).

Jory, R. and Jones, S., "The Aged Accused," *Counsel*, November, 2016, www.counselmagazine.co.uk/articles/the-aged-accused.

Keane, A., "Is There a Weakness in the Current Law on 'Similar Fact Evidence'?", Memorandum 32, House of Commons Home Affairs Committee, *The Conduct of Investigations into Past Cases of Abuse in Children's Homes,* Fourth Report of Session (2001–2002), H.C. 836, October 31, 2, 2002, 66–7

Kilcommins, S., "The Victim in Law; The Emergence of a New Juridical Subject in the Crime Conflict" *Criminal Law and Practice Review* 2(1), 2018, 53–68.

Lawlor, A.-M., "Joint Trials Involving Multiple Victims in Sexual Cases" 18th Annual national prosecutors Conference, 26 November 2017, Dublin Castle, www.dppireland.ie/app/uploads/2017/11/PAPER_-_Anne-Marie_Lawlor.pdf

Leahy, S., "The Corroboration Warning in Sexual Offence Trials: Final Vestige of the Historic Suspicion of Sexual Offence Victims or a Necessary Protection for Defendants?" *International Journal of Evidence and Proof* 18(1), 2014, 41–64.

Lewis, P., *Delayed Prosecution for Childhood Sexual Abuse* (Oxford: Oxford University Press, 2006).

Maxwell, C. and Byrne, G., "Making Trials Work for Juries: Pathways to Simplification" *Criminal Law Review* 11, 2020, 1034–56.

McGrath, P., "'Tendency and Coincidence Evidence" Tendency and Coincidence Evidence NSW Legal Aid Conference, July 2017.

McLoughlin-Burke, G., "The Effect of Delay in Cases of Historic Child Sexual Abuse" *Irish Criminal Law Journal* 29(2), 2019, 26–38.

Mulla, S., "Facing Victims: Forensics, Visual Technologies, and Sexual Assault Examination" *Medical Anthropology: Cross-Cultural Studies in Health and Illness* 30 (3), 2011, 271–94.

Munday, R., *Evidence* (Oxford: Oxford University Press, 2017).

NSW Government, "New Legislation to Strengthen Child Sexual Abuse Laws. Factsheet for Service Providers" *Media Release,* December 2018, https://www.justice.nsw.gov.au/Documents/Media%20Releases/2018/new-legilsation-strengthen-child-sexual-abuse-laws-factheet-serivce-providers.pdf

O'Malley, T., *Sexual Offences. Law Policy and Punishment, 2nd Edition* (Dublin: Round Hall, 2013).

Ormerod, D., et al., "Bad Character Provisions and Their Application to Sexual Offences" in P. Radcliffe et al. (eds), *Witness Testimony in Sexual Cases* (Oxford: Oxford University Press, 2016), 89.

Pezdek, K., et al., "Interviewing Witnesses: The Effect of Forced Confabulation on Event Memory" *Law and Human Behaviour* 31(5), 2007, 463–78.

Ring, S., "Beyond the Reach of Justice? Victim Delay in Historic Child Sexual Abuse Cases and the Right to a Fair Trial" *Judicial Studies Institute Journal* 2, 2009, 162–203.

Ring, S., "The Victim of Historical Child Sexual Abuse in the Irish Courts 1999–2006" *Social and Legal Studies* 26(5), 2017, 562–80.

Roberts, P., "Theorising Procedural Tradition: Subjects, Objects and Values in Criminal Adjudication" in R.A. Duff, et al. (eds), *The Trial on Trial. Volume Two. Judgement and Calling to Account* (Oxford: Hart: 2006), 37–64.

Royal Commission, Criminal Justice Report Parts III-VI.

Tapper, C., "The Erosion of *Boardman v DPP*" *New Law Journal* 145(6708), 1995, 1223.

Weinberg, W., "Jury Direction – An Antipodean Experiment" *Amicus Curiae* 2016(107), 2019, 2–8.

Winters, G.M., et al. "Why Do Child Sexual Abuse Victims Not Tell Anyone about Their Abuse? An Exploration of Factors that Prevent and Promote Disclosure" *Behavioral Sciences and the Law* 38(6), 2020, 568–611.

8 Tort law

Statutes of limitation

Introduction

Non-recent child sexual abuse (NRCSA) survivors may turn to litigation as an alternative to or in addition to making a criminal complaint to the police.[1] By commencing civil proceedings an NRCSA survivor is engaging with private law, specifically tort law. A 'tort' is a civil wrong for which the law provides a remedy and may be contrasted with a 'crime' in public law. Like criminal prosecutions, litigation, if successful, offers survivors public recognition of the individual abuser's wrongdoing and the harms caused by it.[2] But it is a different kind of recognition to that offered by criminal process. In tort claims, unlike in criminal prosecutions where the prosecution decides how to prosecute the case, survivors and their lawyers are responsible for determining the issues to be resolved and the conduct of the litigation. Litigation offers a degree of agency to survivors, whose agency might have been threatened or compromised by the abuse itself.[3] Litigation also offers survivors a clearer route to accountability than the criminal process; in each of the three countries the standard of proof is lower than in the criminal context and the issues are tried by a judge not a jury.[4] Litigation may be brought against any individual abuser, including parents, siblings, extended family members, teachers, priests, bus drivers, sports coaches and so on. As Chapter 9 explores, litigation also offers survivors the possibility of holding a private organization to account for the sexual abuse perpetrated on them by an individual associated with the organization. Survivors can also sue public bodies such as local authorities or government departments for their failures to protect children. Holding a (public or private) organization to account for NRCSA is generally not possible in the criminal justice system.

In tort law the person who suffered the wrong (the 'plaintiff' in Ireland and Australia, or 'claimant' in England and Wales) is seeking a finding of liability and an award of compensation against the defendant (or 'respondent' in Australia).[5] A survivor can sue an individual perpetrator and/or an organization associated with the abuser, such as the bishop of a diocese or the school that employed the abuser. In a civil case the plaintiff must prove on the balance of probabilities that the defendant caused their injuries and that

DOI: 10.4324/9780429468162-10

they did so intentionally or negligently.[6] If the plaintiff is successful they are entitled to monetary compensation from the defendant. Compensation or 'damages' aim to (at least try to) restore the plaintiff to the position in which they would have been had they not suffered the wrong. If a claim is successful damages may be awarded to the plaintiff. Crucially, the fact that the abuser (or the organization associated with the abuser, or the state) is ordered to pay compensation is an important expression of accountability. General damages may be awarded to the claimant/plaintiff for a recognizable physical or psychological injury, temporary or permanent, as determined by psychiatric expert reports. Special damages may be awarded for specific losses, such as medical costs, counselling/psychotherapy, loss of earnings (past and future) caused by the abuse's impact on the person's education, impaired ability to form relationships or decreased employability. Aggravated damages may be awarded where the defendant's actions caused the plaintiff to suffer to an even greater degree than would be expected.[7] A court may also award punitive exemplary damages for what the court views as particularly outrageous conduct and to deter others. While the calculation of damages is artificial (it is impossible for a court to quantify the impact of sexual abuse on a person over a lifetime), it does offer survivors a form of symbolic recognition that reflects their status as a full legal subject and the varied and enduring harms of CSA. This is something that the criminal process, which focusses on punishment of the abuser,[8] cannot offer.

Bringing a claim also involves considerable drawbacks. The process may be adversarial and stressful for the survivor and their family, costly, lengthy and potentially re-traumatizing.[9] As with the criminal process, the survivor will have to face being cross-examined by the alleged abuser's lawyers. If the plaintiff loses, the court may hold them liable to pay the defendant's costs, which could have a devastating impact on their recovery and financial health. For many NRCSA survivors, suing in tort is simply not an option because the person (or their estate if they are deceased) or the organization they wish to sue has no means, property or insurance that could meet an award of damages.

In this chapter and in Chapter 9, we examine two barriers to civil justice for NRCSA survivors who wish to engage tort law: statutes of limitation and doctrinal frameworks for suing organizations. We have selected these two issues because they are of key importance in NRCSA litigation and they shape legal practice both in and outside the courtroom; a defendant's willingness to settle a case out of court or decision to contest it in court is informed by the state of the law on each of these issues. They are also areas where the legislatures can effectively intervene to improve the tort law response to NRCSA survivors. The discussion in this chapter is part of a much larger context that is ripe for further study. Many other procedural and doctrinal issues shape tort law's response to NRCSA. These include: whether multiple survivors can sue as a group, the legal status of apologies in the tort system, the applicability of insurance indemnities, how to calculate damages and the role of expert evidence.[10] Most importantly, many NRCSA claims settle out of court.[11]

Statutes of limitation

Tort law has developed over centuries in ignorance of the interests of people subjected to sexual and domestic violence.[12] The most obvious example of tort law's deafness to the needs of CSA victims is statutes of limitation. Survivors who commence proceedings for damages incurred from NRCSA risk the defendant(s) arguing the claim is barred by the statute of limitation. Statutes of limitation are legislation that stipulate specific 'limitation periods' within which civil proceedings must be commenced. If the plaintiff does not act within this period, the claim will not be allowed to proceed to a full hearing. In other words, statutes of limitation restrict access to civil justice. The policy rationales offered for them are: that each potential defendant (and, in the case of organizations, their insurer) is entitled at some point to certainty about their exposure to litigation; that it would be unfair for a person/organization to be sued many years after a wrongful act where the plaintiff has delayed in acting and that the evidentiary difficulties involved may impede a just outcome.

Statutes of limitation are of central importance in NRCSA litigation because the typical plaintiff commences proceedings many years, often decades, after the alleged sexual abuse. As the Introduction to this Part explained, there are multiple, sometimes overlapping, reasons why a survivor may take so long to seek justice by pursuing civil litigation against the abuser. A primary reason is the effects of post-traumatic stress disorder (PTSD) and complex post-traumatic stress disorder (CPTSD), whereby adult survivors experience feelings of shame, self-blame, stigma and fear of not being believed. For some, the true impact of the abuse became clear only many years later, when they began to connect the abuse with serious personal and health difficulties in adulthood. Part of this process of awareness was connected to the broader awakening in each country around the wrongfulness and lifelong harms of CSA, which was depicted in media interviews with survivors or in documentaries the 1980s and 1990s. For others, although they understood they had been seriously wronged and had suffered considerably, cultural perceptions of child sexual abuse as taboo meant that it was very difficult to disclose until recently, and even more confronting to incur the publicity and costs of commencing litigation. For survivors of institutional abuse, the power and resources of institutional actors may have made litigation seem impossible.

There are four approaches evident in how the three countries examined here have approached the issue of statutes of limitation for NRCSA cases. The first is the most progressive, involving the complete and retrospective abolition of statutes of limitation for all personal injury claims relating to CSA (and even other forms of child abuse). Since 2015 the Australian states and territories have introduced radical reforms along these lines on the basis that it is well established that for a variety of psychological, societal and cultural reasons, NRCSA survivors have legitimately delayed accessing the civil courts.

The remaining three approaches illustrate how existing concepts in tort law for dealing with 'delay' in bringing proceedings have been adapted to the context of NRCSA cases.

The second approach is the concept of 'disability', according to which the law says that the time limit does not begin to run until the plaintiff has emerged from a particular 'disability'. The usual disability in this context is infancy, so that the time limit (usually of three or six years) does not begin to run until the plaintiff reaches the age of 18. This reflects the reality that children do not have the personal or financial resources to commence legal proceedings. In Ireland the statute of limitations was amended in 2000 to create an exception to the standard time limit for NRCSA plaintiffs, in which the concept of disability was broadened out beyond infancy to capture the inability of an adult NRCSA survivor to sue due to the traumatic effects of abuse. Expert evidence on PTSD and CPTSD is crucial for establishing the fact of the plaintiff's disability flowing from the effects of the sexual abuse, as is the broader societal context in which the public silence around abuse was shattered in the 1990s in Ireland. In England and Wales and Australia disability has not been expanded for NRCSA survivors.

'Date of discovery': under this third approach, a time limit will not begin to run until the date when the plaintiff discovered, or realized, that they could sue in tort for the civil wrong they allege. As with disability, this standard tort law category has been used by the courts in NRCSA cases. Exactly what this discovery means can vary, but it generally comes down to when the plaintiff appreciated (or, should have appreciated) that the personal and/or medical challenges they faced were caused by the sexual abuse they suffered in childhood. As with the 'disability' approach, expert psychological and psychiatric evidence on the effects of PTSD or CPTSD is central to the analysis of discovery; without it, such an assertion would not be accepted. In addition to expert evidence, courts have also drawn on their knowledge of the societal 'discovery' of CSA and its effects in each country, during which awareness of its harms came to form a part of a general common sense.

In all three countries trial judges retain the fourth approach of a judicial discretion to halt or stay the proceedings on the grounds of unfairness to the defendant. This discretion may be part of the court's inherent power (Ireland, Australia), or it may come from legislation (England and Wales). Courts tend to consider the factors described above in terms of delayed recognition of the impacts of the abuse, as well as the disabling effects of the abuse on the plaintiff's ability to sue. Courts may also scrutinize the plaintiff's behaviour after reaching adulthood.

England and Wales

In England and Wales the effective maximum time a claimant has to sue for NRCSA is six years after the age of 18; that is, until they are 24 years old. Of course, this is unhelpful in the majority of NRCSA cases. As will be seen, claimants have been forced to argue that their action comes within certain provisions in the Limitation Act 1980 and that they therefore have not exceeded the statutory time limit.

The Limitation Act 1980 (LA 1980) stipulates a time limit of six years for 'actions founded in tort' (s2). Although, unfortunately, the legislation does not define what this term means, it is taken to mean intentional trespasses to the person such as batteries, which are often claimed in NRCSA cases. When battery is claimed, the Act provides no discretion to a trial judge to extend the limitation period. S11 offers an alternative route for NRCSA claimants—that is, claims for negligence, nuisance or breach of duty. Under s11, the limitation period of three years runs from 'the date of discovery' of the abuse.[13] Under s14, the date of discovery is the date the claimant[14] had sufficient knowledge or would be expected to have knowledge that they were suffering a 'significant' injury which if established justifies the institution of proceedings. However, three years from the date of discovery will only help some NRCSA claimants. Other may be forced to seek to bring themselves under s33.

S33 gives a court discretion to disapply the three-year time-bar for claims under s11 (and s14). In deciding whether to exercise its discretion, a court must consider all of the circumstances of the case, in particular, the length of, and reasons for, the delay; the extent to which the evidence is less cogent than if the claim had been brought 'within time'; the conduct of the defendant after the claim was brought; the duration of any disability of the claimant; the extent to which the claimant acted promptly and reasonably once they knew that there was a possibility of bringing a claim; any steps taken by the claimant to obtain medical, legal or other expert advice and the nature of any such advice. In the absence of political appetite for legislative reform, the focus has been on judicial developments, particularly on whether survivors suing for NRCSA can bring themselves within s11 and therefore the court's s33 discretionary power to disapply the time limit. In the majority of NRCSA cases, a person who wants to bring a case of this kind will have to rely on s33, where the consideration of inability to bring a case sooner will be considered as part of the exercise of judge's discretion. The development of this area of law in NRCSA cases was impeded by the controversial House of Lords decision in *Stubbings v Webb* in 1993 which centred on the delayed recognition of harm by an adult survivor of NRCSA.

Stubbings v Webb and its legacy

Lesley Stubbings brought a claim for intentional trespass to the person, specifically battery, against her adoptive stepfather and her stepbrother for rape. She claimed that Mr Webb had sexually assaulted her on various occasions during her childhood until 1971 when she was aged 14. She also claimed that her stepbrother had raped her on two occasions in 1969. As noted above, s2 LA1980 prohibits any such claim for personal injury made six years after reaching adulthood. Lesley turned 18 in 1975 and so the claim was automatically time-barred. Lesley asserted that the sexual abuse had resulted in psychological disturbance and mental illness which had developed in her adult life but that she had become aware that that condition was attributable to the abuse only after consultations with a psychiatrist commencing about September 1984.

The Divisional Court and Court of Appeal both found in favour of Lesley, finding that s11 could be applied to rape because it involved a breach of duty and that time ran from when she first became fully aware that the injury was 'significantly serious'. They held the date of discovery was the date she first made the causal connection many years after the actual abuse, in September 1984.[15] Bingham J (as he then was) noted the societal context:

> I do not, for my part, think that the plaintiff could reasonably have been expected to acquire knowledge of the causal link from facts observable or ascertainable by her, since mental impairment caused as this allegedly was almost necessarily produces a lack of insight and during the period in question there was not that general awareness among the public of the psychological effects of child abuse which certain well-publicised events since then have caused.

Because the Court found the claim came under s11, it could apply its discretion under s33 to extend the limitation period and thereby allow the claim to proceed. The Court of Appeal agreed with the Divisional Court.

The House of Lords overruled the Court of Appeal's decision with all five male Law Lords unanimously rejecting any possibility of a claim under s11, therefore automatically disengaging s33. They asserted that the nature of the claim meant it could only be brought as a claim under s2 which was subject to the six-year rule, which had long expired. Their Lordships disagreed with the Court of Appeal reasoning and refused to accept that intentional abuse could be articulated as a 'breach of duty' to provide abuse victims with access to more generous and flexible limitation periods. Lord Griffiths wondered:

> If I invite a lady to my house one would naturally think of a duty to take care that the house is safe but would one really be thinking of a duty not to rape her?

This rhetorical question reflected Lord Griffith's focus on the difference between an obligation not to cause personal injury (battery) versus an obligation not to infringe another's legal rights (negligence). Surely, the two are not distinguishable; a duty not to infringe someone's legal rights covers a duty not to cause them personal injuries (otherwise, what would be the justification for any remedies in the case of personal injuries?). Lord Griffiths was also highly sceptical that someone who had been subjected to CSA could be 'unaware' that their mental health problems in adulthood flowed from the abuse: 'I have the greatest difficulty in accepting that a woman who knows that she has been raped does not know that she has suffered a significant injury'.[16] This ignored the fact that victims of sexual abuse often require counselling before they can understand the causal link to later problems (see Chapter 6).[17]

The Lords' decision created the situation that an action against the alleged perpetrator had to be brought within six years, whereas an action against a non-perpetrator (e.g. in the tort of negligence) was subject to the more flexible limitation period under s11.[18] The decision produced 'severe distortions in the lower courts who attempted to distinguish it on grounds which created both anomalies and complexity'.[19] Unsurprisingly, it was heavily criticized[20] not least by the Law Commission which aligned itself with the Court of Appeal. The Commission also recommended that the date of 'discovery' marking the commencement of the primary limitation period 'should not start running against the claimant until the date on which they know or should know the *last piece of information* [italics added] needed for the "date of knowledge" test'.[21] This amounted to suggesting a new approach incorporating delayed constructive awareness for NRCSA and encouraging the acceptance of claims after the three-year time-bar.

It would take 15 years before the House of Lords repaired the damage it had caused and acknowledge the historic disadvantage of NRCSA claimants in the case of *A v Hoare*.

A new approach

A v Hoare[22] concerned five conjoined appeals but is primarily known for the lead appeal from Iorworth Hoare, convicted of attempted rape in 1988. This was not a case of NRCSA; the victim was an adult. While out on day release in 2004 Hoare won £7 million on the National Lottery triggering an action by the claimant, then aged 78, who lodged a civil claim for damages for trespass to the person comprising assault and battery resulting in psychiatric harm. The Divisional Court and the Court of Appeal, following *Stubbings,* ruled the claim time-barred by the six-year rule under s2 and were unable to apply s11 because the injury was intentional. The Lords unanimously departed from its previous decision and ruled that a claim for damages for intentional trespass to the person *did* constitute a claim for damages for breach of duty and specifically included cases of intentional sexual abuse. This gave the claimant the advantage of a more generous limitation period; it gave her access to the discretionary extension of time provisions under s33. It also gave the claimant a period of three years from the 'date of knowledge' of the injury (ss11–14) as opposed to six years from when the tort occurred (s2). The House of Lords remitted the case to the High Court to decide whether the discretion under s33 should be exercised in A's favour. The High Court awarded A £50,000 compensation and made an order against Hoare to pay her legal costs.

The Lords also ruled in favour of the other four claims which all involved NRCSA. Three concerned actions brought in negligence, breach of duty and vicarious liability against local authorities,[23] a Catholic charity[24] and the Home Office for past sexual abuse committed by employees. Now with its first female judge, Lady Hale, the panel allowed the four appeals, opening the door to further potential claims from victims of historical assaults. Lord Hoffman directed judicial attention in future to s33(3) which expressly states that the court must consider: 'the reasons for…the delay on the part of the plaintiff' in reporting the abuse.[25] Lady Hale also dismissed concern about the difficulties of securing a fair trial due to delayed reporting: 'A fair trial can be possible long after the event and sometimes the law has no choice. It is even possible to have a fair trial of criminal charges of historic sex abuse'. She crushed the ongoing debate about how to determine the date of knowledge opining, 'with a properly directed discretion one should not need the date of knowledge provision at all'.[26] The Supreme Court concluded that time should run from when the claimant first had knowledge of various facts, including that the injury was significant.[27]

Hoare was not all good news for claimants, however; the majority[28] also held that the test to be applied for that date of knowledge should be an entirely 'impersonal standard', not whether the claimant would have considered the injuries sufficiently serious to justify proceedings but whether they would 'reasonably' have done so.[29] This objective standard means that the court, in assessing the date of discovery, cannot take into account whether the victim knew that the abuse was wrong when it happened,[30] or whether they subsequently suppressed memory of the abuse.[31] This means the court cannot take into account factors such as education, aspirations, self-esteem and gender when considering whether a claimant knew their injury was significant enough to ground a tort action. *Hoare*, therefore, is a narrower approach than that taken by the Irish statute, discussed below, which centres on the notion of disability.[32]

Following *Hoare* much court time is spent investigating the psychological and other reasons for the passage of time, and the difficulties delay could create for the defendant and the trier of fact. The court will need to hear extensive evidence in respect of the reason for delay before deciding how to exercise its discretion. Where psychiatric factors have contributed to the delay, expert evidence from a psychiatrist will almost always be required as well as the claimant's own evidence.[33]

In *JL v Archbishop Michael George Bowen, The Scout Association*[34] in 2017, the Court of Appeal signalled a more restrictive approach to s33. JL had been groomed by the chaplain of his scout troop from the age of 8 and sexually abused from the age of 16. He continued to visit the priest as an adult and sexual contact took place between them until the priest's arrest in 1999, when the claimant was aged 31. JL claimed that the sexual contact had not been consensual because of the emotional manipulation and grooming it involved. The priest pleaded guilty to sexual assaulting JL and others. JL stated that it was only after receiving counselling in 2010 that he realized the damage caused by the sexual abuse. Litigation was commenced in 2011. The priest died in 2014 but before his death claimed that the sexual contact had been consensual. Lord Burnett provided some further detail on the effects of delayed reporting on the exercise of the s33 discretion. He emphasized that judges should undertake an overall assessment of the evidence presented by both parties to determine whether it is or is likely to be less cogent than if the action had been brought within the requisite time limit. The defendant's conduct after the cause of action arose needs to be assessed and whether the claimant acted promptly or reasonably once aware the injury was significantly serious, for example, seeking out appropriate counselling, psychiatric and medical support as well as reporting the harm to the police. Any adverse findings made against the claimant must be weighed into the equation as this could have a profound impact on the defendant's ability to defend the claim.[35] The Court of Appeal ruled that this case was different to *Hoare* because the reason for delay was not the psychological harm caused by the abuse. Instead, the court held that the so-called consensual nature of the later adult relationship ought to have 'coloured' the judge's approach to the delay issue. It held that although there was a criminal conviction in place, it was not as significant as would otherwise be the case, because the question of consent was relevant to the claim,[36] and the priest had pleaded guilty apparently without appreciating the importance of consent. This 'indulgent'[37] view of the priest's reasons for pleading guilty contrasts with the harsh view taken of the claimant's reasons for not suing sooner. *JL* signals a more restrictive approach than *Hoare* on the delay issue and one that arguably fails to adequately account for the connection between the effects of childhood grooming and putative consent in subsequent sexual activity between the parties.[38] It also shows how the passage of time and its effect on the cogency of the evidence are bound up with substantive issues of liability, causation and quantum of damages.

Submissions to the Independent Inquiry into Child Sexual Abuse (IICSA)'s Accountability and Reparations Investigation demonstrate that this area of law is experienced by claimants as highly discriminatory towards them. Lawyers have raised concerns about the ability of judges to understand the dynamics of sexual abuse and how they prevent timely reporting. They have called for radical reform or suspension of limitation.[39] The IICSA's 2019 report highlighted the lack of specialist judges with experience of handling NRCSA claims.[40] It recommended that the Local Government Association and Association of British Insurers should produce codes of practice for responding to civil claims and that the codes should include guidance that a limitation defence should only be used in exceptional circumstances.[41] It remains to be seen if the IICSA will issue more impactful reform recommendations in its final report, such as abolishing the statute of limitation as it applies for NRCSA cases altogether.

Ireland

The Statute of Limitations 1957 (SOL 1957) mirrors the LA 1980 in that it imposes a six-year time limit on tort actions (that is, actions for trespass to the person)[42] and a two-year time limit on personal injuries claims based on negligence, nuisance or breach of duty.[43] Unlike in England and Wales, there is no provision for judicial discretion to lift the statute bar in the interests of justice.[44] Instead, Irish law has centred on the issue of disability. S48 provides for an exception to the time limits for persons deemed to be 'under a disability', including anyone under the age of 18 or persons of unsound mind. For these plaintiffs, the statutory period does not commence until the plaintiff is no longer under one of these disabilities. For survivors of NRCSA in the 1990s contemplating suing, the exceptions were of little use; they would have to either bring proceedings before reaching the age of 21 (which was not typical) or they would have to show that they were of 'unsound mind' and therefore could not have sued.[45] The relevance of arguments about the psychological effects of sexual abuse was not clear; lawyers could not confidently advise a client whether the courts would be receptive to an argument that the claim was not statute-barred because the client was of unsound mind.[46]

The Statute of Limitations (Amendment) Act 1991 changed the law so that the limitation period for personal injuries actions did not commence until the claimant had knowledge of the fundamental facts concerning their cause of action.[47] However, the 1991 reforms were not helpful to NRCSA survivors[48] because they did not reflect the fact that, for many, the barrier to suing was not lack of knowledge of the sexual abuse but rather it was the effects of the abuse that prevented them from acting on that knowledge.[49]

Reform was prompted by the landmark litigation by Sophia McColgan and her three siblings Gerard, Keith and Michelle against the North Western Health Board and the family doctor. In the first Irish case of its kind, the McColgans sued the defendants for their failure to intervene to address their father's physical and sexual abuse from the mid-1970s until the early 1990s.[50] At trial Sophia's claim was presented first. The defendants argued the action was statute-barred because more than three years had elapsed since Ms McColgan's 18th birthday before she commenced proceedings. Her claim could not come within the 1991 Act because she did not lack knowledge of the cause of action.[51] The plaintiffs adduced expert testimony on Sophia's PTSD from Dr Ivor Browne, a psychiatrist specializing in severe psychological trauma, and Dr Suzanne M. Sgroi, an American psychiatrist specializing in CSA intervention and the treatment of adult survivors of childhood trauma. These experts provided reports and testimonial evidence to the court on the traumatic effects of the abuse on Sophia and how they prevented her from being able to sue sooner.[52]

The litigation settled out of court on the 13th day of the trial for a reported £250,000 per sibling plus costs but without admission of liability.[53] The case and extensive media coverage of it greatly increased the public's awareness of the traumatic effects of child sexual abuse.[54] When the settlement was announced, the McColgan siblings urged other victims not to be afraid. Later that year, a book on their experiences was published.[55]

In March 1998 Labour TD Jan O'Sullivan published a Bill that sought to address the statute's deficiencies for NRCSA survivors. Legislators were slow to take it up, until the issue was forced onto their agenda in the wake of the government's apology to survivors of Industrial Schools (see Chapter 10) in May 1999. At this point, tort actions for NRCSA were becoming a significant feature of the Irish legal landscape. A total of 145 sets of proceedings involving alleged historical sexual or physical abuse of children in institutions had been initiated against the Department of Education and Science.[56] Many cases had been initiated against religious orders, school teachers as well as fathers accused of abusing their own children in the past.[57] The gardaí were investigating 230 historical complaints against 75 Christian Brothers at Artane Industrial School for Boys in Dublin.[58] Actions by residents of the Madonna House children's home had come to trial but had settled out of court.[59]

O'Sullivan's Bill became the Statute of Limitations (Amendment) Act 2000 (SLAA 2000). It inserted a new s48A into the SOL 1957 which extended the definition of disability to accommodate effects of CSA. A person bringing a NRCSA tort claim is to be treated as being under a disability 'while they are suffering from any psychological injury caused by that act (or any other act of the transgressor) and the psychological injury is of such significance that their will, or ability to make a reasoned decision, to bring that action is substantially impaired'.[60] Interestingly, according to the text of the provision, the psychological injury need not have been caused by the sexual abuse itself; it need only have inhibited litigation.[61] In practice, most cases centre on the psychological harms caused by the sexual abuse. The 2000 Act does not define psychological injury, but the courts have been willing to find that sexual abuse has caused such significant psychological injury that the plaintiff qualifies as having being under a disability.[62]

S48A(3) also created a one-year extension for actions claiming damages for NRCSA that did not come within the new expanded definition of disability. The extension ran for one year from 21 June 2000. This option only applied if, before 30 March 2000, the plaintiff had complained to the gardaí about the abuse or obtained professional legal advice which caused them to believe that the action was statute-barred, so it excluded most survivors.

The decision to exclude physical abuse from the expanded definition of disability reflected the greater political and societal importance attached to sexual abuse. This was very controversial among survivors, many of whom had spoken publicly about the extreme brutality with which they were treated in certain industrial schools.[63] The government committee referred the matter to the Law Reform Commission,[64] but ultimately nothing changed for survivors of physical abuse.

Case law on s48

The courts have developed a substantial body of jurisprudence on s48A in NRCSA litigation against family members,[65] as well as school chaplains, members of religious orders[66] and religious congregations.[67] The courts have also been willing to accept that a psychological condition inhibiting the initiation of proceedings may wax and wane over time.

In *Doherty v Quigley*[68] the plaintiff alleged she had been sexually abused by her dancing teacher between 1982 and 1989 when she was 12–19 years of age. She alleged that the action was not statute-barred because the abuse had caused her to suffer from PTSD, dissociation complex and repressed memories. Ryan J in the High Court[69] heard evidence from psychiatrist Professor Ivor Browne, who had also given evidence in the McColgan case. Dr Browne's reports explaining how Doherty continued to be seriously incapacitated by PTSD caused by the abuse clearly influenced Ryan J's decision that Doherty had remained under a statutory disability until the action was brought and that s48A applied.[70] Ryan J also found that Doherty had established on the balance of probabilities that Quigley committed the acts alleged and awarded Doherty €400,000 damages.

On appeal to the Supreme Court, Quigley's counsel argued that Doherty was not so impaired that she could not have sued earlier. In support of this claim, counsel pointed to the fact Doherty reported the abuse to her doctor in 1990, reported to the gardaí in 1993, gave evidence for two unsuccessful criminal prosecutions, graduated from university and pursued a teaching career.

Dismissing the appeal, Murray J noted that that even if there are 'short periods or a window in a person's life where he or she might have the capacity to bring proceedings…the underlying psychological injury which impairs the ability to bring proceedings may intervene before the opportunity to act arises', and they may still gain the benefit of the section. Although having the mental strength to lodge a criminal complaint was a relevant fact, this was fundamentally different to being the initiator of a civil claim, as she was 'personally responsible for the carriage and conduct' of that claim.[71] This approach is more pro-plaintiff than that taken by the English/Welsh Court of Appeal in *JL*, but it is worth remembering that Doherty was required to present extensive expert evidence to demonstrate her psychological injury. Other plaintiffs may not have the same resources at their disposal.

Dismissal of an action for delay is still the ultimate fate of many non-recent institutional abuse cases.[72] Even if a defence based on the Statute of Limitations is not applicable, there is a risk that the court's jurisdiction to dismiss proceedings for 'inordinate and inexcusable' delay will be successfully invoked by defendants.[73] Irish law's focus on the reasonableness or otherwise of the plaintiff's behaviour allows defendants to benefit from a technical defence that ends the action before the merits of the claim have been fully aired and ignores the reality of widespread cultural and societal denial of child sexual abuse until the closing decade of the twentieth century. The Irish position compares unfavourably with that taken in Australia.

Australia

Each state and territory has its own Limitation Act. As with the other two countries in most Australian jurisdictions, the limitation period does not commence until a child turns 18. All states and territories allow for a suspending or lengthening of the limitation period to account for time when the plaintiff was under a disability, although they differ in how they define a relevant disability.[74] In some, the 'date of discovery' approach applies whereby a limitation period begins when the plaintiff becomes aware of their injury or when they could have become aware of their injury.

Statutes of limitation had long been identified as a fundamental obstacle to justice. The Australian NRCSA scandal ignited in 1993 when 240 adult male plaintiffs launched a class action against the Holy Spirit Province of the Christian Brothers for physical and sexual abuse in four residential boys' homes in Western Australia (see Chapter 5).[75] The plaintiffs included former child migrants and the lawsuit signified the beginning of organized campaigns for compensation for this group of survivors and others abused in care. The claim was filed first in New South Wales (NSW) and then Victoria, where several of the plaintiffs resided, in an attempt to avail of the more flexible interpretations of Limitations Acts in those states. The Christian Brothers succeeded in having the proceedings transferred to Western Australia where, due to the *Limitation Act 1935 (WA)*, the case was 'dead in the water'.[76] The plaintiff's lawyers applied to the Supreme Court of Western Australia to have Victorian procedural laws including the limitation period applied in the case, but the judge refused the application. Three applications for special leave to appeal to the High Court of Australia were subsequently refused.[77]

In 1996 the plaintiffs were 'pressured to accept a settlement' of $5.1 million, including $1.5 million for legal fees.[78] A trust was created to make payments to the plaintiffs, with conditions imposed in the settlement forcing their legal representatives to make 'arbitrary' and divisive decisions about the nature and severity of the abuse each had suffered.[79] The trust deed permitted $1.16 million to be used for cases of serious sexual abuse, with $25,000 the maximum amount to be paid to the 30 most seriously affected plaintiffs; another 25 would receive $10,000 each. By early 1997 the number of men claiming for serious sexual abuse had already reached 117.[80] Ultimately, the trustees resolved to make 103 different payments of varying amounts from $2,000 to $25,000.[81] Numerous survivors have since given evidence of their bitter disappointment and dissatisfaction with the level of compensation received and the obstructive legalism of the entire process.[82]

The failed Western Australian class action was an international scandal. When addressing the question of child migrants in 1997, the UK government recommended that Australia immediately suspend its statutes of limitations in all child migrant cases so survivors could be 'awarded the maximum possible damages',[83] but Australian governments refused to act. During the period of the Royal Commission into Institutional Responses to Child Sexual Abuse's inquiries (2013–2017), the settlement was renegotiated with the Christian Brothers, with substantially better financial outcomes for those survivors who were still alive 20 years after the original settlement was finalized.[84] Regardless, the failed class action, which dragged on for three years and was systematically subverted by the Christian Brothers, is known to have deterred other survivors from seeking justice and invoked distrust in law firms and the legal system in many vulnerable people abused in care.

Compared to Ireland and England and Wales, there is relatively little jurisprudence from the High Court of Australia on the question of delay in NRCSA cases. The leading judgment is the 2016 case of *Prince Alfred College Incorporated v ADC*, concerning an appeal by a Protestant boarding school that claims for damages for CSA perpetrated in the 1960s should have been ruled outside the limitation period.[85] ADC had boarded at Prince Alfred College and was sexually abused by a school housemaster in 1962 when he was 12 years old. In 1996 ADC's son started attending Prince Alfred College, which triggered flashbacks for ADC about his own abuse, and he was soon diagnosed as suffering from PTSD. In 1997 ADC took legal advice not to sue the College, and instead initiated proceedings against the perpetrator, his former housemaster, settling for $15,000. ADC entered into an agreement with the College that he would not initiate proceedings, and the College would pay his medical and legal fees and meet his son's school fees. Between 2002 and 2004 ADC's PTSD worsened, and he was admitted to a psychiatric clinic; in 2005 he was advised he would not work full-time again. ADC requested that Prince Alfred College pay him $1 million and refund his school fees, which the College refused. In 2008 ADC brought proceedings against the college in the Supreme Court of South Australia, arguing that among other things, new information had come to light about his PTSD and employment prospects, which could warrant an application being made outside the limitation period. The primary judge dismissed the case on grounds of lack of liability, and in *obiter* asserted that no extension of the *Limitation Act* would have been granted, because the delay between when the issue of liability was first raised (1997) and the court action (2008) left the college in a prejudiced position insofar as it was able to defend the claims. The judge also noted that several witnesses had died, and ADC's original psychiatrist's records had been destroyed. On appeal, the Court overturned this decision.

Prince Alfred College appealed to the High Court of Australia, arguing that the delay in bringing the proceedings was unjustifiable.[86] The Court agreed with the original decision, that the 11-year delay between ADC's last interaction with the College and his bringing of the present claim was unjustifiable in the circumstances and meant that a fair trial was no longer possible. ADC's decision to agree to a deal with the College in 1997 not to initiate proceedings was considered highly relevant to the Court's determination; his 2008 decision to sue was cynically characterized by the College's counsel as made 'because he simply ran out of money and...options for improving his financial position'.[87] The High Court ruled:

> Where an injured party makes a deliberate decision not to commence proceedings, there must be strong reasons to permit proceedings to be brought against a defendant who reasonably considered that the dispute had been laid to rest. In so far as proceedings will be oppressive where a party conveys the impression that he or she will not bring proceedings on certain terms and then, when the terms are met, changes his or her mind.[88]

Prince Alfred College is a relatively rare and important example of the High Court adjudicating on delay. However, the case may come to be of limited relevance on the question of limitation periods, in light of recent legislative reform on recommendation of the Royal Commission and after years of lobbying by survivors and their legal advocates.[89] Since 2015, all states and territories have introduced legislation reforming limitation periods for child abuse.[90] Importantly, unlike the Irish SLAA 2000, in all Australian jurisdictions except Western Australia and the Australian Capital Territory (ACT), the reforms apply to CSA and serious physical abuse and arising/connected psychological abuse. Crucially, all the Acts are retrospective, meaning that NRCSA claims can be heard even if the abuse took place at the time of the old statutory regime. In four jurisdictions (Victoria, Queensland, Western Australia and the Northern Territory), the reforms apply to previously adjudicated or settled claims. Plaintiffs are not required to demonstrate psychological damage caused by the sexual abuse (unlike the Irish SLAA 2000, or the discretionary approach developed by the courts in England and Wales under s33 LA 1980). In recognition of the multitude of factors that might deter a person from initiating a claim for sexual abuse, the new legislation simply amends existing statutes of limitation to permit an action for damages in relation to CSA to be brought at any time.

These reforms are having momentous outcomes for some survivors. In Western Australia, in the 2020 case of *WPM,* which contrasts with the result in *Prince Alfred College,* WPM was successful in seeking the reopening of a suit settled with the Christian Brothers in respect of various forms of child abuse suffered at Bindoon Farm School in the 1950s and 1960s.[91] The plaintiff had previously received over $400,000 from the respondent and others in relation to his abuse. The amount included a 2009 settlement with two Christian Brothers for $40,000 (which the plaintiff was unsatisfied with and for which he had not had legal representation); and a 2014 settlement of $250,000 (which the plaintiff accepted because he understood that the *Limitation Act 2005 (WA)* and other legal obstacles meant that he had no claim against the Brothers). Although the Christian Brothers opposed the 2020 application on account of the 2014 settlement deed being a product of a fair and even process, with all parties having legal advice, the court granted the plaintiff leave to commence an action for damages arising from his sexual abuse, and the deeds were set aside. The Court found that it was *prima facie* apparent and relevant that the claim would be worth a figure higher than either of the amounts awarded by way of settlement; it recognized the essentially hopeless position of the plaintiff when he negotiated the earlier deeds of settlement, given the statute bar in Western Australia.

In another recent Western Australian case, *Lawrence,* the plaintiff, a former child migrant, transported to Western Australia from Liverpool England in 1952, sued the Christian Brothers for seven years of severe sexual abuse perpetrated when he was an orphan resident at St Vincent's Orphanage Clontarf and Castledare Junior Orphanage.[92] The Christian Brothers admitted liability but disputed the quantum of damages, which was ultimately calculated at $1,329,500. Although the 2018 legislation to amend the *Limitation Act 2005 (WA)* applies only to CSA,[93] the judge found that the physical and emotional abuse could not be separated from the sexual abuse, and it had to be considered when calculating damages.[94]

Each state and territory in Australia has retained the judicial discretion to dismiss or stay proceedings, for example, in cases where the defendant has advanced dementia and may not be fit to plead,[95] so the reforms to limitation periods, while profoundly significant, should not be understood as a 'magic bullet' to solve the problems of litigating NRCSA. An example is the 2019 case of *Moubarak* which concerned a claim made by the plaintiff against her uncle for damages arising from sexual abuse alleged to have been perpetrated in 1973 or 1974, when she was 12 years old. By the time of the trial, more than 45 years had elapsed. The defendant's claim that he was not able to participate due to his advanced dementia was accepted, and the proceedings were dismissed.

Conclusion

Litigation by NRCSA survivors has prompted lawmakers and courts in each country to re-evaluate fundamental assumptions around when it is too late to pursue a claim for damages. Thanks to the determination of survivors (and their lawyers, some of whom have acted *pro bono*) courts have been presented with compelling survivor testimony explaining why they could not have initiated proceedings earlier. Expert evidence from psychologists and psychiatrists has provided the necessary frameworks to legitimate survivors' reasons. This has worked primarily through discussions of the harmful effects of CSA in (a) causing health challenges or personal difficulties in adulthood that were not recognized as being connected to the abuse until recently or (b) in preventing plaintiffs from suing. Both approaches reflect the increased receptiveness of courts to arguments based on trauma and their improved understanding of the effects of CSA. They may also be understood as mapping neatly onto existing categories in tort law for dealing with delay in bringing proceedings (delayed discovery, disability and judicial discretion). In a recognition of the dynamics of abuse and its effects, Australian states and territories have recently transcended these categories and introduced legislation removing statutes of limitation for all claims involving CSA. This signifies a very important acceptance of the reasons why abuse survivors should not be expected to commence proceedings as promptly as other plaintiffs. It also signals the positive impact legal responses to NRCSA can have on legal responses to contemporary CSA.

The persistence of limitation periods in England and Wales and Ireland allows defendants to benefit from a technical defence that ignores the real barriers to disclosure and to commencing litigation discussed in the Introduction to this Part. Litigating the limitation issue alone may take years and substantial expense, further adding to the trauma for plaintiffs and defendants. In England and Wales and in Ireland survivors are still required to frame their reasons for not suing sooner primarily in terms of psychiatric or psychological injuries. The focus on the plaintiff's behaviour means their credibility and motives are brought into question before the substance of the claim is fully assessed, undermining the healing potential of litigation. The reliance on technicality may be due to judicial anxieties about adjudicating on the truth of the claim where the events are so remote in time. While such concerns are understandable, survivors deserve better, especially given the law's hostility to abuse victims for so long. Indeed, as Chapter 7 explored, the criminal courts in both jurisdictions have moved away from scrutinizing the reasonableness of a complainant's delay. It is not clear why such scrutiny is required in a civil context where the defendant's liberty is not at stake and the need to ensure due process is accordingly less. Indeed, the Australian example suggests that it is not required. Furthermore, because statutes of limitation prevent much NRCSA civil litigation from ever reaching a full hearing, many other key issues (including the appropriate cause of action, the scope of any duty of care, causation and quantum of damages and organizational liability) are left underdeveloped in the case law of Ireland and England and Wales. Finally, taking a broader view, the focus on reasons for delay impedes sustained consideration of the very real but non-psychological factors inhibiting litigation, such as societal denial of CSA and the law's historical ambivalence to survivors' claims for justice (see Chapters 3–5).

There have been calls for statutory reform of the statute of limitation in Ireland, specifically to reform the test for delay 'to take account of what was reasonable given social reality in Ireland before the liberalization of the 1990s'.[96] In England and Wales, survivor groups have made similar calls for reform of the LA 1980.[97] We believe more radical change is needed. Legislators in Ireland and in England and Wales should follow the example of Australia (and other Western countries[98]) and abolish statutes of limitation as they apply to child abuse claims. To ensure coherence of approach and fairness to all litigants, any such reforming legislation should also expressly limit judicial discretion to dismiss by defining what is 'inordinate and inexcusable delay'. Instead, the courts should be directed to exercise any discretion to dismiss only in cases where the fairness of the trial is unduly threatened, using a residual discretion to dismiss on the grounds of the interests of justice.

In the next chapter, we continue our consideration of tort law responses to NRCSA by examining the question of organizations' liability.

Notes

1 Tort law predates criminal law as a way for victims to achieve justice. See M. Dyson, "The Timing of Tortious and Criminal Actions for the Same Wrong" *Cambridge Law Journal* 70, 2012, 86–117, 89.

2 H.F. Antonsdóttir, "Compensation as a Means to Justice? Sexual Violence Survivors' Views on the Tort Law Option in Iceland" *Feminist Legal Studies* 28, 2020, 277–300. P. Case, *Compensating Child Abuse in England and Wales* (Cambridge: Cambridge University Press, 2007); J.M. Balboni, *Clergy Sexual Abuse Litigation Survivors Seeking Justice* (Boulder and London: First Forum Press, 2011).

3 See C. O'Gorman, *Beyond Belief* (London: Hodder and Stoughton, 2010), 187. See also N. Godden-Rasul, "Retribution, Redress and the Harms of Rape. The Role of Tort Law" in A. Powell, N. Henry, and A. Flynn (eds), *Rape Justice* (London: Palgrave Macmillan, 2015), 112–26, 114.

4 The plaintiff must establish the defendant's liability for the sexual abuse 'on the balance of probabilities' (more likely than not). This is a lower standard of proof than in a criminal trial (beyond a reasonable doubt). In each country examined here an NRCSA tort action is usually heard by a judge or judges sitting alone without a jury.

5 The revolutionary reforms to civil procedure in England and Wales in 1999 followed the Woolf Report which modernized a number of existing legal terms, including replacing 'plaintiff' with 'claimant'. See H. Woolf, *Access to Justice, Final Report* (London: HMSO, 1996). Similarly, the term 'respondent' is used in civil litigation in Australia. For ease of reading, we use the terms 'plaintiff' and 'defendant', apart from the sections dealing with England and Wales or Australia only.

6 Generally speaking, NRCSA is actioned as one of two torts. First, a plaintiff may sue a defendant for trespass to the person, specifically an assault and battery which requires an intentional touching without lawful authority. Assault, false imprisonment and intentional infliction of emotional suffering are also relevant actionable trespasses to the person. For litigation against a public servant tasked with child protection responsibilities, misfeasance in public office is a possible option. Second, NRCSA litigants may sue using the tort of negligence. This tort is usually employed when suing organizations. Bringing an action in negligence requires proof that a (common law or statutory) duty of care was owed by the defendant to the claimant in respect of the type of harm suffered, that the duty was breached and that the breach caused damage. Plaintiffs must show that it was reasonably foreseeable that a failure to take care could result in harm to them. The tort chosen to be litigated by the survivor is crucial in determining the success or otherwise of the claim, as it determines the applicability of limitation period, the defences available and the applicability of insurance indemnities. They must also show a relationship of proximity between the parties and that it is just, fair and reasonable to impose a duty of care. See P. Case op. cit. and E.-A. Gumbel, J. et al., *Guide to Child Abuse Compensation Claims, 3rd edition* (London: Lexis Nexis, 2016).

7 Aggravated damages were awarded against the BBC for its coverage of a police search of Cliff Richard's property in relation to NRCSA allegations: *Richard v the BBC and Anor* [2018] EWHC 1837.
8 While sometimes a convicted person may be ordered to pay a sum of money to a victim, this is rare in NRCSA cases. Victims can apply for criminal injuries compensation but that is outside the scope of the formal criminal process.
9 Royal Commission into Institutional Responses to Child Sexual Abuse, *Consultation on Redress and Civil Litigation* (Commonwealth of Australia, 2015), 196 and Issues Paper 5: Civil Litigation.
10 In England and Wales, s2 of the Compensation Act 2006 goes some way to improving matters by providing that an apology or offer of redress is not an admission of liability.
11 In Australia, plaintiffs are generally required to attempt mediation first. For example, see the *Civil Procedure Act 2005 No 28 (NSW)* Part 4.
12 J. Conaghan, "Tort Law and Feminist Critique" *Current Legal Problems* 56, 2003, 175–209.
13 Or three years from the abuse, which in the case of NRCSA would be superseded by the disability provisions giving plaintiffs six years from the age of 18.
14 We use the term 'claimant' instead of 'plaintiff' in this section because that is the correct term for England and Wales.
15 [1991] 3 All ER 949.
16 [1993] AC 498, 506.
17 J. Conaghan, "Tort Litigation in the Context of Intra-Familial Abuse" *Modern Law Review* 61(2), 1998, 132–61.
18 Case op. cit., 251.
19 F. Burton, "Limitation, Vicarious Liability and Historic Actions for Abuse: A Changing Legal Landscape" *Journal of Personal Injury Law* 2013, 95.
20 Conaghan (1998) op. cit.
21 Law Commission, *Limitation of Actions,* Paper 270, HC 23 (UK: House of Commons, 2001), [3.34].
22 *A v Hoare and conjoined appeals* [2008] UKHL 6.
23 Middlesbrough Council, London Borough of Wandsworth and Suffolk County Council.
24 Catholic Care (Diocese of Leeds).
25 Hoare, [44].
26 Ibid., [60].
27 S14(2) 1980 Act.
28 Baroness Hale dissented.
29 Ibid., Lord Hoffman, [34], [35].
30 *KR v Bryn Alyn Community (Holdings) Ltd* [2003] QB 1441.
31 See M. Canny, *Limitation of Actions, 2nd edition* (Dublin: Round Hall, 2016), [6–21].
32 Statute of Limitations (Amendment) Act 2000. Indeed, in the one Irish case which did consider discoverability in the context of the 1991 Act, O'Higgins J's approach was more consistent with that adopted in *KR v Bryn Alyn Community (Holdings) Ltd* than with *Hoare*: *Delahunty v South Eastern Health Board, St Joseph's Industrial School, Kilkenny and the Minister for Education and Science* [2003] 4 IR 361.
33 Gumbel et al. op. cit., 211.

34 [2017] EWCA Civ 82.

35 *Murray v Devenish* [2018] EWHC 1895 QB.

36 Under s15(1) SOA 1956 the consent of a male over 16 was a defence to a charge of indecent assault.

37 J. Wheeler, *Journal of Personal Injury Law* (3) C181–C184.

38 It contrasts with the latter case of *FZO* which held the defendant school vicariously liable for abuse during the period while the claimant was a pupil at the school, but also for abuse that occurred during the five years after the claimant had left the school. There, the abuser's 'control and manipulation' of the claimant which had begun during the time the claimant was a pupil continued to be operative after he left the school. *FZO v Haringey London Borough Council* [2020] EWCA Civ 180. See also *AB v Chethams School of Music* [2021] EWHC 1419 where the High Court chose not to define grooming.

39 Submissions by Tracey Story, Paul Durkin, Peter Garsden, and Henry Witcomb QC to IICSA Accountability and Reparations Investigation, C: 6. https://www.iicsa.org.uk/publications/investigation/accountability-reparations/part-c-civil-just ice-system . See also N. Godden, "Sexual Abuse and Claims in Tort: Limitation Periods after *A v Hoare (and Other Appeals)* [2008] and *AB and Others v Nugent Care Society; GR v Wirral MBC* [2009]" *Feminist Legal Studies* 18, 2010, 179–90.

40 IICSA Issue No.1, Civil Justice System, p.5.

41 G3: Recommendation 2.

42 s11(2)(a)

43 The limitation period for personal injury claims was originally set out in ss11(2)(b). This was replaced by Statute of Limitations (Amendment) Act 1991 (18/1991), s3, which was amended to reduce the limitation period to two years by Civil Liability and Courts Act 2004, s7. A litigant must apply to the Personal Injuries Board prior to issuing proceedings.

44 s33 Limitation Act 1980.

45 The phrase meant 'unable to manage one's own affairs': *Rohan v Bord na Móna* [1990] 2 IR 425.

46 J. Nugent, "The Statute of Limitations in Sexual Abuse Cases" *Bar Review* 3(5), 1998, 222–24.

47 S3. The date of knowledge is defined in s2. The limitation period for personal injuries caused by negligence, nuisance or breach of duty was changed in 2004 to two years from the cause of action or the date of knowledge: s3(1).

48 S3 was successfully pleaded in *Delahunty v South Eastern Health Board, St Joseph's Industrial School, Kilkenny and the Minister for Education and Science* [2003] 4 IR 361.

49 See *Devlin v Roche* [2002] 2 IR 360 in which Geoghegan J. followed the approach in *Stubbings v Webb* and held the 1991 Act did not apply to personal injuries actions founded on trespass to the person.

50 The health board had child protection responsibilities at the time.

51 Nugent op. cit., 223.

52 S.M. Sgroi, "The McColgan Case: Increasing Public Awareness of Professional Responsibility for Protecting Children from Physical and Sexual Abuse in the Republic of Ireland" *Journal of Child Sexual Abuse* 8(1), 1999, 113–27, 124.

53 *The Irish Independent*, 24 January 1998.

54 Sgroi op. cit., 125.

55 S. McKay, *Sophia's Story* (Dublin: Gill & Macmillan, 1998).

56 Minister for Education and Science, Micheál Martin, Dáil Debate, Wednesday, 3 March 1999, Vol 501, No 4. Written Answer to Parliamentary Question.
57 Jan O'Sullivan TD, Statute of Limitations (Amendment) Bill, 1998: Second Stage (Resumed), Dáil Eireann Debate, Thursday, 27 May 1999, Vol 505, No 5.
58 *The Irish Independent*, 25 May 1999.
59 Law Reform Commission, *Consultation Paper on The Law of Limitation of Actions Arising from Non-Sexual Abuse of Children* (Dublin: LRC CP16–2000), para.1.28.
60 S48A(1)(b) (i) and (ii) Statute of Limitations 1957.
61 S48A(3) also created a one-year extension for actions claiming damages for child sexual abuse that did not come within the new expanded definition of disability. The extension ran for one year from 21 June 2000. This option only applied if, before 30 March 2000, the plaintiff had complained to the gardaí about the abuse or obtained professional legal advice which caused them to believe that the action was statute-barred, so it excluded most survivors.
62 For example, *McDonald v Conroy* [2017] IEHC 559.
63 See, e.g., L. Lentin, *Stolen Lives* (TV3, 1999).
64 see Chapter 10.
65 *MW v SW* [2011] IEHC 201.
66 For example, *McDonald v Conroy* op. cit. 2017.
67 *Brennan v Mullan* [2014] IEHC 61.
68 [2015] IESC 54.
69 Mr Justice Ryan chaired the Commission to Inquire into Child Abuse from 2003–2009.
70 [2011] IEHC 361.
71 Ibid.
72 Smith and Duff op. cit., 114, referring to litigation relating to all forms of historical institutional abuse.
73 There is further extensive jurisprudence exploring the principles to be applied to defence arguments about delayed commencement of proceedings, see *Cassidy v The Provincialate* [2015] IECA 754; *McDonald v Conroy* [2020] IECA 239.
74 Compare s50F(2) of the *Limitation Act 1969* (NSW) with s45(2) of the *Limitation of Actions Act 1936* (SA) and s4 (1) of the *Limitation Act 1918* (NT).
75 Bindoon Farm School, Castledare Junior Orphanage, St Vincent's Orphanage Clontarf and St Mary's Agricultural School Tardun.
76 Senate Standing Committees on Community Affairs, *Lost Innocents: Righting the Record – Report on Child Migration* (Canberra: Parliament of Australia, 2001), 221.
77 Royal Commission into Institutional Responses to Child Sexual Abuse, *Redress and Civil Litigation Report* (Commonwealth of Australia, 2015), 437.
78 Senate Standing Committees on Community Affairs op cit., 221, 224.
79 Royal Commission into Institutional Responses to Child Sexual Abuse, *Report of Case Study No 11. Christian Brothers* (Canberra: Commonwealth of Australia, 2014), 57.
80 Ibid.
81 In total, 30 payments of \$25,000, 25 payments of \$10,000, 12 payments of \$9,750, 50 payments of \$6,750 and 6 payments of \$2,000, 58.
82 Ibid.

83 Senate Standing Committees on Community Affairs op cit., 222, quoting Health Committee, House of Commons, *The Welfare of Former British Child Migrants* (1998), [111].
84 7 July 2015.
85 *Prince Alfred College Incorporated v ADC* [2016] HCA 37.
86 This case was decided before the *Limitation of Actions (Child Abuse) Amendment Act 2018 (SA*) which retrospectively removed limitation periods for child abuse claims.
87 Ibid., 91.
88 Ibid., 106.
89 See Royal Commission Report on Redress, op cit, 437.
90 *Limitation of Actions Amendment (Child Abuse) Act 2015 (VIC) and the Children Legislation Amendment Act 2019 (No. 30) (VIC); Limitation of Actions (Child Sexual Abuse) and Other Legislation Amendment Act 2016 (QLD) and the Civil Liability and other Legislation Amendment Act 2019 (QLD); Civil Liability Legislation Amendment (Child Sexual Abuse Actions) Act 2018 (WA); Limitation Amendment (Child Abuse) Act 2017 (No 10) (NT); Limitation Amendment (Child Abuse) Act 2016 (NSW); Limitation Amendment Act 2017 (TAS); Justice and Community Safety Legislation Amendment Act 2016 (No 2) (ACT); Limitations of Actions (Child Abuse) Amendment Act 2018 (SA).*
91 *WPM v Trustees of the Christian Brothers* [2020] WADC 112.
92 *Lawrence v Province Leader of Oceania Province of Congregation of Christian Brothers* [2020] WADC 27.
93 *Civil Liability Legislation Amendment (Child Sexual Abuse Actions) Act 2018 (WA).*
94 *Lawrence v Province Leader of Oceania Province of Congregation of Christian Brothers* [2020] WADC 27, 102.
95 *Moubarak by his tutor Coorey v Holt* (2019) 100 NSWLR 218.
96 C. Smith and A. Duff, "Access to Justice for Victims of Historic Institutional Abuse" *Éire-Ireland* 55 (1 & 2), 2020 100–19, 117.
97 IICSA, Accountability and Reparations Report, 37.
98 s1 Limitation (Childhood Abuse) (Scotland) Act 2017; L. Sarmas, "Mixed Messages of Sexual Assault and the Statute of Limitations: *Stringer v. Clark*, the IPP 'Reforms' and an Argument for Change" *Melbourne University Law Review* 32, 2006, 609–38; D. Katner, "Delayed Responses to Child Sexual Abuse, the Kavanaugh Confirmation Hearing, and Eliminating Statutes of Limitation for Child Sexual Abuse Cases" *American Journal of Criminal law* 47(1), 2020, 1–46.

References

Antonsdóttir, H.F, "Compensation as a Means to Justice? Sexual Violence Survivors' Views on the Tort Law Option in Iceland" *Feminist Legal Studies* 28, 2020, 277–300.

Balboni, J.M., *Clergy Sexual Abuse Litigation Survivors Seeking Justice* (Boulder and London: First Forum Press, 2011).

Burton, F., "Limitation, Vicarious Liability and Historic Actions for Abuse: A Changing Legal Landscape" *Journal of Personal Injury Law* 2013, 95.

Canny, M., *Limitation of Actions, 2nd edition* (Dublin: Round Hall, 2016).

Case, P., *Compensating Child Abuse in England and Wales* (Cambridge: Cambridge University Press, 2007).

Conaghan, J., "Tort Litigation in the Context of Intra-Familial Abuse" *Modern Law Review* 61(2), 1998, 132–61.

Conaghan, J., "Tort Law and Feminist Critique" *Current Legal Problems* 56, 2003, 175–209.

Dyson, M. "The Timing of Tortious and Criminal Actions for the Same Wrong" *Cambridge Law Journal* 70, 2012, 86–117.

Godden, N., "Sexual Abuse and Claims in Tort: Limitation Periods after *A v Hoare (and Other Appeals)* [2008] and *AB and Others v Nugent Care Society*; *GR v Wirral MBC* [2009]" *Feminist Legal Studies* 18, 2010, 179–90.

Godden-Rasul, N., "Retribution, Redress and the Harms of Rape. The Role of Tort Law" in A. Powell, N. Henry, and A. Flynn (eds), *Rape Justice* (London: Palgrave Macmillan, 2015), 112–26, 114.

Gumbel, E.-A., et al., *Guide to Child Abuse Compensation Claims, 3rd edition* (London: Lexis Nexis, 2016).

Katner, D., "Delayed Responses to Child Sexual Abuse, the Kavanaugh Confirmation Hearing, and Eliminating Statutes of Limitation for Child Sexual Abuse Cases" *American Journal of Criminal Law* 47(1), 2020, 1–46.

Law Commission, *Limitation of Actions*, Paper 270, HC 23 (UK: House of Commons, 2001), [3.34].

Law Reform Commission, *Consultation Paper on The Law of Limitation of Actions Arising from Non-Sexual Abuse of Children* (Dublin: LRC CP16–2000).

McKay, S., *Sophia's Story* (Dublin: Gill & Macmillan, 1998).

Nugent, J., "The Statute of Limitations in Sexual Abuse Cases" *Bar Review* 3(5), 1998, 222–24.

O'Gorman, C., *Beyond Belief* (London: Hodder and Stoughton, 2010).

Royal Commission into Institutional Responses to Child Sexual Abuse, *Report of Case Study No 11. Christian Brothers* (Canberra: Commonwealth of Australia, 2014).

Royal Commission into Institutional Responses to Child Sexual Abuse, *Consultation on Redress and Civil Litigation* (Canberra: Commonwealth of Australia, 2015), 196.

Royal Commission into Institutional Responses to Child Sexual Abuse, *Redress and Civil Litigation Report* (Canberra: Commonwealth of Australia, 2015).

Sarmas, L., "Mixed Messages of Sexual Assault and the Statute of Limitations: *Stringer v. Clark*, the IPP 'Reforms' and an Argument for Change" *Melbourne University Law Review* 32, 2006, 609–38.

Senate Standing Committees on Community Affairs, *Lost Innocents: Righting the Record – Report on Child Migration* (Canberra: Parliament of Australia, 2001), 221, 224.

Sgroi, S.M., "The McColgan Case: Increasing Public Awareness of Professional Responsibility for Protecting Children from Physical and Sexual Abuse in the Republic of Ireland" *Journal of Child Sexual Abuse* 8(1), 1999, 113–27.

Smith, S. and Duff, A., "Access to Justice for Victims of Historic Institutional Abuse" *Éire-Ireland* 55 (1 & 2), 2020 100–19, 117.

Wheeler, J., *Journal of Personal Injury Law* (3) C181–C184.

Woolf, H., *Access to Justice, Final Report* (London: HMSO, 1996).

9 Tort law

Organizational liability

Introduction

Litigation against an organization can serve important accountability goals for non-recent child sexual abuse (NRCSA) survivors by holding organizations that did not protect children responsible for their acts of omission and commission. It is usually not possible to hold an organization to account in criminal prosecutions because criminal liability generally only attaches to individuals. Organizational accountability in tort is achieved through both the litigation process and the finding. Discovery, or disclosure, as it is known in England and Wales, is the pre-trial procedure whereby a litigant obtains documents of relevance to the issues in dispute and which are in the possession of another party[1] prior to the trial of the action. Through this crucial process, litigation can expose as untrue an organization's claims; for example, that it did not understand the harms of child sexual abuse (CSA), or that it was not aware of its members who abused children. Through discovery, a lawyer may be able to access important documents revealing systemic wrongdoing by organizations, such as not acting on reports of sexual abuse, or moving abusers to different locations without informing state authorities or parents.[2]

A civil action against an organization can also have a broader deterrent effect beyond that seen in a criminal process or in a lawsuit against an individual abuser, because it may force the organization to reform its reporting and oversight practices. Survivors cite the desire to prevent other children being abused as a key motivation in the pursuit of any form of legal response for NRCSA.[3] Exposing organizational practices implicated in abuse and holding organizations to account through a finding of liability and requiring them to pay damages can also compel other organizations that wish to avoid being sued to improve their child protection policies and practices.

Litigation may also result in the issuing of an apology on behalf of the organization as part of the terms of settlement. This can be seen as a form of recognition of the survivor's suffering and the organization's role in it. High-profile Irish examples include apologies by the Christian Brothers and the state read into the record of the High Court in settlement of litigation

DOI: 10.4324/9780429468162-11

brought by survivor Ron McCartan,[4] and the apology read into the record of the High Court by Éamonn Walsh, Bishop of the Diocese of Ferns for failing to 'recognize and act on the threat posed by the late Fr Fortune to Colm O'Gorman' and for the harm suffered by O'Gorman as a consequence.[5]

Tort litigation may also be seen as informing the development of state responses to NRCSA, with governments sometimes forced to act to initiate public inquiries by the groundswell of litigation against state entities (see Chapter 10). This may be understood as a form of recognition of the survivor as a rights-bearing citizen whose knowledge and experience warrants being taken seriously by the state.

There are also practical reasons for pursuing organizations rather than individuals; an organization is usually insured or has means. Suing an organization implicated in abuse may be the only option for survivors who do not qualify for statutory redress schemes, or for survivors abused by someone of no means, or someone who is deceased or is now gravely ill. There are serious personal risks in suing an organization, many of which mirror those discussed in the Introduction to this Part and in Chapter 8 in relation to litigation against an individual. Survivors risk having an award of costs made against them. Religious orders in both Ireland and Australia have been vigorous in seeking costs against litigants whose claims against them have failed.[6] Survivors must endure cross-examination and challenge by defence lawyers, without the special rules governing the questioning of vulnerable witnesses that apply in the criminal context, and typically they must confront a wall of institutional denial and deflection maintained by an organization with infinitely greater financial and legal resources than the survivor and their community. As with litigation against an individual, survivors suing an organization must reckon with the possibility of publicity. The observations made in Chapter 8 about statutes of limitation also apply to anyone commencing litigation against an organization.

In this chapter we consider the legal developments around holding organizations to account in NRCSA litigation focusing on the relevant doctrinal issues. We use 'organization' to describe any entity, whether incorporated or not, that is organized for some purpose or work. This includes charities, religious congregations and orders, religious, educational, spiritual and other institutions and state authorities.

The doctrinal framework

An organization may be directly liable for negligently failing to prevent the plaintiff being sexually abused, or because it has breached a non-delegable duty of care to them. Alternatively, an organization may be indirectly (vicariously) liable for the sexual abuse.

An organization may be directly liable if it has negligently failed to prevent the sexual abuse from taking place. An organization may be liable in negligence in one of four ways: (1) negligence in employing or continuing to employ staff the organization knew/should have known were abusers; (2) failing to exercise reasonable supervision and direction of employees; (3) failing to investigate abuse following reports by victims and (4) failing to take reasonable steps to prevent or stop sexual abuse, such as by not taking reasonable steps to provide safeguards for children or to train staff properly, or a continued practice of turning a blind eye to credible claims of sexual abuse.[7]

Alternatively, a plaintiff[8] may argue the organization has a 'non-delegable duty' of care to them, which means that the nature of the relationship between the organization and the plaintiff is such that the duty cannot be delegated to an employee or agent or independent contractor. Instead, the defendant is responsible for ensuring that reasonable care is taken.[9] This form of liability holds the organization liable to victims injured due to the torts of any employees or independent contractors to whom it has delegated its duty of care. Examples include a school and a pupil[10] or a health authority and a patient.[11] Non-delegable duties in NRCSA cases involve a higher standard of care and are broader in scope than vicarious liability, discussed next. Courts are reluctant to find non-delegable duties in NRCSA cases.

The most common form of claim raised in NRCSA litigation against an organization is that the organization should be held vicariously liable for the tortious acts of relevant individuals.[12] Vicarious liability is a form of indirect or secondary liability whereby an employer can be held liable for the wrongdoing of an employee, or someone deemed equivalent to an employee. The law on vicarious liability has traditionally focused on whether two conditions could be satisfied: (1) a relationship of employer-employee between the wrongdoer and the organization and (2) the wrongdoer was acting in the course of their employment when they committed the tort. When assessing the latter, the courts have historically relied on the 'Salmond test' of 1907, configured in terms of master and servant and asking whether the employee's act was 'a wrongful and unauthorised mode of doing some act authorised by the master'.[13] By excluding liability for criminal acts such as sexual violence, which an employer could never authorize, the Salmond test effectively insulated organizations from being held liable for CSA.

To say that the law in this area is complex would be an understatement. Much more so than the criminal law, tort for organizational liability in NRCSA cases has been characterized by rapid developments since the start of the new millennium. It continues to evolve, with new decisions emanating from the higher courts on a regular basis, especially in Canada and in England and Wales. Comprehensive discussion is beyond the scope of this chapter. Here we explore how each country has responded to attempts by survivors to sue organizations for abuse by their employees or members or other individuals connected to the organization. We focus on vicarious liability and we consider the particular challenges facing litigants pursuing organizations that do not possess independent legal status separate from their members.

England and Wales

The first major case on vicarious liability for NRCSA was *Lister v Hesley Hall Limited* in 2001.[14] The defendants employed an in-house warden at a private school boarding house who had been convicted of sexually abusing vulnerable 12 to 15-year-old boys from 1979 to 1982. The warden was responsible for running the school, but in the evenings he and his wife supervised the boys. Unbeknownst to the employer, the warden groomed the boys, showed them pornographic videos and committed acts of gross indecency including oral sex and buggery. In 1997 some survivors made claims against Hesley Hall for personal injury, specifically that the company was vicariously liable for the warden's wrongdoing.

Lord Steyn stated that an employer might not be 'at fault', but it may be 'fair' that they should bear some responsibility.[15] The warden's 'sexual abuse was so inextricably interwoven with the carrying out of his duties and so closely connected with his employment that it would be fair and just to hold the employers vicariously liable'.[16] The decision paved the way for more generous interpretations of vicarious liability and its application in educational and care home settings where there is an employment contract. Employers are liable for potential as well as actual risks requiring them to mitigate against any likely adverse consequences, for example, by conducting more rigorous employment checks and introducing better monitoring and safeguarding measures as part of their risk management practices.

Vicarious liability 'on the move'

Establishing vicarious liability has been challenging in relation to the non-corporate structures of religious organizations,[17] but the series of cases culminating in *JGE v The Trustees of the Portsmouth Roman Catholic Diocesan Trust*[18] (holding that Trustees of a Catholic diocese may be liable for priests' actions) and *Catholic Child Welfare Society and Others v Various Claimants and the Institute of the Brothers of the Christian School and others* (CCWS)[19] has firmly established that representatives of Catholic dioceses or religious orders may be vicariously liable for the actions of clergy/members.[20]

CCWS concerned abuse of children by brother teachers at a Catholic school for children in care. The school was run by a Board of Managers (the Catholic Child Welfare Society) with legislative responsibility which had recruited those teachers from the Catholic Institute of the Brothers of the Christian Schools, also known as the De La Salle Institute (the Institute). The case was highly complex, involving a group action with 170 male claimants and 35 defendants, comprising 34 members or representatives of the Board of Managers or the Institute and one individual abuser.

The Board of Managers took over the school in 1979 and inherited, under statute, the liabilities of the managers of the school before that date. The judge at first instance ruled that the Board of Managers was vicariously liable for the teachers' acts of abuse but that the Institute was not. The Board accepted responsibility and was willing to pay damages in part but appealed on the basis that the Institute was jointly liable and should also make a financial contribution. The Institute refused, albeit 146 of the claimants alleged that they had been assaulted by its members, arguing that the relationship of the individual Brothers to the Institute was 'insufficiently close'. The issue on appeal was whether the Institute could be jointly vicariously liable with the Board of Managers for the abuse by teachers.

The head of the Institute is the Superior General of the Christian Brothers in Rome who delegates authority to local 'Provinces' to manage its members. Brothers are bound by detailed and very strict rules of conduct and take vows of chastity, poverty and obedience. If employed by a third party (technically the Board of Managers) as a teacher they must surrender all their worldly goods. The Board allowed the local Provincial to designate a brother to act as headmaster.

Delivering the majority judgment, Lord Phillips asserted that 'the law of vicarious liability is on the move'[21] but that 'the precise criteria for imposing vicarious liability for sexual abuse are still in the course of refinement by judicial decision'.[22] He mandated a two-stage test: first, whether the relationship between the member teachers and the Institute was capable of giving rise to vicarious liability; and second, examination of the connection that linked that relationship with the individual member's wrongful act or omission.[23]

Lord Phillips identified five policy reasons that justify the imposition of vicarious liability: (i) the employer is more likely to have the means to compensate the victim than the employee and can be expected to have insurance; (ii) the tort will have been committed as a result of the activity being undertaken by the employee on behalf of the employer; (iii) the employee's activity is likely to be part of the employer's business activity; (iv) the employer, by employing the employee to carry on the activity, will have created the risk of the tort committed by the employee; (v) the employee will, to a greater or lesser degree, have been under the control of the employer.[24] Where there is no contract of employment but the relationship has these features, that relationship can be treated as *akin* to employment.[25] Here, this stage was satisfied because the relationship between the teaching brothers and the Institute had all the essential elements of the relationship between employer and employees: the Institute's hierarchical structure, which was analogous to that of a corporate body, the brothers' teaching activity was undertaken because of the Provincial's direction; the teaching was in furtherance of the Institute's objective or mission and the Institute's rules dictated how brothers were obliged to conduct themselves as teachers.[26] Lord Phillips acknowledged that the relationship between the brothers and the Institute differed from an employer–employee relationship in that the brothers were bound to the Institute not by contract but their vows, the brothers entered into deeds obliging them to transfer all their earnings to the Institute and it provided for their needs from these funds. These elements rendered the relationship between the brothers and the Institute closer than that of an employer and its employees.[27]

Second, was there a 'close connection' between the relationship and the sexual abuse perpetrated? This stage was satisfied because the brothers were 'employed' by the school to *care for* boys who were vulnerable in three different ways; as children, in effect 'imprisoned' in the school and because their personal history and experience made it less likely that they would be believed. The brother teachers were placed in the school to care for the pupils' educational and religious needs. Abusing the boys in their care was diametrically opposed to those objectives but, 'paradoxically, that very fact was one of the factors that provided the necessary close connection between the abuse and the relationship between the brothers and the Institute'.[28] The status of a brother was no doubt treated by the managers as an assurance that children could safely be entrusted to his care. The placement of teacher brothers in a residential school greatly enhanced the risk of abuse by them if they had a propensity for such misconduct.

The Supreme Court allowed the appeal and held both the Board of Management and the De La Salle Institute vicariously liable for sexual abuse by the brothers.

The position of religious 'orders' other than Catholic orders

In 2020 the High Court expanded the scope of vicarious liability to Jehovah's Witnesses in *A v The Trustees of the Watchtower Bible and Tract Society*.[29] The High Court held that the trustees of the society of Jehovah's Witnesses were vicariously liable for sexual assaults carried out by one of their ministerial servants on a four-year old girl during congregational activities between 1989 and 1994. He determined that the 'high level of control over all aspects of the life of a Jehovah's Witness is arguably a closer relationship than that to be found in an employer/employee relationship. It is at least akin to such a relationship'.[30] He concluded that the relationship between the elders and their congregation was therefore sufficiently 'close in character' to that of a typical employer/employee and that it was just and fair to impose vicarious liability.[31] Regarding stage two of Lord Phillip's test, Globe J held that the 'progressive acts of intimacy were only possible because [the perpetrator] had the actual or ostensible status of a ministerial servant that meant no one who saw him questioned his being alone with the claimant'.[32] He concluded that the defendants should be held responsible for what the abuser did.[33]

Subsequently, Davies LJ in *The Trustees of Barry Congregation of Jehovah's Witnesses v BXB*[34] reviewed the development of the law, including other cases where adults had been assaulted in non-religious settings. B had been raped by an elder in 1990. In 2020, the High Court judge had allowed the claim to proceed under s33 Limitation Act 1980 (see Chapter 8) and awarded £62,000 for psychiatric injuries. Approving Globe J's reasoning in *A*, the CA unanimously confirmed that in relation to the 'business' of the congregation, an elder is equivalent to a priest in terms of his authority to conduct the 'business' of the Roman Catholic Church, thereby satisfying stage one. Regarding stage two, the close connection test was met by the conferral of authority by the Jehovah's Witnesses organization upon its elders and the latter's physical proximity to the congregation.[35] Implicitly, in approving both High Court decisions, the Court of Appeal also acknowledged the impact of PTSD.

Further expansion

The flexibility of the common law is evident in *Armes v Nottinghamshire County Council*.[36] Armes had been abused as a child by two sets of foster parents during the 1980s. A majority of the Supreme Court was prepared to extend the principle of vicarious liability.[37] It held that the relationship between a local authority (responsible for children put into its care) and foster parents (in whose homes those children were placed) was akin to employment. The authority was vicariously liable for abuse carried out by the foster parents. The Court justified its decision by the five factors identified in *CCWS* and concluding that they were all present in the relationship between the authority and the foster parents. Lord Reed noted that the placement of children with foster parents may create a risk of potential sexual abuse over which they may have limited control but that such risk is relevant to the imposition of vicarious liability because 'it may be considered fair that they should compensate the unfortunate children for whom that risk materialises'.[38] He confirmed that the local authority's powers enabled it to exercise a significant degree of control over foster parents including 'approval, inspection, supervision and removal' to ensure that the child's needs are met, unlike 'any parallel in ordinary family life'. Furthermore, councils have the means or can take out insurance to cover the consequences of criminal acts, something that foster parents are unable to do.[39]

In 2020 referring to the Supreme Court delivered two companion judgments addressing the scope of the doctrine of vicarious liability generally. Both decisions respond to academic and practitioner concerns that the doctrine was being stretched too far[40] and sought to restrain further expansion. In *Barclays Bank v Various Claimants*[41] the Court indicated a more cautious approach should be taken to the 'akin to employment' relationship and that the starting point should be the details of the parties' relationship.[42] There, the Bank was held not to be vicariously liable for the non-recent sexual abuse of adults by an independent contractor. In the companion case of *Morrison*[43] (which did not involve sexual abuse), the Court also sought to reduce the number of cases where policy could be used to justify future extensions of vicarious liability doctrine. However, both cases indicate that there is a sub-category of sexual abuse cases where Lord Phillips' policy concerns in *CCWS* will continue to be relevant.[44] This is welcome. While such nuances may create uncertainty and complexity in vicarious liability law generally, the case law examined earlier indicates that such an exception is justified for sexual abuse cases, where the factors identified by Lord Phillips, especially an organization's creation of a risk to children (of being sexually abused), and its role in supervising (or not) its employees, remain central to the court's determination regarding vicarious liability in NRCSA cases.

Ireland

The question of vicarious liability for an employee's perpetration of sexual abuse was first explored in the 2003 case of *Delahunty v South Eastern Health Board, St Joseph's Industrial School and the Minister for Education and Science.*[45] Delahunty had been sexually assaulted by a housemaster working in an industrial school, when at the age of 11 he had visited a classmate resident at the school. Visits were encouraged by the school. Delahunty suffered serious psychiatric and psychological injuries in adulthood caused by the assault, including severe bouts of depression. Having considered *Lister* and progressive Canadian jurisprudence, O'Higgins J held that there was not a sufficient degree of connection between the housemaster's employment and the sexual assault of a visitor to justify holding the school vicariously liable for his actions. However, O'Higgins J left 'open the question on a fuller analysis' whether sexual abuse could ever be within the scope of a housemaster's employment.[46]

The importance of the test for vicarious liability was thrown into stark relief by *O'Keeffe v Hickey*.[47] *O'Keeffe* highlights the disjunction between the Irish state's professed commitment to addressing NRCSA in industrial schools via public inquiry and acts of reparation (Chapters 10 and 11), and its approach to survivors of abuse in a day primary school. Louise O'Keeffe was sexually assaulted in 1973 by her school principal while attending Dunderrow National School, Cork. Almost two years prior to her abuse, a complaint of sexual abuse had been made against the principal, Leo Hickey. Following more complaints later in 1973 he resigned and moved to another school where he remained for 22 years. In 1998 he pleaded guilty to 21 sample charges relating to sexual abuse of 21 girls who had been former pupils at the Dunderrow school, including O'Keeffe. In this litigation she claimed that the state[48] was vicariously liable for the sexual abuse. The hierarchical structure of the school was typical of Irish national schools. The bishop acted as the school patron, while the management duties were conferred on a school manager who was the parish priest, and who was responsible for the employment and discharge of teachers. The Department of Education paid teachers' salaries and checked their qualifications. It also exercised a supervisory role over a teacher's activities in the school.

Fennelly J, giving the majority judgment explored the international cases, considering *Lister* and the Australian case of *Lepore*, discussed below. He concluded that the close connection test should be adopted and that sexual abuse should not be excluded from this type of liability. However, Fennelly J concluded that because the state did not directly employ Principal Hickey, it was not vicariously liable.[49] Unfortunately, there was no consideration of the broader 'akin to employment' test.

Hardiman J held that the Minister could hardly be responsible for failing to protect children, when he was 'quite unaware' of the pattern of sexual abuse and the prior complaint against principal Hickey. This ignored the state's abdication of its role in child protection and its failure to create a child protection system in schools.[50] *O'Keeffe* placed Irish plaintiffs suing for NRCSA in a far weaker position than comparators under English and Australian law.[51]

Institutional responsibility of Catholic religious orders

In *Hickey v McGowan*[52] the Supreme Court explored the institutional responsibility of religious orders for NRCSA. Pádraig Hickey sued for injuries flowing from sexual abuse perpetrated by his teacher and former Marist Brother, Christopher Cosgrove, from 1968 to 1972 while he was a pupil at St John's National School in Sligo. A criminal investigation resulted in Cosgrove's conviction.[53] Hickey sued Cosgrove and Brother McGowan, the Provincial of the Marist Order. The High Court awarded him €250,000 general damages against Cosgrove and €100,000 for general damages against McGowan. On appeal, the Supreme Court held that the close connection test represented the law in Ireland on vicarious liability.[54] Delivering the majority judgment, O'Donnell J held that although the school had no residential dimension, and that the children were not especially vulnerable, the test was met.[55] O'Donnell J noted that as the abuse took place 'during the very act of teaching in the classroom', there was no question as to whether the close connection test had been met.[56] Echoing Lord Phillips in *CCWS*' identification of the reasons justifying vicarious liability, O'Donnell J stated 'it is fair to impose liability on those who choose a general activity of value to them, which creates or exacerbates attendant risks'.[57]

O'Donnell J. was satisfied that the Marist Order (or its members), as represented by McGowan, could be vicariously liable for Cosgrove's actions. He considered the close connection test in *CCWS* and stated

> to apply tests drawn from the modern world of commerce and industry to religious organisations which have existed for centuries is in my view to miss the sheer scale and impact of religious institutions on people's daily lives particularly in the Ireland of the first three-quarters of the 20th century.[58]

He described the relationship between the member of a religious order and his or her fellow members and the order itself as 'much more intense, constant and all pervasive than the relationship between an employer and an employee'; instead, everything in the organization of religious orders is directed towards emphasizing the collective.[59] The vows of obedience, poverty and celibacy created a particular relationship between a member and the order that involved subjugation of the member's will, economic dependency on the order and the primacy of relationships with the order and with God. The objective of teaching young people was not incidental to the order's work but 'the manner in which the order seeks to achieve its object'.[60] Cosgrove's teaching was not merely a job, but a religious vocation.[61] O'Donnell J noted

> once it is accepted that there can be vicarious liability of acts of abuse, a religious order (or its members) may be vicariously liable for acts of abuse which are sufficiently closely connected to the object and mission of the order.[62]

That included Cosgrove's actions. However, that was not the end of the Court's analysis.

The challenges posed by unincorporation

O'Donnell J in *McGowan* criticized the finding in *CCWS* that the Christian Brothers (the Institute) was a corporate association. He stated that the issue was not addressed in argument or discussed adequately in *CCWS*. Rather, the cases referred to as establishing that the Christian Brothers were a corporate body, *Heaton's* and *Dubai,*[63] were cases about trade unions and partnerships, both of which had been conferred with legal status by statute.[64] There was no such statutory intervention in the case of religious orders or the Catholic Church. O'Donnell J held the Marist Order was an unincorporated association.[65] Because it was unincorporated, only the members *at the time of the abuse* were liable.[66] For the plaintiffs, this means that the appropriate course of action when suing a religious order is to

> write to the order or provincial threatening to sue all individual members of the order unless a defendant is nominated. If that course is not taken, then all members who can be identified can be joined as defendants.

O'Donnell J acknowledged that if no nomination is made, any judgment obtained against members is individual and whether damages will be paid by insurance or the order's assets will depend largely on the terms of the insurance policy and the order's willingness to make funds available. The majority's approach allows defendant orders (and other unincorporated associations) to minimize their exposure to liability by simply refusing to nominate a defendant, thus forcing the plaintiff to sue each person who was a member of the order at the time of the abuse. This further complicates things for plaintiffs, who will not easily (if at all) be able to access the records of the relevant order (or diocese in the case of clerical abuse) to identify all the members. Even if they do, and even if they successfully sue, the plaintiff must then attempt to recover damages from each individual member of the religious order, who will have taken a vow of poverty and given their earnings to the order. Much will depend on 'the willingness and ability of the order to make funds available to satisfy any judgment against an individual'.[67] O'Donnell J[68] acknowledged that this was a narrow and technical approach and that reform of the law might be considered.[69]

The decision in *McGowan* is deeply frustrating for survivors and their allies. For centuries religious communities have created legal bodies, usually charitable trusts, capable of owning property, such as schools and hospitals, and which can enter into legal relations in pursuance of the order or diocese's mission. An order/diocese's work in pursuance of that mission, such as the teaching of children and employment of teachers, is carried out by the unincorporated association which has no legal status independent of its members. It is unjust to allow members of a religious order or diocese to have the benefits of historical ownership of property and assets through the law of trusts, without the responsibilities that come from incorporation. The unfairness is highlighted by the Marist Order's legal ability to sell property worth €20 million in 2020.[70] It is possible that another case, in which evidence is adduced demonstrating an organization's corporate structure, may lead a court to take a different view.[71] These arguments are underscored by the adoption of insurance against NRCSA claims by dioceses and orders, the indemnification of certain orders by the state (see Chapter 10), the exposure of unincorporated associations to criminal liability[72] as well as the constitutional rights of plaintiffs to equal treatment[73] and access to the courts.[74]

Australia

The leading decision is *NSW v Lepore & Anor; Rich v Queensland; Samin v Queensland,*[75] concerning appeals of three cases involving NRCSA perpetrated in state schools, brought together in 2003 at the High Court of Australia from New South Wales (NSW) and Queensland. For present purposes we focus on the case of Angelo Lepore who was sexually assaulted as a seven-year-old student by his teacher in 1978. At the time, the teacher was convicted of common assault, fined, sentenced to a good behaviour bond and resigned from teaching. In 2001, as an adult, Lepore initiated proceedings against the perpetrator for trespass to the person (battery) and the NSW government for negligence in failing to protect him from sexual abuse. In the final appellate judgment, the High Court proposed four separate confusing tests for the circumstances in which an authority should be held vicariously liable for the intentional torts of an employee, and it is this mixed ruling that informs Australian doctrine. An 'insistence on scrutiny of the detail of the employment as a way of deciding on whether the employee acted in the course of employment' prevailed in the judgment in which three judges decided that sexual assault cannot be considered part of the course of employment and three judges decided that it can be considered as such.[76]

Lepore is widely criticized for its confusing ratio and its outcomes for survivors. The UK Supreme Court described the decision as a 'bewildering variety of analysis'[77] while Australian lawyers state, 'that would be the understatement'.[78] Feminist scholars note the decision exhibits a 'lack of appreciation of the context and nature of sexual assault in schools' especially in its failure to acknowledge the role of 'power exercised by a teacher over a pupil, the narrow focus on child sexual assault within the frameworks of intimacy and pseudo-parental care situations and the failure to consider the issue from the child's point of view'.[79] *Lepore* has since been affirmed in two important cases, albeit each with a different outcome for each plaintiff.

Vicarious liability and direct liability in Erlich

In *Erlich* in 2015 the Supreme Court of Victoria applied *Lepore* when it upheld findings of both vicarious and direct liability regarding the sexual abuse of a female pupil by the headmistress of the ultra-orthodox Adass Israel School.[80] The Court held that for vicarious liability to arise in the case of sexual abuse by a teacher, there must have been a sufficient connection between that abuse and what the teacher was employed to do. In *Erlich*, the close connection was made out to the judge's satisfaction.[81] *Erlich* is very significant, but far from usual. It involved reasonably contemporary allegations concerning highly particular situations of intimacy and power, including a female perpetrator within a little-understood closed community. In the 2016 census, only 0.4 per cent of the Australian population identified as Jewish; fewer would identify as ultraorthodox.[82]

Children of the closed Adass Community 'were not raised having knowledge of world events and were completely isolated from anything "beyond the community [they] were within"'.[83] Plaintiff Hadassa Sara (Dassi) Erlich had attended the school from 1990 to 2006, from kindergarten until the end of her first year after high school, when she was employed as a teacher. She then left the school when she was married within the community. Erlich alleged that headmistress Malka Leifer sexually abused her during Jewish Studies classes, at her own home, while on school camps and elsewhere, often in the guise of instruction about marriage. On learning of Erlich's allegations in 2008, the school immediately flew Leifer to Israel before she could be investigated. Erlich sued the school, claiming that it was both directly and vicariously liable for Leifer's conduct and that it was negligent.[84]

The Court determined that the relationship between Erlich and Leifer in the context of an ultraorthodox, sex-segregated Jewish school and closed community was invested with a high degree of power and intimacy to which Erlich was especially vulnerable. The school was therefore liable for the creation of the risk of sexual abuse and, because Leifer represented the 'mind and the will of the school' as its headmistress, it was also found directly liable for the abuse.[85] This was a rare finding by a court of institutional fault for sexual abuse.[86]

Assessing vicarious liability, citing *Lepore*, Rush J found that: the connection between the assaults and Leifer's employment made it 'just to treat such contact as occurring in the course of employment'; the plaintiff was particularly vulnerable; there was a close connection 'between the enterprise and the wrong'; and, as such, the school was estopped from asserting that Leifer was not acting as its servant or agent. $1.3 million was awarded, including $100,000 in exemplary damages relating to the school's 'deplorable' conduct in flying Leifer to Israel. After a protracted legal battle, in September 2020, Israel's Supreme Court finally ruled that Leifer should be extradited to face 74 criminal charges of CSA against Dassi Erlich and her two sisters, who have each obtained a settlement from the school.[87] Leifer was extradited in January 2021.[88]

Power and intimacy restated

Immediately following *Erlich*, the High Court then affirmed *Lepore* in the *Prince Alfred College* case discussed in Chapter 8. While the Court did not address whether liability was made out in this case, it did make pronouncements on the vicarious liability tests in *Lepore*. The majority held that when an employee has committed an intentional criminal act, the relevant test is

> whether the institution (or employer) had placed that individual in a position of power and intimacy *vis-à-vis* the [injured party], such that [the perpetrator's] apparent performance of [their appointed role] gave the occasion for the wrongful acts, and that because he misused or took advantage of his position, the wrongful acts could be regarded as having been committed in the course or scope of his employment.[89]

Therefore, the court should consider any special role that the employer has assigned to the employee and the position in which the employee is thereby placed vis-à-vis the victim. In determining whether the apparent performance of such a role may be said to give the 'occasion' for the wrongful act, particular features may be taken into account. They include authority, power, trust, control and the ability to achieve intimacy with the victim. The latter feature may be especially important. Where, in such circumstances, the employee takes advantage of their position with respect to the victim, that may suffice to determine that the wrongful act should be regarded as committed in the course or scope of employment and as such render the employer vicariously liable.[90] This clear articulation of the applicable legal principles, which even the two dissenting judges accepted as the approach to be applied in Australia,[91] has been welcomed.[92] However, the *Prince Alfred College* case did not address the question of whether it is necessary for a plaintiff to prove that their abuser was an employee rather than a contractor. This is an important question for victims of clerical NRCSA in particular, because it is not clear whether parish priests and religious ministers are employees in Australian law.[93]

The problem of the unincorporated association

Both *Erlich* and the *Prince Alfred College* case involved schools that are incorporated associations. Incorporated Anglican dioceses responsible for boarding schools have also been sued for the sexual abuse of children.[94] For many years the great scandal in Australia was the inability to sue Catholic schools, churches, dioceses or religious orders that had historically refused to incorporate, ostensibly for reasons of recognizing the autonomy of each entity and individual. Throughout the twentieth century and beyond, Catholic bodies in Australia continued to organize their finances in an unincorporated manner to make it impossible for them to be sued.

The leading case was that of John Ellis who in 2002 approached the Catholic Church claiming to have been repeatedly abused as a child by his parish priest, Aiden Duggan, from 1974 to 1979. Ellis was offered $30,000 *ex gratia* on the basis of confidentiality and a waiver of liability, which he did not accept. In 2004, after Duggan had died leaving no assets, Ellis brought a common law claim suing both the Trustees of the Catholic Church and the then Archbishop of Sydney, Cardinal George Pell, for and on behalf of the Catholic Church in the Archdiocese of Sydney.[95] The Trustees were appointed under the *Roman Catholic Church Property Trust Act 1936 (NSW)* as guardians of property estimated to be currently worth tens of billions of dollars.[96] Ellis sued the Trust rather than the Catholic Church, presumably because the church is an unincorporated association.

Ellis submitted that both defendants were liable directly or in a representative capacity (representing the unincorporated association known as the Catholic Archdiocese of Sydney) for the wrongdoing of Duggan. On appeal the NSW Supreme Court upheld both the Trust's and Pell's claims of immunity, ruling that the Trust was not liable for the behaviour of clergy, nor was Pell liable for the Sydney Diocese at the time of Ellis's abuse, because he had 'no relevant connection with the Sydney Archdiocese' prior to 2001. Moreover, the Court affirmed that an unincorporated association (such as the Catholic Church in Australia) cannot (at common law) sue or be sued in its own name because, among other things, 'it does not exist as a juridical entity'.[97] The church refused to nominate a defendant to represent it and continued with this legal strategy for 25 years. Ellis was ordered to pay costs and declined leave to appeal to the High Court. He was pursued for three years for $750, 000 before the church waived costs[98] in a case that is stated to have cost the church A$1.5 million, including ultimately $568,000 in *ex gratia* payments.[99] Ellis was left with no legal remedy, and for years, both survivors and the church referred to the church's legal strategy simply as 'the Ellis defence' in Australia. The 'Ellis defence' has meant that Australian courts have not had to rule on the nature of the employment relationship of Catholic priests or brothers (or nuns) and have not had to consider judgments such as *CCWS* or *Hickey v McGowan*.

By 2020 all jurisdictions except the Northern Territory had introduced legislation to require unincorporated associations with responsibility for children to appoint a proper defendant with suitable assets could be named in a lawsuit to overcome the obstacle of the 'Ellis Defence'. If a defendant is not named, the court can appoint one, or it can appoint the trustees of an associated trust to respond to the claim, for example, the Trustees of the Catholic Church.[100] Importantly, these reforms are retrospective, so they may be used by plaintiffs claiming NRCSA.

Conclusion

The progressive developments in each country in respect of organizational liability indicate that tort law is gradually departing from historically narrow understandings of CSA as a problem of individual deviance ('the bad apples theory') and is increasingly recognizing it as a product of situations of power and control in which organizational cultures are gravely implicated. In England and Wales and in Ireland judicial expansion has been based on the recognition that it is just to impose liability on an organization that pursues an activity of value to them that creates or exacerbates risks to children. In Australia the courts have been more reluctant to expand vicarious liability on this basis in NRCSA cases, but there are indications of an increased openness to evaluating certain factors, including whether the organization had placed an employee or associate in a position of power and intimacy in relation to the child, which they abused.

The scope of organizational liability also needs expansion if justice is to be realized. Imposing direct liability on an organization for breach of a non-delegable duty is one potential way forward. It is possible that a future court in any of the three countries would allow a claim for NRCSA under this form of liability. The UK Supreme Court and the High Court of Australia have both considered this issue in recent years but have not yet extended a non-delegable duty to intentional torts such as sexual abuse.[101] Arguably, a non-delegable duty is more appropriate in NRCSA cases than vicarious liability, because it better captures the managerial or organizational fault involved. Unlike vicarious liability, which is a form of secondary liability and focuses on the organization's control over the abuser, a non-delegable duty, as a form of primary liability, better reflects the relationship between the organization and the child, specifically the responsibility for the child's welfare. In *Armes*, the UK Supreme Court refused to rule out the possibility of extending common law non-delegable duties to intentional torts.[102] This is a complex area of law and would, as Giliker notes, require careful conceptual and doctrinal work,[103] but the courts and parliaments in each country should consider it.

Survivors suing unincorporated associations face particular legal obstacles in identifying suitable defendants and in attaching liability to the organization rather than its members. Legislators in Ireland[104] and in England and Wales should look to Australia for inspiration in this regard and empower courts to require organizations to nominate defendants, or appoint one if they refuse to do so. In the meantime, doctrinal and conceptual uncertainty pervades this area of law, restricting law's power to hold organizations to account. Furthermore, organizations are not incentivized to improve their child protection practices if they are unlikely to be sued.

In some Australian states, following recommendations of the Royal Commission into Institutional Responses to Child Sexual Abuse, lawmakers have reformed key aspects of vicarious liability for future claims.[105] NSW, Tasmania, Queensland and Victoria have created a new form of statutory duty, also for future plaintiffs.[106] These developments are at least a positive legacy of the efforts of survivors and their lawyers and should be mirrored in England and Wales and Ireland.

As Chapter 8 and this chapter have shown, tort litigation is an immensely powerful legal response for NRCSA survivors who offer accountability and recognition. Through a judicial finding of liability and the award of damages, it can hold individuals and organizations to account for past, ongoing and future harms of NRCSA while offering survivors a measure of agency and control in the conduct of their litigation. Tort law also offers valuable outcomes to society by incentivizing organizations to improve their child protection practices through the publicity associated with litigation and awards of damages.

Both the Australian Royal Commission and the Independent Inquiry into Child Sexual Abuse have noted that NRCSA survivors have very little confidence in the civil law to deliver justice.[107] The challenges outlined in this chapter and in Chapter 8 show they have good reason to hold this view. Radical reform of statutes of limitation and organizational liability is needed in each country if tort law is to deliver justice in NRCSA claims.

Having examined both public (criminal law) and private law (tort) responses to NRCSA, we now turn to measures of governments to address and redress institutional NRCSA. The next chapter considers public inquiries, and the penultimate chapter, Chapter 11, examines reparations made to survivors.

Notes

1 This can be a person party to the proceedings or a person not party to the proceedings.

2 See T.D. Lytton, *Holding Bishops Accountable. How Lawsuits Helped the Catholic Church Confront Clergy Sexual Abuse* (Massachusetts: Harvard University Press, 2008), 146–52.

3 Royal Commission into Institutional Responses to Child Sexual Abuse Final Report Vol 4, 9; Accountability and Reparations Investigation Report at A:3; See also the submissions by survivors to Ireland's Oireachtas Committee on the Retention of Records Bill November 2019, http://jfmresearch.com/retention-of-records-bill-2019/.

4 M. Raftery, "Cheating Abuse Victims" *Irish Times*, 26 April 2006.

5 See C. O'Gorman, *Beyond Belief* (London: Hodder and Stoughton, 2010), 272–3.

6 C. Smith and A. Duff, "Access to Justice for Victims of Historic Institutional Abuse" *Éire-Ireland* 55 (1 & 2), 2020, 100–19, 109; K. Gleeson, "The Money

Problem: Reparation and Restorative Justice in the Catholic Church's Towards Healing Program" *Current Issues in Criminal Justice* 26(3), 2015, 317–32.

7 L. Hoyano and C. Keenan, *Child Abuse Law and Policy Across Boundaries*, (Oxford: Oxford University Press, 2010), 286–98 and P. Giliker, "Analysing Institutional Liability for Child Sexual Abuse in England and Wales and Australia: Vicarious Liability, Non-Delegable Duties and Statutory Intervention" *Cambridge Law Journal* 77(3), 2018, 506–35, 534.

8 As with Chapter 8, we use plaintiff and defendant throughout the chapter for clarity, and claimant and respondent in the sections on England and Wales and Australia, respectively.

9 *The Pass of Ballater* [1942] P 112, 117, Langton J.

10 *Woodland v Essex County Council* [2013] UKSC 66.

11 *Morrissey and Another v Health Service Executive and Others* [2020] IESC 6.

12 On the issues involved in claiming direct liability, see Giliker op. cit.

13 J.W. Salmond, *Law of Torts: A Treatise on the English Law of Liability for Civil Injuries* (London: Stevens and Haynes, 1907), 83–4.

14 [2001] UKHL 22, 10. In *Trotman v North Yorkshire County Council* [1998] EWCA Civ 1208 the CA held a local authority could not be vicariously liable for non-recent sexual assaults committed by one of its employees.

15 He was influenced by the Supreme Court of Canada's landmark decision in *Bazley v Curry* (1999) 174 DLR (4th) 45 which, along with *John Doe v Bennett* [2004] 1 SCR 436, has shaped the development of vicarious liability in NRCSA cases in courts across the common law world.

16 Ibid., 28.

17 See R. Scorer, "'Can I sue the Pope?' Child Abuse Litigation Against the Holy See" *Journal of Personal Injury Law* 25, 2012.

18 [2012] EWCA Civ 938.

19 [2012] UKSC 56.

20 K. Stevenson, et al., "Reparation for Betrayal of Trust in Child Sexual Abuse Cases: The Christian Duty of Care, Vicarious Liability and the Church of England" *Australian Feminist Law Journal* 41(2), 2015, 253–70.

21 *Catholic Child Welfare Society*, [19].

22 Ibid., [85].

23 [2012] UKSC 56, [21].

24 Ibid., [35].

25 Ibid., [47].

26 Ibid., [55].

27 Ibid., [58].

28 Ibid., [92].

29 [2015] EWHC 1722.

30 Ibid., [65].

31 Ibid., [71]

32 Ibid., [90].

33 Ibid., [152].

34 [2021] EWCA Civ 356.

35 Ibid., [89]

36 [2017] UKSC 60.

37 Lady Hale, Lord Kerr, Lord Clarke and Lord Reed. Lord Hughes dissented.

38 [61].

39 Ibid., [62].
40 See P. Giliker op. cit.
41 *Barclays Bank v Various Claimants* [2020] UKSC 13.
42 P. Giliker, "Can the Supreme Court Halt the Ongoing Expansion of Vicarious Liability: Barclays and Morrison in the UK Supreme Court?" *Journal of Professional Negligence* 37(2), 2021, 55–72 at 62.
43 *Morrison Supermarkets plc v Various Claimants* [2020] UKSC 12.
44 See Giliker op. cit. 2021, 68.
45 [2003] 4 IR 361. The case also dealt with the scope of the non-delegable duty of employers and others to children in their care.
46 [2003] 4 IR 349, 377.
47 [2008] IESC 72.
48 The Minister for Education and Science, Ireland and the Attorney General.
49 Geoghegan J dissented.
50 Ms O'Keeffe later succeeded on this point in the European Court of Human Rights. In a landmark judgment, the Court found Ireland had violated Article 3 of the European Convention on Human Rights (ECHR)'s prohibition of torture and inhuman and degrading treatment and punishment by failing to establish an effective system to protect pupils from abuse and had violated Article 13 ECHR (right to a remedy) by not compensating O'Keeffe. *O'Keeffe v Ireland*, Grand Chamber 35810/09, 28 January 2014; C. O'Mahony and U. Kilkelly, "*O'Keeffe v Ireland* and the Duty of the State to Identify and Prevent Child Abuse" *Journal of Social Welfare and Family Law* 36(3), 2014, 320–29. O'Mahony has also argued for state liability on the basis of constitutional law: C. O'Mahony, "State Liability for Abuse in Primary Schools: Systemic Failure and *O'Keeffe v Hickey*" *Irish Educational Studies* 28(3), 2009, 315–31.
51 J. Gallen, "Vicarious Liability and Historical Abuse: A Critical Analysis of Hickey v McGowan" *The Irish Jurist* 58, 2017, 184–92, 186.
52 [2017] IESC 6.
53 Along with five other teachers, including Cosgrove. See Sinéad Ring, "Representations of Justice in Sexual Abuse Cases" *The Guardian*, 9 May 2010, accessed 25 May 2021, www.theguardian.com/law/2010/may/11/guidance-trial-judges-sexual-abuse-cases; *Irish Independent*, 30 January 2008.
54 [24].
55 Denham CJ, O'Donnell, MacMenamin, Dunne JJ.
56 [26].
57 [41].
58 [37].
59 Ibid.
60 [37]. This approach is not very different to Lord Phillips in *CCWS* [56]
61 Ibid.
62 [38].
63 *Heaton's Transport (St Helens) Ltd v Transport and General Workers' Union* [1973] AC 15; *Thomas v National Union of Mineworkers (South Wales Area)* [1986] Ch 20; *Dubai Aluminium Co Ltd v Salaam* [2002] UKHL 48.
64 [49].
65 [52] 52.
66 Here, the liability was confined to the members for whom the wrongful act was done and at the time it was done.

67 [57]. Charleton J would have remitted the case to the High Court to see if liability could be established against Brother McGowan in his capacity as Provincial and on the basis that such an office is a *corporation sole*. See [55–67].
68 [56].
69 The Court reduced general damages to €75,000.
70 "Marist Fathers Secure €20 Million from Sale of South Dublin Lands" *The Irish Times*, 2 December 2020.
71 Trusts law could be employed to hold institutions to account. In *McDonald v Conroy* [2020] IECA 239 the Court of Appeal noted the development of the law in Canada on this area, as well as the academic writing on this area [151–152]. See also *JGE* op cit.
72 At least for statutory offences: *DPP v Wexford Farmers Club* [1994] 2 ILRC 295.
73 Article 40.1 Irish Constitution.
74 Article 40.3 Irish Constitution.
75 [2003] HCA 4.
76 P. Vines, "*NSW v Lepore*; *Samin v Queensland*; *Rich v Queensland*. Schools' Responsibility for Teachers' Sexual Assault. Non-delegable Duty and Vicarious Liability" *Melbourne University Law Review* 27(2), 2003, 625.
77 *Catholic Child Welfare Society v The Institute of the Brothers of the Christian Schools & Others* [2012] UKSC 56, [82].
78 A. Morrison QC in Royal Commission into Institutional Responses to Child Sexual Abuse, *Redress and Civil Litigation Report* (Commonwealth of Australia, 2015), 480.
79 J. Wangmann, "Liability for Institutional Child Sexual Assault: Where Does *Lepore* Leave Australia?" *Melbourne University Law Review* 28(1), 2004, 169–202, 170.
80 *Erlich v Leifer & Adass Israel School Inc* [2015] VSC 499.
81 [2003] HCA 4, [40].
82 Australian Bureau of Statistics, Media Release: 2016 Census data reveals "no religion" is rising fast, www.abs.gov.au/ausstats/abs@.nsf/a59af5c52fda0c7dca25704c001d21fa/7e65a144540551d7ca258148000e2b85.
83 *Erlich*, [11].
84 Erlich also claimed that the school breached its non-delegable duty of care owed to her, but the court held that in cases of intentional torts of an employee, the appropriate test to apply is vicarious liability, rather than non-delegable duty.
85 [2015] VSC 499, [78].
86 Erlich also claimed the school was liable in negligence. Rush J rejected this claim, finding that there was insufficient evidence to prove the school had breached its duty of care owed to her to take reasonable care, as there was no evidence that Leifer was previously known to be abusive.
87 A. Maguire, "Israeli Court Rules Malka Leifer Should be Extradited to Australia, but Obstacles Remain" *The Conversation*, 21 September 2020, accessed 25 May 2021, https://theconversation.com/israeli-court-rules-malka-leifer-should-be-extradited-to-australia-but-obstacles-remain-146549.
88 BBC News, "Malka Leifer: Israel Extradites Ex-Principal Accused of Child Sex Abuse in Australia," 25 January 2021, accessed 25 May 2021, www.bbc.com/news/world-middle-east-55795075.
89 (2016) 335 ALR 1 [84]. French CJ, Kiefel, Bell, Keane and Nettle JJ.
90 Ibid., 159–60 [80]–[81].

91 Gageler and Gordon JJ.

92 See A. Gray, "Liability of Educational Providers to Victims of Abuse: A Comparison and Critique" *Sydney Law Review* 39(2), 2017, 167–97.

93 L. Griffin and G. Briffa, "Still Awaiting Clarity: Why Victoria's New Civil Liability Laws for Organisational Child Abuse are Less Helpful than They Appear" *UNSW Law Journal* 43(2), 2020, 452, 475.

94 *S v The Corporation of the Synod of the Diocese of Brisbane* [2001] QSC 473. The Anglican Corporation of the Synod of the Diocese of Brisbane was sued for a teacher's sexual abuse of a boarding student at a preparatory school in 1990 and ordered to pay $494,000 including exemplary damages.

95 *Trustees of the Roman Catholic Church for the Archdiocese of Sydney v Ellis* [2007] NSWCA 117 (24 May 2007).

96 *Sydney Morning Herald*, 12 February 2018.

97 *Trustees of the Roman Catholic Church v Ellis* [47].

98 J. Ellis and N. Ellis, "A New Model for Seeking Meaningful Redress for Victims of Church-related Sexual Assault" *Current Issues in Criminal Justice* 26(1), 2018, 34–35.

99 Australian Lawyers Alliance, *Towards Healing: Designed Primarily for the Church, not Victims. Submission to the Royal Commission into Institutional Responses to Child Sexual Abuse* (Sydney: Australian Lawyers Alliance, 2013).

100 *Civil Liability Amendment (Organisational Child Abuse Liability) Act 2018 (NSW); Civil Liability and other Legislation Amendment Act 2019 (QLD); Legal Identity of Defendants (Organisational Child Abuse) Act 2018 (VIC); Justice Legislation Amendment (Organisational Liability for Child Abuse) Act 2019 (TAS); Civil Law (Wrongs) (Child Abuse Claims Against Unincorporated Bodies) Amendment Act 2018 (ACT)*. In Western Australia, a person may sue an unincorporated association by naming an office holder as the respondent. *Civil Liability Legislation Amendment (Child Sexual Abuse Actions) Act 2018 (WA)*.

101 In Australia, in *Erlich*, the court found a school's non-delegable duty extended to the care, supervision and control of children but not to intentional torts such as sexual abuse *Erlich* [2015] VSC 499 [78]. N. Foster, "Convergence and Divergence: The Law of Non-Delegable Duties in Australia and the United Kingdom" in A. Robertson and M. Tilbury (eds), *Divergences in Private Law* (Oxford: Hart Publishing, 2016), 119.

102 Lord Reid for the majority at [54] and [55]. In a non-NRCSA case, the UK Supreme Court has found that a school has a duty to ensure a safe environment for its students. *Woodland v Essex County Council* [2013] UKSC 66.

103 See Giliker 2018 op. cit.

104 The Law Reform Commission is exploring this issue under its fifth programme of Law Reform: 'Current Projects', Law Reform Commission, www.lawreform.ie/press-room/civil-liability-and-commercial-law.766.html.

105 NSW has extended vicarious liability to include liability for the actions of individuals 'akin to an employee' including contractors and clergy. *Civil Liability Amendment (Organisational Child Abuse Liability) Act 2018 (NSW)*. The provisions reflect *ADC's* focus on power and intimacy. Tasmania has similar provisions *Justice Legislation Amendment (Organisational Liability for Child Abuse) Act 2019. (TAS)*.

106 Following the recommendations of the Royal Commission (89 and 91), NSW, Victoria, Queensland and Tasmania created a new form of liability of

organizations for abuse of children in their care. In these jurisdictions it is now presumed that institutions are liable for the treatment of children and that individuals who are 'associated' with an institution attach this liability. *Civil Liability Amendment (Organisational Child Abuse Liability) Act 2018 (NSW)*, s6A; *The Wrongs Amendment (Organisational Child Abuse) Act 2017* (Victoria), s3.; *Civil Liability and Other Legislation Amendment Act 2019 s33D. (Queensland); Justice Legislation Amendment (Organisational Liability for Child Abuse) Act 2019 (TAS) s49F*. The definition of 'organization' has typically been broadened to include community, not-for-profit and volunteer organizations as well as organizations administering foster care or kinship care. Some of these have traditionally not fallen within the scope of liability at common law (such as foster care) and so the statutory inclusion enables causes of action not available at common law. See A. Silink and P. Stewart, "Tort Law Reform to Improve Access to Compensation for Survivors of Institutional Child Sexual Abuse" *University of NSW Law Journal* 39(2), 2016, 553–95.

107 Royal Commission into Institutional Responses to Child Sexual Abuse, *Redress and Civil Litigation Report* (Commonwealth of Australia, 2015), 431. IICSA, *Accountability and Reparations Report*.

References

Australian Lawyers Alliance, *Towards Healing: Designed Primarily for the Church, not Victims. Submission to the Royal Commission into Institutional Responses to Child Sexual Abuse* (Sydney: Australian Lawyers Alliance, 2013).

Ellis, J. and Ellis, N., "A New Model for Seeking Meaningful Redress for Victims of Church-related Sexual Assault" *Current Issues in Criminal Justice* 26(1), 2018, 34–35.

Foster, N., "Convergence and Divergence: The Law of Non-Delegable Duties in Australia and the United Kingdom" in A. Robertson and M. Tilbury (eds), *Divergences in Private Law* (Oxford: Hart Publishing, 2016), 119.

Gallen, J., "Vicarious Liability and Historical Abuse: A Critical Analysis of Hickey v McGowan" *The Irish Jurist* 58, 2017, 184–92.

Giliker, P., "Analysing Institutional Liability for Child Sexual Abuse in England and Wales and Australia: Vicarious Liability, Non-Delegable Duties and Statutory Intervention" *Cambridge Law Journal* 77(3), 2018, 506–35.

Giliker, P., "Can the Supreme Court Halt the Ongoing Expansion of Vicarious Liability: Barclays and Morrison in the UK Supreme Court?" *Journal of Professional Negligence* 37(2), 2021, 55–72.

Gleeson, K., "The Money Problem: Reparation and Restorative Justice in the Catholic Church's Towards Healing Program" *Current Issues in Criminal Justice* 26(3), 2015, 317–32.

Gray, A., "Liability of Educational Providers to Victims of Abuse: A Comparison and Critique" *Sydney Law Review* 39(2), 2017, 167–97.

Griffin, L. and G. Briffa, G., "Still Awaiting Clarity: Why Victoria's New Civil Liability Laws for Organisational Child Abuse are Less Helpful than They Appear" *UNSW Law Journal* 43(2), 2020, 452, 475.

Hoyano, L. and Keenan, C., *Child Abuse Law and Policy Across Boundaries*, (Oxford: Oxford University Press, 2010).

IICSA, *Accountability and Reparations Investigation Report* (2019), www.iicsa.org.uk/reports-recommendations/publications/investigation/accountability-reparations.

Lytton, T.D. *Holding Bishops Accountable. How Lawsuits Helped the Catholic Church Confront Clergy Sexual Abuse* (Massachusetts: Harvard University Press, 2008).

O'Gorman, C., *Beyond Belief* (London: Hodder and Stoughton, 2010).

O'Mahony, C., "State Liability for Abuse in Primary Schools: Systemic Failure and *O'Keeffe v Hickey*" *Irish Educational Studies* 28(3), 2009, 315–31.

O'Mahony, C. and Kilkelly, U., "*O'Keeffe v Ireland* and the Duty of the State to Identify and Prevent Child Abuse" *Journal of Social Welfare and Family Law* 36(3), 2014, 320–29.

Raftery, M., "Cheating Abuse Victims" *Irish Times*, 26 April 2006.

Royal Commission Final Report Vol 4, 9; *Accountability and Reparations Investigation Report* (Canberra: Commonwealth of Australia, 2015).

Royal Commission into Institutional Responses to Child Sexual Abuse, *Redress and Civil Litigation Report* (Canberra: Commonwealth of Australia, 2015), 431.

Salmond, J.W., *Law of Torts: A Treatise on the English Law of Liability for Civil Injuries* (London: Stevens and Haynes, 1907), 83–84.

Scorer, R., "'Can I Sue the Pope?' Child Abuse Litigation Against the Holy See" *Journal of Personal Injury Law* 2012, 25.

Silink, A. and Stewart, P., "Tort Law Reform to Improve Access to Compensation for Survivors of Institutional Child Sexual Abuse" *University of NSW Law Journal* 39(2), 2016, 553–95.

Smith, C. and Duff, A., "Access to Justice for Victims of Historic Institutional Abuse" *Éire-Ireland* 55 (1 & 2), 2020, 100–19.

Stevenson, K., et al., "Reparation for Betrayal of Trust in Child Sexual Abuse Cases: The Christian Duty of Care, Vicarious Liability and the Church of England" *Australian Feminist Law Journal* 41(2), 2015, 253–70.

Vines, P., "*NSW v Lepore*; *Samin v Queensland*; *Rich v Queensland*. Schools' Responsibility for Teachers' Sexual Assault. Non-delegable Duty and Vicarious Liability" *Melbourne University Law Review* 27(2), 2003, 625.

Wangmann, J., "Liability for Institutional Child Sexual Assault: Where Does *Lepore* Leave Australia?" *Melbourne University Law Review* 28(1), 2004, 169–202.

10 Public inquiries

Introduction

This chapter considers three public inquiries established to examine non-recent child sexual abuse (NRCSA) (specifically institutional abuse); the Irish Commission to Inquire into Child Abuse (the CICA) which ran from 2000 to 2009; the Australian Royal Commission into Institutional Responses to Child Sexual Abuse (the Royal Commission) of 2013–2017 and the Independent Inquiry into Child Sexual Abuse of England and Wales (the IICSA) created in 2013 and which is due to report in 2022. Each is recognized as internationally groundbreaking.[1] This is the first in-depth examination of the three inquiries together.

The wave of public inquiries into child abuse in the West in the twenty-first century,[2] of which the three examined here are paradigmatic, draws significantly on ideas and practices of transitional justice. Transitional justice used for addressing historical violence is rooted in the regime changes of totalitarian South American states in the 1980s, and the internationally groundbreaking South African Truth and Reconciliation Commission (TRC) of 1996. Associated responses embrace the discrete but linked 'pillars' of: investigation and truth-seeking, accountability, reparation, guarantees of non-repetition and reconciliation.[3] Increasingly, scholars have used the transitional justice lens to evaluate state responses to historical and institutional child abuse, pointing to a coherent pattern of responses including: state apologies; the establishment of statutory redress schemes; (limited) criminal prosecutions and public inquiries.[4]

While none of the governments in the three countries examined here described their public inquiry explicitly as an exercise in 'transitional justice', each may be understood as conforming to its principles of centring of victims' experiences, truth recovery and non-repetition. Each was part of larger packages responding to institutional child abuse, including parallel processes of financial redress and civil and criminal law reforms. The CICA was the first national inquiry framed in terms of healing for victims and society, through listening to survivors and uncovering the past. The Irish government envisaged the CICA as 'rather like a truth commission' designed to provide as complete

DOI: 10.4324/9780429468162-12

a picture as possible of the causes, nature and extent of abuse and thereby help Irish society 'come to terms with a very negative, very black period in our history'.[5] Accountability underpinned the CICA's investigative function and although it was empowered to make future-oriented recommendations, its emphasis was on the past.[6] The Royal Commission was initially presented as one part of doing 'everything we can to make sure that what has happened in the past is never allowed to happen again' through a process of discovering the truth of the past.[7] The Australian government also aimed for 'healing', but when compared to Ireland, greater emphasis was placed on future-oriented recommendations and research to achieve non-repetition of abuse. The IICSA was modelled largely on the Australian example and is also tasked with considering 'the growing evidence of institutional failures to protect children from child sexual abuse, and to make recommendations to ensure the best possible protection for children in future'.[8] Similar to Ireland and Australia, a core strand of the IICSA's work is to 'consider the experience of survivors of child sexual abuse; providing opportunities for them to bear witness to the Inquiry'.[9]

The idea of bearing witness to historical injustice and healing through speaking publicly of personal pain would make little sense without an understanding of trauma discourse which came to prominence in Western societies from the mid-twentieth century.[10] The incorporation of PTSD in knowledge about child sexual abuse (CSA) in the 1980s is regarded by some scholars as the single most important factor by which to explain the shift away from what Carol Smart identified as a general historical 'ambivalence' about this form of abuse, to contemporary understandings of it as necessarily devastating, and the accompanying transformation of perceptions of survivors from 'inherently suspicious' to embodying our 'common humanity'.[11] Each inquiry's work might seem nonsensical without appreciation of the role of trauma discourse in informing the reception of adults presenting decades after their abuse to tell of their life-changing, harrowing experiences, sometimes for the first time.

We now expand on these themes in examining each country's inquiry beginning with Ireland which was the first country to establish a national inquiry into NRCSA.[12]

Ireland

The work and Final Report of the CICA are watershed moments in Ireland's national story for their laying bare the country's long history of sexual, physical, and emotional abuse of children in institutions. The CICA formed a core element of a package of measures announced on 11 May 1999 by Taoiseach Bertie Ahern in his apology to victims of NRCSA perpetrated in institutions. Ahern's announcement of the package of measures had its roots in years of activism by survivors, raising public awareness of the harms they suffered (see Chapter 4). The government's approach was in direct contrast to its refusal to create a public inquiry into the Catholic Church's handling of allegations of clerical abuse. Indeed, in 1998 in a letter to survivor and activist Andrew Madden, Taoiseach Bertie Ahern had stated that such a public inquiry was 'not considered as appropriate or practical to the issues of child abuse'.[13] Most directly, the state response was prompted by the increase in civil litigation being taken against the Department of Education and Science by survivors of institutional abuse, and the increase in the number of Freedom of Information requests coming into it from survivors seeking access to their records.[14] A Cabinet sub-committee on sexual abuse was set up in 1998. Chaired by the Minister for Education and Science and future Taoiseach Micheál Martin, it comprised the Tánaiste, ministers at the departments of Marine and Natural Resources, Health and Children; Social, Community and Family Affairs and Justice, Equality and Law Reform and the Attorney General. A related working group of secretaries general and officials from all the Departments involved and the Tánaiste's office was created in January 1999. At the time Minister Martin stated that the Commission 'would lead to fundamental change in official attitudes to child abuse in [Ireland]'.[15]

Ireland was undergoing multiple transformations at the close of the twentieth century. It had the fastest growing economy in the world;[16] the government was increasingly powerful in areas the Catholic Church once monopolized, like the provision of healthcare, welfare and education; feminist lawyer Mary McAleese was President and progress was being made in human rights, including ratification of the UNCRC in 1992; legislation on employment equality, domestic and sexual violence, and the decriminalization of sex between men.[17] In 1998 The Good Friday Agreement had ushered in relative peace in Northern Ireland for the first time in a generation and displayed the power of the Republic of Ireland on the international relations stage. It is no surprise the government in 1999 was keen to draw a figurative line in the sand demarcating a brutal past, including the maltreatment of children, from a more progressive political, economic and social present and future.

The CICA was conceived by politicians and civil servants as a form of truth commission, inspired by the South African TRC.[18] However, the version of reconciliation imagined at these early stages arguably preferred a balancing of narratives over truth recovery. As a senior civil servant puts it:

> This wasn't exclusively a story about abuse. The Commission was meant to be a way of finding out the full story. Perhaps for too long Irish society had heard the State's and the congregations' story unchallenged. More recently survivors of abuse had had their say to a greater extent. The idea was to find out what happened in all its colours.[19]

With respected High Court judge Mary Laffoy appointed as Chair and two fellow commissioners who were child abuse and social care experts,[20] the CICA was initially established on an administrative non-statutory basis and was charged with developing its terms of reference and making recommendations on the powers and protections it would need. It reported in autumn 1999 and the CICA was established on 23 May 2000 by the *Commission to Inquire into Child Abuse Act 2000*. The Act marked a radical break with the existing model of public inquiry,[21] which was very public, highly adversarial and costly in terms of time and resources.[22] The definition of abuse was very broad, encompassing acts of sexual and physical abuse, failure to prevent physical injury, neglect and any other act or omission resulting in serious impairment of the physical or mental health or development of a child, or serious adverse effects on a child's behaviour or welfare.[23] The CICA was initially given two years to complete its work[24] on the expectation that hundreds of survivors would come forward.[25] This vision would be frustrated by lack of cooperation from various actors (including state actors) a vast underestimation of the number of survivors involved and legal challenges.

The Act's key innovation was that the CICA was to have both therapeutic and investigative functions. Its primary objective was therapeutic: to help survivors to 'overcome the lasting effects of abuse' by 'giv[ing] their account to an experienced and sympathetic forum'.[26] A Confidential Committee (CC) was created for this purpose.[27] This marked an important departure from previous inquiries into child abuse in the implicit recognition of the traumatic effects of CSA. It also resonates with a transitional justice ideal of bearing witness to lived experiences of abuse. Its second objective aligned more with that of a 'truth commission'; to determine the facts about institutional child abuse in Ireland.[28] The Investigation Committee (IC) was required to inquire into institutional abuse and, where satisfied that abuse had occurred, determine its causes, nature, circumstances and extent.[29] The IC was also required to inquire into the extent to which the individual institutions, and the systems of management and regulation, contributed to abuse.[30] Respondents in the IC could be an individual, a management body (usually religious organizations) or a regulatory body. A survivor could only appear before either the IC or the CC. Third, the CICA was to report to the public about the incidence of abuse to identify 'the institution and the persons who committed the abuse'[31] and make public findings about the management, administration, operation, supervision and regulation (direct or indirect) of an institution and the persons in whom those functions were vested, and, controversially, to identify those persons.[32] The CICA was also empowered to make future-oriented recommendations, although the statutory requirement was cursory (that any recommendations should include action to be taken to address the effects of abuse on survivors and to reduce the incidence of child abuse in institutions).[33]

The membership of the CICA's therapeutic and fact-finding arms represented an important shift away from the traditional public inquiry model of centring legal expertise, towards one that valued specialist expertise in childcare, health and psychology. The CC was chaired by a social worker and childcare director at Barnados.[34] The other members were a consultant paediatrician,[35] a retired Chief Inspector with the Social Services Inspectorate in Northern Ireland[36] and, from 2002, a senior social worker.[37] Justice Laffoy chaired the IC. Its ordinary members included a clinical psychologist,[38] and a psychiatrist who was director of Ireland's main CSA assessment and treatment unit.[39] The Commission had no ordinary members who were lawyers until 2004, when solicitor Marian Shanley was appointed to the IC.

Scope

The CICA was empowered to investigate and hear testimony relating to a range of institutions, including day schools, industrial schools, reformatory schools, orphanages, hospitals, children's homes and any other form of out of home care.[40] Abuse by parish priests or abuse in community or (foster) family settings were outside its terms of reference.[41] The inclusion of hospitals and schools, both public and private, was welcomed.[42] Its broad remit, coupled with a flexible definition of the 'relevant period',[43] meant that the CICA could have considered contemporary care provision. However, the focus remained on non-recent child abuse in industrial schools and reformatories.[44] The period to be considered was 1940–1999 but could be extended. The IC exercised this power by considering matters from 1936. The CC heard from survivors relating experiences between 1914 and 2000.

Structure and procedures

Under the 2000 Act the CICA was empowered to create its own procedures.[45] These were set out in its first public hearing and on its website. Close examination of these procedures shows that the CICA was working hard to try to achieve truth-telling and accountability for wrongdoing while protecting the legal rights of individuals accused of abuse.

The CC performed the CICA's therapeutic function. This 'healing forum'[46] was intended to provide an informal, private forum for survivors to share their experiences. Hearings took place over a six-year period between 2000 and 2006. Over 2,000 hours of evidence was recorded, either by audio recording or by contemporaneous written record, and was archived in a specially created database.[47] Most hearings were conducted by two Commissioners.[48] Survivors were allowed to bring one companion, with more men attending without a companion than women.[49] The overall gender split of witnesses was 54 per cent men and 46 per cent women.[50] However, this rose to 66 per cent men and 34 per cent women for survivors based in Ireland.[51] Survivors were invited to bring supporting documentation to their hearing if they wished. Witnesses brought admission records, documents from institutional centres, medical records, birth certificates, letters from the Department of Education, court orders, correspondence between their families the institutions and relevant authorities, letters from the gardaí and others seeking payments from parents, general correspondence, newspaper cuttings relating to their admission and personal photographs from their time in the institution. Their testimony and documentation formed the basis of a report containing general findings. In keeping with the CC's listening role, individuals implicated in abuse described by witnesses were not informed of the testimony about them and no findings were made against them. The CC was prohibited from identifying or publishing information that could lead to the identification of survivors, alleged abusers or institutions.

The IC performed the CICA's investigative function and could hold both private and public hearings. To date, it is the only abuse inquiry in Ireland to have held public hearings. It had powers to compel attendance of witnesses and discovery of documents and punish non-cooperation or obstruction.[52] It took evidence on oath. It was only to consider evidence which would have been admissible in a court (hearsay, for example, was not admissible).[53] In making findings of fact the IC applied the civil standard of proof, the balance of probabilities.[54] As noted above, the CICA was empowered to identify individuals and institutions responsible for abuse in its Final Report. This statutory power provoked strong opposition from religious congregations, especially the Christian Brothers.

Respondents giving evidence to the IC could not rely on the privilege against self-incrimination; they were not entitled to refuse to answer a question on the ground that the answer might be incriminating.[55] However, witnesses were granted immunity from liability in respect of their testimony. Commentators argued this created an effective amnesty for individuals who admitted abuse, but this was incorrect; it was simply that if someone were later to be prosecuted or sued, the case against them could not include their incriminating statement or admission to the CICA. In its First Public Statement the CICA emphasized that coming forward to give evidence would not affect survivors' right to testify to the abuse in a criminal or civil court.[56] More worryingly, in legislation in 2004 that covered later commissions, including the Murphy Commission into the handling of allegations of abuse in the Dublin Archdiocese[57] the cover of inadmissibility attached to participation in a commission was broadened to include documents given or sent to a commission pursuant to a direction/request of the commission, or documents specified in an affidavit and given to a commission pursuant to a direction/request of the commission.[58] This amounts to an effective sealing of documents that could be of critical importance in a criminal prosecution or civil action and could frustrate justice for NRCSA survivors. Perhaps the 2004 provisions are the reason why civil servants have argued against creating a statutory inquiry into the handling of NRCSA reports in Scouting Ireland, discussed in Chapter 3.

The Laffoy years

The first few years of the CICA were fraught and progress was slow. Survivors adopted a cautious approach to the IC. This was well founded, and the CICA found that the majority of religious orders adopted 'an adversarial, defensive and legalistic approach'.[59] Most allegations were contested or the orders' lawyers demanded strict proof. The Department of Education, whose duty it was to inspect and regulate the institutions, did not fully cooperate with the CICA's requests for documentary evidence, forcing it to schedule procedural hearings and even require the attendance of the Secretary General of the Department, in an effort to procure compliance with statutory requests and directions.[60]

The IC imposed a deadline of 30 June 2002 for complainant statements by which time statements had been provided by 1,800 people.[61] It responded by issuing a new framework, including a procedure for hearing together all allegations relating to an institution.[62] The Congregation of the Christian Brothers, against whom more allegations were made than all of the male orders combined, issued legal proceedings. It argued that the new procedures did not ensure natural and constitutional justice, claiming it was unfair that findings of fact relating to abuse could be made against members of the congregation who were dead or too infirm to defend themselves. The High Court agreed that the procedures needed to be amended but upheld the CICA's power to name abusers.[63]

In 2002, the government reviewed the Terms of Reference with the stated purpose of making the Commission more cost and time effective. Without having published that review, in September 2003 the government announced it would engage in another review that would radically change the CICA's mandate. This proved to be the final straw for Justice Laffoy. The day after the press release announcing the second review, she resigned as Chair. Laffoy cited a range of factors for her resignation, including the government's delay in dealing with redress for survivors,[64] which affected their cooperation with the CICA; the issue of payment of legal costs of complainants and respondents in the IC; inadequate resources and delays in concluding the 2002 review. The effect was that the CICA could not be independent and reasonably efficient in the performance of its functions.[65]

The Ryan years

In 2003, Senior Counsel Seán Ryan was chosen to replace Laffoy as Chair and was appointed as a High Court judge. Ryan had been former counsel to the inquiry into clerical sexual abuse in the Diocese of Ferns and had chaired the Compensation Advisory Committee which prepared guidelines on compensation to be paid by the Residential Institutions Redress Board. His appointment was widely welcomed. Solicitor Marian Shanley joined the IC in 2004. In June 2004 the Commission published consultation documents aimed at speeding up its work.[66] These proposals were translated into legislation. The Commission to Inquire into Child Abuse (Amendment) Act 2005 removed the obligation to hear every allegation of abuse. The IC could now decide which cases to hear based on a prior examination of the documentation associated with each complain. This new discretionary 'sampling' approach was reminiscent of the approach adopted by the Forde Inquiry in Queensland, Australia. This compromise was heavily criticized by survivor groups.[67]

The 2005 Act added a new function: to inquire into how children were placed in institutions and the circumstances in which they continued to be resident there. This was surprising given that in 2000 the government resisted efforts to include a review of the actions of the courts in sending children to industrial schools.[68] This could have involved investigating the issue of the alleged criminality of those who had been committed to an institution following a conviction, or the complicity of the legal profession and the judiciary in the abusive system. This was not to be.

The most significant change was that the Final Report would not identify any abusers and pseudonyms would be used instead.[69] This satisfied the Christian Brothers, who dropped their appeal against the High Court's rejection of their challenge to the IC's new procedures.[70] For many survivors, the decision to use pseudonyms fatally undermined the CICA's goals of truth-telling and accountability.[71]

Under Justice Ryan's stewardship, the IC conducted its work in three phases:

- First, public hearings allowed religious congregations to describe how the institutions were managed. The aim was to establish the context in which abuse occurred. However, the effect was to create a public platform for institutions without any contextualization or contestation by historians or survivors.
- In the second phase, private hearings were conducted into specific allegations of abuse. Statements from survivors, individuals, religious congregations and Departments of Education/Health/Justice were obtained before the hearings. The IC had sought to limit the number of lawyers present at the private hearings in order to assist complainants in giving evidence; but the High Court found that was an interference of the constitutional rights of respondents and Congregations.[72] As a consequence, it was impossible to limit the numbers of lawyers who attended, making the experience daunting for witnesses.[73]
- In the third phase, public hearings examined particular institutions, the Department of Justice, Equality and Law Reform and the Irish Society for the Prevention of Cruelty to Children. The CICA appointed eight firms of solicitors to represent complainants' interests at these hearings.[74]

The CICA also held public 'emergence hearings' which heard evidence from survivors, political leaders and representatives of the state institutions and the religious congregations, as well as from academic Dr Eoin O'Sullivan on the historical context of the emergence of child abuse in Ireland.[75]

By the time both Committees concluded their inquiries in 2006, the IC had received 2,107 applications, of which 1,007 had proceeded to hearing,[76] and 552 people had been interviewed by the IC.[77] The CC had received 1,541 applications and heard from 1,090 witnesses.[78]

The final report

The CICA published its Final Report on 20 May 2009.[79] Every copy of the five-volume, 2,600-page report was sold that morning. Survivors were banned from attending the press conference held at the Report's launch.[80] The strength of feeling, shock, disgust and horror it evoked is difficult to convey. The force of the testimony of so many survivors, underscored by the authority and sheer length of the Final Report, made the reality of institutional abuse unavoidable. The Report painted a devastating picture of the industrial school system, the Department of Education and the various religious orders. Sexual abuse was endemic in boys' schools and that physical and emotional abuse and neglect were pervasive across the entire system.[81] Cases of sexual abuse were hidden by the congregations and abusers were transferred to other locations where they were free to re-offend. Abusers were able to operate undetected for long periods at the core of institutions.[82] Sexual abuse by members of religious orders was seldom brought to the attention of the Department of Education by religious authorities because of a culture of silence.[83] The state failed to protect children in industrial and reformatory schools and the Department of Education generally dismissed or ignored complaints of sexual abuse[84] and 'the deferential and submissive attitude of the Department towards Congregations compromised its ability to carry out its statutory duty of inspection and monitoring of the schools'.[85] The Department's inspection system was 'fundamentally flawed and incapable of being effective'.[86]

The Report made several recommendations aimed at addressing the effects of abuse on survivors and preventing abuse in institutions.[87] The first, the construction of a memorial to survivors, has yet to be fulfilled (see Chapter 11). The second simply urged the state and the congregations to learn the lessons of the past and to examine their attitudes and processes. It is impossible to evaluate whether or how that recommendation has been acted on. Other recommendations include the continuation of the existing provision of counselling, educational services and family tracing. 16 other recommendations aimed at preventing abuse. The most specific related to the accountability of management and the need for independent inspections of institutions. These recommendations, along with the Report's findings, have contributed to the implementation of the Children First Guidelines, the Children's Rights Referendum in 2012, the creation of the Child and Family Agency and the introduction of mandatory reporting (see Chapter 4).

The Church of Ireland Bishop of Cork Paul Colton summed up the atmosphere of shock at the time saying that the country was in the midst of 'a national trauma'.[88] The media reaction was one of shock, disgust, shame and anger. The Irish Times described the report as 'a map of an Irish hell' that 'define[d] the contours of a dark hinterland of the State, a parallel country whose existence we have long known but never fully acknowledged'.[89] Alongside expressions of horror, there were public expressions of solidarity with survivors. Thousands gathered in the Garden of Remembrance in Dublin to take part in a silent march to the Dáil in solidarity with survivors and thousands signed a book of solidarity. President Mary McAleese hosted hundreds of survivors at a reception at which she apologized for their suffering on behalf of the people of Ireland.[90] In Northern Ireland, thousands of people wrote to the Stormont Assembly demanding an inquiry along the lines of the CICA. In 2011, the Stormont Executive agreed to create a major inquiry into abuse in institutions run by the Catholic Church and the state. The Historical Institutional Abuse Inquiry was chaired by Sir Anthony Hart to review abuse perpetrated between 1922 and 1995. It reported in 2017.[91]

Notwithstanding its immensely significant findings and recommendations, its national and international impacts, and its provocation of subsequent academic and social commentaries and research, the Final Report was far from definitive in terms of establishing the truth for the participants and the public. No quantitative analysis of the incidence of abuse was offered. In 2019 the Final Report's figure for the number of children in the institutions was announced as incorrect.[92] Although the terms of reference covered a broad range of institutions, the CICA's work focussed almost exclusively on industrial schools and reformatories run by religious congregations on behalf the state.[93] Of these, only institutions that attracted more than 20 complainants were examined by the IC, with varying degrees of scrutiny. This partial and fragmented history limits the ability to understand the abusive past and to prevent recurrence of abuse.

The Report examined each institution separately, frustrating analysis of the system and of how abusers were transferred between schools.[94] The use of pseudonyms prevented comparison with information about institutions or abusers already in the public domain.[95] The focus on selected testimonies excluded certain accounts of victimhood and subordinated the experiences of some survivors.[96] Although the Report noted 'the deferential and submissive attitude of the Department of Education towards the Congregations [which] compromised its ability to carry out its statutory duty of inspection and monitoring of the schools',[97] it did not investigate the state's responsibility for allowing the industrial schools system to operate effectively unregulated for so long, for ignoring pleas for reform and for allowing children to continue to be incarcerated despite evidence of abuse. The Report also failed to consider the question of race in the systemic institutionalization and abuse of racialized groups such as Mincéirí and those of mixed-race heritage.[98] It also underestimated the role of the Irish Society for the Prevention of Cruelty to Children in the transfer of children to industrial schools.[99]

As well as these failures of truth recovery, the CICA did not lead to increased accountability in terms of criminal justice. Only 11 cases of abuse were forwarded to the Director of Public Prosecutions and only three resulted in a prosecution.[100]

Crucially, the Final Report was also unable to examine the connections between institutional abuse and cover-ups in the distant past and abusive institutional practices in more recent times. The focus of most of the CICA's investigations and its findings and recommendations was on the historical period between 1936 and 1970.[101] Mary Raftery, whose States of Fear documentary had exposed suppression of sections of an inquiry into CSA at the Madonna House in Dublin (arguably provoking Ahern's apology), highlighted the CICA's failure to investigate recent abuse in residential childcare facilities and suppression of inquiries into abuse in the 1990s. She noted:

> Unless those connections are rammed home, it remains far too easy to avoid confronting the legacy of the past, slipping again into the kind of generalised denial which so bedevils the area of child abuse in this country.[102]

The state's official response in the years since the publication of the Final Report has been defensive. At Ireland's hearing before the UN Committee Against Torture in 2011 the state was criticized for failing to implement all of the CICA's recommendations.[103] The Department of Justice representative, Seán Aylward, stated that 'some of the issues that are raised and looked at in the Ryan report…relate to a very distant, far-off time' and later, 'many of the people who suffered in that period or were victims of it are no longer with us and it would be very difficult for the State to rewrite its history or right the wrongs that were done'. Mr Aylward also stated that there was 'a need to have a sense of proportion in what people say' about these issues.[104]

Australia

The Royal Commission into Institutional Responses to Child Sexual Abuse of 2013–2017 (the Royal Commission) is one of the most significant public inquiries in Australia's history in terms of duration, resources and potential for influence by way of its 400+ once-in-a-generation recommendations. In its combination of inquisitorial determinations of fact and therapeutic hearing of survivor testimony, the Royal Commission is described as 'one of the most important public inquiries into child abuse globally'[105] and was used partly as a model in England and Wales.[106] The Royal Commission was highly original in scope and mandate, but its antecedents should not be forgotten. Internationally, while the South African Truth and Reconciliation Commission of 1996 proved an important global milestone in survivor-centred transitional justice, Australia had pioneered listening to survivors and their communities in the 1987 landmark Commonwealth Royal Commission into Aboriginal Deaths in Custody (RCIADIC).

Although it was a fact-finding investigation that did not promise the therapeutic outcomes of the recent Royal Commission, the RCIADIC extended its processes beyond strictly inquisitorial legal methods to interview affected families and explore the life and death of a deceased person, through which 'issues of wider social significance' emerged.[107] Evidence about deaths of Aboriginal men and women in custody came 'mainly from the oral testimony of family members in the hearings as well as from the voluminous welfare department files or from reports by police, probation officers or psychologists'.[108] This hybrid collation of a profile of an individual and their untimely death served to humanize the deceased and create empathy and understanding about the discriminatory social, political and legal contexts in which their precarious and ultimately fatal social existence was embedded. The *Bringing Them Home* Inquiry, established in May 1995 as one outcome of the RCIADIC recommendations, continued in this tradition. The tireless work of First Nations survivors, lobbyists, legal representatives and the families of those who did not survive should never be underestimated in the shaping of justice for survivors of many forms of historical and contemporary abuses in Australia.

Calls had been made for a Commonwealth Royal Commission into CSA, particularly in religious institutions, since at least 1998, and they intensified following the scandals associated with Governor-General Peter Hollingworth in 2003 (see Chapter 2).[109] In 2004 the *Forgotten Australians* Senate Inquiry into out-of-home-care recommended that the government 'consider establishing a Royal Commission into State, charitable, and church-run institutions and out-of-home care during the last century'[110] and provide redress for care leavers, but successive governments failed to act on its recommendations. Advocacy groups such as Care Leavers Australasia Network (CLAN), Broken Rites (for survivors of abuse by Catholic clergy), and Bravehearts (for all survivors of CSA) began to gain political traction supported by news media campaigns in communities beset with scandals concerning NRCSA by Catholic clergy.

International developments were also influential. The release of the 'landmark'[111] Final Report of the CICA in 2009 was met with outrage among Australian survivors, prompting responses from the Catholic Church about the possibility that offending Irish priests had been transferred to Australia.[112] Demands for a Royal Commission heightened as survivors condemned the anonymity of the CICA report and lack of prosecutions in Ireland. Mainstream Australian newspapers criticized the Irish process, arguing that

> the vast body of evidence obtained by the report, including the testimony of more than 1,700 men and women about the abuse they suffered, cannot be used for prosecutions. The guilty are, in effect, still being protected. It also makes it more difficult to establish which perpetrators might have been transferred to countries such as Australia while casting a shadow over Irish clergy who are innocent of wrongdoing.[113]

However, other aspects of the CICA and the Irish Catholic diocesan inquiries into CSA that followed it were quickly recognized as setting a new international standard for the national reckoning of institutional child abuse and reform of the church.

In response to revelations of a Victorian government inquiry into 'systemic problems' in the state's child protection system,[114] Labor MP Ann Barker travelled to Ireland to consult with former chair of the CICA, Mr Justice Seán Ryan, and returned calling for an Australian inquiry with comparable statutory powers.[115] The Victorian government responded with a parliamentary inquiry with limited powers, but which did identify systemic abuses in various churches.[116] The two Victorian inquiries invigorated campaigns for a national inquisitorial inquiry with powers to compel witnesses to testify about criminal matters against children.

The tipping point came when a senior detective from the Newcastle region in New South Wales NSW appeared on national television to allege police corruption in the covering up of sex crimes committed by Catholic clergy, including those of suspected prolific offender Father Denis McAlinden, who was transferred from Ireland to Australia in 1949.[117] The NSW government immediately announced *The Special Commission of Inquiry into matters relating to the police investigation of certain child sexual abuse allegations in the Catholic Diocese of Maitland-Newcastle.*[118] Three days later, on 12 November 2012, Labor Prime Minister Julia Gillard announced the national Royal Commission. Gillard had previously resisted calls for a public inquiry out of fears it would re-traumatize survivors but 'came to the decision that it would offer more healing than its potential capacity for hurt'.[119] She described the abuse scandals as 'heartbreaking…insidious, evil acts to which no child should be subject. There have been too many revelations of adults who have averted their eyes from this evil'.[120] And she explained that what she wanted to achieve was twofold:

> for the survivors of child sexual abuse, I want this to be a moment of healing, for us to say to them as a nation we hear you, you're valued and you're believed…And second, I want the Royal Commission to provide for us recommendations about the future.[121]

Seán Ryan was immediately interviewed by the Australian media because Ireland 'is the only other country to have launched a national child abuse inquiry similar to that announced yesterday by Australia's Prime Minister'.[122] When asked for his advice, Ryan emphasized survivors' needs for recognition and belief, and for the state to acknowledge the extent of abuse.[123] Considering practicalities, Ryan advised that the Royal Commission should employ the 'sampling' methodology used in the CICA, whereby: 'We decided that we would not hear everybody in every institution so we said we will hear a selection of people that we will choose from the documentary evidence'.[124]

Ryan also supported the Australian focus on institutional factors implicated in child abuse because, in Ireland,

> we found it difficult to envisage a trial of every allegation somebody made...There was some consideration given to us recommending prosecutions [of individual perpetrators]. I know what I think of going down that path, but Australians will have to make their own decisions on that.[125]

Establishment of the Royal Commission

The Royal Commission was established by way of Letters Patent (a written order by a head of state or equivalent constituting Terms of Reference), requiring it to inquire, *inter alia* into institutional responses to allegations of CSA including what institutions and governments should now do to protect children; appropriate redress and justice responses for survivors; and legal and other impediments to reporting crime. It was to carry out its investigations while having regard to 'the experience of people directly or indirectly affected by child sexual abuse' including through 'the provision of opportunities for them to share their experiences in appropriate ways'.[126] Its work was informed by three 'pillars': public hearings, private sessions and research and policy and commenced in February 2013.

Australian 'Royal' Commissions bear no relation to the British legal system. The title is a colonial legacy of the Westminster system that was never relinquished even with the passage of the *Australia Act 1986* which eliminated any avenue of legal appeal to the English Privy Council. Royal Commissions constitute *ad hoc* committees established by the executive of the Australian government (state, territory or federal) and appointed by the Governor-General (or state Governor) as the representative of the Queen of Australia, to inquire into matters of serious public interest, including the behaviour of the government. Unlike their counterpart public inquiries in the UK, Australian Royal Commissions are governed by special laws that confer coercive powers on the Commission. They were used in the colonies from at least 1892, but the most significant legislation is the Commonwealth *Royal Commissions Act 1902* (*The Act*), passed as one of the first acts of the Australian parliament.[127] When compared to other forms of Australian public inquiries, Royal Commissions are considered to be independent of the government (because Commissioners are appointed by the Crown) and to be of the highest transparency with investigations and evidence publicly reported on.[128] They are described as the 'most exalted' and even the 'most dignified' form of Australian public inquiry.[129] While they have been regularly used to investigate corruption in the states, there have been relatively fewer federal Royal Commissions. The recent child abuse Royal Commission was a landmark not only for survivors but also for the political and legal tradition of this form of investigation.

Australia's political federation necessitated processes of intergovernmental cooperation that were not required for a national inquiry in Ireland or England and Wales. As a means of protecting state sovereignty, the Australian constitution limits what the Commonwealth may inquire into.[130] The constitutionality of an investigation into matters of state affairs such as welfare and child protection, which could be deemed to fall outside the Commonwealth's 'legislative competence', may be understood by reference to s51(xxxix) of the Constitution: the external affairs power granting the Australian parliament power to legislate to meet international treaty obligations.[131] The Letters Patent of the Royal Commission made explicit mention of the UNCRC 1989 ratified by Australia in 1990 and requiring (s19(1)) that state parties 'take all appropriate legislative, administrative, social and educational measures to protect children from all forms of ...violence... including sexual abuse'.[132] While the Royal Commission did not pass laws to protect children or make findings of guilt or liability in a criminal or civil sense, its investigations may be interpreted as an 'appropriate and adapted measure to meet Australia's s19(1) obligations'.[133] Despite the lack of Commonwealth human rights mechanisms and culture in Australia, it was human rights discourse that legitimized the investigations.

The cooperation of the states and territories was imperative to ensuring the respectful treatment of survivors who may have participated in different inquiries in the past. The Letters Patent included provisions to request, but not compel, this cooperation:

> To establish appropriate arrangements in relation to current and previous inquiries, in Australia and elsewhere, for evidence and information to be shared...in ways consistent with relevant obligations so that the work of those inquiries, including, with any necessary consents, the testimony of witnesses, can be taken into account...in a way that avoids unnecessary duplication, improves efficiency and avoids unnecessary trauma to witnesses.[134]

States were highly cooperative, ensuring the Royal Commission was nationally informed and would set the tone for the definitive debate about NRCSA throughout the country.

There is no formal requirement that judges chair Royal Commissions, but they often do, and Justice Peter McClellan, Judge of Appeal in NSW, was appointed Chair. The appointment of an otherwise relatively diverse range of Commissioners including Senator Andrew Murray, a former child migrant, and Professor Helen Millroy, a Palyku (Aboriginal) child psychiatrist, and three legal representatives including Justice Jennifer Coate AO, a former judge of the Family Court of Australia, aimed for a breadth of expertise and national inclusivity, but its membership was more legalistic than the CICA (although less so than the IICSA). Unlike the CICA and the IICSA, the Royal Commission maintained its Chair and team throughout its five-year tenure and is regarded as a great success in terms of stability and continuity. Investigations were not bound by a historical period, and it was soon apparent that heightened resources would be required. Commissioners were initially required to report by December 2015, but due to the massive volume of complaints received, their tenure was extended until December 2017. Over 15,000 individuals contacted the Royal Commission and were within its Terms of Reference.[135]

Scope

At the time, the Royal Commission's scope was unique internationally in its focus only on sexual, not other forms of abuse, in the past and the present, and in its broad definition of institutions which saw it examine the abuse of children in care as well as those who were not in care but were abused in the context of institutions (for example, by a parish priest or scout leader). There were political reasons for these parameters and inevitably they were not satisfactory to all. The range of institutions investigated reflects the Australian public-private hybridity and religious pluralism in welfare provision and denominational education. Media focus on Catholic clerical CSA had led some religious representatives to claim that investigations were disproportionately targeting Catholics.[136] In part to dispel these claims, Prime Minister Gillard consulted with the then leader of the Catholic Church in Australia, Cardinal George Pell, before announcing the Royal Commission and she ensured its investigations included a very broad range of institutional settings defined as:[137]

> any public or private body, agency, association, club, institution, organisation or other entity or group of entities of any kind (whether incorporated or unincorporated), and however described…for example, an entity or group of entities (including an entity or group of entities that no longer exists) that provides, or has at any time provided, activities, facilities, programs or services of any kind that provide the means through which adults have contact with children, including through their families.[138]

As with the CICA and the IICSA, the family was excluded from investigations.

One criticism of the Australian approach is that the distinct needs of survivors who were sexually abused in care and survivors of clerical CSA were fused in the investigations and, therefore, in some government responses (such as redress).[139]

Care leavers had long been lobbying for a national inquiry into all aspects of abuse in out-of-home-care including forced labour,[140] but the Royal Commission was tasked with investigating only CSA, reflecting the media focus of the day. Particularly since the publicity surrounding lawsuits against the Catholic Church for NRCSA in Boston in 2003, international and Australian media had focused overwhelmingly on sexual abuse, which also emerged as a fundamental problem of the Catholic Church in the Victorian and Newcastle inquiries of 2012.

While the Royal Commission's focus on CSA was generally received as important, even crucial, many survivors of other forms of abuse and neglect remain disappointed with what was withheld from public scrutiny. Leonie Sheedy, CEO of CLAN, implored:

> how do I tell the members of CLAN that were left dangling over orphanage balconies and never knew whether they were going to be dropped on their heads, and that they'd live or die, how can I tell them that, well, sorry, if you'd have been sodomised, they'd be interested? But that sort of torture's not covered?[141]

CLAN vice-president Frank Golding described the Royal Commission as elevating sexual abuse to the 'the core transgression of childhood innocence' in the public mind, thereby suggesting that other forms of child abuse are 'subordinate or inferior'.[142] Gillard went part way to acknowledging this disappointment when she rationalized the focus of investigations in terms of resources:

> Of course physical mistreatment, neglect, are very evil things.... Anything that stops a child having a safe and happy childhood is an evil thing. But we've needed to make some decisions about what makes this a process that can be manageable and can be worked through in a time frame that gives the recommendations real meaning.[143]

While some care leavers suggest they still feel 'betrayed' by the failure of the Royal Commission to investigate all forms of child abuse, others state they have gained great comfort from its harnessing of the 'power of collective testimony' and its shattering of illusions that 'the child welfare system always acted with the best interests of the child'.[144]

Structure and procedures

A Royal Commission has coercive and inquisitorial powers to compel the production of documents and require witnesses to answer questions, even those that might incriminate them.[145] Any evidence given in its proceedings is not admissible in evidence against the person in any Australian court (criminal or civil).[146] A Royal Commission can make referrals to the police and other authorities. In this sense, the Royal Commission had powers similar to the CICA, but it made far greater use of police referrals: over 2,000 were made, with charges laid in 'a number of cases'.[147] The Royal Commission was also empowered to override any confidentiality agreements survivors and other witnesses might have signed, to allow them to testify with full frankness.[148] Public hearings took the form of 57 case studies investigating institutional responses to allegations of child sexual abuse where: criminal convictions had been made; there was overwhelming evidence of abuse (such as a series of credible complaints made to the institution or elsewhere); or civil liability had been admitted. Case studies were generally selected based on the number of allegations received about an institution, weighed up in the context of the potential for future reform, rather than justice for survivors. Commissioners considered 'whether or not the hearing would advance an understanding of systemic issues and provide an opportunity to learn from previous mistakes so that any findings and recommendations for future change the Royal Commission made would have a secure foundation'.[149]

Most case studies opened with survivor testimony. Each aimed to allow those affected by child sexual abuse to give evidence with legal representation and to 'examine the response of the institution to complaints made and importantly, to raise community awareness and understanding of child sexual abuse and the institutions in which it occurred'.[150] Witnesses were subject to cross-examination. The government established a free legal advice service for those who appeared (*knowmore*), but representation was funded privately or through the Attorney General's department.

Normal rules of evidence such as discovery did not apply. Evidence that might be inadmissible in a criminal trial, such as opinion evidence, was often important in forming an impression of how an institution functioned and how child abuse might have been concealed. Anyone with the potential to have an adverse inference made against them had the opportunity to respond to allegations including viewing evidence and submissions provided before the hearing, to ensure natural and procedural justice. In total, 1,302 witnesses appeared in public hearings examining 134 institutions in 11 locations across the country.[151] Again to deflect any potential charges of sectarianism, the first case study did not examine religious organizations, but the activities of a convicted perpetrator associated with an Aboriginal children's service and the Boy Scouts. The second concerned the YMCA. Ultimately, however, most case studies concerned religious schools and institutions. The Catholic Church was identified as the source of most reported abuse.[152]

The Royal Commission was committed to transparency, with public hearings live-streamed on the internet and testimonies, submissions and evidence uploaded quickly for maximum public access in processes meeting the terms of The Act. The educational function of the Royal Commission ('raising community awareness') was highlighted through its website and engagement with social and mainstream media. All case studies were written up as reports with findings made about the responses of institutions according to the civil standard of proof. Identities of witnesses were protected with pseudonyms if required, pursuant to The Act, which provides for non-publication orders.[153] Unlike the CICA, convicted perpetrators and deceased persons with allegations made against them were usually named. Aside from the vulnerability of witnesses, considerations informing non-publication included the special status of schools and the potential to prejudice current or forthcoming criminal proceedings (in which case pseudonyms were always used). Some information remains redacted in the Royal Commission's final outputs.[154]

Although Gillard initially framed the Royal Commission as a means by which to ensure history was not repeated, its investigations were not constrained to the past. Unlike the CICA and like the IICSA, several case studies involved contemporary allegations. These included a high-profile investigation into a Sydney dance instructor for child abuse and child pornography offences committed over some time until his arrest in 2013.[155] The Terms of Reference had always included making recommendations to safeguard the future, and much of the Royal Commission's extensive research programme was dedicated to this aim. In a departure from comparable inquiries overseas, the Royal Commission reserved nine of its ten final case studies for 'institutional reviews' of organizations it had scrutinized in earlier case studies. This way, institutions could demonstrate the progress they had made (or not) on modifying their procedures for detecting and responding to child abuse.

Much like the CICA's CC, the Royal Commission also provided confidential 'private sessions' for survivors to tell their stories unchallenged, a mechanism that suggests a different way of producing and documenting 'truth' than inquisitorial or adversarial processes and which aimed to go partway to Gillard's objective of 'healing' for survivors through hearing and believing their experiences.[156] In recognition that the Royal Commission was 'as much about assisting victims of past abuse to be heard, as it is about investigating systemic failures to prevent future abuse',[157] the Act was amended to enable individual Commissioners to receive 'information from persons directly or indirectly affected by child sexual abuse in a manner less formal than a hearing', which is 'appropriate given the deeply personal and distressing nature of people's experiences of child sexual abuse'.[158] According to the amended Act, which was justified with reference to the right to privacy outlined in the International Covenant on Civil and Political Rights and elsewhere, a private session was not a hearing; individuals testifying were not witnesses and were not considered to be giving evidence. Survivors participating in private sessions 'were expected to tell the truth' and were not required to take an oath or affirmation or to be subject to cross-examination.[159] Freedom of Information legislation does not apply to information obtained at a private session, and under the Archives Act, associated records are not accessible for 99 years.[160] After much deliberation, the Commissioners determined that institutions named in private sessions would not be identified in the Royal Commission's final report.[161]

Over 8,000 individuals attended private sessions in over 90 locations. A further 1,000 submitted statements in writing.[162] Some private sessions were conducted with children; some with men and women in prison.[163] Sessions were trauma-informed, meaning that Royal Commission officers and staff were 'aware of the diverse and far-reaching impacts of childhood trauma on survivors' and sought to engage people 'in ways that affirmed their experiences and responses while minimizing interactions or processes that could increase their trauma'.[164] Survivors were offered counselling, and they could request a written copy of their transcript. One perhaps unexpected outcome of the Royal Commission's public profile has been an education of the public about the enduring effects of CSA and the grave need to revolutionize the way traumatized survivors are received and responded to. Numerous Royal Commission recommendations include reference to trauma-informed principles that should be adopted by services and agencies including welfare, child protection and the police.

Some commentators are very enthusiastic about these aspects of the Royal Commission, describing it as taking on a 'broad new understanding of trauma into its institutional practices' and creating an 'organizational culture that was humanistic and inclusive'.[165] Still, concerns remain about participation and the experiences of those who did participate. Early on, some Aboriginal legal and community representatives voiced fears that the Royal Commission could re-traumatize survivors who had cooperated with the 1996 *Bringing Them Home* inquiry into the Stolen Generations, only to be let down by the Commonwealth's failure to provide redress and find that, in reality, 'little has changed; children continue to be sexually abused and services to support and prevent such abuse are still lacking'.[166] Participation of First Nations' Australians in the Royal Commission was significant—14 per cent of people who attended a private session identified as Aboriginal or Torres Strait Islander.[167] But when considering their over-representation in institutions and other indicators about prevalence of abuse, the Aboriginal Legal Service of Western Australia considers it to have potentially been under-representative.[168] Many First Nations people believe they have already informed the 'authorities' about what happened to them, and 'there is no logical reason for them to come forward again and experience the re-traumatization of providing their story to a different government "agency"'.[169]

Research outputs and recommendations

The Royal Commission was tasked with producing research (its third pillar) along with a report and recommendations. Together with a written analysis of the 57 case studies, the Royal Commission produced a lengthy 17-volume report making recommendations grouped in topics such as *Understanding Child Sexual Abuse in Institutional Contexts*, *Redress and Civil Litigation*, *Criminal Justice*, *Working with Children* and analysis of different types of institutions. The Report found that:

> Tens of thousands of children have been sexually abused in many Australian institutions. We will never know the true number. Whatever the number, it is a national tragedy, perpetrated over generations within many of our most trusted institutions.

> The sexual abuse of children has occurred in almost every type of institution where children reside or attend for educational, recreational, sporting, religious or cultural activities. Some institutions have had multiple abusers who sexually abused multiple children. It is not a case of a few "rotten apples". Society's major institutions have seriously failed. In many cases, those failings have been exacerbated by a manifestly inadequate response to the abused person. The problems have been so widespread, and the nature of the abuse so heinous, that it is difficult to comprehend.[170]

Individual institutions were named as harbouring specific incidents of abuse as well as abusive organizational cultures. Different religious organizations were identified as demonstrating 'remarkable similarities in the institutional responses', including 'in-house' responses where alleged perpetrators were treated with leniency and secrecy; victims were disregarded, blamed, punished and lied to; criminality was ignored; and perpetrators were not removed from ministry or contact with children.[171] Only one volume was dedicated solely to examining historical residential institutions. In practice, many of the investigations culminated in contemporary analyses, with Commissioners imploring that 'although, inevitably, the Royal Commission has looked at past events, it is important that the momentum for change initiated by the Royal Commission's work is not lost and that lasting changes to protect children are implemented'.[172] As part of its research 'pillar', the Royal Commission commissioned a diverse programme of research addressing institutional child sexual abuse according to the following themes: causes; prevention; identification; institutional responses; government responses; treatment and support needs; institutions of interest; ensuring a positive impact.

Generally, the report and research are highly regarded. The public conversation about the impact of CSA, risk factors and the need for continued efforts at prevention has irrevocably changed, often in ways that have altered people's perceptions of once-revered institutions. One national survey found that 48 per cent of practising Catholics lost confidence in church leaders throughout the Royal Commission hearings.[173] Recommendations have begun to be implemented including reforms to civil and criminal law procedures, state and institutional child protection policies and practices, and redress (see Chapters 7, 8 and 9). However, some religious bodies such as the Catholic Church continue to resist recommendations for reform such as the removal of the confessional seal. In 2019, Justice McClellan, the former Chair of the Royal Commission, publicly excoriated Catholic Church leaders, stating that he could not comprehend 'how any person, much less one with qualifications in theology...could consider the rape of a child to be a moral failure but not a crime'.[174]

One ideal of transitional justice is to address the past in order to prepare for the future. Both the *Forgotten Australians* and *Lost Innocents* inquiries into out-of-home-care and child migration fit this mandate, in that they examined the treatment of children in the past and potential remedies and compensation for survivors in the present. In contrast, *Bringing Them Home* was a hybrid approach examining past practices of child removal and current child protection policies, as well as the question of reparations. Similarly, the Royal Commission examined contemporary case studies alongside those of the past. The Royal Commission's phenomenal social science research programme was aimed at generating new understandings of how to safeguard children in the future, and yet the Commissioners were also tasked with making recommendations about redress and compensation for adult survivors of NRCSA. In this sense, the Royal Commission can be read as a radical, comprehensive deployment and transformation of traditional transitional justice remedies. This internationally influential hybrid inquiry performed the profound discursive function of connecting NRCSA with the present and the future in the public mind by addressing institutional CSA as a historical yet linear and potentially ongoing phenomenon if left unchecked. The Royal Commission has proven that CSA may be endemic to any institution, secular or religious, and that at the same time all children are at risk of abuse, all adults are at risk of participating in hierarchical organizational cultures that dehumanize the vulnerable. Perhaps most crucially of all, in its taking of private hearings, the Royal Commission has determined that survivors have a right to be believed and to determine the conditions of their disclosures. It has undoubtedly elevated sexual abuse above other forms of child abuse and perhaps deterred political discussion of CSA within the family. In its focus on institutions and organizations, the Royal Commission performed at times an elision of feminist analyses of the gendered power relations that inform the sexual abuse of children.

England and Wales

In 1996 Wales was one of the first countries to establish a statutory public inquiry into NRCSA with the Waterhouse Tribunal Inquiry into abuse at children's homes in North Wales (see Chapter 2).[175] In 2012 the Tribunal was at the heart of controversy when accusations emerged of cover-ups, secrecy, failure to acknowledge the full extent of abuse or refusal to disclose the identities of those responsible. A reinvestigation by the National Crime Investigation, Operation Pallial, and a review of the scope and conduct of the Waterhouse Tribunal, the Macur Review, was ordered by government.[176] Macur found 'no reason to undermine the conclusions of the Tribunal in respect of the nature and the scale of abuse'. It also found no evidence of the involvement of prominent individuals in the abuse of children in care in North Wales during the relevant period. But the IICSA was conceived of in Westminster, by a government under pressure to respond to the seemingly never-ending scandals involving allegations of NRCSA in every corner of British society. In 2014 with the nation still reeling from Operation Yewtree (the joint National Society for the Prevention of Cruelty to Children [NSPCC] and Metropolitan Police report into Jimmy Savile), reports implicating other celebrities in NRCSA,[177] and Baroness Jay's Rotherham inquiry,[178] there were increasing demands for a more substantive examination of police practices and institutional responsibilities. In Parliament, survivor of NRCSA and Liberal Democrat MP, Tessa Munt together with six other MPs had lobbied hard for an independent public inquiry. On 7 July 2014 Theresa May, then Home Secretary, and future Conservative Prime Minister, informed the House of Commons that:

> I want to address two important public concerns: first, that in the 1980s the Home Office failed to act on allegations of child sex abuse; and, secondly, that public bodies and other important institutions have failed to take seriously their duty of care towards children.[179]

May announced the commissioning of two new non-statutory inquiries into matters relating to CSA. The first was termed 'an independent Review' and was to be conducted by Peter Wanless, Chief Executive of the NSPCC and Richard Whittam Queen's Counsel. Wanless and Whittam were tasked with reviewing two previous reviews commissioned by May's Permanent Secretary. The first of these, conducted in 2013, was into repeated concerns raised in the 1980s by the late Geoffrey Dickens Conservative MP (whose letters had mysteriously disappeared) about allegations of organized CSA involving senior politicians and officials, including senior diplomat Sir Peter Hayman.[180] The second review, conducted in 2014, concerned suggestions that in the 1970s the Home Office had approved grant funding to the Paedophile Information Exchange,[181] a pro-paedophile group that lobbied to abolish the age of sexual consent. Both original reviews had found no evidence of specific allegations against named individuals or improper financial support, although it was revealed that in respect of the former '114 potentially relevant files' were 'presumed lost or destroyed'.[182] The Wanless and Whittam Review into the previous two reviews was to be guided by three key principles: to allow the full investigation of CSA and prosecution of its perpetrators; adopt a presumption of maximum transparency; and expose and learn from the failures of individuals and institutions in managing sexual abuse to revive public confidence. Wanless and Whittam's subsequent report concluded there had been no improper funding allocation or cover-ups but recognized that child protection in the 1980s and 1990s was 'given seriously less consideration than would be expected today, the risk to children was not considered at all' by the Home Office and 'senior government figures were putting fear of political embarrassment above the risks to children'.[183]

The Wanless and Whittam review was very much a sideshow to the overarching super-inquiry into CSA announced by May on 7 July 2014. Initially, May chose to establish a non-statutory panel inquiry 'to consider whether public bodies and other non-state institutions have taken seriously their duty of care to protect children from sexual abuse'.[184] Over the past few decades, the use of non-statutory inquiries, as opposed to full statutory inquiries, has been increasingly perceived as preferable by politicians and civil servants because of the flexibility for those in charge (such as the Home Secretary or Chair) to determine an inquiry's operational procedures. Non-statutory inquiries have less power, however. For example, only a statutory inquiry can compel witnesses to attend and require disclosure of documents. May's inquiry was not limited to those who had caused or committed out-of-home CSA but also embraced the responses of institutions, or their lack of reaction, to such allegations. It was tasked with undertaking 13 separate and highly complex investigations into primarily sexual and physical abuse and, like the Australian Royal Commission, included both historic, or to use the inquiry's preferred term 'non-recent', and contemporary incidents. This Independent Inquiry into Child Sexual Abuse (IICSA) would be guided by the same three principles as the Wanless review.[185] May also promised conversion of the IICSA to a full statutory inquiry under the Inquiries Act 2005 if the Chair subsequently deemed it necessary[186] (which occurred in 2015). May acknowledged it would be impossible for the IICSA to conclude its work before the next general election in 2015. It was only later that the project's true ambition was understood when Dame Lowell Goddard, the third Chair, publicly confirmed to MPs on her resignation in August 2016 that 'there was an inherent problem in the sheer scale and size of the inquiry'.[187]

Scope and structure

The scope of the IICSA is unprecedented in British parliamentary history and of the three public inquiries discussed here is arguably the most multi-faceted, challenging and infinite. Its work is divided into three strands: the first addresses the goal of accountability and involves 15 investigations into institutional responses to CSA in a variety of settings (custodial institutions, residential schools, via the Internet; Nottinghamshire Councils, Lambeth Council; outside the UK; Cambridge House, Knowl view and Rochdale institutions: the Roman Catholic Church, the Anglican Church, Westminster; and child sexual exploitation by organized networks). There is also an investigation into the institutional responses (of Leicestershire County Council, the Crown Prosecution Service, the Labour Party, Parliament, government departments and the security and intelligence services) to allegations of CSA involving the late Labour politician Lord Janner (see Chapter 3). These are overlain with two macro-level investigations, one into the provision of accountability and reparations for survivors in the form of availability of support services and accessibility to legal procedures, the other into effective leadership in child protection within institutions covered by the Inquiry's terms of reference.[188] The investigations underpinned the public hearings, which lasted 323 days and involved 648 witnesses giving evidence in person. Of those, only 94 witnesses were survivors. During the hearings 24,565 documents totalling over 590,000 pages were disclosed. As with the Australian Royal Commission, but unlike the Irish CICA, survivors afforded core participant status were allowed legal representation.

The IICSA's second major strand is a Research Project that engages stakeholders in a range of seminars to enhance current understandings of institutional CSA. The emphasis on research underscores a transitional justice style commitment to preventing a repetition of the failures of the past.

The third strand is a version of the CICA's CC and the Royal Commission's Private Sessions and explicitly embodies the goal of truth-telling. The Truth Project is a facility 'for victims and survivors to share their experiences and be respectfully heard and acknowledged'.[189] Survivors' accounts inform the IICSA's research and will inform its recommendations.

An eight-member Victims and Survivors' Consultative Panel (established by Dame Lowell Goddard in 2016) assists and advises the IICSA on its work. The IICSA also sponsors a Victims' and Survivors' Forum, which holds regular events and seminars offering support and information to anyone affected by (NR)CSA or interested. Regular updates and events are live-streamed and published on the IICSA website and quarterly statistics about the Inquiry's progress are published and disseminated. Both the Panel and the Forum are important mechanisms for survivors to engage with the IICSA's work, something that was missing from the Irish CICA.

Despite criticism of the implementation, complexity and unwieldiness of the IICSA it is undeniable that Theresa May delivered on her promise to *enable* comprehensive investigations of those institutions responsible for countenancing CSA, past and present.

However, the unprecedented ambitious scope was not without its limitations. No account of the IICSA would be complete without a reflection on the challenges in finding a Chair who could claim complete distance from the allegations involving the political classes and who was not daunted by the sheer scale and scope of the enterprise. We explore the long road to establishing the IICSA here.

Shambolic beginnings

The IICSA had an inauspicious start, dogged by delays and disagreements about the suitability of the nominated Chairs. First to be appointed, on 8 July 2014, was Dame Elizabeth Butler-Sloss whose tenure was short-lived; she stepped down just six days later. The retired first female Court of Appeal judge, although aged 80, was an obvious choice having chaired the landmark 1988 Cleveland Inquiry (see Chapter 3). But journalist Bea Campbell, who covered the Cleveland scandal, was critical of the nomination. Campbell was sceptically dismissive of the judge's missed opportunity to uncover the extent of CSA during the Cleveland inquiry in 1988. She 'neither asked nor answered the question: Were the children abused?'.[190] However, it was the storm of controversy surrounding Butler-Sloss's late brother, Sir Michael Havers that ended her appointment. Havers, who was Attorney General during the 1980s, allegedly tried (and failed) to stop Geoffrey Dickens MP using parliamentary privilege to name diplomat Sir Peter Hayman as a paedophile.[191]

Butler-Sloss was adamant that she knew nothing about the incident but the family tie to the very establishment the IICSA was created to examine not only compromised her position but challenged Theresa May's wisdom in selecting her.

Fiona Woolf, Lord Mayor of London, was appointed to replace Butler-Sloss on 5 September, but she too stepped down seven weeks later, on 31 October 2014. Woolf was a friend of former Conservative Home Secretary Sir Leon Brittan who at the time was under 'suspicion' in relation to the perceived government cover-up of paedophile activity in Westminster in the 1980s. Woolf denied any 'close association' with Brittan, insisting he was 'one of thousands of friends' she knew in London[192] but when it transpired that Home Office officials had helped Woolf redraft a letter seven times to downplay her relationship with Brittan, May's reputation hit rock bottom.[193] The series of false starts underscored the enmeshed nature of the British ruling class.

With no immediate alternative and two Chairs already discredited because of their perceived ties to the 'establishment', the need to ensure the next incumbent was unassailable. The IICSA was dissolved and put on hold.

May had initially intended for the IICSA to be conducted as an independent non-statutory panel inquiry with experts similar to the Hillsborough[194] and Iraq inquiries.[195] Lord Justice Scott, Chairman of the Arms to Iraq Inquiry summarized the three overriding objectives of how such inquiries should operate:

> the need to be fair and to be seen to be fair to those whose interests, reputations or fortunes may be adversely affected by the proceedings, that inquiries should be conducted efficiently and expeditiously and that the costs must be kept within reasonable bounds.

He concluded that 'The golden rule is that there should be procedural flexibility with procedures to achieve fairness tailored to suit the circumstances of each inquiry'.[196] However, non-statutory panels have no legal authority to compel witnesses to attend or for evidence to be taken on oath and, under the Inquiries Act 2005 must operate in public, which is of particular concern when sensitive or confidential information is sought. On 12 March 2015, May announced that the IICSA had been reconstituted as a statutory inquiry with powers to compel witnesses to 'determine whether state and non-state institutions have taken seriously their duty of care to children'.[197] She also extended its jurisdiction to institutions implicated in, or that showed disregard for, the trafficking and abusing of children outside England and Wales. Four new panel members were appointed, and it was estimated that the work would take at least half a decade at a cost of £100 million.[198] There are mixed reports about the selection process for the next Chair. The official line was that the due diligence and selection processes used by the Home Office were carried out in unprecedented depth and detail according to lead counsel to the inquiry.[199] But investigations by Andrew Norfolk, The Times' reputable reporter who has uncovered and publicized a range of sexual abuse scandals, hinted at the Home Office's 'desperation' to find someone not tainted by links to the British establishment.[200]

May must have been relieved when Dame Lowell Goddard, a New Zealand High Court judge, former Queen's Counsel and human rights expert, accepted the post. The first woman of Māori ancestry promoted to New Zealand's Court of Appeal,[201] Goddard assumed her post as IICSA Chair on 9 July 2015 on a remuneration package of almost £500,000 and with a £17.9 million budget for the forthcoming year.[202] But on 4 August 2016, after criticism that she had spent three months of her role at taxpayers' expense in New Zealand, Goddard offered her resignation to the Home Secretary. Goddard's short resignation letter was implicitly critical of the magnitude of the task and 'legacy of failure' she had inherited. According to newspaper reports, Goddard had lost the trust of her staff; insiders supposedly accused her of rudeness, and, when asked why there were so many paedophiles in Britain, of allegedly responding 'because it has so many Asian men', prompting accusations of racism.[203] Goddard strenuously denied the allegations, calling them 'false' and 'malicious'.[204] Peter Saunders, founder of the National Association for People Abused in Childhood and core participant of the IICSA said that survivors had a good working relationship with Goddard and that 'it was a pity that it was all done in haste because she certainly listened to survivors'.[205] Graham Wilmer, founder of the survivor support organization Lantern Project and a Consultative Panel member under former Chair Fiona Woolf agreed the structure of the IICSA was 'far too complicated...[with] too many people involved trying to cause difficulties', intimating that one of the existing main panel members should be appointed as the next Chair as they were now more knowledgeable and informed than any outsider.[206]

Back on track?

From this point on, although independent, the IICSA was in danger of becoming politicized with the need to co-ordinate and manage 13 investigations, 155 staff, 188 core participants, 2,200 communications from the public and 35,000 documents.[207] Labour MP Chuka Umunna campaigned to be the fourth Chair but was rejected in favour of Baroness Professor Alexis Jay, another controversial appointee. Jay, a child protection expert, had been recruited as a panel member in March 2015 and became Chair on 11 August 2016. She was well-regarded politically for having led the independent inquiry into child sexual exploitation in Rotherham between 1997 and 2013 involving at least 1,400 children and multiple perpetrators (see Chapter 3). Her 2014 report was highly critical of the police, council and child protection agency responses and has prompted further investigations.[208] In 2014 the National Crime Agency created Operation Stovewood to investigate allegations of abuse in Rotherham between 1997 and 2013. It is the single largest police investigation into non-familial child sexual exploitation and abuse in the UK. To date 20 people have been convicted. Also following Jay's Report, the Independent Office for Police Conduct created a wide-ranging independent investigation into alleged police misconduct in respect of CSE in Rotherham between 1997 and 2013.[209] It is due to report in 2022.

The Survivors' Alliance, an umbrella group of several victim organizations, welcomed Jay's appointment as Chair of the IICSA, but lawyers appeared less enamoured with her as she does not have a legal background. In October 2016 Imran Khan, a lawyer representing 40 survivors, criticized Jay for lack of legal expertise in the questioning of witnesses and in legal decision-making and said she could not fulfil the inquiry's terms of reference.[210] Similar perceptions about Jay persisted. In November, the Shirley Oaks Survivors Association representing 600 victims in residential care homes in Lambeth from the 1950s withdrew on the basis it had lost confidence in the IICSA and (arguably somewhat unfairly) that Jay would make it a 'social work talk shop'.[211] Further tensions and conflicting perspectives led to the formal withdrawal, 'with deep regret', in June 2017 of the Survivors of Organised and Institutional Abuse who criticized the IICSA as 'not fit for purpose'. Survivors claimed they had been 'totally marginalised', and it had become a 'very costly academic report writing and literature review exercise'.[212] Balancing such competing interests was always going to be a major challenge especially as one of the key objectives of the IICSA, the Research Project, was intended to supplement the existing literature on CSA, known to have significant knowledge gaps.

Jay remained on as Chair, and the IICSA progressed through its substantial work programme, although the IICSA continued to face criticism from some survivor groups.

Accountability through investigations

By autumn 2021 the IICSA had commissioned 15 investigations, four of which were ongoing, into residential schools, religious settings, organized networks and allegations against Lord Janner. Its last public hearing was conducted in December 2020. Each investigation has or will culminate in a dedicated report. It is a far broader investigation than the CICA, which focused on industrial schools and reformatories run by religious orders. It also is broader than the Australian Royal Commission which although it examined a wide range of institutions, came to focus predominantly on religious organizations and did not examine organized paedophile activity outside of institutions. In the IICSA, abuse in religious settings receives comparatively less attention than either Ireland or Australia. It is the subject of three investigations out of 15 (the Anglican and Roman Catholic Churches, and abuse in other religious organizations and settings) and is explored in relation to accountability and reparations and support services for survivors, as well as in the Truth Project.

However, the investigations by the IICSA extend far beyond religious contexts and embrace public institutions such as the custodial institutions, children's homes and other forms of state residential care, as well as the police, the Crown Prosecution Service, security and intelligence services and the armed forces. It also considers the responses of some private institutions.

Relaunching the IICSA as a Statutory Inquiry in March 2015, May promised there would be 'no geographical boundaries' limiting any investigation or curtailing accountability. She confirmed that the IICSA would liaise with other UK national inquiries: the Historical Institutional Abuse Inquiry in Northern Ireland,[213] the Scottish Child Abuse Inquiry[214] and the Independent Jersey Care Inquiry[215] and that all would be connected via joint protocols. The IICSA also collaborated with the Australian Royal Commission. Perhaps the most significant instance of this broadened scope is the inclusion of child migration schemes. The abuse of child migrants had been the subject of numerous government inquiries in Australia (including the Royal Commission) and in the UK dating back to the mid-1990s.[216] No public inquiry in England and Wales had undertaken a sustained analysis of allegations of sexual abuse of child migrants and failings by institutions based in England and Wales (and Northern Ireland) in relation to that abuse. The IICSA clearly decided to prioritize this internationally significant issue by making it the subject of its first case study and report, recommending that the UK government establish a redress scheme available to all surviving child migrants, regardless of whether they had personally suffered CSA, which the Australian government had failed to do. The UK government subsequently agreed to accept the IICSA's recommendation and established a redress scheme to former child migrants that provided a flat payment of £20,000 to all eligible applicants.[217]

The Truth Project

The Truth Project was influenced by South Africa's post-apartheid TRC model, and its objective in facilitating survivors sharing their experiences resonates with the work of the CC of the Irish CICA and the Private Sessions of the Australian Royal Commission. Like the Royal Commission the Truth Project allowed survivors to share their experiences in person or in writing, and the IICSA also offered the option of a telephone or video call, but most survivors shared their experiences in writing.[218] Those attending a private session at the IICSA were offered a support worker and two companions, indicating the IICSA's sensitivity to survivors' needs. By mid-2021 5,861 people had shared their accounts of sexual victimization.[219] While many accounts provided to the Truth Project were harrowing there was also evidence of positivity and healing with cathartic narratives around rebuilding lives and relationships. The Truth Project published on the IICSA website includes an online anthology of accounts from survivors collected throughout the duration of the inquiry.[220]

The Truth Project offers invaluable insights into the experiences of those survivors who participated. Ten per cent of participants reported that they shared an experience of (NR)CSA for the first time through the Truth Project. Also, 50 per cent reported abuse involving penetration[221] and 24 per cent of participants had been groomed. Almost half (48 per cent) reported that the perpetrator was a family member. This figure points to the major flaw with the IICSA and all three inquiries examined here, none of which investigated sexual offending in the family, despite evidence emerging of its prevalence. The profile of those who participated in the Truth Project contrasts directly with the profile of those who gave evidence to the Irish CC or the Royal Commission's private sessions. In the Irish and Australian commissions, the great majority of participants were male.[222] In contrast, 70 per cent of survivors who spoke to the IICSA's Truth Project were female, which correlates with the numbers of survivors who came forward who had been abused within their families. Girls remain the primary victims of incest and intrafamilial abuse. The publicity around the Truth Project seems to have elicited testimony of incest in a way that the other two public inquiries did not. The failure of all three public inquiries to investigate abuse in families is a missed opportunity for understanding and responding to the most common form of NRCSA and CSA.

A further difference concerns the age of those who testified: in all three public inquiries, most survivors who engaged with the truth-telling forum were over the age of 50,[223] but the IICSA had a much larger proportion of young people. While the Irish CC had no participants under 30 years of age,[224] and the Royal Commission only had 6.3 per cent of Private Sessions participants aged under 30, in the IICSA's Truth Project, some 25 per cent of participants were aged under 30. It is likely that both the gender and age demographic differences reflect the IICSA's broader remit in terms of the institutions and types or forms of abuse it is considering when compared to the other two public inquiries. The increased proportion of younger people is a welcome reflection of the increased engagement with survivors of NRCSA dating to the late 1990s and suggests a more heightened awareness that CSA is not a relic of a supposed distant past but an urgent contemporary problem.

Importantly, the Truth Project has led directly to changes in the IICSA's work; in May 2019, as 11 per cent of survivors had reported abuse in religious settings,[225] an additional thematic investigation was launched to review child protection practices in major religions in England and Wales. This demonstrates a degree of responsiveness and engagement with survivors that was also seen in the Royal Commission but was far greater than that seen in the CICA.

Referrals to the criminal process

The IICSA is required to refer all allegations of CSA to the police, which responds to them as part of Operation Hydrant, the national non-recent abuse coordination hub established in June 2014. This is a significant innovation on past child abuse public inquiries and connects the IICSA's work with broader accountability functions of criminal justice. Personal details will not be provided without survivors' consent (unless there is a risk to a child or someone is at risk of serious harm). Anonymized information is still valuable; providing even general circumstances of a case 'may reveal important information about particular locations or institutions that may be of assistance to the police'.[226] As at March 2018 the majority of referrals by the IICSA (78 per cent) resulted in 'no further action' following consideration by the receiving police force or agency.[227] The IICSA stated that the reasons for this include a lack of evidence, being unable to trace or identify a perpetrator, a perpetrator being deceased, or a survivor no longer wanting to continue with the criminal process. The IICSA did not expand on which reasons were the most common, so it is difficult to infer anything about the activities of the prosecution service or police. What is clear however is that the kind of accountability being delivered by the IICSA is not criminal justice.

Predictably, with such a groundbreaking and ambitious project, there have been setbacks. In November 2017 a serious error was made when the name of an alleged victim was published online, the seventh time this had happened, constituting a contempt of court under the IICSA's rules.[228] Despite the systematic approach adopted by the IICSA, survivors have expressed dissatisfaction with how it has engaged with them, either in respect of the Truth Project or in relation to hearings for particular investigations.[229] Many survivors have criticized what they describe as inadequate scrutiny of institutional responses to child sexual exploitation by organized networks. The controversies surrounding the IICSA from its earliest days have generated a sense of disconnection from the investigative process for many survivors.[230]

The IICSA has made recommendations which have been, or now are being, implemented by the government: these include the award of redress to child migrants; removal of the unfair 'same roof' rule preventing awards of criminal injuries compensation to those abused in family settings before 1979 (see Chapter 11), and the extension of the criminal offence of 'breach of trust' to clergy and sports coaches. More far-reaching recommendations about key issues such as regulation of organizations charged with the care of children, mandatory reporting, and access to civil and criminal justice for survivors are yet to come in its final report.

Conclusion

Public inquiries perform invaluable functions, but at the same time, they can be a way for governments to attempt to take the political sting out of a controversial issue, to be seen to 'overcome' the past and move on. The centring of survivors' experiences, first performed by the CICA, and expanded upon in the Royal Commission and the IICSA, has made any such 'overcoming' in the case of NRCSA implausible. A new cultural frame informed the design of each public inquiry, one in which traumatic experiences are linked to legitimate victimhood, and in which speaking about trauma has an epistemic and symbolic value for truth-telling and accountability.

Each of the public inquiries examined here embodied private goals of 'healing' for survivors and public goals of understanding children's suffering through 'truth-telling' and the use of adult survivors' testimonies and voices, the uncovering of abuse and the prevention of future abuse through reform of children's institutions and child protection laws and policies.

The focus on the extent to which institutions have failed in their duty of care to protect children from sexual abuse means that each inquiry's findings (may) expose important institutional structural and systemic contributors to past and contemporary victimization of children, serving all three goals of transitional justice. However, both the CICA and the Royal Commission tended to examine institutions individually.

The major difference between the three is the scope of institutions examined. The difference in scope matters for truth-telling (only some survivors are able to donate their testimony to the public record), accountability (only some institutions/individuals are held to account) and non-repetition (only some forms of abuse will be understood and addressed by preventative measures). While the CICA interpreted its terms of reference narrowly and focused primarily on institutions run by religious orders on behalf of the state, the other two inquiries considered a broader range of public and private institutions. As was the case with both the CICA and the Royal Commission, (NR)CSA in the family is not being investigated by the IICSA (even though its research with survivors and some of the academic work commissioned do consider familial abuse). This represents the major flaw in each form of inquiry, since research demonstrates that children are as much at risk, if not more, in intra-familial relationships than other kinds of relationships.[231] Similarly, as in Ireland and Australia, foster care has fallen largely beneath the IICSA's radar, despite this being a significant form of out-of-home residential care especially post-institutional living.

There is also a difference in terms of temporal scope between the three inquiries; while the CICA focused primarily on the past, the Royal Commission and the IICSA both explored historical and contemporary CSA and made recommendations that impact present and future children. The goal of non-repetition was also served by each public inquiry commissioning research that has contributed to greater public and scholarly understanding of key issues for institutions/and the state.[232] The CICA included research on the psychological adjustment of adult survivors of institutional abuse, and on the social and historical contexts of industrial schools and residential child welfare. The theme of research and analysis was greatly expanded upon first by the Royal Commission and then by the IICSA to form a key pillar of each inquiry's programme of work. The scope of public inquiries internationally is continually evolving as countries learn from each other and respond to survivors' critiques.

Publicity is an important element in both truth-telling and accountability, and each inquiry has prioritized it. The CICA is the first and only Irish abuse inquiry to have held public hearings, albeit these were relatively limited in scope and number. Transcripts of the hearings were published on the CICA's website.[233] The Royal Commission's website contains the witness lists, transcripts, exhibits, images and associated submissions for its 57 public hearings which were live-streamed.[234] Daily transcripts of the IICSA's public hearings are published on its website, along with detailed information about the legal procedures and protocols, as well as witness lists, exhibits and submissions.[235] In 2017 Former Australian Labor MP Ann Barker, who first called for the CICA to be emulated in Australia, stated that both the Irish and Australian public inquiries had 'changed the nation. They now talk about it [CSA]. They now talk about it in clubs and communities, where nobody talked about that before, but now they do'.[236] It is already evident that the IICSA is having a similar cultural and political effect.

However, each example also illustrates the limits of public inquiries used in this context. In the CICA the systemic nature of abuse in industrial schools and reformatories and, crucially, the state's role in it, was not subjected to sustained scrutiny. The decision not to name abusers, even those who were deceased or convicted, precluded accountability of individual perpetrators and obscured the accountability of the religious orders of which they were members. The anonymization of institutional staff (both lay and religious), the civil service, and other figures representing society, 'create[d] a barrier between the truths of the report and the reality'.[237] The lack of engagement with the gardaí contrasts with the police referral policies of the Royal Commission and the IICSA. It is also far from clear what child protection measures were taken following of disclosures of abuse made by survivors at the CICA against living persons. Even though the automatic referrals of the Royal Commission and the IICSA were imperfect in terms of rates of conviction, they symbolized an important formal effort to hold individual abusers to account.

Public inquiries cannot serve the other important goal of transitional justice: symbolic and material reparations to individual survivors. In the next chapter we examine state reparations for NRCSA.

Notes

1 K. Wright, "Challenging Institutional Denial: Psychological Discourse, Therapeutic Culture and Public Inquiries" *Journal of Australian Studies* 42(2), 2017, 177–90; K. Wright et al., "The Australian Royal Commission into Institutional Responses to Child Sexual Abuse" *Child Abuse and Neglect* 74(1), 2017, 1–9.

2 S. Swain, K. Wright, and J. Sköld, "Conceptualising and Categorising Child Abuse Inquiries: From Damage Control to Foregrounding Survivor Testimony" *Journal of Historical Sociology* 31(3), 2017, 282–96.

3 UN Secretary-General, *The Rule of Law and Transitional Justice in Conflict and Post-Conflict Societies: Report of the Secretary-General* (23 Aug. 2004), S/2004/616.
4 K. Gleeson and S. Ring, "Confronting the Past and Changing the Future? Public Inquiries into Institutional Child Abuse Inquiries, Ireland and Australia" *Griffith Law Review* 29(1), 2021, 109–33; S. Winter, "Towards a Unified Theory of Transitional Justice" *International Journal of Transitional Justice* 7(2), 2013, 224–44; J. Gallen, "Transitional Justice and Ireland's Legacy of Historical Abuse" *Éire-Ireland* 55 (1&2), (2020), 35–67; A.-M. McAlinden and B. Naylor, "Reframing Public Inquiries as Procedural Justice for Victims of Institutional Child Abuse: Towards a Hybrid Model of Justice" *Sydney Law Review* 38(3), 2016, 277–308; M. Enright and S. Ring, "State Legal Responses to Historical Institutional Abuse: Shame, Sovereignty and Epistemic Injustice" *Éire-Ireland* 55 (1&2) 2020, 68–99.
5 Commission to Inquire into Child Abuse, *Final Report* (Dublin: Government Publications, 2009), Vol 1, Chapter 1, [1.64].
6 Ss5(2)(a) and (b).
7 Royal Commission into Institutional Responses to Child Sexual Abuse, *Final Report* Vol 1 (Commonwealth of Australia: Royal Commission into Institutional Responses to Child Sexual Abuse, 2017), 3.
8 www.iicsa.org.uk/background
9 Terms of Reference.
10 D. Fassin and R. Rechtman, *The Empire of Trauma* (Princeton: Princeton University Press, 2009).
11 C. Smart, "A History of Ambivalence and Conflict in the Discursive Construction of the 'Child Victim' of Sexual Abuse" *Social and Legal Studies* 8(3), 1999, 391–409; S. Ring "The Victim of Historical Child Sexual Abuse in the Irish Courts 1999–2006" *Social and Legal Studies* 2017, 562–80.
12 The Forde Inquiry in Queensland was the only similar endeavour. It took one year and sampled survivors. L. Forde AC, *Report of the Commission of Inquiry into Abuse in Queensland Institutions* (Brisbane: Commission of Inquiry into Abuse in Queensland Institutions, 1999). www.qld.gov.au/__data/assets/pdf_file/0023/54509/forde-comminquiry.pdf.
13 Letter from the Private Secretary to the Taoiseach to Andrew Madden, 9 June 1998, reproduced in A. Madden, *Altar Boy* (Dublin: Penguin Ireland, 2004), 209–12.
14 See CICA (2009) Volume 1 [1.48]. Transcript of Evidence of Tom Boland, former Head of Legal Affairs at the Department of Education and Science (24 June 2004). www.childabusecommission.ie/public_hearings/documents/04/Transcript-24June2004.PDF.
15 Micheál Martin in L. Lentin, *Our Boys' Stories. Stolen Lives* (documentary, Louis Lentin), episode 1, https://ifiarchiveplayer.ie/our-boys-stories/.
16 P. Sweeney, *The Celtic Tiger Ireland's Economic Miracle Explained* (Dublin: Oak Tree Press, 1998).
17 T. Inglis, *Moral Monopoly. The Decline and Fall of the Catholic Church in Modern Ireland* (Dublin: University College Dublin Press, 1998).
18 Boland op. cit., 2004, 34.
19 Ibid., 80.
20 Psychiatrist Dr Imelda Ryan, director of St Louise's Child Sexual Abuse and Assessment Unit at Our Lady's Hospital in Dublin and Bob Lewis, a former director of social services in Stockport, England.

21 Under the Tribunals of Inquiry Act (Evidence) 1921.
22 With the notable exceptions of the Hepatitis C Tribunal and HIV Compensation Tribunal.
23 S1.
24 S 5(5)(b) CICAA 2000.
25 *The Irish Times*, 14 January 2000.
26 516 *Dail Debates* Col 293.
27 Ss 4(1)(a) and 10(1)(a) CICAA 2000.
28 S1 CICAA 2000. See Boland 2004 at 45–46.
29 Ss 4(b)(i) and (ii) and Statement Delivered at First Public Sitting of the Commission to Inquire into Child Abuse held on 29 June 2000; s10(1)(b).
30 Ss 4(1)(b) (i)–(iii).
31 S5(3)(a).
32 S5(3)(b). The Commission was not allowed to identify the survivors of abuse.
33 S5(2)(a) and (b).
34 Norah Gibbons, preceded by Bob Lewis CBE, a former director of social services in Stockport, England.
35 Dr Paddy Deasy.
36 Dr Kevin McCoy.
37 Anne McLoughlin.
38 Fred Lowe.
39 Dr Imelda Ryan.
40 S1 Commission to Inquire into Child Abuse Act 2000.
41 Other Commissions of Inquiry established later examined clerical sexual abuse in certain dioceses: Department of Justice Equality and Law Reform (2005); Commission of Investigation (2009) and (2010).
42 *The Irish Times*, 5 February 2000.
43 S1 Commission to Inquire into Child Abuse Act 2000.
44 The Final Report included a chapter prepared by an academic on Residential Child Welfare from 1956–2008, and a chapter on interviews with people who did not proceed to an oral hearing, some of whom recounted abuse in orphanages, hospitals, national schools, special schools and other institutions.
45 S7(4).
46 516 *Dáil Debates* Col 293.
47 [2.28].
48 [2.21].
49 [2.26].
50 CICA op. cit., 2009, Vol III, [2.20].
51 Table 1, [2.20]. By contrast, 58 per cent of survivors based in the UK were women.
52 S14 Commission to Inquire into Child Abuse Act 2000.
53 Statement at first Public Hearing June 2000 available at www.childabusecommission.ie/publications/documents/29-06-2000.pdf
54 Ibid. and see Third Interim Report, 2003, Ch 10.
55 S21(1) of the 2000 Act. This did not apply to survivors.
56 *The Irish Times*, 14 January 2000.
57 Commission of Investigation, *Report in the Catholic Archdiocese of Dublin* (Dublin: Stationery Office, 2009), available at www.justice.ie/en/JELR/Pages/PB09000504.
58 S19 Commissions of Investigation Act 2004.

59 IC Framework of Procedures, 2002, www.childabusecommission.ie/publications/documents/Child%20Abuse%20Commission%20Framework%20of%20Procedures.pdf.

60 Third Interim Report, 2003, Ch 10, www.childabusecommission.ie/publications/documents/abuse.pdf.

61 Legal Team's Statement 7 May 2004, www.childabusecommission.ie/events/documents/SC%20Address%20-%20070504.pdf.

62 The High Court rejected the Commission's attempt to limit the number of legal representatives for a person attending the IC: *Re Commission to Inquire into Child Abuse* [2002] 3 IR 459.

63 *Michael Murray and David Gibson v the Commission to Inquire into Child Abuse the Minister for Education and Science, Ireland and the Attorney General* [2004] IEHC 102.

64 This was finally addressed in 2002.

65 M. Laffoy, 'Letter of Resignation', www.irishtimes.com/news/justice-mary-laffoy-s-letter-of-resignation-1.373996.

66 'A Position Paper on Identifying Institutions and Persons under the Commission to Inquire into Child Abuse Act 2000'; 'Opening Statement by Judge Ryan' and 'Statement by The Legal Team' (7 May 2004), www.childabusecommission.ie/publications/index.html.

67 *The Irish Times*, 18 September 2003.

68 Seanad Éireann Debate 20 April 2000, Dr Michael Woods. The provision was s58 *Children Act 1908*.

69 S8 2005 Act. There was an exception for those convicted of crimes, but even convicted abusers were given a pseudonym in the Final Report.

70 *Michael Murray and David Gibson v the Commission to Inquire into Child Abuse the Minister for Education and Science, Ireland and the Attorney General* [2004] IEHC 102.

71 Reclaiming Self, *Ryan Report Follow-Up. Submission to the United Nations Committee Against Torture* Session 61 (Dublin: Reclaiming Self, 2017), https://tbinternet.ohchr.org/_layouts/15/treatybodyexternal/SessionDetails1.aspx?SessionID=1132&Lang=en; S. Pembroke, "Historical Institutional Abuse in Ireland: Survivor Perspectives on Taking Part in the Commission to Inquire into Child Abuse (CICA) and the Redress Scheme" *Contemporary Justice Review* 22(1), 2019, 43–59.

72 *In Re Commission to Inquire into Child Abuse* [2002] 3 IR 459.

73 CICA [5.05].

74 Historian Dr Diarmaid Ferriter was commissioned by complainants to produce a report on the historical context of sexual abuse in Ireland, which was published as an appendix to the Final Report.

75 See O'Sullivan, E., "*Residential Child Welfare in Ireland,1965-2008: An Outline of Policy, Legislation and Practice: A Paper Prepared for the Commission to Inquire into Child Abuse,"* Commission to Inquire into Child Abuse, *Final Report* Vol IV, Ch 4 (Dublin: Commission to Inquire into Child Abuse, 2009).

76 Comptroller and Auditor General, *Cost of Child Abuse Inquiry and Redress*, 2016, 21. This excluded three schools for deaf children: CICA op. cit., 2009, Vol I, [5.109–5.10].

77 Ibid. [5.19].

78 Totally, 136 cases were transferred to the IC. Comptroller and Auditor General op. cit., Figure 2.2, 21.

79 CICA op. cit., 2009.
80 E. Pine, *The Politics of Irish Memory* (London: Palgrave Macmillan, 2011), 24.
81 CICA 2009 op. cit., Executive Summary, [18].
82 [6.19].
83 [6.29].
84 Final Report Volume VI, [6.30]. The report also included research on the history and operation of the residential childcare system and the psychological adjustment of adult survivors.
85 Executive Summary, [3].
86 Executive Summary, [6].
87 CICA (2009) Vol IV, Ch 7.
88 *The Irish Times*, 15 June, 2009.
89 21 May 2009.
90 *Irish Independent,* 29 June 2009.
91 www.hiainquiry.org.
92 The 2009 Report put it at 170,000, but the correction in 2019 stated that the correct figure, based on flow and not stock figures, was closer to 42,000. See Statement 25 November 2019, published on www.childabusecommission.ie.
93 See Chapter 3 for a discussion of a history of these institutions in Ireland.
94 The Industrial Memories Project led by Emilie Pine has digitized the Report and made it fully searchable: see https://industrialmemories.ucd.ie/project.
95 Reclaiming Self op. cit.
96 Enright and Ring op. cit.; McAlinden and Naylor op. cit.
97 CICA op. cit., 2009, Vol IV, 451.
98 See contributions by Mixed Race Ireland and Dr Rosaleen McDonagh to Reclaiming Self op. cit.
99 S.-A. Buckley (2013).
100 C. Holohan, *In Plain Sight: Responding to the Ferns, Ryan, Murphy and Cloyne Reports* (Dublin: Amnesty International Ireland, 2011); UN Committee Against Torture (CAT), *Consideration of reports submitted by States parties under article 19 of the Convention – Ireland*, 17 June 2011, CAT/C/IRL/CO/1, [20].
101 The CICA did examine abuse at a group home St Michael's Care Centre in Co Waterford managed by the Sisters of Mercy in the 1980s and abuse at the Christian Brothers-run school for deaf boys in Cabra, Dublin.
102 M. Raftery, "Secretive State Might Mislead You to Think Abuse Is Thing of the Past" *The Irish Times*, 1 June 2009.
103 And for failing to establish a statutory inquiry and redress scheme for Magdalene women.
104 *The Irish Times* 2011.
105 K. Wright, S. Swain and K. McPhillips, "The Australian Royal Commission into Institutional Responses to Child Sexual Abuse" *Child Abuse & Neglect* 74, 2017, 1–9.
106 Ibid.
107 G. Cowlishaw, "Inquiring into Aboriginal Deaths in Custody. The Limits of a Royal Commission" *Journal of Indigenous Policy* 1991, 28–40, 33.
108 Ibid.
109 *The Australian*, 21 January 1998.
110 Community Affairs References Committee, *Forgotten Australians: A Report on Australians who Experienced Institutional or Out-of-Home Care as Children* (Canberra: Australian Parliament, 2004), Recommendation 11.

111 *The Age*, 22 May 2009, 14.
112 *BBC Monitoring Asia Pacific*, 21 May 2009.
113 Anonymous, "An Unholy Conspiracy Against Children Exposed" *The Age*, 22 May 2009, 14.
114 P. Cummins et al., *Report of the Protecting Victoria's Vulnerable Children Inquiry* (Melbourne: Department of Premier and Cabinet, 2012).
115 *ABC News*, 13 December 2017.
116 Family and Community Development Committee, *Betrayal of Trust: Inquiry into the Handling of Child Abuse by Religious and Other Non-government Organisations* (Melbourne: Parliament of Victoria, 2013).
117 *Sydney Morning Herald*, 22 May 2009.
118 M. Cunneen, *Special Commission of Inquiry into Matters Relating to the Police Investigation of Certain Child Sexual Abuse Allegations in the Catholic Diocese of Maitland-Newcastle Report* (Sydney: NSW Department of Premier and Cabinet, 2014).
119 *ABC 7.30 Report*, 14 December 2017.
120 *ABC News*, 12 November 2012.
121 *ABC News*, 3 April 2013.
122 E. Alberichi, 'Interview with High Court Judge Sean Ryan from Dublin' *Australian Broadcasting Corporation Transcripts*, 13 November 2012.
123 Ibid.
124 *The Australian*, 14 November 2012.
125 Ibid.
126 Royal Commission (2013) *Terms of Reference* www.childabuseroyalcommission.gov.au/terms-reference.
127 L. Beck, "Institutional Responses to Child Sexual Abuse. The Constitutionality of a Royal Commission" *Alternative Law Journal* 38(1), 2013, 14–9.
128 Ibid.
129 S. Donaghue, *Royal Commissions and Permanent Commissions of Inquiry* (Sydney: Butterworths, 2001), 4–5.
130 Beck op. cit., 5.
131 Ibid., 6.
132 United Nations Convention on the Rights of the Child 1989.
133 Beck op. cit., 6.
134 Royal Commission, *Terms of Reference.*
135 Royal Commission into Institutional Responses to Child Sexual Abuse, *Final Report* Vol 1 (Commonwealth of Australia, 2017), 23.
136 For example, see G. Henderson, "The Royal Commission, the Media and the Church" *Quadrant* 61(7/8), 2017, 46.
137 J. Gillard, *My Story* (Sydney: Random House, 2014), 278.
138 Royal Commission, *Terms of Reference.*
139 K. Daly and J. Davis, "Unravelling Redress for Institutional Abuse of Children in Australia" *University of New South Wales Law Journal* 42(4), 2019, 1254–93.
140 F. Golding, "Sexual Abuse as the Core Transgression of Childhood Innocence: Unintended Consequences for Care Leavers" *Journal of Australian Studies* 42(2), 2018, 191–203.
141 Cited in B. Hall and J. Lee, 'Child Abuse Inquiry Criticised', *Sydney Morning Herald*, 16 January 2013.
142 Golding op. cit., 202.
143 Cited in Hall and Lee op. cit.

144 Golding op. cit., 203.
145 S. Prasser, "Royal Commissions in Australia: When Should Governments Appoint Them?" *Australian Journal of Public Administration* 65(3), 2006, 28–47, 32.
146 S6DD of the *Royal Commission Act*.
147 Royal Commission (2017) *Final Report Vol 1*, 25.
148 K. Cripps and R. McCreery, "Indigenous Engagement with the Royal Commission into Institutional Responses to Child Sexual Abuse" *Indigenous Law Bulletin* 8, 2013, 22–25, 24.
149 Royal Commission into Institutional Responses to Child Sexual Abuse op. cit., 3.
150 Royal Commission op. cit., 23.
151 Ibid, 34.
152 T. Jones, "Royal Commission Recommends Sweeping Reforms for Catholic Church to End Child Abuse' *The Conversation*, 15 December 2017, https://theconversation.com/royal-commission-recommends-sweeping-reforms-for-catholic-church-to-end-child-abuse-89141.
153 S6D.
154 Report of Case Study 43 – *The Response of Catholic Church Authorities to Allegations of Child Sexual Abuse in the Maitland–Newcastle Region*.
155 *ABC News,* 21 October 2016.
156 *ABC News*, 3 April 2013.
157 M. Dreyfus MP 'Legislation to Amend Royal Commissions Act 1902' *Australian Government News*, 13 February 2013.
158 *Royal Commissions Amendment Bill* (Cth) 2013. Explanatory memorandum.
159 Royal Commission, *Final Report Vol 1,* p. 26.
160 Anonymous, "Private Sessions to Enable People to Share Stories to Commissioner Voluntarily" *Australian Government News,* 22 March 2013.
161 Royal Commission, op. cit., p. 32.
162 Ibid.
163 Ibid.
164 Ibid., 28.
165 K. McPhillips, "Traumatic Isolation: Institutional Stigma and the Australian Royal Commission into Institutional Responses to Child Sexual Abuse" *Health and History* 20(2), 2018, 75–90.
166 A. Barter, et al., "Why the Caged Bird Sings: Issues with the Royal Commission into Institutional Responses to Child Sexual Abuse" *Indigenous Law Bulletin* 8(13), 2014, 7–10.
167 Royal Commission op cit., 10.
168 Cripps and McCreery op. cit.
169 Barter et al. op. cit., 8.
170 Royal Commission op. cit., 6.
171 Royal Commission into Institutional Responses to Child Sexual Abuse (2017) *Final Report Vol 16*, 26.
172 Royal Commission, *Final Report Preface and Executive Summary*, 4.
173 *Sydney Morning Herald*, 8 February 2018.
174 In M. Perkins, '"I Cannot Comprehend'. Sex Abuse Royal Commissioner Slams Religious Leaders," *Sydney Morning Herald*, 10 December 2019.

175 *Lost in Care, Report of the Tribunal of Inquiry into the abuse of children in care in the former county council areas of Gwynedd and Clwyd in North Wales since 1974* (UK: HMSO, 2000), available at www.childrenshomes.org.uk/NorthWales/LostInCare.pdf. See Chapter 2.

176 J.W. Macur, *The Report of the Macur Review* (UK: HMSO, 2016). Macur Review of Child Abuse in Wales – Redacted Version. An independent review of the Tribunal of Inquiry into the abuse of children in care in the former county council areas of Gwynedd and Clwyd in North Wales since 1974, 2016 www.gov.uk/government/publications/the-report-of-the-macur-review.

177 Including Rolf Harris and Stuart Hall.

178 See Chapter 2.

179 HC Debates, 7 Jul 2014 vol.584 col.23

180 Including Sir Leon Brittan (criticized by Dickens for not dealing appropriately with documents sent to him and who had been interviewed but not charged in relation to an allegation of NRCSA declaring it 'wholly without foundation') and Lord McAlpine, incorrectly identified online after a BBC Newsnight programme had wrongly implicated him in the Bryn Estyn children's home scandal, *The Times*, 8 July 2014.

181 The PIE was active 1974–1984.

182 HL Debates 7 July 2014, vol.755 col.54. Both investigation reports are attached to the Wanless and Whittam Report: P. Wanless and R. Whittam, *An Independent Review of Two Home Office Commissioned Independent Reviews Looking at Information Held in Connection with Child Abuse from 1979-1999* (London: NSPCC, 2015).

183 Ibid.

184 HC Debates 7 July 2014, vol 584 col 23.

185 www.IICSA.org.uk/

186 HC Debates, 7 July 2014 vol.584 col.25.

187 *The Telegraph,* 16 December 2016.

188 see www.IICSA.org.uk/investigations.

189 https://www.iicsa.org.uk/victims-and-survivors/truth-project

190 B. Campbell, "A Child Abuse Inquiry Requires a Truth-Seeker. Grabbing a Grandee Isn't Enough," *The Guardian*, 14 July 2014. Bea claimed, 'The government squandered a generation of professionals. And it denied justice—or if not justice, at least honour—to the survivors', B. Campbell, *Unofficial Secrets*; Interview, *The Guardian*, 12 September 2016.

191 *The Telegraph*, 14 July 2014.

192 *The Guardian*, 21 October 2014.

193 *The Guardian*, 31 October 2014.

194 Into responsibility for the deaths of 96 Liverpool football fans crushed at Hillsborough football stadium in 1989, *Hillsborough: The Report of the Hillsborough Independent Panel,* September 2012, HC 581.

195 Into decisions leading up to the Iraq conflict, *The Report of the Iraq Inquiry,* July 2016, HC 264.

196 R. Scott, "Procedures at Inquiries: the duty to be fair" *Law Quarterly Review* 1995, 596–616.

197 Statement from the Home Secretary, made on 12 March 2015 Statement UIN HCWS371, available at https://questions-statements.parliament.uk/written-statements/detail/2015-03-12/HCWS371.

198 *The Telegraph*, 9 July 2015.
199 *BBC News*, 4 February 2015.
200 *The Times,* 14 October 2016.
201 *The Guardian*, 5 February 2015.
202 *RTE News*, 9 July 2015.
203 *The Times*, 14 October 2016.
204 *BBC News*, 14 October 2016.
205 *The Tablet*, 10 August 2016.
206 *The Guardian,* 5 August 2016.
207 IICSA Transcript, www.IICSA.org.uk/key-documents/607/view/2016-07-26-general-matters-relating-to-investigations-transcript.pdf, 26 July 2016.
208 A. Jay, *Independent Inquiry into CSE in Rotherham 1997-2013*, Rotherham Borough Council, 21 August 2014.
209 Operation Linden is the IOPC's biggest investigation since its investigation into the Hillsborough disaster and is due to report in 2022.
210 *The Guardian*, 17 October 2016.
211 *The Independent*, 19 November 2016.
212 *The Times,* 14 June 2017.
213 HIAI or Hart inquiry, 13 January 2014 to 30 June 2017, www.nidirect.gov.uk/articles/historical-institutional-abuse; www.hiainquiry.org.
214 "Investigating the Abuse of Children in Care in Scotland," Scottish Child Abuse Inquiry, www.childabuseinquiry.scot/, opened 1 October 2015.
215 "Independent Jersey Cary Inquiry," Jersey Care Inquiry, www.jerseycareinquiry.org/, 10 December 2013 to 3 July 2017.
216 See Lynch G. Lynch, *UK Child Migration to Australia, 1945-1970. A Study in Policy Failure* (Palgrave MacMillan, 2021) at 5, footnote 11.
217 Department of Health and Social Care, Payment Scheme for former British Migrants, www.gov.uk/government/news/payment-scheme-for-former-british-child-migrants.
218 www.iicsa.org.uk/key-documents/26712/view/victims-survivors-engagement-with-inquiry-q2-2021.pdf
219 *The Times,* 1 November 2017.
220 Truth Project Team, *Truth Project Experiences Shared. Victims and Survivors Speak Out* (UK: IICSA, 2018), available at www.truthproject.org.uk/key-documents/5462/view/truth-project-experiences-shared-june-2018.pdf.
221 Defined as relating to vaginal, anal or digital penetration, cunnilingus, fellatio.
222 In the Irish CICA, 54.3 per cent of participants at the Confidential Committee were male. Volume 3, Ch 2 at 2.45. 64.3 per cent of participants in the Royal Commission private sessions were male. Volume 5 at 3.2.
223 83 per cent for the Irish CC. This figure is for those participants who were industrial school and reformatory survivors; see ICC Vol 3, Chapter 3. Information was provided on the 259 witnesses who reported abuse in 'Other institutions', but there appears to be some double counting so the age breakdown is not estimated here. The comparators are 61 per cent (Royal Commission) and 51 per cent (Truth Project Dashboard August 2021 at 2).
224 Based on information provided for people who attended industrial schools or reformatories.
225 Thematic Report: Child Sexual Abuse in the context of religious institutions.
226 www.iicsa.org.uk/news/inquiry-clarifies-operation-hydrant-referrals.

227 www.iicsa.org.uk/news/inquiry-clarifies-operation-hydrant-referrals.
228 *BBC News*, 9 November 2017.
229 See Centre for Women's Justice 'Credibility of Child Sexual Abuse Inquiry under Threat' (2020), www.centreforwomensjustice.org.uk/news/2020/9/24/credibility-of-child-sexual-abuse-inquiry-under-threat.
230 J. Aldridge, "'This is Not Just About History…' Addressing the Disconnect in Historic (Non-Recent Child Abuse Investigations" *Child Abuse Review* 27, 2018, 24–9.
231 Children's Commissioner, *Protecting Children from Harm: A Critical Assessment of Child Sexual Abuse in the Family Network in England and Priorities for Action* (2015), www.childrenscommissioner.gov.uk/wp-content/uploads/2017/06/Protecting-children-from-harm-full-report.pdf and see Chapter 2.
232 Such as abuse in custodial institutions. The IICSA Research Team, *Safe Inside? Child Sexual Abuse in the Youth Secure Estate* (UK: HMSO, 2019), www.iicsa.org.uk/key-documents/9536/view/safe-inside%3F-child-sexual-abuse-youth-secure-estate-full-report.pdf and has prompted reconsideration of how child abuse is measured nationally: See "Exploring the Feasibility of a Survey Measuring Child Abuse in the UK: January 2021," Office for National Statistics, 21 January 2021, www.ons.gov.uk/peoplepopulationandcommunity/crimeandjustice/articles/exploringthefeasibilityofasurveymeasuringchildabuseintheuk/january2021.
233 www.childabusecommission.ie.
234 www.royalcommission.gov.au.
235 www.iicsa.org.uk.
236 P. Kennedy, 'Undeniable: Politicians Must "Resist Religious Influence" when Child Abuse Royal Commission makes Recommendations' ABC News, 13 December 2017, https://www.abc.net.au/news/2017-12-13/child-abuse-royal-commission-church-forces-cant-dilute-response/9222662.
237 E. Pine, *Irish Examiner,* 19 May 2019.

References

Aldridge, J., "'This is Not Just About History…' Addressing the Disconnect in Historic (Non-Recent Child Abuse Investigations" *Child Abuse Review* 27, 2018, 24–9.

Barter, A. et al., "Why the Caged Bird Sings: Issues with the Royal Commission into Institutional Responses to Child Sexual Abuse" *Indigenous Law Bulletin* 8(13), 2014, 7–10.

Beck, L., "Institutional Responses to Child Sexual Abuse. The Constitutionality of a Royal Commission" *Alternative Law Journal* 38(1), 2013, 14–9.

Campbell, B., "A Child Abuse Inquiry Requires a Truth-Seeker. Grabbing a Grandee Isn't Enough," *The Guardian*, 14 July 2014.

Children's Commissioner, *Protecting Children from Harm: A Critical Assessment of Child Sexual Abuse in the Family Network in England and Priorities for Action* (2015), www.childrenscommissioner.gov.uk/wp-content/uploads/2017/06/Protecting-children-from-harm-full-report.pdf.

Commission of Investigation, *Report in the Catholic Archdiocese of Dublin* (Dublin: Stationery Office, 2009), www.justice.ie/en/JELR/Pages/PB09000504.

Commission to Inquire into Child Abuse (CICA), *Final Report* (Dublin: Government Publications, 2009).

Community Affairs References Committee, *Forgotten Australians: A Report on Australians who Experienced Institutional or Out-of-Home Care as Children*, (Canberra: Australian Parliament, 2004).

Comptroller and Auditor General's *Report on Cost of Child Abuse Inquiry and Redress* (Dublin: Stationery Office, 2016).

Cowlishaw, G., "Inquiring into Aboriginal Deaths in Custody. The Limits of a Royal Commission" *Journal of Indigenous Policy* 1991, 28–40.

Cripps, K. and McCreery, R., "Indigenous Engagement with the Royal Commission into Institutional Responses to Child Sexual Abuse" *Indigenous Law Bulletin* 8, 2013, 22–5.

Cummins, P. et al., *Report of the Protecting Victoria's Vulnerable Children Inquiry* (Melbourne: Department of Premier and Cabinet, 2012).

Cunneen, M., *Special Commission of Inquiry into Matters Relating to the Police Investigation of Certain Child Sexual Abuse Allegations in the Catholic Diocese of Maitland-Newcastle Report* (Sydney: NSW Department of Premier and Cabinet, 2014).

Daly, K. and Davis, J., "Unravelling Redress for Institutional Abuse of Children in Australia" *University of New South Wales Law Journal* 42(4), 2019, 1254–93.

Donaghue, S., *Royal Commissions and Permanent Commissions of Inquiry* (Sydney: Butterworths, 2001), 4–5.

Enright, M. and Ring, S., "State Legal Responses to Historical Institutional Abuse: Shame, Sovereignty and Epistemic Injustice" *Éire-Ireland* 55 (1&2), 2020, 68–99.

Family and Community Development Committee, *Betrayal of Trust: Inquiry into the Handling of Child Abuse by Religious and Other Non-government Organisations* (Melbourne: Parliament of Victoria. 2013).

Fassin, D. and Rechtman, R., *The Empire of Trauma* (Princeton: Princeton University Press, 2009).

Forde L., AC, *Report of the Commission of Inquiry into Abuse in Queensland Institutions* (Brisbane: Commission of Inquiry into Abuse in Queensland Institutions, 1999). www.qld.gov.au/__data/assets/pdf_file/0023/54509/forde-comminquiry.pdf.

Gallen, J., "Transitional Justice and Ireland's Legacy of Historical Abuse" *Éire-Ireland* 55 (1&2), 2020, 35–67.

Gillard, J., *My Story* (Sydney: Random House, 2014).

Gleeson, K. and Ring, S., "Confronting the Past and Changing the Future? Public Inquiries into Institutional Child Abuse Inquiries, Ireland and Australia" *Griffith Law Review* 29(1), 2021, 109–33.

Golding, F., "Sexual Abuse as the Core Transgression of Childhood Innocence: Unintended Consequences for Care Leavers" *Journal of Australian Studies* 42(2), 2018, 191–203.

Hall, B. and Lee, J., 'Child Abuse Inquiry Criticised', *Sydney Morning Herald*, 16 January 2013.

Henderson, G., "The Royal Commission, the Media and the Church" *Quadrant* 61(7/8), 2017, 46.

Hillsborough: The Report of the Hillsborough Independent Panel, September 2012, HC 581.

Holohan, C., *In Plain Sight: Responding to the Ferns, Ryan, Murphy and Cloyne Reports* (Dublin: Amnesty International Ireland, 2011).

IICSA Research Team, *Safe Inside? Child Sexual Abuse in the Youth Secure Estate* (UK: HMSO, 2019), www.iicsa.org.uk/key-documents/9536/view/safe-inside%3F-child-sexual-abuse-youth-secure-estate-full-report.pdf.

Inglis, T., *Moral Monopoly. The Decline and Fall of the Catholic Church in Modern Ireland* (Dublin: University College Dublin Press, 1998).

Jay, A., *Independent Inquiry into CSE in Rotherham 1997-2013*, Rotherham Borough Council, 21 August 2014.

Jones, T., "Royal Commission Recommends Sweeping Reforms for Catholic Church to End Child Abuse' *The Conversation*, 15 December 2017, https://theconversation.com/royal-commission-recommends-sweeping-reforms-for-catholic-church-to-end-child-abuse-89141.

Kennedy, P., 'Undeniable: Politicians Must "Resist Religious Influence" when Child Abuse Royal Commission makes Recommendations' *ABC News*, 13 December 2017, https://www.abc.net.au/news/2017-12-13/child-abuse-royal-commission-church-forces-cant-dilute-response/9222662

Lost in Care, Report of the Tribunal of Inquiry into the Abuse of Children in Care in the Former County Council Areas of Gwynedd and Clwyd in North Wales since 1974 (UK: HMSO, 2000), www.childrenshomes.org.uk/NorthWales/LostInCare.pdf.

Macur, J.W., *The Report of the Macur Review Macur Review of Child Abuse in Wales – Redacted Version. An Independent Review of the Tribunal of Inquiry into the Abuse of Children in Care in the Former County Council Areas of Gwynedd and Clwyd in North Wales since 1974, 2016* (UK: HMSO, 2016) www.gov.uk/government/publications/the-report-of-the-macur-review.

Madden, A., *Altar Boy* (Dublin: Penguin Ireland, 2004), 209–12.

McAlinden, A.-M. and Naylor, B., "Reframing Public Inquiries as Procedural Justice for Victims of Institutional Child Abuse: Towards a Hybrid Model of Justice" *Sydney Law Review* 38(3), 2016, 277–308.

McPhillips, K., "Traumatic Isolation: Institutional Stigma and the Australian Royal Commission into Institutional Responses to Child Sexual Abuse" *Health and History* 20(2), 2018, 75–90.

O'Sullivan, E., "*Residential Child Welfare in Ireland,1965-2008: An Outline of Policy, Legislation and Practice: A Paper Prepared for the Commission to Inquire into Child Abuse*," Commission to Inquire into Child Abuse, *Final Report* Vol IV, Ch 4 (Dublin: Commission to Inquire into Child Abuse, 2009).

Pembroke, S., "Historical Institutional Abuse in Ireland: Survivor Perspectives on Taking Part in the Commission to Inquire into Child Abuse (CICA) and the Redress Scheme" *Contemporary Justice Review* 22(1), 2019, 43–59.

Perkins, M., '"I Cannot Comprehend'. Sex Abuse Royal Commissioner Slams Religious Leaders," *Sydney Morning Herald*, 10 December 2019.

Pine, E., *The Politics of Irish Memory* (London: Palgrave Macmillan, 2011), 24.

Prasser, S., "Royal Commissions in Australia: When Should Governments Appoint Them?" *Australian Journal of Public Administration* 65(3), 2006, 28–47.

Raftery, M., "Secretive State Might Mislead You to Think Abuse Is Thing of the Past" *The Irish Times*, 1 June 2009.

Reclaiming Self, *Ryan Report Follow-Up. Submission to the United Nations Committee Against Torture* Session 61 (Dublin: Reclaiming Self, 2017), https://tbinternet.ohchr.org/_layouts/15/treatybodyexternal/SessionDetails1.aspx?SessionID=1132&Lang=en.

Ring, S., "The Victim of Historical Child Sexual Abuse in the Irish Courts 1999-2006" *Social and Legal Studies* 2017, 562–80.

Royal Commission into Institutional Responses to Child Sexual Abuse, *Final Report* (Canberra: Commonwealth of Australia, 2017).

Scott, R., "Procedures at Inquiries: The Duty to be Fair" *Law Quarterly Review* 1995, 596–616.

Smart, C., "A History of Ambivalence and Conflict in the Discursive Construction of the 'Child Victim' of Sexual Abuse" *Social and Legal Studies* 8(3), 1999, 391–409.

Swain, S. et al.., "Conceptualising and Categorising Child Abuse Inquiries: From Damage Control to Foregrounding Survivor Testimony" *Journal of Historical Sociology* 31(3), 2017, 282–96.

Sweeney, P., *The Celtic Tiger Ireland's Economic Miracle Explained* (Dublin: Oak Tree Press, 1998).

Wanless, P. and Whittam, R., *An Independent Review of Two Home Office Commissioned Independent Reviews Looking at Information Held in Connection with Child Abuse from 1979-1999* (London: NSPCC, 2015).

Winter, S., "Towards a Unified Theory of Transitional Justice" *International Journal of Transitional Justice* 7(2), 2013, 224–44.

Wright, K., "Challenging Institutional Denial: Psychological Discourse, Therapeutic Culture and Public Inquiries" *Journal of Australian Studies* 42(2), 2017, 177–90.

Wright, K. et al., "The Australian Royal Commission into Institutional Responses to Child Sexual Abuse" *Child Abuse and Neglect* 74(1), 2017, 1–9.

11 State reparations

Introduction

This chapter continues the analysis of state responses to non-recent child sexual abuse (NRCSA) begun in Chapter 10, exploring the various forms of reparations offered in Ireland, Australia, and England and Wales to NRCSA survivors. Reparations are a core feature of transitional justice[1] aimed at repairing harms and relationships caused by wrongs. Reparations may include: symbolic measures; financial compensation practical and therapeutic supports and access to personal information for survivors; and legislation to ensure the non-repetition of abuse. Engaging in reparations is a deeply sensitive political exercise for a state. A haste to acknowledge responsibility and 'move on' might make survivors feel reparations are being used to buy their silence and end their quest for truth and justice'.[2] On the other hand, waiting too long to deliver reparations may exacerbate survivors' sense of abandonment by the state and provoke accusations that the state is waiting for aged survivors to die.

In this chapter we examine how each country has sought to deliver on its promises of reparations for institutional child abuse and how they have been received by survivors.

The first section describes the various forms of reparations in more detail and the remaining sections explore each country's engagement with reparations.

Forms of reparation

State apologies

State apologies have become a routine part of addressing past institutional abuses. There is a vast literature on what constitutes a legitimate apology,[3] on the politics of apologies[4] and the relationship between a state apology and a nation's sense of itself.[5] Sköld and Swain have begun the conversation about apologies for historical institutional child abuse which this chapter seeks to develop.[6] State apologies have repeatedly been requested by survivors of

DOI: 10.4324/9780429468162-13

institutional child abuse.[7] Through acknowledgement of wrongdoing and the vindication they can offer survivors, apologies may contribute to individual and societal healing.[8]

To be accepted as legitimate, state apologies need to include specific acknowledgement of responsibility for wrongdoing and an unequivocal expression of regret. They must have consequences,[9] including 'direct and immediate actions (such as payments of compensation) that manifest responsibility for the violation'.[10] State apologies are bound up with other acts of reparation.[11] In Ireland the value of the state apology to survivors of institutional abuse has been seriously undermined by the adversarial and secretive approach to financial redress.

Memorialization

State apologies and public inquiries are often accompanied by promises of memorialization, which aims to honour the past and serves as a reminder of the continuing potential for abuse in the present. While memorials have historically tended to take the form of statues, trees or plaques, recently, scholars, advocates and survivors have called for more active forms of memorialization, including Sorry Books, educational initiatives for younger generations and research projects such as oral history archives or the creation of an international 'site of conscience'. Others have called for active destruction of institutions or the removal of perpetrators' gravestones from local landscapes.[12] If delayed, memorials may create a sense of abandonment or lack of recognition amongst survivors. For some survivors, however, any form of memorial is inappropriate while other forms of state responses remain unfinished or unsatisfactory. Commemorative practices in each country are as yet inadequate and are typically characterized by a lack of engagement with survivors.

Financial redress schemes

Redress schemes provide compensation for personal injuries caused by institutional abuse and are an alternative to civil litigation. Schemes may be publicly funded or paid for wholly or in part by the state and/or by organizations responsible for the abuse (or their insurers).[13] Redress schemes are different from settlement schemes to compensate groups of claimants taking civil litigation such as the scheme used in the litigation arising from Jimmy Savile's actions.[14] For survivors, the importance of financial redress goes far beyond the material and is linked to 'a sense of validation'.[15] Financial redress schemes formed part of the package of state responses to NRCSA in Ireland and in Australia. In England and Wales, a redress scheme was created for child migrants following a recommendation by the Independent Inquiry into Child Sexual Abuse (IICSA) (see Chapter 10). It remains to be seen if the IICSA will recommend a redress scheme for other survivors of institutional abuse. The Irish and Australian schemes are *ex gratia*, meaning that the state is not admitting a survivor's right to compensation and it is not admitting any legal liability. The payment is entirely discretionary and it does not commit the state to an ongoing practice of treating like cases alike.[16] As a form of acknowledgement, it is not as powerful as civil litigation which involves a finding of liability (see Chapters 8 and 9). States may institute redress schemes as a way of containing their exposure to civil claims and evading the question of legal liability.[17] Redress schemes in contexts other than institutional abuse are designed to be non-adversarial forums in which applications for financial compensation are considered, usually on the basis of written applications, but the Irish and Australian redress schemes have been described by survivors as unnecessarily adversarial and have involved hearings.

There has been very limited use of redress schemes in England and Wales, although the IICSA is considering recommending a large-scale redress scheme.[18] Here we include the state-funded scheme to compensate victims of crime because it is one of the main avenues for redress for survivors of institutional child abuse in England and Wales.

Practical and therapeutic supports for survivors and their families

Therapeutic counselling and practical supports such as access to education and accommodation or assistance with healthcare needs are necessary to address the heightened vulnerability to economic and social marginalization experienced by many adult survivors of CSA.[19] Survivors may have particular needs regarding their ageing processes, for example, a fear of living in nursing homes due to a history of institutionalization. Ideally, support should be tailored to each person's needs. Schemes to provide practical supports in Ireland and Australia have been controversial and in England and Wales they are very underdeveloped.

The importance of personal information for the individual and for society

Often institutions held personal information in the form of records about a survivor who was abused in care. The importance of accessing personal records cannot be overstated.[20] Access to institutional records can form an important component of recognition of state responsibility for abuse and is a tangible way for survivors to learn about their past and experience a personal and meaningful form of reparations. Records may help a survivor understand their family history. These records are important to survivors' sense of identity and belonging and provide key information about medical histories. If abuse was recorded, institutional records can reveal important information about what, if any, actions were taken by responsible adults. Records can also be an important source of evidence for criminal trials and civil litigation, for redress schemes and for accessing support services. Under data protection laws survivors have the right to access their personal files held by the state and bodies such as religious orders or charities,[21] but many are unaware of their rights or how to search for their information, and they can face resistance from institutions. States can improve reparations to survivors by making records more readily available to them. Providing access to researchers, practitioners and the public to (appropriately anonymized) records can further the goal of non-repetition facilitating the writing of accurate histories and learning the lessons of the past. Australia has introduced the most progressive initiatives in relation to records. In recent years, governments in Ireland and England and Wales have finally started to admit the value of these arguments, but they have a long way to go.

Ireland

In its response to institutional child abuse the Irish state developed a framework of apology, report and redress that has now become standard in responding to other forms of institutional abuse that formed part of Ireland's network of coercive confinement.[22]

A state apology

Taoiseach Bertie Ahern's apology to the survivors of institutional child abuse was one of the first issued on behalf of any state for child abuse. A state response to institutional child abuse survivors had been discussed by a Working Group of senior civil servants and politicians since 1998 but an apology had not been part of these discussions. The apology was issued prior to the airing of the third episode of States of Fear which highlighted years of state inaction on child abuse in institutions and the previous government's suppression of details of an official report into child abuse in a residential home. It marked the beginning of an international trend toward public contrition by politicians for institutional abuse.[23] On 11 May 1999 Ahern made the following statement at a specially convened press conference:

> On behalf of the state and all its citizens, the government wishes to make a sincere and long overdue apology to the victims of childhood abuse for our collective failure to intervene, to detect their pain, to come to their rescue [...] Too many of our children were denied [..] love, care and security. Abuse ruined their childhoods and has been an ever-present part of their adult lives reminding them of a time when they were helpless. I want to say to them that we believe they were gravely wronged, and that we must do all we can now to overcome the lasting effects of their ordeals. [...] A light has been shone into the dark corners of both our past and present, and these victim-survivors have performed an immense service in challenging our collective complacency. They have shown us that we cannot put the past behind us by ignoring it. We must confront it and learn its lessons. That is the least we can do to address the injustices of the past and the dangers of the present.[24]

The apology was welcomed by many survivors of institutional abuse as key to their healing and restoration as full citizens. Prominent campaigner and survivor Christine Buckley (see Chapter 4) stated that Ahern's apology 'lifted the veil of secrecy, stigma and injustice which had dogged our lives and impeded our futures'.[25]

The apology can also be read as performing a 'double displacement of the past'.[26] It situated institutional child abuse in a distant past, far removed from Ireland in 1999. By connecting the state's and its citizen's failures 'to come to children's rescue', both leaders diluted the state's culpability. Culpability should attach to the state (the courts and health services) for sending children to industrial schools, engaging in inappropriate deference to the Catholic Church in relation to reports of abuse, ignoring official reports recommending improvements to industrial schools[27] and for completely ignoring its legal duties of inspection and regulation. The rhetoric of the apology failed to acknowledge the state's legal and moral responsibility for violation of children's rights to life, dignity, privacy, care and education in industrial schools.

In his apology Ahern promised a commission of inquiry (see Chapter 10), changes to the statute of limitations to allow for victims to sue for childhood abuse (see Chapter 8), a fund for counselling, a sex offender register and mandatory reporting of CSA (see Chapter 4). Redress was not mentioned.

Financial redress: the 2002 indemnity and the residential institutions redress board

Despite the tone of Ahern's apology, the state was slow to create redress mechanisms. The Law Commission of Canada's 2000 report *Restoring Dignity: Responding to Child Abuse in Canadian Institutions*[28] was an important influence on the government's approach to redress. Officials from the Department of Education and the Attorney General's office travelled to Canada to learn about negotiated settlements and redress schemes for institutional child abuse at federal and provincial levels.[29] Solicitors representing survivors told the department they could not co-operate with any commission of investigation unless an offer of compensation was on the table. The government decided not to make redress part of the work of the CICA because it could 'lead to an excessively adversarial environment'.[30]

Plans for a redress scheme were delayed by negotiations between the representatives of religious orders and the State around the costs of redress. Although a compensation scheme was approved by government in February 2001, further negotiations continued around the religious orders' contribution. Much of the negotiations were conducted by the Minister for Education Dr Michael Woods and his secretary general for the state, and the chief negotiators on behalf of the 18 religious orders[31] (Sr Helena O'Donoghue[32] and Sr Elizabeth Maxwell[33]) without the Attorney General.[34] A compensation advisory committee chaired by lawyer Seán Ryan, future chair of the Commission to Inquire into Child Abuse, presented its assessment to Government in January 2002.[35] On 5 June 2002 an indemnity agreement between the state and the leaders of the religious orders was brought to the final cabinet meeting of the Fianna Fáil/Progressive Democrats government by the Minister for Education. Despite warnings from the Attorney General, the deal was agreed.[36] It was not subjected to public scrutiny in the Oireachtas and was never published. Under the agreement the orders promised to make a capped contribution of €128 million in cash and property transfers[37] to the costs of redress, including funding for educational programmes for survivors and counselling support services for survivors and their families. This turned out to be a significant underestimate of the final cost of €1.5 billion. In return for this contribution, the state indemnified each of the 18 congregations against liability in civil litigation. The agreement was criticized by the then Attorney General (and later Minister for Justice) Michael McDowell Senior Counsel for 'throw[ing] away' the State's right to claim as of legal right any contribution from the religious orders.[38]

As a meaningful acknowledgement of wrongdoing, the agreement was flawed. Survivors have criticized its failure to apportion responsibility for abuse to the congregations.[39] During the negotiations a senior official noted that the congregations saw 'the making of a financial contribution to help people who are in pain as consistent with their pastoral mission, as opposed to any making of amends for abuse which has not been proven'.[40]

A Redress Board was eventually established in 2002, two years after the issue of financial redress was first raised by a group of solicitors acting for a large number of survivors.[41] It was established by the Residential Institutions Redress Act 2002.[42] By this time, some 2,500 related High Court cases were underway or threatened.[43] The scheme was described as providing 'an alternative method of…redress' to those who were abused as children in the residential institution listed in the 2002 Act.[44] A review committee was also established, chaired by a retired Supreme Court judge.[45]

The Board was chaired by High Court judge Seán O'Leary. Applicants could seek redress for sexual abuse, physical and emotional abuse and neglect.[46] The amount was determined by reference to five redress bands which differentiated payments according to severity of abuse and injury/effects of the abuse. These bands ranged from maxima of €50,000 for band I, to €200,00–€300,000 for band V.

The redress scheme was fully operational for only three years,[47] in violation of the state's ongoing obligation to provide redress under international human rights law.[48] It made 16,650 financial awards. When the scheme's details were originally announced, it was declared that payments would be broadly equivalent to those awarded in the courts for similar cases.[49] However, the average award was €62,250,[50] roughly half that awarded in successful civil cases against religious orders (and in which, under the indemnity agreement, the state was liable)[51] and far below the €350,000 awarded to Ron McCartan in 2017 in settlement of his case against the Christian Brothers for injuries arising from repeated rapes and physical assaults during his time at Artane Industrial School,[52] or the €370, 000 awarded by the High Court to Raymond Noctor for sexual abuse at St Joseph's industrial school, Kilkenny run by the Irish Sisters of Charity.[53]

According to the legislation establishing the Redress Board, a person named as an abuser was formally notified of the existence of the complaint and could request a copy of the completed application form. If a person named as an abuser wished they could also take part in the proceedings before the Board, submit a statement denying the allegations and seek an oral hearing. The Board could also allow the person to cross-examine the applicant and anyone giving evidence on the applicant's behalf. According to the founding legislation, the purpose of such cross-examination was 'to allow the alleged abuser to contest allegations or to protect and vindicate their personal and other rights'.[54] The alleged abuser could also be cross-examined by the applicant's counsel.[55]

The environment of panel hearings distressed many of those who came before them.[56] They have described the Board as re-traumatizing[57] and as discouraging future help-seeking.[58] Some felt so strongly about their treatment that they never spent their awards.[59] Partners or friends were not allowed to be present. One psychiatrist who gave evidence in respect of three patients described it as 'contraven[ing] the most basic of human and civil rights'.[60] In contravention of normal legal procedure, survivors taking part in panel hearings were subjected to cross-examination by legal advisors to the Redress Board on the information provided by the religious orders but without any oral evidence having been given by the orders.[61] Despite the no-fault basis of the Scheme, the Christian Brothers were still permitted to issue letters denying that any abuse took place in their institutions,[62] adding to survivors' distress. Even when awards were made, apologies did not form part of the redress package. This contrasts with the apologies that may attach to settlements of civil litigation (see Chapter 8). The Christian Brothers continued to issue denials right up until five days before the CICA report was published.

The legal framework for redress was characterized by secrecy and control. Survivors were not automatically given a copy of the transcript of their evidence to the Board, and many who requested one did not receive it or important information was missing.[63] Successful applicants were required to accept their *ex gratia* 'award' on the basis that there was no admission of liability and were required to sign a formal waiver relinquishing certain rights of action against the Department of Education and Science and public bodies, and the religious orders who had signed the Indemnity Agreement and who made a contribution to awards under the Act. Survivors accepting an award were also required to sign a confidentiality agreement promising not to talk about their experience of the Scheme or how much compensation they were awarded.[64] While this may be standard practice in settlements of legal actions, it was not appropriate to the redress context. Survivors were also sent a letter quoting legislation criminalizing the publication of information relating to a redress application/award that could lead to identification of a person or institution.[65] The maximum punishment for breach is a fine of €25,000 and two years' imprisonment.[66] While no prosecutions have been brought to date, this section has been interpreted by survivors as preventing them from speaking or writing publicly about their own experience of abuse.[67] The alienation and distress felt by many survivors in their engagement with the Redress Board and the continued fear of the consequences of speaking publicly about their experiences has left many feeling that the harms they suffered have not been recognized.[68] On a broader societal level, the creation of collective knowledge about the nation's history of institutional abuse was impeded by the statutory prohibition on publication of the information provided by the religious orders to the Board.[69]

Despite Ahern's promise to learn the lessons of the past, the state continues to extend extraordinarily deferential treatment to the religious orders who were party to the Indemnity Agreement. Following the publication of the 2009 CICA Report, the state asked the orders to increase their contributions to redress (financial and counselling/education). They offered a further €226 million in cash, property and other resources. The total offers made by the congregations amount to €436.95 million, of which €239.93 million has been realized to date.[70] The costs of the commission, redress and survivor supports are approximately €1.5 billion.[71] The orders' contributions come to approximately 16 per cent of the total cost, far short of the 50–50 split originally envisaged by the Department of Finance during the 2002 indemnity agreement negotiations.[72] Despite the huge shortfall, and statements from senior politicians criticizing the deal,[73] the state continues to protect the religious orders from legal liability and refuses to consider compulsory acquisition of their assets. Instead, there have only been appeals to the orders' 'moral responsibility'.[74]

Redress for survivors of abuse in day schools

Survivors of victims of abuse in day schools were excluded from the Redress Board's process. The reason given was that children in such schools were resident with their families, unlike children in industrial schools who were resident in the institution.[75] The fallacy of this distinction was laid bare by the European Court of Human Rights in 2014 when it ruled that Ireland had violated Articles 3 and 13 of the European Convention on Human Rights by failing to establish an effective system to protect children in day schools from abuse and by failing to provide compensation to the applicant, Louise O'Keeffe (see Chapter 9).[76] As part of the state measures to implement *O'Keeffe* an *ex gratia* scheme was established to provide out of court settlements payments of up to €84,000 to survivors of abuse in primary schools. To be eligible applicants had to satisfy three highly restrictive and discriminatory conditions by showing: (1) they had previously commenced and then discontinued litigation against the state for the abuse, (2) the abuse had occurred in the aftermath of a 'prior complaint' against the abuser and (3) their claim was precluded by the Statute of Limitations. By July 2019 every single application to the scheme had been rejected for failure to satisfy the 'prior complaint' criterion.[77] The Independent Assessor tasked with examining the scheme found that the requirement to demonstrate prior complaint was 'an inherent inversion of logic and a fundamental unfairness to applicants' and was 'inconsistent with the core reasoning of the judgment of the ECtHR'.[78] Following this, both the Taoiseach and the Minister for Education publicly committed to dispensing with the prior complaint criterion and re-opening the scheme. As of November 2021, the government had reopened the scheme, but only for people who had begun legal proceedings against the State prior to July 2020 and that those who did initiate proceedings are not allowed to claim their legal expenses as part of redress.

Survivors' access to their records and memorialization

The theme of censorship begun with the criminalisation of people who spoke of their experiences of the Redress Board, was continued in draft legislation in 2015 and again in 2019 that proposed to seal the archives of the CICA and the Redress Board and Review Committee for 75 years. Under the Retention of Records Bill 2019, no one would be allowed access to these bodies' records, including people who gave evidence, their family members and researchers. These records are diverse, including personal testimony from people who engaged with one of these bodies, as well as public documents from government departments which would normally be archived according to the practices of the National Archives. The legal position regarding all files that refer to individual survivors is unambiguous: records containing personal information of survivors are the data of survivors and they are entitled to them under European Union law and domestic data protection law.[79] Survivors' personal data (which they own) includes transcripts of their own testimony provided to the CICA or the Redress Board, accounts of their own redress application or personal files which may include records created by schools or religious bodies, records created by the state and witness statements or other documents produced by people involved in the running of the schools, which mention or concern individual survivors.[80]

Minister for Education Joe Mc Hugh stated that the Bill was needed to strike a balance between the original confidentiality provisions around the work of the three bodies and the need to preserve the records for future generations.[81] An array of survivors, and practitioner allies working on archives, history and data protection law and psychology, as well as scholars working on historical abuse[82] published arguments collectively[83] and individually explaining that the Bill breached survivors' rights to access their personal data,[84] contravened established practice in relation to public records relating to the Department of Education, and contravened existing legislation that would allow the records to be accessed in the future by the gardaí and the courts. In November 2019 the Joint Oireachtas Committee on Education and Skills convened a special session where survivors, along with lawyers and archivists, called for survivors to have unrestricted access to their own complete files, including their birth certificates, records of institutionalization, as well as their transcripts of their testimony to the CICA or the Redress Board, and copies of submissions made by religious orders in response to their application to the Redress Board.[85] They also called for the repeal of criminalization of survivors who choose to speak publicly about their experiences of the Redress Board.

In her evidence to the parliamentary committee, survivor and academic Dr Mary Lodato highlighted the importance of Redress Board records, and 'the need for the state to prioritize the openness and transparency needed to facilitate reconciliation and healing while survivors are still alive'. She stated:

> These files belong to survivors, and no time barriers should be imposed on their access. …The state has already robbed survivors of so much already and profited off that suffering. Can you really not give survivors their history? Let them see and share *their* past.[86]

Survivors also pointed to the importance of the records of the industrial school system being made available to researchers. The activism by survivors and academics proved successful, ensuring the Bill was delayed. Since then the government has agreed to 'delay and re-examine' the Bill.[87] The episode made clear that the state is continuing to seek to control victim-survivors' access to their own testimony and is preventing academic and community exploration of Ireland's histories of institutional abuse, information that, among other things, could usefully inform child-care policy and practice in the present.[88]

One of the outcomes of the campaigning against the Retention of Records Bill 2019 was the state was forced to reckon with arguments around survivors' rights to access their own testimony and any information on them held by the state. A broader conversation has also opened up in relation to access to the records of religious orders that ran industrial schools and reformatories, the records of other institutions that formed part of Ireland's architecture of containment in the twentieth century and the records of Catholic dioceses.[89] The questions around access to personal information and the need for scholars to access institutional files in order to better understand the social histories of Ireland are growing as survivors of other coercive institutions such as Magdalene Laundries and Mother and Baby Homes seek records about themselves and their families from the state and religious orders and from dioceses.[90]

In January 2020 a coalition of 72 abuse survivors and individuals affected by adoption, along with academic and practicing archivists, historians, psychologists, sociologists and lawyers, issued a public statement calling for the establishment of an archive to hold and make available historical institutional and care-related records.[91] This archive would facilitate survivors to access their own personal files and allow for them and others to deposit testimony and other information for public access now or in the future. It would also provide for public access to the (anonymized) administrative records of the systems of institutionalization and adoption in twentieth century Ireland, whether currently held by private or state bodies. In 2021 the government committed to creating the Independent National Archive of Care-Related Records, but it has yet to commit resources to it.[92]

Supports for survivors

Following the 1999 apology, the National Counselling Service (NCS) created a dedicated service for survivors of childhood abuse. Since 2000, more than 40,000 people have been referred to it for counselling in relation to experiences of childhood abuse.[93] This was in addition to existing services provided by the Catholic Church.[94] The State also created the Origins family tracing service run by Barnado[95] and the Education Finance Board, established in 2006[96] to provide financial assistance for training and education to former residents of institutions and their relatives from a contribution of €12 million made by religious congregations under the Indemnity Agreement. The Residential Institutions Statutory Fund Act 2012 created the state agency Caranua (which translates to New Friend) to manage a fund of €111.38 million for survivors of institutional child abuse. This money came from religious congregations that signed the 2002 Indemnity Agreement.[97] Caranua was tasked with making arrangements for the provision of services to support survivors and paying grants to survivors to avail of approved services, ranging from medical, dental services, hospital treatment, to education and housing support (i.e. adaptation of the home to suit a person's needs).[98] Caranua was also to promote understanding among service providers of the effects of abuse on survivors.[99] It began accepting applications from 6 January 2014.[100] Eligibility was conditional on an award of damages from the courts, or through settlement with religious congregations or redress from the Redress Board.

Many who engaged with Caranua have described it as abusive and disempowering.[101] Survivors' primary interaction with it was through a website, which posed a barrier to engagement for illiterate people and elderly survivors unfamiliar with computers. They were threatened with 'audits' and criminal proceedings if found to be fraudulently making claims.[102] This was a disproportionate response to the tiny number of suspected fraud cases (19 out of 5,000) and at odds with the organization's reparative goal.[103] Survivors reported delays in processing applications and lack of action following successful appeals. An upper limit of €15,000 for each claim was imposed, despite evidence that some survivors have ongoing medical and related housing needs that will inevitably exceed that amount.[104] In 2018 Tom Cronin, a survivor of St Joseph's industrial school, Cork, resigned from Caranua's board citing 'mistreatment of survivors'. The state refused requests to carry out a review of the operation of the scheme, incorrectly claiming that Caranua was independent of the state.[105] The Caranua scheme closed in 2020.

Memorialization

Demonstrating the important links between acknowledgement, memorialization and apology, the CCA Final Report recommended that lines from the Ahern apology be inscribed on the memorial 'as a permanent public acknowledgement' of the experiences of victims and survivors.[106] A budget of up to €500,000 was reserved for the project,[107] and a committee was established to obtain the views of survivor groups in relation to the location and nature of the memorial. However, due to disagreements regarding the type and location of the planned memorial, no memorial has been erected.[108]

In recent years, following the repeated revelations of historical abuse involving women and children in the Magdalene Laundries and Mother and Baby Homes, survivors and other activists have been exploring ways to memorialize historical abuse.[109] The Open Heart City was established to explore opportunities for a Site of Conscience for institutional abuse at the site of the last Laundry to close in Ireland.[110] The volunteer-led project is consulting on memorialization with survivors of Magdalene institutions, Mother and Baby Homes and people affected by forced and secret adoption and related abuses, as well as survivors of residential schools. A key proposal is that the site will house the proposed Independent National Archive of Care-Related Records.

Australia

The notion of 'apology' in Australia may forever be tainted by the painful stalemate over the national *Apology to the Australia's Indigenous Peoples* that ensued in response to the *Bringing Them Home Report* commissioned by the Keating Labor Government in 1994. *Bringing Them Home* recommended restitution and rehabilitation for adults who had been removed from their families as children, financial compensation and the acknowledgement of the responsibility of predecessors including 'formal apologies' from governments, churches and other organizations involved in the practice of child removal.[111] On the change to a conservative administration under Prime Minister John Howard in 1996, the trajectory of Indigenous Affairs altered markedly. On the first anniversary of the release of *Bringing Them Home*, rather than apologize, the government introduced National Sorry Day as a day of observance including the use of Sorry Books for 'ordinary citizens' to sign (at least a million people are thought to have signed in 1998). By 2001 all states and territories and many churches and other organizations had offered an apology, but the Howard government refused out of fear of liability[112] and because,

> such an apology could imply that the present generations are in some way responsible and accountable for the actions of earlier generations, actions

> that were sanctioned by the laws of the time, and that were believed to be in the best interests of the children concerned'.[113]

Throughout this divisive political period, the government vigorously defended a Stolen Generations lawsuit and passed laws to undermine Native Title.[114]

At the federal level the meaning and promise of an apology was highly politicized along partisan lines. After years of lobbying and discontent among the community, in 1999 Howard finally delivered a parliamentary 'Motion of Regret', expressing 'deep and sincere regret that Indigenous Australians suffered injustices under the practices of past generations and for the hurt and trauma that many Indigenous people continue to feel as a consequence of those practices', along with a commitment to 'practical reconciliation' rather than financial redress.[115] Then Opposition Leader and leader of the Australian Labor Party, Kim Beazley, immediately tabled a motion to replace Howard's with an 'unreserved apology' including support for 'restitution'.[116] Beazley's motion was unsuccessful but a national Apology remained the policy of the Labor Party and was finally delivered by Labor Prime Minister Kevin Rudd on 13 February 2008 (without the accompanying restitution).

Rudd's greatly-anticipated *Apology to Australia's Indigenous Peoples* was a watershed moment in Australian history. Rudd did not speak of child abuse, but of the 'mistreatment' of Aboriginal and Torres Strait Islander peoples at the hands of 'the laws and policies of successive Parliaments and governments that have inflicted profound grief, suffering and loss on these our fellow Australians'.[117] Rudd would then go on to offer the first *National Apology to the Forgotten Australians and Former Child Migrants* in 2009 when he delivered on one of the mutual recommendations of the *Lost Innocents* inquiry into child migration and the *Forgotten Australians* inquiry into abuse in out-of-home-care.

Rudd apologized for the 'ugly chapter in Australia's history' concerning the 500,000 children placed in care who 'did not receive proper care',[118] and he named the forms of abuse children endured, stating:

> We look back with shame that so many of you were left cold, hungry and alone and with nowhere to hide and nobody – absolutely nobody – to whom to turn. We look back with care that so many of these little ones who were entrusted to institutions and foster homes instead were abused physically, humiliated cruelly, violated sexually.[119]

The *Apology to Australia's Indigenous Peoples* acknowledged the responsibility of past governments for laws and practices governing child removal and the future-oriented transitional justice goal of 'healing' the entire country so that 'a new page in the history of our great continent can now be written'.[120] The *National Apology to the Forgotten Australians and former Child Migrants* was more comprehensive in terms of descriptions of children's pain and suffering, but it was less concerned with questions of legality and state responsibility. The focus was on the shame of 'the nation' (meaning, the people), rather than the practices of parliaments and governments. When the two Australian apologies are compared, it is apparent that the foundational basis of the experiences of the Stolen Generations, colonization, which inflicted harmful laws and governance on entire populations, was represented as the core injustice for First Nations children. In the case of the Forgotten Australians (a population that included a proportion of Indigenous children), injustice was instead represented as a form of non-intervention or, at most, a *failure of guardianship*. Only in the case of former child migrants was it tacitly acknowledged that international legal regimes (which had sent children from the UK and Malta to Australia without their informed consent) may have been unjust and directly implicated in their abuse.[121]

Building on these apologies, and those of the states and territories, on 22 October 2018 Liberal Prime Minister Scott Morrison became the first conservative leader to offer a national apology for past wrongs when he delivered the *Apology to the Australian Survivors and Victims of Institutionalised Child Sexual Abuse* on the recommendation of the Royal Commission into Institutional Responses to Child Sexual Abuse.[122] Morrison opened the Apology by addressing survivors directly, acknowledging 'your journey to where you are today has been a long and painful one'.[123] He spoke of acknowledging a 'trauma' and an 'abomination' that was 'hiding in plain sight for too long'.[124] He posed questions about why children were not believed and why it had taken so long to act, but then dictated, 'we can't be so vain to pretend to answers'.[125] Morrison's was a daring rhetorical evasion of responsibility, given that the Royal Commission had just spent five years ascertaining and documenting answers to these exact questions and more. Much like Rudd in the *Forgotten Australians* apology, Morrison spoke of the nation, rather than the government, failing children and he highlighted examples of mothers not believing children before finally acknowledging that priests abused children and that churches concealed crimes. The only mention of governments concerned praise for establishing the Royal Commission and associated initiatives. Still, Morrison would appear to have finally transcended the conservative argument that present generations of Australians cannot apologize for acts of the past. Representatives of institutions were not welcome to attend the apology. Parliament was instead filled with survivors, their families and supporters.

The Royal Commission recommended that any financial redress provided for institutional CSA must include the provision of 'direct personal responses', including apologies from institutional representatives to those survivors who seek a response, as well as financial payments. The legislation enacting these recommendations diluted them substantially. Under the *National Redress Scheme for Institutional Child Sexual Abuse (Consequential Amendments) Act 2018*, an institution is required only to take 'reasonable steps' to provide a personal response to a survivor and a 'motion of regret' may be issued instead of an apology.[126]

Memorialization

The use of Sorry Books was an inventive way to involve the community in reconciliation with First Nations Australians who had been removed from their families and suffered abuse as children, while distracting from the fundamental question of state responsibility for their mistreatment. Other community events followed, such as the Reconciliation Walk of 2000 which saw more than 250,000 people walk over Sydney Harbour Bridge in support of Reconciliation. More formal forms of memorialization of historical child abuse have also been promoted by governments such as in Prime Minister Morrison's pledge to establish a national museum and research centre as 'a place of truth and commemoration, to raise awareness and understanding of the impacts of child sexual abuse'[127] and 'ensure the nation does not forget the untold horrors they experienced'.[128] The promise of a museum was based on the recommendations of the Royal Commission and followed years of negotiations between care leavers and the government. The Gallery of First Australians at the National Museum of Australia hosts the permanent exhibition *Losing Our Children,* exploring the experiences of the Stolen Generations. For two decades representatives of Care Leavers Australasia Network (CLAN) have lobbied the National Museum to create a similar exhibition about all children in care.[129] This request also formed part of CLAN's submission to the *Forgotten Australian's* inquiry, which recommended that the museum be 'urged to consider establishing an exhibition, preferably permanent, related to the history and experiences of children in institutional care, and that such an exhibition have the capacity to tour as a travelling exhibition'.[130] The recommendation was finally met with a temporary exhibition. *Inside: Life in Children's Homes and Institutions* represented the experiences of both groups of care leavers and the Stolen Generations at the National Museum from November 2011 to February 2012. Despite being developed as a touring exhibition, uptake was limited in the states with only Melbourne and Queensland museums agreeing to host it.[131] In contrast, *On Their Own: Britain's Child Migrants*, an exhibition created by the Australian National Maritime Museum, was hosted by six other museums.[132]

Curators of *Inside* speculate about the ability of the elite Australian historical and museum community to integrate the Forgotten Australians into the 'consensus history' that dominates the public record and remains beholden to the Australian myth of a classless society.[133] Acknowledging the Stolen Generations is now a routine practice in elite and educational institutions, and the international experiences of up to 7,000 child migrants are memorialized in numerous films and other cultural accounts of relationships to Empire. The experiences of up to 500,000 Australian children in care, constituting mostly a 'white underclass', appear to be more difficult to reconcile with the national identity.[134] Responses of individuals who attended *Inside*, were, however, empathetic and profound.[135] Groups of Forgotten Australians travelled to Canberra to view it, stating they 'felt overwhelmed that their history was on display, that finally, their history was recognised', although some were disappointed that not all relevant institutions were featured.[136] The National Library of Australia was also funded to conduct an oral history project collecting testimonies of over 200 former residents and staff of children's institutions, including $500,000 for counselling support for those who participated.[137]

Memorialization performed at local sites of incarceration, such as the former Haye Institute for Girls, have been troubled endeavours, reflecting limited political will and resources to represent survivors' experiences.[138] The recent listing of the 1921 Parramatta Female Factory (Australia's oldest continuous institutional site) as an international Site of Conscience does however suggest burgeoning international support for reclaiming 'sites of human suffering to forge common ground for dignity, respect and civil participation, instead of abuse and neglect'.[139] While the museum and research centre promised by Morrison in 2018 have not yet been established, in 2020 the Museum of Australian Democracy launched the online exhibition *Citizen Activism: Reclaiming Childhood Rights* profiling select campaigners who were instrumental in bringing about the Royal Commission.[140]

Local communities have provided some of the most poignant and organic forms of memorialization. The Loud Fence movement began in the Victorian town of Ballarat following repeat revelations of the sexual abuse of children in Catholic schools and its aftermath including devastating suicide rates among victims. In 2015 during the course of Royal Commission hearings conducted in Ballarat, brightly coloured ribbons began appearing tied to front fences of the schools and churches named as sites of abuse. Local resident Maureen Hatcher was inspired to organize the community in response to the actions of local school principals who tied ribbons to the fences of schools.[141] The name 'Loud Fence' signifies a defiance of silence about child sexual abuse and the bright colours aim to signal 'a bold protest against the misuse of power and authority'.[142]

Survivors' access to their records

Services for locating and accessing records have long been identified as crucial to providing truth recovery for care leavers, as well as potential family reunion. The NRSCA scandal first catalysed once former child migrants were able to access their records following reform of Freedom of Information laws in the 1980s.[143] Aboriginal community and grassroots organizations have also been providing services for family reconnection since the 1980s, such as those offered by the Link-Up (NSW) Aboriginal Corporation. Accessing information in the web of Australian state-based welfare has been very challenging for all. In 2015 CLAN developed a *Charter of Rights to Records* for care leavers informed by three principles: *participation* through the application of the legislated right to challenge historic records where they are inaccurate, misleading or out-of-date and to submit alternative material for inclusion;

control including the right to know who has access to the file, and a right to veto readers who 'do not have the subject person's permission to read'; and *ownership* through an assertion of the right to full and unredacted access to all original documents.[144] If implemented, the CLAN charter would represent a radical departure from current practices.

Although records and recordkeeping were not explicit in the terms of reference of the *Bringing them Home, Forgotten Australians* and *Lost Innocents* inquiries, records 'emerged as a core issue in each instance' and each inquiry came to make recommendations about records.[145] In 2010 on the anniversary of the *Apology to the Forgotten Australians and Former Child Migrants*, the federal government announced that $26.5 million would be invested in a range of 'Find & Connect' services for care leavers. This included funding for CLAN, the Alliance for Forgotten Australians, the Child Migrants Trust and the International Association of Former Child Migrants and their Families, to expand their counselling, advocacy, outreach and information-sharing services. The government also provided funding to develop the *Find & Connect* website to provide 'counselling and family tracing services' for care leavers.[146] The development of 'the largest non-military public history project in Australia'[147] involved university-based archivists, history and social work academics and a full-time public historian funded in each state and territory. *Find & Connect* aims to record information on every organization that provided care since the colonial period (1788–1900) with 'links to its predecessor and successor organizations, legislation governing child removal and placement, and importantly, listings of its records holdings and links to the organisations controlling records access'.[148] Historians characterize their role in the project as 'mediators' who update the website and database on the basis of information provided by care leavers who often know the system better than the academic 'experts'.[149]

Locating records is only half of the odyssey. Records first need to be kept and made available. Since the 1980s legislation has been enacted to govern general recordkeeping obligations by institutions, such as the *Australian Charities and Not-for-profits Commission Act 2012* (Cth) and the *Corporations Act 2001* (Cth). Each state and territory has also enacted 'public records laws' applicable to government agencies and public bodies. But the shift to a culture of comprehensive record-taking and keeping has been slow. One recommendation of *Forgotten Australians* in 2004 was that 'all government and non-government agencies immediately cease the practice of destroying records relating to those who have been in care'.[150] Although recordkeeping was not part of its terms of reference, the Royal Commission examined the contemporary situation for care leavers, publishing a *Consultation Paper* including many submissions from care leavers.[151]

The Royal Commission found that despite some progress over the past 30 years, survivors often found that their institutional records were non-existent, sparse, inaccurate and completely void of any information about their sexual abuse and the perpetrator, even in instances when the abuse had been reported. Along with causing emotional distress, incomplete records have hampered survivors' abilities to seek redress and compensation or pursue criminal charges. In response to reports of 'obstructive and unresponsive processes for accessing records' by some institutions, the Royal Commission recommended that all relevant institutions should retain records relating to CSA that has occurred or is alleged to have occurred, for 45 years, and:

> individuals whose childhoods are documented in institutional records should have a right to access records made about them. Full access should be given unless it is contrary to law. Specific, not generic, explanations should be provided in any case where a record, or part of a record, is withheld or redacted. Individuals should be made aware of, and assisted to assert, their existing rights to request that records containing their personal information be amended or annotated; and to seek review or appeal of decisions refusing access, amendment or annotation.[152]

The Royal Commission concluded that the keeping of complete records is central to meeting obligations under the UNCRC associated with rights to 'identity, nationality, name and family relations' and to preventing child abuse.[153]

Practical supports

The Howard government systematically subverted campaigns for rights and reparations for First Nations Australians, including through the promise of 'practical reconciliation', a phrase suggesting the symbolic and *impractical* nature of financial redress and enhanced Native Title or Treaties as restitution and natural justice.[154] In response to *Bringing Them Home* the government allocated $63 million for practical assistance in the form of counselling, family reunion services, parenting support programmes, preservation of Indigenous languages and culture, oral history recordings and archiving of records.[155] The programmes offered responded to only 17 of the 54 recommendations contained in *Bringing Them Home* and have meant that the phrase 'practical reconciliation' is forever politicized in Australia.[156]

Similar forms of practical assistance were recommended by the *Lost Innocents* and *Forgotten Australians* inquiries in 2001 and 2004 and funds were established for family reunion, adult learning and advocacy services including CLAN and The Alliance for Forgotten Australians.[157] However, on review of the implementation of the recommendations in 2009, it was determined that many had not been acted on. Counselling services for care leavers were mostly introduced in response to previous state (not national) inquires 'which means that in effect there has been no take-up of this recommendation' about providing enhanced national counselling.[158] Again, the Australian federal political system and the states' historical control of social policy have undermined possibilities for national uniformity. Services available in the states and territories vary, with some offered by government providers and others by private entities, churches and other implicated institutions.[159]

In Victoria, home to over 30 per cent of care leavers, in 2008, the government committed $7.1 million in funding for services over four years, intended to 'support and assist care leavers who have experienced significant disadvantage', promising *a single access point* for obtaining advice on accessing available services, including: housing, mental health, aged care, counselling, alcohol and drugs, literacy and numeracy, dental and medical services, peer support and support from professionals; search and support services, including locating siblings; developing life skills; and support for families of carers, including counselling and information about claims processes and referrals for assistance with legal claims.[160] For Frank Golding, Vice-President of CLAN, it was 'a nice start, but we need a lot more'.[161]

The Royal Commission canvassed the experiences of survivors accessing treatment and advocacy support, to find that little had changed in 2017. Survivors are still required to negotiate a complex web of providers and there is 'no single entry point to the service system', which is often ill-equipped to deal with complex trauma or the treatment needs of survivors of institutional abuse.[162] The Commissioners heard from many survivors that institutional CSA was often compounded by sexual abuse within the family, and they required specialist treatment that can be difficult to access. There are 'gaps in services' for all groups, but particularly children, male survivors, survivors entering aged care and survivors in and transitioning out of prisons.[163] Moreover, survivors reported facing 'stigmatising community and professional attitudes about child sexual abuse' when seeking treatment.[164] Support for secondary victims, such as family members, carers and friends and others in the institution where the abuse occurred, is often lacking. The Royal Commission identified a non-exhaustive list of what survivors require, including mainstream services;[165] community support services;[166] specialist services[167] and advocacy services and legal advice.[168]

In contradiction of the Royal Commission's recommendations, the *National Redress Scheme for Institutional Child Sexual Abuse Assessment Framework* provides only limited counselling attached to its financial redress scheme discussed below. The state-funded, privately-delivered counselling sessions are capped based on arbitrary distinctions made between different forms of sexual abuse. Victims who have been determined to be eligible for redress for penetrative abuse are eligible for 20 counselling sessions throughout their lifetime ($5000); those who experienced 'contact abuse' are eligible for 10 sessions ($2500) and those who experienced 'exposure abuse' are offered five counselling sessions ($1250).[169] In a cruel contradiction, while the redress scheme has the capacity to award extra financial payments on the recognition of 'extreme circumstances of sexual abuse', no extra counselling is available for survivors who meet this criterion. Survivor advocates describe this sliding scale as creating a divisive hierarchy and sending a message that CSA can be recovered from quickly; non-penetrative abuse can be recovered from twice as quickly as penetrative abuse.[170]

Financial redress

The federal political system and hybridity of Australian welfare provision including the diverse range of institutions historically involved has meant that Australia has implemented the second highest number of financial redress schemes relating to child abuse of any country in the world (second only to Norway).[171] Most states and territories established limited redress schemes for care leavers and members of the Stolen Generations including financial payments and minimal counselling services. Resources have typically been stretched and politicized. None of the state and territory schemes were dedicated solely to redressing *sexual* abuse, and on recommendation of the Royal Commission, in 2018, the federal government introduced the *National Redress Scheme for People who have Experienced Institutional Child Sexual Abuse* (the 'NRS').

The NRS is available to Australian citizens and permanent residents born before 2010 who were sexually abused as children in closed settings such as institutionalized care and open settings such as church services, in the past and until July 2018. Designing the NRS was legally and politically challenging as the Commonwealth is not necessarily empowered to spend into programmes of state portfolios such as child protection or welfare.[172] In part to manage the complex relationship of state and Commonwealth powers, the Australian government agreed to provide the architecture of an 'opt-in' NRS, to which state and territory governments and individual institutions could choose to contribute and participate in.[173] After protracted negotiations with the states (especially Western Australia) to refer their powers for Commonwealth legislation to be enacted, the NRS became operational in 2018. Extended public and political pressure has meant that almost all the institutions named in the Royal Commission have now agreed to participate in the scheme.[174]

The NRS has been criticized by survivors, parliamentary inquiries, lawyers and academics for departing from the Royal Commission's recommendations to the detriment of survivors, many of whom are elderly and frail. Contrary to Royal Commission findings that the 'consequences for people who are abused may not be proportionate to the severity of their abuse', redress is determined based on a schedule of damages arbitrarily distinguishing between penetrative abuse (maximum $150,000), 'contact' abuse (maximum $50,000) and 'exposure' abuse (maximum $20,000). The schedule also includes minimal scope for the recognition of 'related non-sexual abuse' ($5000) and instances where an individual was 'institutionally vulnerable' ($5000) (for example, they resided at the institution and did not have friends outside the institution).[175] Claims are determined *prima facie* on the basis of a survivor submitting a written statement outlining their abuse suffered. Unlike the award of damages in the civil justice system, survivors are not required to prove the enduring effects of their abuse, but they are required to provide detailed accounts of its occurrence—a situation that many find traumatizing. It is likely that complex claims could 'drag on for years'.[176]

While survivors do not require legal representation to make a claim on the NRS, the government has made free legal advice available through the service *knowmore*. Legal advice can be very important. The NRS requires claimants to waive their rights to sue any entity directly associated with their claim, and if a survivor has received a relevant prior payment from an institution or a different redress scheme, that payment will be deducted from their total NRS payment. If a claim involves multiple institutions, as is not uncommon, the institutions will share the costs of redress. However, a survivor might, on legal advice, instead issue legal proceedings (litigation) against one entity and pursue another through the NRS. Redress recipients are not sworn to confidentiality, but they may request that their claim remains confidential. Individuals in prison are not eligible to apply until their release, and anyone who has served a five-year prison sentence may not be eligible at all. These exclusions may have greatest impact on First Nations Australians, who experience the highest incarceration rates in the world.[177] All of these factors could be very confusing and overwhelming to negotiate without legal advice.

Despite the positive elements of the NRS, including that survivors need not prove the extent of the harm they have suffered, a 2019 parliamentary review concluded that because the NRS did not closely follow the recommendations of the Royal Commission or the expert advisory group established to inform it, it is:

> unjust; has no capacity to recognise individual circumstances; does not reflect survivors' experience or research findings; does not align with medical knowledge or common law assessment of damages; fails to accommodate relevant factors such as frequency and duration of abuse and co-existing forms of abuse; is ill-informed, insulting and re-traumatising for survivors.[178]

By July 2020 a total of 2,852 applications for redress had been finalized, including 2,795 payments totalling around $229 million, with an average payment of $82,000.[179] Given that over 8,000 individuals testified to the Royal Commission in person, this suggests that most eligible survivors have not accessed the NRS and/or its processes are drawn out and obstructive.

England and Wales

Apologies

Until recently, government ministers, including the Prime Minister, have been reticent about the consequences of issuing apologies for historically significant events. Following Tony Blair's apologies for the British government's inaction in respect of the Irish famines of the 1840s (1997) and for miscarriages of justice suffered by the Guildford Four (2000) and Britain's historic role in the slave trade (2007) there are signs of a less cautious approach.[180] The first government expression of contrition with respect to specific institutional NRCSA came in February 2000 after the publication of the Waterhouse Inquiry (see Chapter 2) when the Secretary of State for Wales, said 'we all say "sorry" but "sorry" is not enough'.[181] In December 2004 Scotland became the first country in the UK to issue a collective national apology for institutional abuse. First Minister Jack McConnell, made a 'sincere and full' apology on behalf of the *people* of Scotland to those who had suffered physical, sexual and emotional abuse in care homes putting pressure on the English government to emulate his initiative.

It would take another six years until the first national collective apology was issued by Westminster. In February 2010 Prime Minister Gordon Brown apologized in Parliament on behalf of the government to former child migrants sent abroad between the 1920s and 1960s to Canada, Australia, New Zealand, Rhodesia (now Zimbabwe) and other former colonies as part of Britain's child migration programmes. Particularly after the Second World War, the government knowingly condoned the role and activities of many voluntary agencies and local authorities in conveying some 4,000 children overseas, many on the pretext of saving on care costs rather than for the welfare of the child. Many were permanently separated from their families or physically or sexually abused in foster homes, orphanages and religious institutions. Brown avowed:

> To all those former child migrants and their families, to those here with us today and those across the world – to each and every one – I say today that we are truly sorry. They were let down. We are sorry that they were allowed to be sent away at the time they were most vulnerable. We are sorry that instead of caring for them, this country turned its back, and we are sorry that the voices of these children were not always heard and their cries for help not always heeded. We are sorry that it has taken so long for this important day to come, and for the full and unconditional apology that is justly deserved to be given.[182]

As the IICSA's subsequent child migrants' inquiry confirmed, the policy was 'fundamentally flawed', successive governments had 'failed to ensure that there were in place sufficient measures to protect children from sexual abuse', children were lied to about their parents not caring for them or having died and countless institutions kept incomplete or no documentation.[183]

Brown put aside £6 million to help reunite families affected but the IICSA later insisted that approximately 2,000 living former migrants should be offered equal financial reparation through a government funded Redress

Scheme managed by the Child Migrants' Trust.[184] Implemented in February 2019, the scheme allows all former British child migrants[185] to apply for a redress payment on the basis that they were exposed to the risk of sexual abuse. Successful applicants each receive an *ex gratia* payment of £20,000.[186] The payment was payable to all applicants regardless of whether they had received payments from other governments or through private legal action. In a parliamentary debate in February 2019 Labour MP Lisa Nandy raised concerns about the scheme, including that the fixed sum was lower than the average payment issued to claimants under the Australian NRS, open to former British child migrants, which is the equivalent of £43,000 with a cap at £82,000. Nandy also raised the concerns of many former child migrants about their lack of involvement in the scheme's development.[187]

In the absence of a national redress scheme for NRCSA, survivors must seek redress through the civil courts (see Chapters 8 and 9) or apply to the Criminal Injuries Compensation Scheme.

Criminal injuries compensation scheme

In the personal injuries case of *Stubbings* (Chapter 8), Lord Griffiths advocated that survivors should seek compensation from the Criminal Injuries Compensation Scheme (CICS) rather than the courts. He was oblivious to the fact that not only has there been a time-bar on NRCSA applications to the CICS but that often harsh and sometimes indefensible conditions apply.[188] The CICS is governed by s1 of the Criminal Injuries Compensation Act 1995 authorizing the implementation of various schemes, currently the Criminal Injuries Compensation Scheme 2012. While claims may be made up to a capped amount of £500,000 for injuries resulting from a criminal act, there are limitations. Awards may be withheld or reduced because of the applicant's character.[189] A 2015 BBC investigation found that compensation had been reduced for more than 400 sexual abuse victims in Britain who had subsequently committed criminal offences.[190] This contrasts with the approach increasingly being taken by the civil courts which see addiction and its consequences as part of the lifelong impact of abuse.

Decisions are made according to the civil standard of a balance of probabilities and may be appealed to the First Tier Tribunal, Upper Tribunal (Administrative Appeals Chamber) or challenged by judicial review. Applications are not conditional on securing a conviction but are contingent on reporting the crime to the police.

The advantage of recruiting specialist legal advice can make a significant difference, as illustrated in an application 16 years out-of-date concerning a woman abused as a child by her uncle for years. The Criminal Injuries Compensation Authority offered £22,000 but failed to take account of her psychiatric injury. The First Tier Tribunal ordered the Authority to reconsider; on reappraisal the award was increased to £221,000.[191]

One of the most incomprehensible aspects of the CICS was the rejection of claims from victims of familial sexual abuse who lived in the same house as their abuser at the time of the offence: the 'same-roof rule'. It was changed in 1979 to enable future victims to access compensation, but not retrospectively, meaning victims from before that time were still refused awards. In *JT v First Tier Tribunal* 2018,[192] the applicant had been raped by her stepfather from the age of five until 17 between 1968 and 1975. He was convicted in 2012. Another relative of JT who had given evidence at the criminal trial had also been abused but because she had not lived under the 'same roof' was entitled to an award of £1,000. Sir Terence Etherton MR ruled that the differential treatment of victims depending on when they were abused was unlawful discrimination and held that JT was entitled to an award. In response, the Ministry of Justice amended the 2012 Scheme to remove the rule in relation to criminal injuries sustained before 1 October 1979. It also allowed survivors who may not have applied to the scheme because of the rule to make an application and to allow for applicants previously refused compensation on the basis of the pre-1979 same roof rule to reapply.

At the time of writing the entire Criminal Injuries Compensation Scheme in England and Wales is under review by the Ministry of Justice.[193] The review was partly prompted by the IICSA's Interim Report which recommended revision of the scheme to remove some of the barriers faced by NRCSA survivors, including eligibility, time limits and previous convictions.[194] In its 2020 consultation, the government rejected calls by the IICSA and other stakeholders[195] to relax the two year time limit for claims, proposing instead that the Victims' Code should be amended to include explicit information on the scheme time limits.[196]

The IICSA Interim Report also recommended reform of the CICA's rules around applicant's unspent convictions and evidence relating to their 'character and conduct'. It recommended that each case be handled by specialist caseworkers trained in the impact and consequences of NRCSA. The Victims' Commissioner for England and Wales also called for greater discretion to benefit victims of exploitation, abuse and coercive control.[197] The All-Party Parliamentary Group for Adult Survivors of Childhood Sexual Abuse called for the unspent convictions rule to be abolished.[198] However, in its consultation the Ministry of Justice stated 'we do not believe it is possible to commit to making any change to this rule, without undermining the core principles of the Scheme and introducing significant potential discrimination and operational challenge'.[199] In the 2021 updated guide to the scheme convictions and character are still relevant to the decision to make an award.[200]

The majority of those who provided evidence to the IICSA Accountability and Reparations Investigation said that both civil claims and the CICS are not suitable for victims and survivors and can have a damaging impact.[201] The IICSA is currently considering whether to recommend a national redress scheme. Given the CICS's restrictive approach to NRCSA survivors and the barriers to accessing civil justice described in Chapter 8, such a scheme is clearly necessary if the state is to fully acknowledge the harms suffered by survivors.

Survivors' access to their records and memorialization

In 2020 the IICSA published a report of a consultation with its victims and survivors' forum on access to records.[202] A majority of forum members described institutions' reluctance to share records and that they encountered a lack of sensitivity and a defensive culture. Forum members had been told that institutions were not obliged to share information or that data had been lost during a transfer from paper to digital records.[203] The consultation will inform the recommendations in the IICSA Final Report. A resource for care-experienced people has been developed by the charity Family Action, working with experts David Holmes CBE and Julia Feast OBE and scholars at University College London[204] and the Care Leavers Association. The website familyconnect.org.uk helps adults who have been in care or who have been adopted access their information and prepare them for the (sometimes very difficult) journey. Such supports are clearly necessary.

Scholars have also highlighted the importance of records and recordkeeping for children experiencing the care system today,[205] demonstrating that records are a vital resource for the construction of identity and belonging into adulthood.[206] In 2020 the British Association of Social Workers provided a guidance booklet. 'Top 10 Tips: Recording in Children's Social Work'.[207]

It remains to be seen what recommendations will be made by the IICSA in respect of records and memorialization in its final report in 2022.

Conclusion

In each country apologies have been an important feature of the state's response to institutional child abuse. A fundamental flaw in the Irish and English and Welsh apologies was the temporal confinement of the harms and injustice of CSA (and all child abuse) to a remote past. In all three countries, there has been a failure to fully recognize the ongoing nature of the harms of CSA and its impacts on survivors today and their families. This leaves unanswered questions about how to repair the ongoing harms of NRCSA into adulthood and the ongoing needs of adult victims. The apologies and the accompanying material and symbolic reparations have shown governments eager to 'overcome' the dark past and move towards a bright national future. Structural factors relating to race, gender and class, underlying the abuse and responses to it remain hidden in this supposedly national process of overcoming.

Financial redress has developed in different ways in each country. In Ireland the RIRB has been an exercise in containing the state's and the religious orders' exposure to civil claims for damages (see Chapters 8 and 9) and has been accompanied by problematic practices of adversarial confrontation and control of victims. In Australia the NRS has proved to be more survivor-centred than the Irish Redress Board, but survivors also criticize it for its retraumatizing effects. In England and Wales proposals for state-based redress for institutional CSA have yet to be developed as survivors await the IICSA's final report.

While all three countries have provided therapeutic supports for survivors, there has been different provision of practical life and health supports. In England and Wales this area of reparations is the most underdeveloped. In Australia a differentiated scheme has created an impression of a hierarchy of suffering. In Ireland the agency for providing supports has been heavily criticized by survivors, and now that the agency is closed, survivors are left feeling abandoned by the state.

Commemorative practices for institutional CSA are as yet wholly inadequate, indicating an enduring contestation by each state of its responsibility in relation to institutional abuse. In each country further engaged and sustained consultation with survivors on how to appropriately memorialize the harms suffered by survivors of institutional child abuse and their families is urgently needed.

Survivors' access to their records is an essential form of reparation for institutional child abuse. It is acknowledgement that the information is owned by the survivor and not by the institution and involves an acceptance that the information contained within may be used to hold the institution (or the state itself) to account. Each country still has a long way to go towards addressing these core needs of survivors. More broadly, access to archives of institutional abuse is essential to the telling of social histories of each country, which can help ensure that the lessons of the past are finally learned. A national repository of archives relating to institutional abuse could allow for the donation by survivors of their testimonies of survivors to redress mechanisms or public inquiries. This would in itself be a form of commemoration of suffering and would work towards ensuring that the mistakes of the past are not repeated.

Each country has yet to fully engage with its responsibility to deliver reparations for the past and ongoing harms of institutional CSA suffered by survivors and their families. The experience of survivors in Ireland in particular shows how ideas of reparation can be frustrated by excessive legalism. The role of reparations in each country has been about overcoming the dark past and moving on without fully engaging with the ethical necessity of listening to and fully addressing survivors' ongoing material and other needs. Structural factors relating to race, gender and class underlying the abuse and responses to it remain hidden in this supposedly national process of overcoming. In Ireland this has been linked to control of survivors' access to information and resources without attention to questions of accountability. In Australia and in England and Wales the work of reparations has been shaped by a desire to move on from their colonial histories. In no country have survivors' needs and justice interests been prioritized.

Notes

1 United Nations Basic Principles on the Right to a Remedy and Reparation for Victims of Gross Violations of International Human Rights Law and Serious Violations of International Humanitarian Law (UNPBG) (2005) A/RES/60/147, Principle 19–23; P. de Greiff, "Justice and Reparations" in P. de Greiff (ed), *The Handbook of Reparations. International Center for Transitional Justice* (Oxford: Oxford University Press, 2006), 451.

2 B. Hamber and R. Wilson, "Symbolic Closure through Memory, Reparation and Revenge in Post-Conflict Societies" *Journal of Human Rights* 1, 2002, 35–53.

3 P. Lundy and B. Rolston, "Redress for Past Harms? Official Apologies in Northern Ireland" *International Journal of Human Rights* 20(1), 2016, 104–22.

4 M. Gibeny, et al. (eds), *The Age of Apology: Facing up to the Past* (Philadelphia, University of Pennsylvania Press, 2009).

5 D. Celermejer, "Apology and the Possibility of the Ethical Nation" in D. Cuypers et al. (eds), *Public Apology between Ritual and Regret: Symbolic Excuses on False Pretenses or True Reconciliation out of Sincere Regret?* (Brill Publishing, 2013) and *The Sins of the Nation and the Ritual of Apologies* (Cambridge: Cambridge University Press, 2009); J.K. Olick, *The Politics of Regret. On Collective Memory and Historical Responsibility* (London: Routledge, 2007).

6 J. Sköld and S. Swain, "Introduction" in J. Sköld and S. Swain (eds), *Apologies and the Legacy of Abuse of Children in "Care"* (Palgrave MacMillan, 2015), 1. and see A.-M. McAlinden, "Apologies as 'Shame Management': The Politics of Remorse in the Aftermath of Historical Institutional Abuse" *Legal Studies* 2021. doi:10.1017/lst.2021.39

7 P. Lundy, " 'I Just Want Justice': A Critical Analysis of the Historical Institutional Abuse Inquiry in Northern Ireland" ire-Ireland, 55(1, 2), 2020, 252–78. Law Commission of Canada, *Restoring Dignity: Responding to Child Abuse in Canadian Institutions: Executive Summary* (Ottawa: Law Commission of Canada, 2000); Royal Commission into Institutional Responses to Child Sexual Abuse, *Redress and Civil Litigation* report (Commonwealth of Australia, 2015); L. Taft, "Apology Subverted: The Commodification of Apology," *Yale Law Journal* 109(5), 2000, 1135–60, 1137.

8 A.-M. McAlinden op. cit., 7.

9 P. Lundy, "I Just Want Justice Assessing the Impact of Historical Institutional Child Abuse Inquiries from the Perspective of Survivors" *Éire-Ireland* 55(1&2), 2020, 252–78, 261.

10 M. Minow, *Between Vengeance and Forgiveness: Facing History After Genocide and Mass Violence* (Boston: Beacon Press, 2000), 115.

11 M. James, et al., "Impermanent Apologies: on the Dynamics of Timing and Public Knowledge in Political Apology" *Human Rights Review* 19(1), 2018 1–23.

12 McAlinden op. cit., 19.

13 For example, the Catholic diocese of Dromore has created a redress scheme for victims of clerical abuse in the diocese: *The Irish Times*, 29 September 2021. Dromore is in Northern Ireland, but administration of the Catholic Church is on an all-island basis.

14 "Jimmy Savile Victims' Compensation Scheme Approved By Appeal Court," *The Guardian*, 16 December 2014.

15 K. Daly, "Money for Justice? Money's Meaning and Purpose as Redress for Historical Institutional Abuse" in Y. Smaal et al. (eds), *The Sexual Abuse of Children: Recognition and Redress* (Melbourne: Monash University Publishing, 2016), 160.

16 S. Winter, "Australia's Ex Gratia Redress" *Australian Indigenous Law Review* 13(1), 49–61.

17 M. Enright and S. Ring, "State Responses to Historical institutional Abuse: Shame, Sovereignty and Epistemic Injustice" ire-Ireland 55(1, 2), 2020, 68–99.

18 Save the Children, *Global Accountability and Investigations Report* (London: Save the Children International, 2018).

19 A. Barrett et al., "Childhood Sexual Abuse and Later-life Economic Consequences" *Journal of Behavioural and Experimental Economics* 53, 2014, 10–16.

20 Lundy (2020) op. cit.

21 F. Logue, "Submission on the Retention of Records Bill to the Joint Committee on Education and Skills," available at http://jfmresearch.com/wp-content/uploads/2019/10/Fred-Logue-Submission.pdf; "Your Right of Access," Information Commissioner's Office, https://ico.org.uk/your-data-matters/your-right-to-get-copies-of-your-data/; "Access to Your Personal Information," Australian Government Office of the Australian Information Commissioner, www.oaic.gov.au/privacy/your-privacy-rights/your-personal-information/access-your-personal-information/.

22 H. Kehoe, "The Irish State's Responses to Its Gendered and Historical Human Rights Violations," *Irish Law Times*, 1, 2018, 15.

23 E. Catterall, *Apologies and Institutional Abuse* (Belfast: Queen's University Belfast, 2018), 4.

24 "Taoiseach Apologises to Victims of Child Abuse," RTÉ News, www.rte.ie/news/1999/0511/1662-abuse/.

25 C. Buckley, Letter to the Editor, *Irish Independent*, 7 April 2008.

26 J.M. Smith, "Knowing and Unknowing Tuam: State Practice, The Archive, and Transitional Justice" *Eire-Ireland* 55(12), 2020, 142–80, 145.

27 The Commission of Inquiry into the Reformatory and Industrial School System 1934–1936, *Report* (Dublin: Stationery Office, 1936), the Report of the Inter-Departmental Committee on the Prevention of Crime (1962) and the Commission of Inquiry into the Reformatory and Industrial School System *Report of the Commission of Inquiry into the Reformatory and Industrial School System* (Dublin: Stationery Office, 1970) had made recommendations on reformatories and industrial schools, many of which were ignored or only partially implemented. Department of Health and Children, *Report on the Inquiry into the Operation of Madonna House* (Dublin: Stationery Office, 1996) was not published. See Chapter 4.

28 Available at www.attorneygeneral.jus.gov.on.ca/inquiries/cornwall/en/hearings/exhibits/Peter_Jaffe/pdf/Restoring_Dignity.pdf.

29 See T. Boland, Evidence Before the Commission to Inquire into Child Abuse, 24 June 2004, 51, www.childabusecommission.ie/public_hearings/documents/04/Transcript-24June2004.PDF, 56.

30 Ibid., 64.

31 The Institute of Charity (Rosminians), the Sisters of Mercy, the Christian Brothers, the Daughters of Charity of St Vincent de Paul, the Daughters of the

Heart of Mary, the De La Salle Brothers, the Dominican Order, the Oblates of Mary Immaculate, the Hospitaller Order of St John of God, the Presentation Brothers; the Presentation Sisters; Religious Sisters of Charity; the Sisters of Our Lady of Charity of the Good Shepherd; the Sisters of St Clare; Sisters of St Louis; the Sisters of Our Lady of Charity of Refuge; the Sisters of Nazareth; the Brothers of Charity.

32 Head of the south-central province of the Congregation of the Sisters of Mercy.

33 The Conference of Religious in Ireland (CORI)'s secretary general and leader of the Presentation Sisters' Northern Province.

34 *The Irish Times,* 4 October 2003; *The Irish Times*, 2 October 2003; *The Irish Times*, 5 April 2019.

35 Compensation Advisory Committee, *Report to The Minister for Education and Science* (2002), www.rirb.ie/documents/cac_report2002.pdf.

36 *The Irish Times,* 2 March 2000.

37 Including €40 million in property already transferred since May 1999: see Murphy 2005.

38 *The Irish Times*, 2 October 2003.

39 CICA (2009), Vol 1, 14; S. Pembroke, "Historical Institutional Abuse in Ireland: Survivor Perspectives on Taking Part in the Commission to Inquire into Child Abuse (CICA) and the Redress Scheme" *Contemporary Justice Review* 22(1), 2019, 43–59.

40 T. Boland memorandum to the Secretary General of the Department of Education, cited in C. Murphy, "Indemnity Deal Dress up to Disguise Massive Shortfall," Magill, 16 November 2005, https://magill.ie/archive/indemnity-deal-dressed-disguise-massive-shortfall.

41 See T. Boland, Evidence Before the Commission to Inquire into Child Abuse, 24 June 2004, 51, www.childabusecommission.ie/public_hearings/documents/04/Transcript-24June2004.PDF.

42 Which also made clear that anyone detained in an industrial school as a child without a criminal offence having been committed by them is not to be regarded as having a criminal record s35 of the Residential Institutions Redress Board Act 2002. s251 The Children Act 2001 had clarified that children who were convicted of a criminal offence were to be treated as a person who has not been charged prosecuted or found guilty or dealt with for an offence.

43 C. Brennan, "Facing What Cannot Be Changed: The Irish Experience of Confronting Institutional Child Abuse" *Journal of Social Welfare and Family Law* 29, 2007, 245–63, 252.

44 Residential Institutions Redress Board, *A Guide to the Redress Scheme under the Residential Institutions, 3rd ed.* (Dublin: The Residential Institutions Redress Board, 2005) 3; Residential Institutions Redress Act 2002.

45 Ibid.

46 s1 Residential Institutions Redress Act 2002.

47 16 December 2002–15 December 2005; late applications were accepted in exceptional circumstances until 16 September 2011 (Residential Institutions Redress Board, *Annual Report* 2012 (Dublin: Stationery Office, 2013).

48 See United Nations Committee against Torture, *General Comment (no 3)* (2012), [40].CAT/C/GC/3.

49 *The Irish Times,* 1 February 2002.

50 Residential Institutions Redress Board Op. cit., 2016.

51 Comptroller and Auditor General, *Special Report on Costs of Child Abuse Inquiry and* Redress (Dublin: Government of Ireland, 2017), 11; *The Irish Times,* 3 March 2005.
52 M. Raftery, "Cheating Abuse Victims," *The Irish Times*, 26 April 2007.
53 *Noctor v Ireland and Others* [2005] IEHC 50.
54 s11(8)(c) Residential Institutions Redress Board Act 2002.
55 For example, see *KMM v Residential Institutions Redress Board* [2015] IEHC 66.
56 K. Coleman, *Haunting Cries, Stories of Child Abuse from Industrial Schools.* (Dublin: Gill and MacMillan, 2010), 237; B. Walshe and C. O'Connell, *Consultations with Survivors of Institutional Abuse on Themes and Issues to be Addressed by a Survivor Led Consultation Group* (Department of Education and Skills, 2019), <www.education.ie/en/Publications/Education-Reports/consultations-with-survivors-of-institutional-abuse-on-themes-and-issues-to-be-addressed-by-a-survivor-led-consultation-group.pdf.
57 Pembroke op. cit.
58 Moore, J., et al. "On the Road to Resilience: the Help-Seeking Experiences of Irish Emigrant Survivors of Institutional Abuse" *Child Abuse Review* 26, 2015, 375–87.
59 Reclaiming Self, *Ryan Report Follow-Up. Submission to the United Nations Committee against Torture Session 61* (Reclaiming Self, 2017), 26, https://tbinternet.ohchr.org/Treaties/CAT/Shared%20Documents/IRL/INT_CAT_CSS_IRL_27959_E.pdf.
60 *The Irish Times*, 19 May 2005.
61 Reclaiming Self op. cit., Appendix IV (c).
62 This ended in 2009 when the Ryan Report was published. P. McGarry, "Order Denied Abuse Five Days Before Report," *The Irish Times,* 3 June 2009.
63 See Crean, A.M., *Submission to the Joint Oireachtas Committee, 26 November 2019*, http://jfmresearch.com/retention-of-records-bill-2019/. and Lodato, M., Submission to the Oireachtas Joint Committee on Education and Skills, 26 November 2019, http://jfmresearch.com/wp-content/uploads/2019/10/Mary-Lodato-Submission.pdf.
64 They were sent a letter directly quoting the relevant section of the legislation. The punishment for breach of this section is a fine of €25,000 and two years' imprisonment. The punishment was not mentioned in the letter but was well known about by survivors.
65 ss 28(6), (9) RIRBA 2002.
66 s34 RIRBA 2002.
67 See, e.g. Redress (2020) RTÉ and *The Irish Times,* 18 March 2010; *Irish Examiner*, 14 March, 2021.
68 See Reclaiming Self at 26.
69 s28.
70 *The Irish Times*, 17 April 2021.
71 Comptroller and Auditor General, *Special Report.*
72 Comptroller and Auditor General, *Annual Report* 83.
73 In 2020, Taoiseach Micheál Martin described it as 'a mistake': M. Peelo, "*Redress: Breaking the Silence*" (2020; Dublin: RTÉ Television).
74 *The Irish Times*, 9 March 2017.
75 M. Woods, Written Answers-Victims of Abuse, Dail Eireann debate, Tuesday, 28 November 2000.
76 *O'Keeffe v Ireland,* Grand Chamber 35810/09, 28 January 2014.

77 C. O'Mahony, *Special Rapporteur on Child Protection. Annual Report* 26 (2020), 25.
78 Decision of the Independent Assessor at [46] and [52], www.education.ie/en/Learners/Information/Former-Residents-of-Industrial-Schools/ECHR-OKeeffe-v-Ireland/independent-assessment-process/okeeffe-v-ireland-decision-of-the-independent-assessor.pdf.
79 General Data Protection Regulation and Data Protection Act 2018.
80 Gallen submission to the Joint Oireachtas Committee, on the Retention of Records Bill, http://jfmresearch.com/retention-of-records-bill-2019/, 7.
81 Department of Education, Minister McHugh announces publication of the Retention of Records Bill 2019 to Transfer Records Relating to Residential Institutional Child Abuse to the National Archives, 28 February 2019, www.education.ie/en/Press-Events/Press-Releases/2019-press-releases/PR19-02-28.html.
82 M. O'Rourke, et al., *Submission to the Oireachtas Joint Committee on Education and Skills on the provisions of the Retention of Records Bill 2019*, 13 November 2019. Available at http://jfmresearch.com/retention-of-records-bill-2019/.
83 *The Irish Times*, 4 December 2019.
84 General Data Protection Regulation; The Data Protection Act 2018
85 For example, see submissions by Dr Mary Lodato and Eileen Molloy, http://jfmresearch.com/retention-of-records-bill-2019/ and see https://www.oireachtas.ie/en/debates/debate/joint_committee_on_education_and_skills/2019-11-26/3/.
86 [1.1] of the submission by Dr Mary Lodato to the Oireachtas Joint Committee on Education and Skills, http://jfmresearch.com/wp-content/uploads/2019/10/Mary-Lodato-Submission.pdf.
87 *The Sunday Times*, 2 August 2020.
88 There is no legislation requiring religious organizations to make their archives accessible to victim-survivors and their families, researchers, the child protection services or the gardaí.
89 C. Crowe, "Guilt Shame, Acknowledgement, and Redress: A Personal Reflection on Ireland's Institutional Treatment of Women and Children" in M. Corcoran and P. Cullen (eds), *Producing Knowledge, Reproducing Gender* (Dublin: UCD Press, 2020), 235.
90 *The Irish Times*, 24 October 2020.
91 "Justice for Magdalenes Research," National Archive, http://jfmresearch.com/retention-of-records-bill-2019/archive_election2020/.
92 Government Statement on the Final Report of the Commission of Investigation (Mother and Baby Homes and certain related matters) https://www.gov.ie/en/press-release/4f64f-government-statement-on-the-final-report-of-the-commission-of-investigation-mother-and-baby-homes-and-certain-related-matters/.
93 See "History," Towards Healing, https://towardshealing.ie/history/.
94 Since 1996 the Conference of Religious in Ireland had funded a telephone help-line, Faoiseamh and face-to-face counselling service. Following the apology, this continued until 2011, when it was taken over by a new service called Towards Healing.
95 See www.childabusecommission.ie/findinghelp/documents/Tracing%20Information.pdf.
96 Commission to Inquire into Child Abuse (Amendment) Act 2005, ss 22–33.
97 See definition of 'relevant trust' in s2 of the 2012 Act.
98 70 per cent of payments were spent on housing, and 28.1 per cent was spent on health. Anonymous, *Caranua Evaluation Report* (Dublin: Caranua, 2021), 2.
99 s7 (1) 2012 Act.

100 Evaluation Report op. cit., 1.
101 *The Irish Times* 2017; Reclaiming Self op. cit.
102 Caranua 2016, 3.
103 Reclaiming Self op. cit.
104 Ibid.
105 R. Bruton, "Residential Institutions Statutory Fund: Motion (Resumed) [Private Members]" *Dáil Éireann Debates*, 24 May 2017, www.oireachtas.ie/en/debates/debate/dail/2017-05-24/29/.
106 CCIA Report Viol IV Ch 7 para 7:02.
107 Department of Children and Youth Affairs, *Ryan Report Implementation Plan: Second Progress Report* (2001), 11, www.dcya.gov.ie/documents/20180831RyanRepImplPlanSecProgRep.pdf.
108 *Irish Examiner,* 15 January 2021.
109 Magdalene Flowers project.
110 Open Heart City, http://openheartcitydublin.ie.
111 Human Rights and Equal Opportunity Commission, *Bringing them Home: Report of the National Inquiry into the Separation of Aboriginal and Torres Strait Islander Children from Their Families* (Sydney: HREOC, 1997), Appendix 9.
112 C. Dow, *Sorry. The Unfinished Business of the Bringing Them Home Report* (Australia: Parliamentary Library, 4 February 2008). www.aph.gov.au/About_Parliament/Parliamentary_Departments/Parliamentary_Library/pubs/BN/0708/BringingThemHomeReport.
113 In R. Manne, "In Denial: The Stolen Generations and the Right" *The Australian Quarterly Essay* 2001, 75. Howard also used fear of liability as an excuse not to apologize, claiming to have received advice to the effect that, 'a formal unqualified apology' would have 'certain legal implications'. Such advice, if received, would appear to contradict the protections of the *Parliamentary Privileges Act 1987*, concerning all statements made in parliament, including apologies. Dow op. cit.
114 *Kruger v Commonwealth* [1997] HCA 27; *Native Title Amendment Act 1998*.
115 Dow op. cit.
116 Ibid.
117 K. Rudd, *Apology to Australia's Indigenous Peoples*, 13 February 2008. www.aph.gov.au/Visit_Parliament/Whats_On/Exhibitions/Custom_Media/Apology_to_Australias_Indigenous_Peoples.
118 K. Rudd, *National Apology to the Forgotten Australians and Former Child Migrants*, 16 November 2009, http://parlview.aph.gov.au/mediaPlayer.php?videoID=314492&operation_mode=parlview#/3.
119 Ibid.
120 Rudd op. cit., 2008.
121 Rudd op. cit., 2009.
122 For many survivors the Royal Commission was indelibly associated with Julia Gillard, who had established it as her last act as Prime Minister in 2012. Gillard was greeted with a standing ovation and 'mobbed' by grateful survivors when she appeared in parliament for the Apology. *Sydney Morning Herald*, 22 October 2018.
123 S. Morrison, *National Apology to Victims and Survivors of Institutional Child Sexual Abuse,* 22 October 2018, www.pm.gov.au/media/national-apology-victims-and-survivors-institutional-child-sexual-abuse.

124 Ibid.
125 Ibid.
126 K. Daly and J. Davis, "Unravelling Redress for Institutional Abuse of Children in Australia" *University of New South Wales Law Journal* 42(4), 2019, 1254–93, 1277.
127 Morrison op. cit.
128 *ABC News*, 22 October 2018.
129 A. Chynoweth, "Forgotten or Ignored Australians? The Case for an Inclusive Museum" in P. Ashton and J.Z. Wilson (eds) *Silent System. Forgotten Australians and the Institutionalisation of Women and Children* (North Melbourne: Australian Scholarly Press, 2014), 172.
130 Ibid.
131 Ibid.
132 Ibid.
133 Ibid., 174.
134 Ibid., 176
135 Ibid., 178. Reviewers of the exhibition noted that 'many visitors noticeably wept at the content'.
136 Ibid., 179.
137 "Forgotten Australians Remembered," National Library of Australia, 12 November 2012, www.nla.gov.au/news/2012/11/16/forgotten-australians-remembered-1.
138 Chynoweth op. cit.
139 L. Steele, et al., "Parramatta Female Factory Precinct as a Site of Conscience: Using Institutional Pasts to Shape Just Legal Futures" *University of New South Wales Law Journal* 43(2), 2020, 521–51, 524.
140 "Citizen Activism: Reclaiming Childhood Rights," Museum of Australian Democracy, available, www.moadoph.gov.au/democracy-are-you-in/citizen-activism-reclaiming-childhood-rights/#.
141 *The Courier*, 22 May 2018.
142 Ibid.
143 F. Golding, "Sexual Abuse as the Core Transgression of Childhood Innocence: Unintended Consequences for Care Leavers" *Journal of Australian Studies* 42(2), 2018, 191.
144 F. Golding, "'Problems with Records and Recordkeeping Practices Are Not Confined to the Past:' A Challenge from the Royal Commission into Institutional Responses to Child Sexual Abuse" *Archival Science* 20, 2020, 9.
145 Ibid., 2.
146 S. Swain, "Stakeholders as Subjects. The Role of Historians in the Development of Australia's Find & Connect Web Resource" *The Public Historian* 36(4), 2014, 38–50, 40.
147 Ibid., 39.
148 Ibid., 41.
149 Ibid.
150 Senate Community Affairs Committee, *Forgotten Australians: A Report on Australians Who Experienced Institutional or Out-of-Home Care as Children* (Canberra: Commonwealth of Australia, 2004), Chapter 9.
151 Golding 2020 op. cit.
152 Royal Commission into Institutional Responses to Child Sexual Abuse, *Final Report Volume 8. Record Keeping and Information Sharing* (Commonwealth of Australia, 2017), 11.

153 Golding 2020 op. cit., 7.

154 Howard promoted 'practical reconciliation' to explicitly counter 'the particular kinds of symbolism articulated by Indigenous people when they derived their entitlements to land or to government services from prior ownership, historical dispossession or Indigeneity': M. Phillips in A. Pratt, *Practising Reconciliation. The Politics of Reconciliation in the Australian Parliament 1991–2000* (Canberra: Parliamentary Library, 2003), 135. www.aph.gov.au/binaries/library/pubs/monographs/pratt/practisingreconciliation.pdf.

155 K. Daly, *Redressing Institutional Abuse of Children* (United Kingdom: Palgrave and Macmillan, 2014), 150.

156 A. Durbach, "'The Cost of a Wounded Society:' Reparations and the Illusion of Reconciliation" *University of New South Wales Faculty of Law Research Series 4. 2008*. (2008), www.austlii.edu.au/au/journals/UNSWLRS/2008/4.html.

157 Daly op. cit., 152.

158 Senate, *Inquiry into the Implementation of the Recommendations of the Lost Innocents and Forgotten Australians Reports* (Australia: Parliament of Australia), Chapter 3.

159 In NSW the Department of Family and Community Services (FACS) subcontracts the privately-run services Aftercare Resources Centre and Wattle Place to provide counselling for adults who have experienced care. FACS also provided limited funding to CLAN to continue its advocacy and provide support to care leavers.

160 Clare in Ibid.

161 Golding in Ibid.

162 Royal Commission into Institutional Responses to Child Sexual Abuse, *Final Report Volume 9. Advocacy, Support and Therapeutic Treatment Services* (Commonwealth of Australia, 2017), 10.

163 Ibid., 9.

164 Ibid., 11.

165 Including mental health services, alcohol and other drugs services, community health services, general practitioners (GPs) and private practitioners such as psychologists.

166 Ibid, 30.

167 Such as child and adult sexual assault services.

168 Ibid., 10.

169 National Redress Scheme for Institutional Child Sexual Abuse Assessment Framework 2018.

170 P. White, "The Role of Monetary Redress in Shaping Perceptions of Child Abuse and Neglect," paper presented to the *Society for the History of Children and Youth Conference,* Australian Catholic University, 28–30, June 2019.

171 K. Daly, "Redress for Historical Institutional Abuse of Children" in A. Deckert and R. Sarre (eds), *The Palgrave Handbook of Australian and New Zealand Criminology, Crime and Justice* (London: Palgrave MacMillan, 2017), 449–66.

172 G. Ryall, "*Williams v Commonwealth* – A Turning Point for Parliamentary Accountability and Federalism in Australia?" Papers on Parliament No. 60 March 2014, www.aph.gov.au/sitecore/content/Home/About_Parliament/Senate/Powers_practice_n_procedures/pops/pop60/c07.

173 *National Redress Scheme for Institutional Child Sexual Abuse (Consequential Amendments) Act 2018*.

174 At 30 June 2020 the following had not committed to the NRS: Boys' Brigade NSW, Fairbridge Restored Limited, Lakes Entrance Pony Club, Jehovah's Witnesses and Kenja Communications.

175 National Redress Scheme for Institutional Child Sexual Abuse Assessment Framework 2018.

176 *ABC News*, 20 August 2020.

177 Daly and Davis op. cit., 1287.

178 In P. White, op. cit. See Joint Select Committee on oversight of the implementation of redress related recommendations of the Royal Commission into Institutional Responses to Child Sexual Abuse, Getting the National Redress Scheme Right: An Overdue Step Towards Justice (Commonwealth of Australia, 2019), www.aph.gov.au/Parliamentary_Business/Committees/Joint/Royal_Commission_into_Institutional_Responses_to_Child_Sexual_Abuse/RoyalCommissionChildAbuse/Report.

179 "Ministers Redress Scheme Governance Board Communique," Department of Social Services, Last updated 10 July 2020, www.dss.gov.au/about-the-department/news/62056.

180 Gordon Brown: Prosecution of Alan Turing (2009); David Cameron: Amritsar Massacre and Unnecessary Deaths at Staffordshire Hospital (2013) Hillsborough Disaster (2012), Bloody Sunday (2010).

181 *The Guardian,* 7 December 2004.

182 HC, Hansard, 24 February 2010, vol.506, col.301.

183 IICSA, *Child Migration Programmes Investigation Report* (London, IICSA, 2018), vii–viii.

184 See IICSA, *Interim Report of the Independent Inquiry into Child Sexual Abuse* (London: IICSA, 2018), www.iicsa.org.uk/publications/inquiry/interim and IICSA, *Child Migration Programmes* op. cit., www.iicsa.org.uk/key-documents/4265/view/child-migration-programmes-investigation-report-march-2018.pdf.

185 However, problematically, those accompanied by an adult family member or guardian were not eligible.

186 "Payment Scheme for Former British Child Migrants," Gov.UK, Last modified: 26 February 2019, www.gov.uk/government/news/payment-scheme-for-former-british-child-migrants.

187 Former British Child Migrants: Payment Scheme Hansard vol. 655 col. 107WH Tuesday, 26 February 2019.

188 See N. Sugarman, "The Criminal Injuries Compensation Scheme 2012 and Its Impact on Victims of Crime" *Journal of Personal Injury Law* 2016, 231; D. Miers, "Compensating Deserving Victims of Violent Crime: The Criminal Injuries Compensation Scheme" *Legal Studies* 34, 2014, 242–78; IICSA, Interim Report, December 2018, Recommendations 5,6,7. Similar schemes are also operative in Ireland and in Australia.

189 See Ministry of Justice, *The Criminal Injuries Compensation Scheme 2012* (London: HMSO, 2012), [25–27].

190 31 July 2015.

191 "Farleys Secure Damages of Over £220,000 for Victim of Abuse," Farleys Solicitors LLP, Last modified: 21 May, 2019, www.farleys.com/farleys-secure-damages-of-over-220000-for-victim-of-abuse/.

192 [2018] EWCA Civ 1735.

193 Ministry of Justice, *Criminal Injuries Compensation Scheme Review 2020* (London: Ministry of Justice, 2020), https://assets.publishing.service.gov.uk/government/uploads/system/uploads/attachment_data/file/901140/cics-review-2020.pdf.

194 Interim Report, December 2018, Recommendations 5,6,7. It also recommended changes to awards thresholds.

195 All-Party Parliamentary Group for Adult Survivors of Childhood Sexual Abuse, *Can Adult Survivors of Childhood Sexual Abuse Access Justice and Support? Part Three* (London: HMSO, 2019), 6, https://static1.squarespace.com/static/5c8faf788d97401af928638c/t/5daf7856b44b5003d766ee7c/1571780697125/EMBARGOED+until+Wed+23+Oct+-+Adult+Survivors+of+CSA.pdf.

196 Ibid., [28.2].

197 The Victims' Commissioner, *Compensation without Re-traumatisation: The Victims' Commissioner's Review into Criminal Injuries Compensation* (United Kingdom: Victims' Commissioner, 2019), https://victimscommissioner.org.uk/published-reviews/compensation-without-re-traumatisation-the-victims-commissioners-review-into-criminal-injuries-compensation/.

198 All-Party Parliamentary Group for Adult Survivors of Childhood Sexual Abuse, op. cit., 6.

199 Ibid., 30.

200 www.gov.uk/guidance/criminal-injuries-compensation-a-guide.

201 Ibid., 92.

202 IICSA, *Victims and Survivors Forum Consultation on Access Records: Summary* (London: IICSA, 2020).

203 Ibid., 4.

204 See the MIRRA Project based at UCL: https://blogs.ucl.ac.uk/mirra/.

205 See P. Williams, "Care Leavers Rights to Records. MIRRA Project," UCL, Last modified: 22 February 2021, https://medium.com/policy-postings/care-leavers-access-to-childhood-records-leveraging-grassroots-initiatives-to-impact-national-5c83957bc67b.

206 V. Hoyle, et al., "Recordkeeping and the Life-Long Memory and Identity Needs of Care-Experienced Children and Young People" *Child and Family Social Work* 25(4), 2020, 935–45.

207 BASW England, Recording in Children's Social Work (BASW, 2020), www.basw.co.uk/system/files/resources/basw_recording_in_childrens_social_work_aug_2020.pdf.

References

All-Party Parliamentary Group for Adult Survivors of Childhood Sexual Abuse, *Can Adult Survivors of Childhood Sexual Abuse Access Justice and Support? Part Three* (London: HMSO, 2019), https://static1.squarespace.com/static/5c8faf788d97401af928638c/t/5daf7856b44b5003d766.

Anonymous, *Caranua Evaluation Report* (Dublin, Caranua, 2021), https://caranua.ie/wp-content/uploads/2021/03/Caranua-Evaluation-Report-Executive-Summary.pdf.

Barrett A., et al., "Childhood Sexual Abuse and Later-life Economic Consequences" *Journal of Behavioural and Experimental Economics* 53, 2014, 10–16.

BASW England, *Recording in Children's Social Work* (BASW, 2020), www.basw.co.uk/system/files/resources/basw_recording_in_childrens_social_work_aug_2020.pdf.

Brennan, C., "Facing What Cannot Be Changed: The Irish Experience of Confronting Institutional Child Abuse" *Journal of Social Welfare and Family Law* 29, 2007, 245–63.

Bruton, R,. "Residential Institutions Statutory Fund: Motion (Resumed) [Private Members]," *Dáil Éireann Debates*, 24 May 2017, www.oireachtas.ie/en/debates/debate/dail/2017-05-24/29/.

Buckley, C., Letter to the Editor, *Irish Independent*, 7 April 2008.

Catterall, E., *Apologies and Institutional Abuse* (Belfast: Queen's University Belfast, 2018).

Celermejer, D., *The Sins of the Nation and the Ritual of Apologies* (Cambridge: Cambridge University Press, 2009).

Celermejer, D., "Apology and the Possibility of the Ethical Nation" in D. Cuypers, et al. (eds), *Public Apology between Ritual and Regret: Symbolic Excuses on False Pretenses or True Reconciliation out of Sincere Regret* (Brill Publishing, 2013).

Celermejer, D., '"Problems with Records and Recordkeeping Practices Are Not Confined to the Past:' A Challenge from the Royal Commission into Institutional Responses to Child Sexual Abuse" *Archival Science* 20, 2020, 9.

Chynoweth, A., "Forgotten or Ignored Australians? The Case for an Inclusive Museum" in P. Ashton and J. Z. Wilson (eds), *Silent System. Forgotten Australians and the Institutionalisation of Women and Children* (North Melbourne: Australian Scholarly Press, 2014), 172.

Coleman, K., *Haunting Cries, Stories of Child Abuse from Industrial Schools* (Dublin: Gill and MacMillan, 2010), 237.

Compensation Advisory Committee, *Report to The Minister for Education and Science* (2002), www.rirb.ie/documents/cac_report2002.pdf.

Comptroller and Auditor General, *Annual Report, 2002* (Dublin: Government of Ireland, 2003).

Comptroller and Auditor General. *Special Report on Costs of Child Abuse Inquiry and Redress* (Dublin: Government of Ireland, 2017).

Crean, A.M., *Submission to the Joint Oireachtas Committee,* 26 November 2019, http://jfmresearch.com/retention-of-records-bill-2019/.

Crowe, C., "Guilt Shame, Acknowledgement, and Redress: A Personal Reflection on Ireland's Institutional Treatment of Women and Children" in M. Corcoran and P. Cullen (eds), *Producing Knowledge, Reproducing Gender* (Dublin: UCD Press, 2020), 235.

Daly, K., *Redressing Institutional Abuse of Children* (United Kingdom: Palgrave and Macmillan, 2014).

Daly, K., "Money for Justice? Money's Meaning and Purpose as Redress for Historical Institutional Abuse" in Y. Smaal, et al. (eds) *The Sexual Abuse of Children: Recognition and Redress* (Melbourne: Monash University Publishing, 2016), 160.

Daly, K., "Redress for Historical Institutional Abuse of Children" in A. Deckert and R. Sarre (eds) *The Palgrave Handbook of Australian and New Zealand Criminology, Crime and* Justice (London: Palgrave MacMillan, 2017), 449–66.

Daly K. and Davis, J., "Unravelling Redress for Institutional Abuse of Children in Australia" *University of New South Wales Law Journal* 42(4), 2019, 1254–93.

de Greiff, P. "Justice and Reparations" in P. de Greiff (ed), *The Handbook of Reparations. International Center for Transitional Justice* (Oxford: Oxford University Press, 2006), 451.

Department of Children and Youth Affairs, Ryan Report Implementation Plan: Second Progress Report (2001), 11. www.dcya.gov.ie/documents/20180831RyanRepImplPlanSecProgRep.pdf.

Department of Health and Children, *Report on the Inquiry into the Operation of Madonna House* (Dublin: Stationery Office, 1996).

Dow, C., *Sorry. The Unfinished Business of the Bringing Them Home Report* (Australia: Parliamentary Library, 4 February 2008), www.aph.gov.au/About_Parliament/Parliamentary_Departments/Parliamentary_Library/pubs/BN/0708/BringingThemHomeReport.

Durbach, A., '"The Cost of a Wounded Society:' Reparations and the Illusion and Reconciliation" *University of New South Wales Faculty of Law Research Series 4.* (2008), www.austlii.edu.au/au/journals/UNSWLRS/2008/4.html.

Enright, M. and Ring, S., "State Responses to Historical institutional Abuse: Shame, Sovereignty and Epistemic Injustice" ire-Ireland 55(1, 2), 2020, 68–99.

Gibeny, M. et al. (eds), *The Age of Apology: Facing up to the Past* (Philadelphia: University of Pennsylvania Press, 2009).

Golding, F., "Sexual Abuse as the Core Transgression of Childhood Innocence: Unintended Consequences for Care Leavers" *Journal of Australian Studies* 42(2), 2018, 191.

Golding, F., "'Problems with Records and Recordkeeping Practices Are Not Confined to the Past:' A Challenge from the Royal Commission into Institutional Responses to Child Sexual Abuse" *Archival Science* 20, 2020, 9.

Hamber, B. and Wilson, R., "Symbolic Closure through Memory, Reparation and Revenge in Post-Conflict Societies" *Journal of Human Rights* 1, 2002, 35–53.

Hoyle, V., et al., "Recordkeeping and the Life-Long Memory and Identity Needs of Care-Experienced Children and Young People" *Child and Family Social Work* 25(4), 2020, 935–45.

Human Rights and Equal Opportunity Commission, *Bringing them Home: Report of the National Inquiry into the Separation of Aboriginal and Torres Strait Islander Children from their Families* (Sydney: HREOC, 1997).

IICSA, *Child Migration Programmes Investigation Report* (London: IICSA, 2018).

IICSA, *Interim Report of the Independent Inquiry into Child Sexual Abuse* (London: IICSA, 2018).

IICSA, *Victims and Survivors Forum Consultation on Access Records: Summary* (London: IICSA, 2020).

James, M., et al., "Impermanent Apologies: on the Dynamics of Timing and Public Knowledge in Political Apology" *Human Rights Review* 19(1), 2018 1–23.

Joint Select Committee on oversight of the implementation of redress related recommendations of the Royal Commission into Institutional Responses to Child Sexual Abuse, Getting the National Redress Scheme Right: An Overdue Step Towards Justice (Canberra: Commonwealth of Australia, 2019).

Kehoe, H., "The Irish State's Responses to Its Gendered and Historical Human Rights Violations" *Irish Law Times* 1, 2018, 15.

Law Commission of Canada, *Restoring Dignity: Responding to Child Abuse in Canadian Institutions: Executive Summary* (Ottawa: Law Commission of Canada, 2000).

Lodato, M., Submission to the Oireachtas Joint Committee on Education and Skills, 26 November 2019, http://jfmresearch.com/wp-content/uploads/2019/10/Mary-Lodato-Submission.pdf.

Logue, F., "Submission on the Retention of Records Bill to the Joint Committee on Education and Skills," http://jfmresearch.com/wp-content/uploads/2019/10/Fred-Logue-Submission.pdf.

Lundy P. and Rolston, B., "Redress for Past Harms? Official Apologies in Northern Ireland" *International Journal of Human Rights* 20(1), 2016, 104–22.

Lundy, P., "I Just Want Justice Assessing the Impact of Historical Institutional Child Abuse Inquiries from the Perspective of Survivors" *Éire-Ireland* 55(1&2), 2020, 252–78.

Manne, R., "In Denial: The Stolen Generations and the Right" *The Australian Quarterly Essay* 2001, 75.

McAlinden, A.-M, "Apologies as 'Shame Management': The Politics of Remorse in the Aftermath of Historical Institutional Abuse" *Legal Studies* 2021. doi:10.1017/lst.2021.

McGarry, P., "Order Denied Abuse Five Days Before Report," *The Irish Times,* 3 June 2009.

Miers, D., "Compensating Deserving Victims of Violent Crime: The Criminal Injuries Compensation Scheme" *Legal Studies* 34, 2014, 242–78.

Ministry of Justice, *The Criminal Injuries Compensation Scheme 2012* (London: HMSO, 2012).

Ministry of Justice, *Criminal Injuries Compensation Scheme Review 2020* (London: Ministry of Justice, 2020), https://assets.publishing.service.gov.uk/government/uploads/system/uploads/attachment_data/file/901140/cics-review-2020.pdf.

Minow, M., *Between Vengeance and Forgiveness: Facing History After Genocide and Mass Violence* (Boston: Beacon Press, 2000).

Moore, J, et al., "On the Road to Resilience: The Help-Seeking Experiences of Irish Emigrant Survivors of Institutional Abuse" *Child Abuse Review* 26, 2015, 375–87.

Morrison, S., *National Apology to Victims and Survivors of Institutional Child Sexual Abuse,* 22 October 2018, www.pm.gov.au/media/national-apology-victims-and-survivors-institutional-child-sexual-abuse.

Olick, J.K., *The Politics of Regret. On Collective Memory and Historical Responsibility* (London: Routledge 2007).

O'Mahony, C., *Special Rapporteur on Child Protection. Annual Report* 26, 2020.

O'Rourke, M., et al., *Submission to the Oireachtas Joint Committee on Education and Skills on the provisions of the Retention of Records Bill 2019*, 13 November 2019, http://jfmresearch.com/retention-of-records-bill-2019/.

Peelo, M., "*Redress: Breaking the Silence*" (Dublin: RTÉ Television, 2020).

Pembroke, S., "Historical Institutional Abuse in Ireland: Survivor Perspectives on Taking Part in the Commission to Inquire into Child Abuse (CICA) and the Redress Scheme" *Contemporary justice Review* 22(1), 2019, 43–59.

Phillips, M. in A. Pratt, *Practising Reconciliation. The Politics of Reconciliation in the Australian Parliament 1991-2000* (Canberra: Parliamentary Library, 2003), 135. www.aph.gov.au/binaries/library/pubs/monographs/pratt/practisingreconciliation.pdf.

Raftery, M., "Cheating Abuse Victims," *The Irish Times*, 26 April 2007.

Reclaiming Self. *Ryan Report Follow-Up. Submission to the United Nations Committee against Torture Session 61* (Reclaiming Self, 2017), 26, https://tbinternet.ohchr.org/Treaties/CAT/Shared%20Documents/IRL/INT_CAT_CSS_IRL_27959_E.pdf.

Residential Institutions Redress Board, *A Guide to the Redress Scheme under the Residential Institutions, 3rd ed.* (Dublin: The Residential Institutions Redress Board, 2005).

Residential Institutions Redress Board, *Annual Report 2012* (Dublin: Stationery Office, 2013).

Royal Commission into Institutional Responses to Child Sexual Abuse, *Redress and Civil Litigation Report* (Canberra: Commonwealth of Australia, 2015).

Royal Commission into Institutional Responses to Child Sexual Abuse, *Final Report Volume 8. Record Keeping and Information Sharing* (Canberra: Commonwealth of Australia, 2017).

Royal Commission into Institutional Responses to Child Sexual Abuse, *Final Report Volume 9. Advocacy, Support and Therapeutic Treatment Services* (Canberra: Commonwealth of Australia, 2017).

Rudd, K., *Apology to Australia's Indigenous Peoples*, 13 February 2008, www.aph.gov.au/Visit_Parliament/Whats_On/Exhibitions/Custom_Media/Apology_to_Australias_Indigenous_Peoples.

Rudd, K., *National Apology to the Forgotten Australians and Former Child Migrants*, 16 November 2009, http://parlview.aph.gov.au/mediaPlayer.php?videoID=314492&operation_mode=parlview#/3

Ryall, G., "*Williams v Commonwealth* – A Turning Point for Parliamentary Accountability and Federalism in Australia?" Papers on Parliament No. 60 March 2014, www.aph.gov.au/sitecore/content/Home/About_Parliament/Senate/Powers_practice_n_procedures/pops/pop60/c07.

Save the Children, *Global Accountability and Investigations Report* (London: Save the Children International, 2018).

Senate, *Inquiry into the Implementation of the Recommendations of the Lost Innocents and Forgotten Australians Reports* (Australia: Parliament of Australia).

Senate Community Affairs Committee, *Forgotten Australians: A Report on Australians Who Experienced Institutional or Out-of-Home Care as Children* (Canberra: Commonwealth of Australia, 2004), Chapter 9.

Sköld J. and Swain, S., "Introduction" in J. Sköld and S. Swain (eds), *Apologies and the Legacy of Abuse of Children in 'Care* (Palgrave MacMillan, 2015), 1.

Smith, J. M. "Knowing and Unknowing Tuam: State Practice, The Archive, and Transitional Justice" *Eire-Ireland* 55(12), 2020, 142–80.

Steele, L., et al, "Parramatta Female Factory Precinct as a Site of Conscience: Using Institutional Pasts to Shape Just Legal Futures" *University of New South Wales Law Journal* 43(2), 2020, 521–51.

Sugarman, N., "The Criminal Injuries Compensation Scheme 2012 and Its Impact on Victims of Crime" *Journal of Personal Injury Law* 2016, 231.

Swain, S., "Stakeholders as Subjects. The Role of Historians in the Development of Australia's Find & Connect Web Resource" *The Public Historian* 36(4), 2014, 38–50, 40.

Taft, L., "Apology Subverted: The Commodification of Apology" *Yale Law Journal* 109(5), 2000, 1135–60.

The Commission of Inquiry into the Reformatory and Industrial School System 1934–1936, *Report* (Dublin: Stationery Office, 1936).

The Commission of Inquiry into the Reformatory and Industrial School System (1970) *Report of the Commission of Inquiry into the Reformatory and Industrial School System* (Dublin: Stationery Office, 1970).

The Victims' Commissioner, *Compensation without Re-traumatisation: The Victims' Commissioner's Review into Criminal Injuries Compensation* (United Kingdom: Victims' Commissioner, 2019), https://victimscommissioner.org.uk/published-reviews/compensation-without-re-traumatisation-the-victims-commissioners-review-into-criminal-injuries-compensation/.

Walshe, B. and O'Connell, C., *Consultations with Survivors of Institutional Abuse on Themes and Issues to be addressed by a Survivor Led Consultation Group* (Department of Education and Skills, 2019), www.education.ie/en/Publications/Education-Reports/consultations-with-survivors-of-institutional-abuse-on-themes-and-issues-to-be-addressed-by-a-survivor-led-consultation-group.pdf.

White, P., "The Role of Monetary Redress in Shaping Perceptions of Child Abuse and Neglect," paper presented to the *Society for the History of Children and Youth Conference,* Australian Catholic University, 28–30, June 2019.

Williams, P., "Care Leavers Rights to Records. MIRRA Project," UCL, Last modified: 22 February 2021, https://medium.com/policy-postings/care-leavers-access-to-childhood-records-leveraging-grassroots-initiatives-to-impact-national-5c83957bc67b.

Winter, S., "Australia's Ex Gratia Redress" *Australian Indigenous Law Review* 13(1), 49–61.

12 Conclusion

Introduction

The efforts of countless adult survivors in speaking out about their sexual abuse in childhood represents a significant breaking of the silence in each country around what had long been a stigmatized form of victimhood. By seeking legal responses adult survivors of non-recent child sexual abuse (NRCSA) have highlighted the inadequacies of established legal norms and doctrines in delivering justice. In this book we have examined the legal responses to NRCSA in England and Wales, Ireland and Australia: criminal trials; civil litigation against individuals and organizations; public inquiries and state reparations. The reforms introduced to each form of legal response have been groundbreaking but it is clear that no one country has delivered full accountability and recognition to NRCSA survivors. Rather, as we have highlighted in the conclusion to each chapter, there are ways in which each country should learn from the others in respect of improving each of its legal responses. In this conclusion we take a step back and argue that ambivalence characterizes the legal responses in each domain in each country. By ambivalence we mean the simultaneous conflicting attitudes to NRCSA survivors' justice needs evident in each country's set of legal responses. We argue that the legal responses to NRCSA reflect the important efforts of courts, parliaments and governments in recognizing survivors' suffering and holding abusers accountable, but that they also betray a persistent reluctance to fully confront the complexities of NRCSA cases and to reckon with survivors' rights to effective and meaningful legal responses. Before turning to this issue of ambivalence, we offer some observations on how the effects of the passage of time impact on the quality of justice possible for NRCSA survivors.

Law, justice and NRCSA

First, in NRCSA cases the law is approaching the past through the present. To some extent, the law, the court, the jury and, by extension, society are

DOI: 10.4324/9780429468162-14

all engaging in a form of time travel, imposing procedural and evidentiary standards on events that, if they had been tried contemporaneously, would have been treated very differently. Criminal prohibitions on indecent assault, rape and buggery, the civil tort of trespass to the person, the statutory duties of inspection and care used to evaluate the conduct of institutions or government agencies in public inquiries, and state reparation measures, were all part of the legal order at the time children were abused. However, in the past these laws were not respected by individual abusers or institutions, nor were they enforced by the state. Through evidentiary and procedural reforms to facilitate the trial of NRCSA claims in civil and criminal courts, and by allowing survivors' testimony to ground determinations of public inquiries and reparations, the legal responses created are contemporary responses that have been constituted in light of each country's reckoning with NRCSA. In each of the legal responses, then, we are judging the past using the tools of the present. Older laws have finally become effective, illustrating each society's attempts to redeem itself for its dismissal of child victims of sexual abuse in the past.

A second observation flowing from the passage of time is the fact that NRCSA survivors who seek justice are doing so *as adults*. When and if the law responds it is not answering to the child they once were, but to the adult they have become. While this may seem like a simplistic observation, it points to something important. In response to NRCSA the law is engaging with adults who necessarily possess greater agency and individual resources to act than a child. While the legal responses explored in this book may involve partial recognition of the survivor's suffering as a child, this is filtered through the incontrovertible reality that the person presenting before the judge or jury or public inquiry is an adult. The adult survivor has been forced to act as an advocate for their child self because no adult performed this role at the time. Therefore, the full experience of the child, their embodied vulnerability, powerlessness, dependence on others and the full impact of the abuse on them *as a child* is never, can never, be fully recognized by the law in the context of NRCSA. Relatedly, any legal response offered in the present is also far too late to adequately recognize the survivor's suffering during those years when they carried the burden of the abuse alone.

Third, the belated accountability offered by law is limited by the fact that the abuser has most likely lived for decades without the stress and stigma of a criminal prosecution or the worry of having to defend a civil action or pay damages to the survivor. Similarly, those (few) organizations and state agencies and regulatory actors, who have been targeted by legal responses in recent years, have escaped public scrutiny for decades and have benefitted from not having been required to pay damages or redress. No contemporary legal response can make abusers, abusive organizations and state agencies accountable for those years when the law itself did not hold them accountable.

Finally, the interval of time and the fact that the survivor is an adult may make NRCSA easier for courts and parliaments to address than contemporary CSA and children as victims. For governments and societies too, it is perhaps less challenging to recognize, judge and attempt to overcome the past than to see the continuities between the past and the present and the continued risk to children including failures in child protection. It is more comfortable to judge grave wrongdoing at the remove of decades than to reckon with the reality of contemporary abuse. It is essential that lawyers, survivors and policymakers remain attentive to the limits of any legal responses to NRCSA, and not confuse action on it with action on CSA.

Accountability, recognition and ambivalence

In her influential 1989 social and cultural history of how adult-child sexual contact came to be understood as harmful,[1] sociologist Carol Smart identified a discursive struggle in England between campaigners and the legal profession/criminal justice system over the seriousness and significance of CSA in the period 1910–1960. At stake in this contest was the question of whether the children had suffered real harm. Smart argued that at this time there was an ambivalence in legal and medical discourses about both the nature and harms of CSA and the nature of victimhood. She identified various sites of ambivalence, but here we focus on one: the idea, evident in the 1920s and 1930s, that children could be victims of the crime of incest (which was recognized by the legal and medical professions as having extremely damaging impacts) but their testimony was often not believed by the criminal justice system to be reliable, precisely because of the effects of the presumed loss of innocence, a result of the abuse. This dual conception of sexually abused children as victims but also as inherently suspicious and not credible witnesses, contributed to a great inertia affecting CSA law and policy and a fundamental ambivalence on the part of the state that continued throughout the later part of the twentieth century and into the twenty-first century.[2]

At the root of this ambivalence is law's (and by extension, society's) historical distrust of sexual abuse survivors, and its failure to fully reckon with the true prevalence and harms of sexual offending of all kinds, but especially against children. We argue that in legal responses to NRCSA a second form of ambivalence is apparent. Although responses to NRCSA may be understood as courts/parliaments/governments recognizing the suffering of survivors, and holding abusers accountable, there persists a reluctance to fully address the realities of NRCSA cases and to reckon with survivors' rights to effective and meaningful legal responses. We have argued that any legal response to NRCSA must deliver both accountability and recognition to survivors. Accountability entails publicly holding the abuser, the abusive organization or the state (if implicated) to account for wrongdoing and ensuring consequences follow. Recognition entails the survivor's status as a person with enforceable legal rights (citizenship) and as a member of the broader community (belonging) who deserves to have their experience and knowledge of injustice believed and acted on. While each legal response in each country has delivered some forms of limited accountability and recognition, it is also apparent that each country has struggled to fully deliver these aspects of justice to NRCSA survivors. Just as the criminal process's treatment of child victims of sexual abuse in 1920s England was characterized by ambivalence around the legitimacy of their status as victims meriting effective legal responses, in the legal responses to NRCSA examined here, the law betrays unstable and contradictory attitudes to delivering justice to survivors.

Criminal prosecutions and trials can deliver the important form of accountability of the conviction of individual abusers. By providing their testimonies in very gruelling, often re-traumatizing circumstances, survivors have forced lawyers and judges to confront the legal and evidential challenges of NRCSA. Courts have overhauled long-established approaches to survivors' 'delays' in seeking criminal justice, refashioning traditional notions of fairness to defendants and liberalizing admissibility rules governing evidence of multiple complainants. These changes signify, at last, a willingness to reimagine embedded norms of criminal procedure and evidence law to address the unique challenges of NRCSA cases.

In the civil law context litigation has provided some survivors with greater autonomy in bringing proceedings to hold individual abusers to account through the award of damages with a legal statement on liability and the wrong committed. In England and Wales courts have re-interpreted statutes of limitation to allow survivors to sue despite being many years too late according to established norms. In Ireland parliament has created an exception to the normal time limit for NRCSA cases. In Australia state and territory parliaments have in recent years, recognized the injustice of statutes of limitation and abolished them for all CSA and NRCSA cases. Courts have been confronted with legal and moral arguments about the need to hold to account organizations that protected abusers or which did not act to protect children from abusers. Civil litigation against organizations has been instrumental in recognizing the culpability of some institutions such as religious schools.

Entirely new procedures and methodologies for judging the past have been created. Through their incorporation of individual testimonies, public inquiries have been central to national acknowledgements of survivors as full rights-bearing citizens deserving of recognition and respect, and national reckonings with each country's abusive histories. The early work of the Irish Commission to Inquire into Child Abuse contributed to embedding these understandings of survivors' citizenship as a form of international common sense through its radical emphasis on testimony, memory and voice, a common sense that is evident in the work of the Australian Royal Commission into Institutional Responses to Child Sexual Abuse and the Truth Project of the Independent Inquiry into Child Sexual Abuse. In turn, survivor testimony to these inquiries in confidential truth-telling fora, in public hearings and in investigations, has destroyed the old myth that CSA is a problem of deviant individuals, and exposed it as endemic to institutional settings.[3]

State efforts to repair fractured relationships with survivors of institutional abuse through symbolic and material reparations have developed in different ways in each country. In Ireland and Australia financial redress has been an important recognition of (some) survivors' suffering and the state's role in that suffering. In England and Wales survivors of sexual abuse (other than child migrants) must instead bring themselves within the inadequate criminal injuries compensation framework, pending the IICSA's final report. We have argued that each of these developments identified in each form of legal response is important not only because of the justice they may deliver but because each signifies the NRCSA survivors (finally) as full subjects of the law deserving of accountability and recognition.

However, in this book we have also identified important gaps in the legal responses to NRCSA. Criminal prosecutions continue to be hampered in each country by confusion about how a judge should decide on the cross-admissibility of evidence of multiple complainants and how they should direct a jury on the issues of delay and corroboration. Survivors contemplating civil litigation against individuals and organizations must reckon with considerable financial costs. Survivors in Ireland and England and Wales must also overcome complex jurisprudence regarding statutes of limitation. In each country inadequate common law doctrines of primary and secondary liability in tort law have largely stymied efforts to effectively hold many organizations and government agencies to account for their roles in institutional child abuse.

A further failure of recognition and accountability is apparent in each country's public inquiry. Although, in principle, all three inquiries could have examined the institutions of the family and foster and kinship care, for the most part they did not.[4] Recent research suggests that familial abuse may be the most common form of abuse, the hardest to uncover, and the most damaging to victims.[5] Throughout the history of the state's engagement with the problem of CSA, from the time of the so-called 'white slavery' scandals of the 1880s, to international focus on 'organized paedophile networks' in the 1980s, the family has been protected from scrutiny.[6] In the twenty-first century, the shocking nature of high-profile scandals involving prominent men associated with religious/state/cultural elites in each country, who were generally portrayed as prolific offenders, allowed this protection to continue largely unchallenged. As public inquiries are the most important legal mechanism in terms of collective knowledge-making about NRCSA (and CSA), this neglect of families including foster care represents a significant gap in terms of recognition and accountability and learning and suggests that the historical reluctance to understand and address this form of offending endures into the present.

Each country has yet to fully engage with its responsibility to deliver reparations for the harms of institutional NRCSA to survivors and their families. For the most part the role of reparations has been concerned with the political priority of being seen to 'overcome' a 'dark past' which needs to be relegated to history, rather than recognizing that survivors' rights were infringed on in ways that have implications for their present lives and that they are entitled to ongoing measures of support and redress from the state. In Australia and England and Wales reparations have been shaped in part by a desire to transcend their entwined colonial histories, as Imperial child migration formed a fundamental catalyst to the movements for justice and redress in each. In Ireland reparations have been concerned with a desire to limit the state and Catholic religious orders' exposure to civil liability. In each country a political drive to overcome the past has resulted in reparations aimed at moving forward without adequately engaging with survivors' ongoing material and other needs.

In short, although each legal response in each country promises accountability and recognition for NRCSA survivors, each remains characterized by a fundamental ambivalence towards survivors. As we have shown, the problems with the legal responses do not lie in the features of NRCSA cases themselves (such as the delayed reporting or the elderly nature of the defendant, for example), but rather in a failure to fully adopt responses that reflect the complex legal and social realities of NRCSA. Criminal trial judges could be given better, more consistent guidance. Barriers to litigation in civil cases could be addressed through statute. Abuse in families could form the focus of political attentions. Reparations could be framed and delivered in survivor-centred ways that avoid excessive adversarialism.

It is difficult to discern exact reasons for this ambivalence which runs consistently through the three countries examined here. Perhaps part of the answer is the common law's reliance on precedent, which is not suited to the comprehensive legal reform needed in this context. Certainly, Australia shows how, in the wake of the Royal Commission, state legislatures have acted to address some key issues by abolishing statutes of limitation and introducing changes to allow unincorporated associations to be sued. In Ireland by comparison, while there has been some important reform of statutes of limitation, with greater political will, the issues around civil litigation in NRCSA cases could be revisited by parliamentarians in light of the past two decades of case law. In England and Wales the continued inertia in respect of law reform in NRCSA cases is perhaps attributable to the political focus on the establishment of the IICSA and the shocking nature of the revelations involving the political classes during the 'discovery' phase. Ultimately, in each country the failure to fully address the challenges of NRCSA cases is indicative of remaining traces of the law's historical suspicion of CSA victims and suspicion of delayed reporting, along with the inherent conservatism of law. The resonances with the ambivalence identified by Smart in relation to the criminal process's treatment of child victims of sexual abuse in the 1920s are clear. In no country are NRCSA survivors afforded access to the complete accountability and recognition that their experiences deserve.

We have suggested reforms in each domain to ensure a more coherent and comprehensive approach to legal responses to NRCSA in each country. These include better directions to criminal trial juries, abolishing civil statutes of limitations (in England and Wales and Ireland) and expanding organizational liability in each country. We have also argued that legislators, policymakers, lawyers and courts must more fully recognize the ongoing nature of the harms of NRCSA and its impacts on survivors today and their families. For institutional abuse survivors, this points to the legal institutions making effective survivors' right to discover the full history of their abuse through access to state and institutional records, as well as to health and wellbeing and supports in later life. For survivors of non-institutional sexual abuse, practical support in initiating criminal prosecutions and civil litigation (through legal aid) is essential to ensure access to justice.

Legal responses to NRCSA in England and Wales, Ireland and Australia have dissolved the temporal boundaries of justice. They have demonstrated law's capacity to adapt and respond to an unprecedented and complex contemporary social problem. As this book has shown, there are still significant gaps in the accountability and recognition offered to NRCSA survivors. It is imperative that courts and legislators work to ensure that these responses deliver recognition and accountability to survivors. This matters for NRCSA survivors in the present, but also for future NRCSA survivors. The lessons of trauma studies and the experiences of survivors tell us that for as long as CSA is allowed to persist in society, adult survivors will continue to seek legal responses. Learning the lessons of law's engagement with NRCSA is a first step towards ensuring they will receive the justice to which they are entitled.

Notes

1 C. Smart, "A History of Ambivalence and Conflict in the Discursive Construction of the 'Child Victim' of Sexual Abuse" *Social and Legal Studies* 8(3), 1999, 391–409.

2 See Chapters 3–5 and J. Kitzinger, "Defending Innocence: Ideologies of Childhood" *Feminist Review* 28, 1988, 77–87; A. Kosaraju, *Exploring Attrition in Cases Involving Crimes of Child Sexual Exploitation in England A Foucauldian Feminist Analysis*, unpublished PhD thesis (Canterbury: University of Kent, 2017).

3 Shurlee Swain also makes this point looking at Australian inquiries. S. Swain, *History of Australian Inquiries Reviewing Institutions Providing Care for Children* (Royal Commission into Institutional Responses to Child Sexual Abuse, 2014), 11.

4 The Royal Commission excluded foster care from its terms of reference but survivors who had been abused in foster care did testify in private sessions. The CICA Confidential Committee heard from 24 witnesses who reported being abused while in foster care. The decision not to investigate abuse in foster care contrasts with the approaches of comparable inquiries in Germany and Jersey: www.aufarbeitungskommission.de; www.jerseycareinquiry.org.

5 J. Benedet and I. Grant, "Breaking the Silence on Father-Daughter Sexual Abuse of Adolescent Girls: A Case Law Study" *Canadian Journal of Women and the Law* 32(2), 2020, 239–87.

6 K. Gleeson, "The 'Hero's Journey': Gender and the Politics of Justice for Child Sexual Abuse" in K. Gleeson and C. Lumby (eds), *The Age of Consent: Young People, Sexual Abuse and Agency* (Crawley: UWA Publishing, 2019), 31.

References

Benedet, J. and Grant, I., "Breaking the Silence on Father-Daughter Sexual Abuse of Adolescent Girls: A Case Law Study" *Canadian Journal of Women and the Law* 32(2), 2020, 239–87.

Gleeson, K., "The 'Hero's Journey': Gender and the Politics of Justice for Child Sexual Abuse" in K. Gleeson and C. Lumby (eds), *The Age of Consent: Young People, Sexual Abuse and Agency* (Crawley: UWA Publishing, 2019), 31.

Kitzinger, J., "Defending Innocence: Ideologies of Childhood" *Feminist Review* 28, 1988, 77–87.

Kosaraju, A., *Exploring Attrition in Cases involving Crimes of Child Sexual Exploitation in England A Foucauldian Feminist Analysis*, unpublished PhD thesis (Canterbury: University of Kent, 2017).

Smart, C., "A History of Ambivalence and Conflict in the Discursive Construction of the 'Child Victim' of Sexual Abuse" *Social and Legal Studies* 8(3), 1999, 392–409.

Swain, S., *History of Australian Inquiries Reviewing Institutions Providing Care for Children* (Royal Commission into Institutional Responses to Child Sexual Abuse, 2014).

Appendix

Terms used in this book

Non-recent child sexual abuse

In this book 'non-recent child sexual abuse' is used as an umbrella term for a range of offences involving the infliction of sexual violence on a child in the past.

Survivors have explained that while incidents of abuse may have occurred in the past, the effects of this abuse can be ongoing.[2] We also consider that 'historical' implies an unhelpful and misleading discursive separation of a dark past from the (more enlightened) present. We use the acronym NRCSA to make the text easier to read. The offences that are charged in these cases include indecent assault, gross indecency, rape, unlawful carnal knowledge, incest and buggery. These offences have different elements, and some require proof of absence of consent (such as rape) and in others only the act, the age of the victim, the identity of the accused as the perpetrator and the required culpable mental state must be proved.[1]

Child sexual abuse

Child sexual abuse (CSA) is one of four types of child maltreatment (the others being physical abuse, psychological abuse and neglect).[3] The World Health Organization defines CSA as:

> The involvement of a child or an adolescent in sexual activity that he or she does not fully comprehend and is unable to give informed consent to, or for which the child or adolescent is not developmentally prepared and cannot give consent, or that violates the laws or social taboos of society.[4]

It includes abuse by a family member or close relative and by adults or other children who are in a position or trust or responsibility or power over the victim. CSA can be (i) non-contact sexual abuse (threats, indecent exposure, exposing a child to pornography) or (ii) contact sexual abuse which may range from kissing to more serious forms of sexual touching and assault. Research suggests that around one in four women have experienced CSA.[5] Secrecy is at the heart of CSA offending; abusers will isolate children physically or emotionally and then engage in efforts (such as verbal or physical coercion, affection or support) to maintain secrecy.[6] CSA is predominantly perpetrated by men; prevalence studies estimate that between 3 per cent and 11 per cent of child sex offenders were women.[7]

The terms used by each country's legal and child welfare systems in relation to sexual offending against children have changed over the years. The term 'child sexual abuse' is a 1980s term, but much NRCSA occurred before then,[8] when different terminology was used, including terms such as incest, unlawful carnal knowledge and indecent assault. Other euphemisms were also regularly used in popular and legal discourse. Although for efficiency's sake we use the term child sexual abuse (CSA), we acknowledge that this was not a term used by practitioners or the public until at least the 1980s.

CSA is a major public health and justice problem that carries immediate and longer-term effects for victims. Experience of CSA is associated with an increased risk of adverse outcomes in all aspects of survivors' lives.[9] In many cases, these outcomes can endure over a survivor's lifetime[10] such as poorer physical health and mental health difficulties including lower self-esteem, difficulties with interpersonal relationships, self-harm and suicidal behaviours, as well as anxiety and depression, post-traumatic stress disorder (PTSD) and personality disorders.[11]

CSA can also have serious economic consequences in adulthood in terms of lower educational attainment, higher unemployment, financial instability and homelessness.[12] Survivors abused by religious figures may find that their entire belief systems and ways of understanding the world are shattered. Institutional responses that minimize or deny the CSA, or require victims and survivors to forgive the perpetrators of the abuse, can compound the original harm.[13] Survivors of institutional CSA may experience a loss of family identity due to fragmentation of relationships. Research suggests that victims and survivors of CSA may be vulnerable to subsequent revictimization and may be two to four times more likely to be revictimized compared with the likelihood of those who have not experienced CSA becoming victims for the first time. Health and behavioural effects of CSA have been found to increase victims' and survivors' vulnerability to revictimization.[14] CSA also impacts the lives of survivors' family members; in particular, the impacts on non-offending mothers can mirror those experienced by survivors.[15]

Surveys of adult survivors indicate that between 70 per cent and 90 per cent of perpetrators of sexual abuse are known to the child as acquaintances or family members.[16] Sexual abuse within a family context is associated with more severe contact abuse.[17] Even adjusting for the severity of the abuse, risk of PTSD for victims of familial sexual abuse are at least double that of similar acts of sexual violence perpetrated by non-family abusers.[18] This book explores whether legal responses to NRCSA have challenged embedded understandings of familial abuse and even abuse within religious organizations as private and outside the focus of public scrutiny.

Institutional abuse

The concept of 'institutional abuse' of children was originally alluded to by David Gil in the mid-1970s and was first addressed in the United States Senate Hearings on Abuse and Neglect of Children 1979. However, it was not until the 1980s that the term became more widely understood and acknowledged.[19] Although comprehensive data is lacking, figures from various studies in the twenty-first century indicate that 9.6 per cent of children have experienced sexual abuse in educational settings, 10 per cent in sporting contexts and 9.5 per cent in juvenile detention centres.[20] Cumulative studies over time suggest that 5 per cent of Catholic priests in the United States[21] and 7 per cent in Australia have sexually abused children.[22] The position of the offender within the institution can instil the necessary authority and trust that facilitates the abuse.[23] As this book shows, there are so many obstacles to disclosing abuse that all data needs to be read with great caution.

Non-recent institutional abuse is different to contemporary institutional abuse.[24] The former relates more to 'closed' or 'total' institutions where children were primarily housed in residential care isolated from society such as private boarding schools, detention centres, mental health hospitals and so on. The latter incorporates more 'open' institutions that may provide 'residential facilities, out-of-home care, and any organised activity outside the family home', for example, charitable youth/youth-serving organizations (girl guides, scouts), sporting and religious or community-based groups.[25] We use the term 'institutional abuse' to mean NRCSA that took place in closed or total institutions[26] specifically residential schools, reformatory schools and industrial schools. Institutional abuse has been a core focus of each country's public inquiry into NRCSA.

Complainants, victims, survivors

'Complainant', 'victim' and 'survivor' all have specific connotations and meanings for those affected by sexually abusive behaviour. 'Complainant' generally refers to an affected individual making a formal report to the police of a crime committed against them and describes their status during any subsequent criminal investigation and prosecution. The term suggests an expectation of agency, but in fact, complainants are witnesses in a prosecution; they have no legal representation and no control over the decision to prosecute.[27] The term 'complainant' can carry with it many legal and societal myths associated with people who report sexual violence (including the idea of the hysterical woman who cannot be believed).[28] The term 'victim' expresses the harm done, but for some, it is associated with an incorrect connotation of passivity.

The term 'survivor' is preferred by many people because it expresses resistance to oppressive conditions and a refusal to being defined by abuse. Others, however, feel that the term implies a pressure to overcome past injuries and to remain silent about any ongoing suffering. We acknowledge these controversies, and we do not wish to contribute to further marginalization or hurt on the part of people who were abused as children. In this book, we generally use the term 'survivor', but we acknowledge the difficulties with the term.

Notes

1 The prosecution must also negative any defence offered.
2 Independent Inquiry into Child Sexual Abuse (IICSA), *Victims and Survivors Consultative Panel, Terms and Phrases Relating to Child Sexual Abuse*, www.iicsa.org.uk/key-documents/1412/view/independent-inquiry-into-child-sexual-abuse-iicsa-vscp-terms-phrases.pdf.
3 World Health Organisation (2017), http://apps.who.int/violence-info/child-maltreatment.
4 World Health Organisation, *Clinical Guidelines for Responding to Children and Adolescents Who Have Been Sexually Abused* (2017), http://apps.who.int/iris/bitstream/handle/10665/259270/9789241550147-eng.pdf;jsessionid=651EF89D30035F34665D9A66AD1BF951?sequence=1.
5 Y. Pan et al., "Prevalence of Childhood Sexual Abuse Among Women Using the Childhood Trauma Questionnaire: A Worldwide Meta-Analysis" *Trauma, Violence, & Abuse* 22(5), 2020, 1181–91.
6 See N. Martschuka et al., "Similarities in *Modi Operandi* of Institutional and Non-Institutional Child Sexual Offending: Systematic Case Comparisons" *Child Abuse and Neglect* 84, 2018, 229–40.
7 J. Cashmore et al., *The Impact of Delayed Reporting on the Prosecution and Outcomes of Child Sexual Abuse Cases* (Royal Commission into Institutional Responses to Child Sexual Abuse, 2016), 20; T. Peter, "Exploring Taboos: Comparing Male- and Female-Perpetrated Child Sexual Abuse" *Journal of Interpersonal Violence* 24, 2009, 1111–28.
8 In recent years a new focus has centred on Child Sexual Exploitation (CSE). This involves children being given money, gifts or affection in exchange for sexual activity and may be linked with trafficking of children for sexual purposes. Although the term CSE is a relatively new one, this type of behaviour is a form of NRCSA.
9 We acknowledge that survivors are not a homogenous group and that the effects of (NR)CSA differ between survivors.
10 IICSA, *The Impacts of Child Sexual Abuse: A Rapid Evidence Assessment Summary Report* (2017), www.iicsa.org.uk/reports-recommendations/publications/research/impacts-csa.
11 A. Browne and D. Finkelhor, "Impact of Child Sexual Abuse: A Review of the Research" *Psychological Bulletin* 99(1), 1986, 66–77. J. Cashmore and R. Shackel, "The Long-Term Effects of Child Sexual Abuse" (Child Family Community Australia Paper No. 11: 2013), https://aifs.gov.au/cfca/publications/longterm-effects-child-sexual-abuse. C. E. Cavanaugh, "Experiences of Mothers Who Are Child Sexual Abuse Survivors: A Qualitative Exploration" *Journal of Child Sexual Abuse* 24(5), 2015, 506–25. R. Alaggia et al. "Facilitators and Barriers to Child Sexual Abuse (CSA) Disclosures: A Research Update (2000–2016)" *Trauma Violence and Abuse* 20(2), 2017, 260–83. S. Easton, "Disclosure of Child Sexu

Abuse Among Adult Male Survivors" *Clinical Social Work Journal* 41(4), 2013, 344–55.

12 A. Barrett et al., "Childhood Sexual Abuse and Later-Life Economic Consequences" *Journal of Behavioural and Experimental Economics* 53, 2014, 10–16.

13 J. Breckenridge and G. Flax. *Service and Support Needs of Specific Population Groups that Have Experienced Child Sexual Abuse* (University of New South Wales/ Royal Commission into Institutional Responses to Child Sexual Abuse, 2016).

14 IICSA op. cit., 2017, 7.

15 Ibid., 10.

16 D. Finkelhor et al., "Sexual Abuse in a National Survey of Adult Men and Women: Prevalence, Characteristics and Risk Factors" *Child Abuse and Neglect* 14, 1990, 19–28. One in Four, *The Experiences of Clients of One in Four in the Criminal Justice System*, www.oneinfour.ie/Handlers/Download.ashx?IDMF= 491615e8-9c8f-4126-ad86-d057838625a6.

17 H. McGee et al., *Sexual Abuse and Violence in Ireland* (Dublin: Liffey Press, 2002).

18 Ibid., 114.

19 D. Gil, "Unravelling Child Abuse" *American Journal of Orthopsychiatry* 45, 1975, 345–56.

20 B. Matthews, "Optimising Implementation of Reforms to Better Prevent and Respond to Child Sexual Abuse in Institutions" *Child Abuse and Neglect* 74, 2017, 86–98.

21 K. Terry et al., *Causes and Context of the Sexual Abuse Crisis in the Catholic Church* (Washington, DC: United States Conference of Catholic Bishops, 2011).

22 Australian Government Royal Commission into Institutional Responses to Child Sexual Abuse, *Analysis of Claims of Child Sexual Abuse Made with Respect to Catholic Church Institutions in Australia.* (Sydney: Commonwealth of Australia, 2017).

23 A.-M. McAlinden, *Grooming and the Sexual Abuse of Children: Institutional, Internet and Familial Dimensions.* (Oxford: Oxford University Press, 2012).

24 K. Daly, "Conceptualising Responses to Institutional Abuse of Children" *Current Issues in Criminal Justice* 26, 2014, 5–29, 6.

5 J. Sköld, "Historical Abuse – A Contemporary Issue" *Journal of Scandinavian Studies in Criminology and Crime Prevention* 14, 2013, 5–23, 7.

E. Goffman, *Asylums: Essays on the Social Situation of Mental Patients and Other mates* (New York: Anchor Books, 1961).

ere is a possibility of judicial review but this is rarely exercised.

Busby, "Not a Victim Until a Conviction is Entered: Sexual Violence, cutions and Legal 'Truth'" in E. Comack (ed), *Locating Law: Race/Class/ /Sexuality Connections* (2nd ed) (Halifax: Fernwood Press, 2006), 258.

Index

For Product Safety Concerns and Information please contact our EU representative GPSR@taylorandfrancis.com
Taylor & Francis Verlag GmbH, Kaufingerstraße 24, 80331 München, Germany

www.ingramcontent.com/pod-product-compliance
Ingram Content Group UK Ltd.
Pitfield, Milton Keynes, MK11 3LW, UK
UKHW020154200926
475702UK00016B/2704
* 9 7 8 1 0 3 2 2 5 3 6 4 0 *